AI Algorithms and ChatGPT for Student Engagement in Online Learning

Rohit Bansal
Vaish College of Engineering, India

Aziza Chakir
Faculty of Law, Economics, and Social Sciences, Hassan II University, Casablanca, Morocco

Abdul Hafaz Ngah
Faculty of Business Economics and Social Development, Universiti Malaysia, Terengganu, Malaysia

Fazla Rabby
Stanford Institute of Management and Technology, Australia

Ajay Jain
Shri Cloth Market Kanya Vanijya Mahavidyalaya, Indore, India

A volume in the Advances in Computational Intelligence and Robotics (ACIR) Book Series

IGI Global
Scientific Publishing
Publishing Tomorrow's Research Today

Published in the United States of America by
IGI Global
Information Science Reference (an imprint of IGI Global)
701 E. Chocolate Avenue
Hershey PA, USA 17033
Tel: 717-533-8845
Fax: 717-533-8661
E-mail: cust@igi-global.com
Web site: http://www.igi-global.com

Library of Congress Cataloging-in-Publication Data

Names: Bansal, Rohit, 1982- editor.
Title: AI algorithms and ChatGPT for student engagement in online learning / Rohit Bansal, Aziza Chakir, Abdul Hafaz Ngah, Fazla Rabby, Ajay Jain.
Other titles: Artificial intelligence algorithms and ChatGPT for student engagement in online learning
Description: Hershey, PA : IGI Global, 2024. | Includes bibliographical references and index. | Summary: "This book provides comprehensive research on the role and applications of Artificial Intelligence Algorithms and ChatGPT in fostering student engagement in online learning. The aim is to bring together readers such as educators, students, researchers and practitioners interested in advancement of the state of role of artificial intelligence algorithms and ChatGPT in online student engagement in digital age"-- Provided by publisher.
Identifiers: LCCN 2024034468 (print) | LCCN 2024034469 (ebook) | ISBN 9798369342688 (hardcover) | ISBN 9798369350904 (paperback) | ISBN 9798369342695 (ebook)
Subjects: LCSH: Artificial intelligence--Educational applications. | ChatGPT. | Web-based instruction.
Classification: LCC LB1028.43 .A397 2024 (print) | LCC LB1028.43 (ebook) | DDC 370.285/63--dc23/eng/20240904
LC record available at https://lccn.loc.gov/2024034468
LC ebook record available at https://lccn.loc.gov/2024034469

This book is published in the IGI Global book series Advances in Computational Intelligence and Robotics (ACIR) (ISSN: 2327-0411; eISSN: 2327-042X)

British Cataloguing in Publication Data
A Cataloguing in Publication record for this book is available from the British Library.

For electronic access to this publication, please contact: eresources@igi-global.com.

Advances in Computational Intelligence and Robotics (ACIR) Book Series

Ivan Giannoccaro
University of Salento, Italy

ISSN:2327-0411
EISSN:2327-042X

MISSION

While intelligence is traditionally a term applied to humans and human cognition, technology has progressed in such a way to allow for the development of intelligent systems able to simulate many human traits. With this new era of simulated and artificial intelligence, much research is needed in order to continue to advance the field and also to evaluate the ethical and societal concerns of the existence of artificial life and machine learning.

The **Advances in Computational Intelligence and Robotics (ACIR) Book Series** encourages scholarly discourse on all topics pertaining to evolutionary computing, artificial life, computational intelligence, machine learning, and robotics. ACIR presents the latest research being conducted on diverse topics in intelligence technologies with the goal of advancing knowledge and applications in this rapidly evolving field.

COVERAGE

- Evolutionary Computing
- Algorithmic Learning
- Neural Networks
- Artificial Life
- Cyborgs
- Heuristics
- Automated Reasoning
- Agent technologies
- Cognitive Informatics
- Artificial Intelligence

IGI Global is currently accepting manuscripts for publication within this series. To submit a proposal for a volume in this series, please contact our Acquisition Editors at Acquisitions@igi-global.com or visit: http://www.igi-global.com/publish/.

The Advances in Computational Intelligence and Robotics (ACIR) Book Series (ISSN 2327-0411) is published by IGI Global, 701 E. Chocolate Avenue, Hershey, PA 17033-1240, USA, www.igi-global.com. This series is composed of titles available for purchase individually; each title is edited to be contextually exclusive from any other title within the series. For pricing and ordering information please visit http://www.igi-global.com/book-series/advances-computational-intelligence-robotics/73674. Postmaster: Send all address changes to above address.

Titles in this Series

For a list of additional titles in this series, please visit:
www.igi-global.com/book-series/advances-computational-intelligence-robotics/73674

Bio-Inspired Intelligence for Smart Decision-Making
Ramkumar Jaganathan (Sri Krishna Arts and Science College, India) Shilpa Mehta (Auckland University of Technology, New Zealand) and Ram Krishan (Mata Sundri University Girls College, Mansa, ndia)
Information Science Reference • © 2024 • 334pp • H/C (ISBN: 9798369352762) • US $385.00

AI and IoT for Proactive Disaster Management
Mariyam Ouaissa (Chouaib Doukkali University, Morocco) Mariya Ouaissa (Cadi Ayyad University, Morocco) Zakaria Boulouard (Hassan II University, Casablanca, Morocco) Celestine Iwendi (University of Bolton, UK) and Moez Krichen (Al-Baha University, Saudi Aabia)
Engineering Science Reference • © 2024 • 299pp • H/C (ISBN: 9798369338964) • US $355.00

Utilizing AI and Machine Learning for Natural Disaster Management
D. Satishkumar (Nehru Institute of Technology, India) and M. Sivaraja (Nehru Institute of Technology, India)
Engineering Science Reference • © 2024 • 340pp • H/C (ISBN: 9798369333624) • US $315.00

Shaping the Future of Automation With Cloud-Enhanced Robotics
Rathishchandra Ramachandra Gatti (Sahyadri College of Engineering and Management, India) and Chandra Singh (Sahyadri College of Engineering and Management, India)
Engineering Science Reference • © 2024 • 431pp • H/C (ISBN: 9798369319147) • US $345.00

Bio-inspired Swarm Robotics and Control Algorithms, Mechanisms, and Strategies
Parijat Bhowmick (Indian Institute of Technology, Guwahati, India) Sima Das (Bengal College of Engineering and Technology, India) and Farshad Arvin (Durham University, UK)
Engineering Science Reference • © 2024 • 261pp • H/C (ISBN: 9798369312773) • US $315.00

Comparative Analysis of Digital Consciousness and Human Consciousness Bridging the Divide in AI Discourse
Remya Lathabhavan (Indian Institute of Management, Bodh Gaya, India) and Nidhi Mishra (Indian Institute of Management, Bodh Gaya, India)
Engineering Science Reference • © 2024 • 355pp • H/C (ISBN: 9798369320150) • US $315.00

Machine Learning Techniques and Industry Applications
Pramod Kumar Srivastava (Rajkiya Engineering College, Azamgarh, India) and Ashok Kumar Yadav (Rajkiya Engineering College, Azamgarh, India)
Engineering Science Reference • © 2024 • 307pp • H/C (ISBN: 9798369352717) • US $365.00

IGI Global
Scientific Publishing
Publishing Tomorrow's Research Today

701 East Chocolate Avenue, Hershey, PA 17033, USA
Tel: 717-533-8845 x100 • Fax: 717-533-8661
E-Mail: cust@igi-global.com • www.igi-global.com

Table of Contents

Detailed Table of Contents

To study and assess the immersive virtual environment experience of ChatGPT on student engagement in online script writing among media students, an experiment was conducted at the VR Experiential Lab, Christ University, between September 2023 and January 2024. The media students were tasked with writing a script for a short film within a VR environment, with ChatGPT displayed using an Oculus HMD (head-mounted display). A total of 180 students were recruited for the study through purposive sampling, and experiment photos are provided in the appendix. The data collection tool utilized was the virtual experience questionnaire developed by Tcha-Tokey.

This study delves into the attitudes of Generation Z (Gen Z) towards ChatGPT within academic contexts, employing a rigorous analysis. With the rise of advanced language models, understanding how the digitally native Gen Z perceives and engages with ChatGPT is crucial for shaping the future of academic technology. The research assesses various factors influencing Gen Z attitudes, including accessibility, academic pressure, time constraints, language barriers, curiosity, instant gratification, fear of missing out, and technology integration. The study utilizes a robust regression model to comprehensively analyze these factors and their impact on Gen Z's anticipation of increased ChatGPT usage in academics. The research underscores the significance of Gen Z's perspectives in shaping the integration of ChatGPT into educational landscapes. By unraveling their attitudes and perceptions, this research aims to provide valuable insights for educators, policymakers, and developers, facilitating informed decisions for optimizing the utility of ChatGPT in academic settings.

The aim of the study is to examine AI tools that will increase student engagement in online courses and provide support to teachers. In this context, AI tools were examined as a result of the literature review. These tools were examined under six headings: adaptive learning platforms, customized material creation tools, feedback and guidance tools, exam and test creation tools, student engagement monitoring tools, and classroom management tools. Some of the tools analyzed are ALEKS, SlidesAI, Squirrel, MagicForm, Quizbot, Nearpod, and Knewton Alta. It can be argued that these tools provide a range of benefits such as improving learning outcomes by increasing student engagement in online courses, personalizing learning experiences, improving teaching quality, providing tailored courses for students, and improving assessment. However, concerns such as unethical use of student data, limitations in measuring and assessing the learning process, and the inability of automated assessment systems to adequately assess emotion and creativity should be taken into account when using these tools.

This study delves into the potential of AI to transform urban conveyance by reinforcing traffic flow and automobile route growth. Improving transportation adeptness, hateful hate journey opportunities, and lowering environmental impacts are all aims of the AI-stimulated answers being grown. This study takes a close look at current systems for traffic signals, instrument expelling, and machine intelligence systems. The research evolves smart finishing algorithms by joining absolute-time traffic dossier accompanying lineaments of the parking lot network and private travel habits. To humble blockage hotspots, the submitted AI plan finds the best routes by analysing current traffic environments and regulating the ruling class utilizing optimisation and machine intelligence methods. Extensive simulations and instances in miscellaneous urban domains judge AI-driven planning.

The degree to which artificial intelligence fosters student participation determines the heutagogical performance. The main ideas of heutagogy, student engagement, and artificial intelligence are covered in this chapter. The chapter discuss how artificial intelligence technology can be used in education to enhance student engagememt in teaching and learning. The analysis demonstrates that heutagogy, student engagement, and student performance are strongly correlated. The chapter goes on to demonstrate the close relationship that exists between student performance and engagement and the use of artificial intelligence technologies in the classroom. The chapter suggests more advancements in the ways that artificial intelligence technology is used in education.

The increasing role of Artificial Intelligence (AI) applications in educational activities is also evident in online education. By providing personalised and adaptive learning experiences and offering support for teachers by tracking student behaviours to make inferences about student success and performance, AI reduces teachers' workload, allowing them to focus more on educational activities. AI applications especially enable the rapid and easy completion of assessment and evaluation activities, which teachers often spend significant time and effort on. Within this scope, AI-supported tools are used in online education activities to perform automatic assessments, provide real-time feedback, and conduct data analysis and performance evaluation activities. In this context, the aim of the study is determined as the examination of measurement, evaluation, and feedback activities in online education with AI-supported tools.

This work outlines the steps necessary to build a cloud-based control-loop performance monitoring system that can centrally monitor data from several industrial facilities in different parts of the world. Given the high expenses associated with on-premises installations (including systems, human resources, maintenance, and upgrades), this is an attractive option for many businesses, and it's all made possible by current Industry 4.0 technology.

Applications now operating on virtual servers will be moved to another virtual or physical server, or perhaps to the same server altogether, to save power consumption in cloud data centres and maximize the use of computing resources. Optimizing resources is directly affected by knowing when to move an application to a virtual machine. Efficiently tracking the use of computer resources is the surest way to optimize performance. Therefore, to assess the efficiency of virtual machines, they require an all-inclusive intelligent monitoring agent. They provide an agent-based system for tracking resource use, namely CPU and memory, in this chapter. Virtual machine resource utilization data is collected and shown on a dashboard by the monitoring agent. The dashboard shows important performance indicators like memory and CPU use. In order to optimize resources, the cloud administrator might use the data provided by the dashboard's statistics report.

Artificial intelligence (AI) is transforming the landscape of education by revolutionizing student engagement. Through personalized learning algorithms, AI analyzes individual student data to tailor educational content, keeping students engaged with material that suits their learning preferences and abilities. AI-driven gamification elements inject fun and motivation into the learning process, incentivizing students to progress. Analyzing engagement metrics with AI enables educators to identify struggling students early on and intervene effectively to keep them engaged. So, this research will investigate the impact of artificial intelligence on student engagement through bibliometric analysis. For the literature database, the Scopus database was examined, and the researcher got 300 research papers in total. After refining and limiting the years from 2014 to 2024, researchers selected 80 papers for the final examination. The selected papers are open-access and in the final stage. A few of the drivers of artificial intelligence on student engagement are also elaborated in this chapter.

With the advent of online education, the traditional classroom setting has undergone a significant transformation. However, one of the key challenges faced by educators in the online environment is maintaining student engagement and active participation. In this chapter, the authors explore the topic of innovative tools and technologies that have emerged to address the issue of boredom and enhance engagement in online classes. Online learning environments often suffer from a lack of face-to-face interaction, leading to diminished student engagement and increased boredom. However, educators and researchers have recognized the need to bridge this gap and have developed various tools and technologies to foster participation and interactivity. As traditional education transitions into digital platforms, the need for effective and engaging online teaching methodologies becomes paramount. This chapter explores the integration of gamification principles, innovative tools, and technologies to enhance the engagement and learning experience in online classes.

The study explores the transformative impact of artificial intelligence (AI) on teacher-learner engagement in virtual education settings. It uses secondary data sources to analyse the evolving landscape of virtual education facilitated by AI technologies The research explores how AI enhances personalized learning experiences, adaptive assessments, and real-time feedback mechanisms, fostering deeper engagement and understanding among learners. It also discusses the role of AI in facilitating collaboration and communication in virtual classrooms, enabling seamless interaction across geographical boundaries. The study also explores the potential of AI to address individual learning needs, promote inclusivity, and optimize learning outcomes through data-driven insights and analytics. The research emphasizes the importance of leveraging AI technologies to enhance teacher-learner engagement, promote active learning, and foster academic success in the digital age.

Among the numerous sorts of Industries 5.0, machine learning incorporates AI, which is both a necessary and promising component. Companies in the food, health, and pharmaceutical industries, among others, consistently provide excellent outcomes, which are good for customers. An AI system that provides data in a way that people can understand and use is proposed in this chapter. Therefore, the chapter's explanation of Food Industry 5.0 is based on the idea that AI and HR are converging. The result will be that businesses will have more information on the most recent innovations in the food industry, including how to save time and money while increasing output. As a result, the food industry can make a lot of money by preparing meals in the most promotional, sanitary, and healthful way possible.

Artificial intelligence (AI) is transforming online education, offering personalized learning experiences and automating administrative tasks. This chapter explores AI's impact on teacher-learner interaction, highlighting opportunities and challenges. AI enables customized instruction, real-time communication, and immersive learning experiences. Yet, a cautious approach is needed to complement human expertise. AI addresses challenges like unequal access and engages diverse learners, revolutionizing content delivery and automating tasks. By combining AI with human insight, educators can create supportive virtual learning environments.

Preface

AI transforms education by offering personalized learning paths, interactive experiences, and real-time feedback. AI enhances engagement by providing customized learning paths based on students' strengths and weaknesses. AI injects variety into tests by creating engaging exercises, such as humorous AI-generated content. Moreover, AI overcomes language barriers with live captions and advanced translation tools. These features enable educators to teach a wider audience, enhancing engagement and learning standards worldwide. One of the most significant benefits of using AI for students is its personalized teaching approach. Artificial intelligence can be used to assess a learner's performance and study tendencies. It allows teachers to understand the strengths and weaknesses of a particular student. This personalization can create ideal learning paths based on the learner's needs. AI tools for student engagement can assess a learner's academic history, tendencies, strengths, and weaknesses. AI algorithms play a crucial role in enhancing student engagement in online learning by leveraging data, personalization, and adaptive technologies.

ChatGPT can facilitate interactive learning experiences by engaging students in discussions, quizzes, and simulations. It can provide instant feedback, encourage active participation and help students grasp concepts more effectively. For language-based subjects, ChatGPT can serve as a language practice tool. It can assist students in developing their writing, speaking, and comprehension skills by generating responses, correcting grammar, and offering language-related tips.

Accordingly, this book provides comprehensive research on the role and applications of Artificial Intelligence Algorithms and ChatGPT in fostering student engagement in online learning. The aim is to bring together readers such as educators, students, researchers and practitioners interested in advancement of the state of role of artificial intelligence algorithms and ChatGPT in online student engagement in digital age.

Chapter 1, "ChatGPT: An Automated Teacher's Guide to Learning," highlights the perspectives of the global education community about ChatGPT's potential impact on learning and education. Chapter 2, "Artificial Intelligence-Based Deep Learning Approach to Identify the Web-Based Attack," examines the effectiveness of deep learning models, including convolutional neural networks impacting animate nerve organ systems (CNNs, or CNN), reiterating impacting animate nerve organ systems (RNNs), and change models, in classifying attacks and identifying the typical attack attribute. Chapter 3, "ChatGPT and Virtual Experience: Student Engagement in Online Script Writing - An Experimental Investigation Among Media Students," assesses the immersive virtual environment experience of ChatGPT on student engagement in online script writing among media students. Chapter 4, "Exploring Gen Z Perspectives Toward ChatGPT in Academic Contexts," delves into the attitudes of Generation Z (Gen Z) towards ChatGPT within academic contexts, employing a rigorous analysis. Chapter Five, "Artificial

Intelligence-Supported Teacher Tools to Increase Participation in Online Courses," examines AI tools that will increase student engagement in online courses and provide support to teachers. Chapter 6, "Artificial Intelligence Techniques to Optimize the Traffic in Urban Areas," delves into the potential of AI to transform urban conveyance by reinforcing traffic flow and automobile route growth. Chapter 7, "Artificial Intelligence-Driven Instruction and Its Impact on Heutagogy and Student Engagement," discusses how artificial intelligence technology can be used in education to enhance student engagement in teaching and learning. Chapter 8, "Assessment, Evaluation, and Feedback in Online Education With Artificial Intelligence-Supported Tools," determines the examination of measurement, evaluation, and feedback activities in online education with AI-supported tools. Chapter 9, "Monitoring, Operations and Performance Assessment Through AI and Cloud-Based Plants," outlines the steps necessary to build a cloud-based control-loop performance monitoring system that can centrally monitor data from several industrial facilities in different parts of the world. Chapter 10, "Cloud Computing Agent-Based Performance Evaluation of Resource Monitoring System in IaaS," provides an architecture for resource monitoring that makes use of an agent-based system. Chapter 11, "Drivers and Impact of Artificial Intelligence on Student Engagement," investigates the impact of artificial intelligence on student engagement through bibliometric analysis. Chapter 12, "Engaging Online Classes Through Gamification: Leveraging Innovative Tools and Technologies," explores the integration of gamification principles, innovative tools, and technologies to enhance the engagement and learning experience in online classes. Chapter 13, "Impact of Artificial Intelligence on Virtual Teacher Learner Engagement Redefining Educational Dynamics: Artificial Intelligence," explores how AI enhances personalized learning experiences, adaptive assessments, and real-time feedback mechanisms, fostering deeper engagement and understanding among learners. Chapter 14, "Integrate the Artificial Intelligence and Human to Develop the Food Processing Unit," proposes an AI system that provides data in a way that people can understand and use. Chapter 15, "The Impact of Artificial Intelligence on Teacher-Learner Interaction in Virtual Education: Addressing Challenges and Embracing Opportunities," explores AI's impact on teacher-learner interaction, highlighting opportunities and challenges.

We highly appreciate everyone involved in the publication of this book.

Rohit Bansal
Vaish College of Engineering, India

Aziza Chakir
Faculty of Law, Economics, and Social Sciences, Hassan II University, Casablanca, Morocco

Abdul Hafaz Ngah
Faculty of Business Economics and Social Development, Universiti Malaysia, Terengganu, Malaysia

Fazla Rabby
Stanford Institute of Management and Technology, Australia

Ajay Jain
Shri Cloth Market Kanya Vanijya Mahavidyalaya, Indore, India

Chapter 1
ChatGPT:
An Automated Teacher's Guide to Learning

Kutubuddin Sayyad Liyakat Kazi
https://orcid.org/0000-0001-5623-9211
Brahmdevdada Mane Institute of Technology, Solapur, India

ABSTRACT

ChatGPT's main advantage in today's classroom is its capacity to offer students automated support. Students can use ChatGPT to pose inquiries and receive personalised feedback on their work. This could enhance students' understanding of the subject matter and boost their performance as a whole. Furthermore, ChatGPT might be utilised to give students access to personalised learning and practice activities, which will enable them to study more efficiently. Teachers can also enhance their instruction by using ChatGPT. Students may develop interactive lessons with ChatGPT and give instructors feedback on how they are teaching. Teachers can better tailor their instruction to their students' needs by using this feedback.

INTRODUCTION

Technology use in education has been growing in popularity recently. Using ChatGPT (Chat-based Generative Pre-trained Transformer) for educational purposes is one of the most recent developments. ChatGPT is AI-artificial intelligence tool that simulates human speech using ML-machine learning and NLP-natural language processing algorithms. This kind of technology possesses the capability to completely change how people interact with and consume educational content.

Students' individualized learning proficiencies will be developed through ChatGPT. With the help of this technology, students can receive pertinent information that is specifically catered to their needs while also understanding their preferences and needs. Additionally, it offers suggestions and feedback to aid students in better understanding the subject matter. Better learning outcomes may result from the interactive and engaging nature of education provided by ChatGPT.

DOI: 10.4018/979-8-3693-4268-8.ch001

Teachers' workloads can be lighter as a result of utilizing ChatGPT. Many of the laborious tasks that teachers must perform, like grouping tests and giving feedback, can be automated by this technology. Teachers will have more time to devote to giving each student individualized attention and guidance as a result of this.

Students can also receive personalized learning paths via ChatGPT. Depending on the needs and progress of the students, this technology can provide assignments and questions for them. This may offer a more effective means of evaluating student performance and determining areas in which they require improvement. Like any technology, using ChatGPT for educational purposes could have some potential disadvantages. The possibility that this technology will be used to replace teachers and decrease human interaction in the classroom is among the primary reasons to be concerned. Additionally, there's a chance that the instruments will be applied unethically, like swaying students' beliefs or spreading misleading information.

All things considered, the utilization of ChatGPT for educational objectives is a promising advancement that could completely transform the way pupils acquire knowledge. With the help of technology, teachers can create more individualized learning experiences and give students more effective ways to evaluate their progress. But it's important to make sure the tools are used ethically and sensibly and don't take the place of a human teacher.

Artificial intelligence (AI) evolved dramatically over the last few decades and changed many facets of society. Numerous research domains, such as robotics, education, autonomous driving, and medical, artificial intelligence (AI) has made a name for itself. In its widest definition, AI refers to an computer system's ability to mimic human brain functions. This means gathering information from external sources, learning through teaching, and achieving the desired outcomes in light of that learning. The field of artificial intelligence (AI) is growing and has the potential to completely transform education by Devi (2022).

ChatGPT has gained a lot of popularity since its November 30, 2022 launch, which indicates AI possesses the capability to significantly change human communication and education. The app's releases created anticipation for ChatGPT's possible effects on education, but they also raised concerns. The potential broad effects of artificial intelligence (AI) in written communication are suggested by Microsoft's announcement that ChatGPT and other programs of a similar nature will soon be available to all users through its office suite of applications. As generative AI tools like ChatGPT are increasingly integrated into the classroom, educators need to address future-focused concerns regarding learning and instruction. Students need to understand artificial intelligence's (AI) workings, benefits, and drawbacks, as well as how to use AI to their own advantage without feeding the system's biases. It will be necessary for instructors to follow along, learning as they go and reinforcing previously learned skills like critical thinking, ethical source use, and source verification and examination by Montenegro-Rueda (2023).

Notable outcomes from the integration of AI in education include improved learning process efficiency, global learning promotion, personalized learning, more intelligent content creation, and more effective and efficient learning supervision. The teaching-learning process can be streamlined with the help of modern technologies. Education is a process that allows learning to be more than just a single product and surpasses the mere acquisition of information. Thus, AI, which has recently emerged as an innovative technology with a vast amount of educational potential, makes possible personalized learning that is catered to each student's unique desires and requirements.

It is reliable to state that there are significant challenges and moral quandaries connected to the application of AI at education. Issues involving knowledge privacy, fair participation in education, along with an influence upon the employment of a teacher must be carefully taken into account. Responsible handling of these issues is essential to ensure that AI is utilized in a way that benefits and makes sense for every student. A harmony between the necessary role of educators and their tools play in society is necessary in order to guarantee that the holistic growth of pupils and their preparedness for an environment which evolves all the time. Because ChatGPT was only launched for a short time (ending in November of 2022), there are currently no systematic reviews available that examine its effects on education. Therefore, this well-organized review's primary goal is to evaluate the body of studies on ChatGPT's applications for education so as to pinpoint advantages, disadvantages, and potential directions for instructional and educational domains in the future by Gill(2023).

ChatGPT uses AI and NLP to generate responses to user-inputted questions that resemble those of a human. Due to its ability to generate responses that are logical, methodical, and instructive, it has garnered interest from people worldwide. Even with its extensive use, ChatGPT has created new risks and challenges for the educational sector. There have been concerns expressed regarding the potential misuse of AI-Generated Content (AIGC), which has the potential to be used to generate tests and homework assignments for students as well as customized responses to assessment questions. As a result, the use of ChatGPT by students is prohibited in a number of educational institutions; one such prohibition covers the entire country. Researchers that examined ChatGPT's impact on learning reported that teachers were apprehensive about using the app in the classroom. They expressed concern that because ChatGPT can produce pertinent content quickly, students might use it to outsource their assignments. Additionally, a number of issues have been discovered, including redundant text, inaccurate answers, and insufficient or nonexistent referencing. Therefore, it is essential to carefully evaluate the effects of ChatGPT-assisted education in order to maximize its benefits and minimize its drawbacks. Similar concerns were expressed when internet searches were first introduced, so this isn't a new phenomenon. Conversely, a content users can use a search engine to cross-reference specific URLs that may have been used to achieve a particular objective. There are not any particular references or URLs in the text that ChatGPT generates Rahman (2023).

Understanding and valuing human language is the primary goal of the artificial intelligence field of natural language processing, or NPL. It is used to communicate with people more naturally and to derive meaning from text, audio, and other digital data types. Among other things, NLP has been applied to tasks like machine translation, sentiment analysis, and text summarization.

With increasing requests for AI-powered applications in recent years, NLP has gained importance. NLP systems are employed in many different sectors, including finance, education, and the legal and medical fields. Additionally, automated customer support, natural language search, and customer service are all being enhanced by NLP technology. NLP is a difficult and complex field that needs a lot of data and processing power to create useful applications. However, NLP has become more widely available and is currently being used in many different fields due to the growing availability of strong hardware and large datasets.

NLP is a significant field of artificial intelligence that is being utilized to maximize the usefulness of digital data and facilitate more organic interactions between people and machines. It is already having a significant impact on a variety of industries, and as advances in AI technology occur, its applications will probably grow by Alfonso (2023).

The field of NLP, has seen rapid growth in the last few years. It has demonstrated promise in a wide range of real-world applications, including text generation, language translation, entity and speech recognition, summarization, and more. Recurrent Neural-Network (RNN) simulations have also been widely used by researchers to remember dependencies in texts due to their recurrent structure. Nevertheless, RNN model is limited and unable to manage the kind of very long-range dependencies that one finds in natural language texts. The Transformer architecture has been developed to address this problem. A self-attention tool that evaluates the significance and connections among various input elements is also included in Transformer. This is why the model is so good at understanding the relationships among words in a phrase, no matter in which they're located. LLMs: Generative pretrained transformer (GPT)-3 is one of the large language models based on the Transformer architecture that has demonstrated notable success in NLP tasks. Large amounts of text data are used to train GPT-3 models, about 570 GB of text and 175 billion parameters that can be trained. As a result, they are able to produce text that is almost human-like and execute other language-related tasks extremely accurately.

OpenAI created the so-called ChatGPT NLP model, which was made available in November of 2022. ChatGPT is a revolutionary LLM that can write text and maintain a formal style similar to a human. Since GPT-3 is suitable for a wide range of downstream tasks and was successfully trained on massive amounts of Internet data, the ChatGPT begins using the GPT-3 pretrained LLM. One of GPT-3's shortcomings is that it displays "poorly characterized behavior". In order to avoid producing negative and dishonest results, ChatGPT decided to use three different approaches:

a. Supervised fine-tuning,
b. Reward modelling, and
c. Reinforcement learning.

To fine-tune GPT-3 using supervised learning, the first step is to collect a dataset of labeler demonstrations. Employing a dataset of rankings of model outputs, the supervised model is then further improved through reinforcement learning based on user feedback. In the end, the generated model is called InstructGPT. Unlike other AI-powered languages, ChatGPT speaks with the user in real-time while producing and displaying entirely original content. Furthermore, ChatGPT is capable of continually sustaining a dialogue technique that engages the handler in a more realistic way rather than responding to every query with an irrelevant response. This distinguishes ChatGPT from other LLMs by Fütterer(2023).

ChatGPT has proven to be extremely effective in a variety of application domains, such as writing coherent essays and content, answering questions, paraphrasing language, and writing programming codes. Additionally, research is being done to optimize such LLMs for specific tasks and apply transfer learning in new domains. Within the context of education, educators and students can use ChatGPT for a range of scholarly and investigative goals. Teachers can create course outlines, lecture and demonstration materials on hypothetical subjects, questions and problem sets, and more by using ChatGPT. Likewise, ChatGPT can expedite learning for students by assisting them with essay composition, deciphering challenging inquiries, and problem-solving. Students can even get assistance with programming here, which will expedite their learning of the language. Despite ChatGPT's significant advancements, concerns regarding abuse persist. Thus, it's critical to weigh the many educational benefits of ChatGPT towards any possible drawbacks (such as the veracity of online tests and Q&A platforms). Some experts have expressed concerns about the prospects of collaborative adheres to like encoding in the ChatGPT era. Therefore, it's imperative to evaluate the circumstances impartially and, with the aid of tools like ChatGPT, develop an appropriate plan for upcoming instruction by Alshater(2022).

In the past few decades, a plethora of technologies have emerged, sometimes challenging established knowledge. People must therefore evaluate and consider the benefits and risks related to these new technologies. There have been previous concerns raised about Google's ability to change people's thinking, reading, and memorization processes. An additional educational resource is the Massive Open Online Course. It garnered quite a bit of curiosity at the beginning of 2010, but because of its corporate structures and strategies, its performance declined. These concerns also apply to ChatGPT because it presents several real risks in addition to its many potential. Above all, ChatGPT can be used not only for tutoring and language modelling purposes but also as a research and teaching assistant. Furthermore, ChatGPT distinguishes itself from other LLMs with a few special features like affordability, customization, accessibility, and a conversational style. Numerous studies have examined the application of artificial intelligence (AI) in education, with particular attention paid to chatbots, language models, programming assistance, and natural language processing (NLP) tools. Having just recently been released, ChatGPT is a comparatively new technology in the educational field. To the best of our knowledge, no study has (i) investigated, using a comprehensive survey of teachers and students, how ChatGPT supports teaching and learning programming, or (ii) investigated the possible risks and strategies related to ChatGPT for research, education, and specifically programming education.

So, we look at the first two months of ChatGPT's global adoption after its launch in this article. Our objective is to understand the perspectives of the global education community about ChatGPT's potential impact on learning and education. This could include anything from the potential for customized instruction to the ethical implications of relying entirely on AI for information and communication. More specifically, we analyze ChatGPT's global reception using social media data.

LITERATURE SURVEY

In this section, we address current research as well as educational studies that make use of ChatGPT from the perspectives of teachers and students. Additionally, we offer an overview of published studies that have used ChatGPT and AI in a range of academic fields, including science, engineering, and medicine. The topic is so new that we were only able to locate a limited number of peer-reviewed scholarly papers. However, we looked at preprints, which are scholarly articles from various academic fields that are not reviewed by peers.

According to a study by Kazi et al.(2022),(2023), professional techniques utilising artificial intelligence (AI) and deep learning have advanced significantly over the past ten years, benefiting a wide range of industries. This is due to the fact that AI-assisted tools, among other media, are capable of classifying a wide range of objects and subjects regardless of the input, including text and pictures. This enables the development of systems that can be used for a variety of tasks, such as automated photo tagging, text generation, scanning, and translation.

Furthermore, the educational applications of ChatGPT have been documented by multiple studies. Using GHOSTS and custom datasets, Frieder et al. (2023) investigated ChatGPT's mathematical prowess. The most comprehensive collection of natural language data produced and updated by working mathematicians is called GHOSTS. It was evident from the results of their experiment that "ChatGPT's mathematical aptitude is markedly less than that of the usual mathematics scholar." Often, ChatGPT understands the question but provides imprecise responses. The contribution that ChatGPT has made to medical education is also noteworthy. Kung(2023) evaluated ChatGPT's efficacy using the US Medical Licencing Exam, which consists of three assessments: Step 1st, Step 2nd CK, and Step 3rd CK. Their test results show that ChatGPT performed all three tests at a level that was near or above the minimum requirement, even in the absence of any specific guidance or help. Gilson(2022) looked at the implementation of ChatGPT on the therapeutic licencing assessment. These remarkable results mean that ChatGPT can support medical education. You can find a list of articles concerning ChatGPT-based medical education in Aydın (2022).

Software design is a challenging task that requires precise implementation of syntax and logic. AI-based models have successfully handled programming tasks like summarization, completion, code repair, correction, classification, and generation. Alphacode is a state-of-the-art LLM that was specifically created and trained to support competitive-level programme design. Humans generate a lot of text to perform coding-related tasks in both ChatGPT and Alphacode processes. Although they both use "virtually the same architecture," Alphacode is more programming-focused than ChatGPT, which is a more general-purpose conversation engine. Moreover, even though ChatGPT was not designed with automatic code repair in mind when it was first developed, it is still suitable for this use. The performance of code debugging with ChatGPT is presented in the study. The results of their tests show that ChatGPT can correct bugs just as well as deep learning (DL) models like Codex and CoCoNut. But ChatGPT has shown to be far more successful than traditional code-repair techniques. Jalil(2023) looked at ChatGPT's effectiveness in answering inquiries about the curriculum for software testing. About 44% and 57% of the time, respectively, ChatGPT was able to offer explanations and answers that were either completely or somewhat accurate.

Malinka (2023) looked into ChatGPT's advantages for college education, mainly in terms of options pertaining to software programming. They demonstrated the effectiveness of ChatGPT for handling homework, exams, and programming assignments using the data they had collected. They also talked about the benefits and drawbacks of ChatGPT for computer science education. The study looked at ChatGPT's programming capabilities for solving mathematical problems. The following tasks were tested with ChatGPT: writing code, rewriting code in different programming languages for numerical algorithms, debugging and optimising human-written code, and finishing code. Among the numerical problems they looked at were the differential equation, Poisson's equation, inviscid flow, Vector equation, solving linear calculations, eigenvalue problems, and sparse matrix storage. The results of the experiment showed that ChatGPT can efficiently produce programme codes for arithmetic problems; nevertheless, there are constraints and challenges related to problem-solving. Furthermore, ChatGPT has been applied recently to a wide range of tasks, such as AI problem solving, code generation, intelligent cars, software engineering, data augmentation, medical education, and the fifth industrial revolution. However, academics are concerned about the general programming techniques that ChatGPT may employ in the future.

Describe ChatGPT

The artificial intelligence-AI research company OpenAI created ChatGPT, a chatbot powered by artificial intelligence. The technology, which was first made available in early 2020, is meant to let people communicate naturally with chatbots driven by artificial intelligence. OpenAI's GPT-3 model, a deep learning-based machine learning model by Vahida(2023), powers ChatGPT, a system focused on natural language processing (NLP). GPT-3 stands for Generative Pre-trained Transformer, and it can produce text output that is similar to what a human would write. Because the GPT-3 model is trained on extensive text datasets, it can produce responses that have the natural tone of a human. Easy to use and compatible with current chatbot technology, ChatGPT is designed with ease of use in mind. AI-powered chatbots and users can have interactive conversations with each other through its use. It could be used, for instance, to develop customer service, chatbots that can respond to inquiries from clients in natural language, or bots that can provide users tailored recommendations.The technology is still being tested and refined and is currently in its early stages. Nonetheless, its capacity to produce responses that sound natural and draw users into deep dialogues has already demonstrated promise. It is anticipated to spread further and become a standard feature of chatbot technology in the future.

ChatGPT's Use in Education

The potential of ChatGPT to increase students' involvement in their education has led to an overabundance of worry about its use in the classroom. With the help of this system, students can receive prompt feedback, customised responses that are tailored to their individual needs, and assistance in understanding complex concepts. This makes it a potentially helpful tool that encourages student interaction and intellectual growth by adapting to their preferred method of learning and offering long-lasting support for their quest for knowledge.

Accordingly, it has proven to be a useful tool for promoting the growth of students' writing abilities. Students who interact with the system and receive thorough feedback on their written work in addition to grammar-related corrections and improvement suggestions can improve their transcribed communication and realise greater efficiency with their transcribed expression. Though this application presents itself as a helpful tool for written scientific assistance, it is important to understand that it is not an all-encompassing solution to producing scientific content. It is the responsibility of writers to employ their experience and knowledge to confirm and improve the information provided by the tool. However, it also excels at promoting cooperative student involvement in assignments and projects and fostering group discussions. Students' sense of community is strengthened as a result of the promotion of communication and idea sharing among them.

The potential effects of AI have been the subject of numerous investigations, especially with the popular educational tool ChatGPT. We looked at a number of AI-related educational applications, such as predictive analytics, chatbots, adaptive testing, and personalised learning environments. As such, it shows great potential for improving the efficiency of learning and providing educators and students with individualised learning support. It is imperative to take into account the hazards and constraints posed by these technologies, including concerns regarding data privacy, cultural disparities, language ability, and the ensuing ethical ramifications.

The last year has seen a rise in interest in education due to its impact. This inventive instrument is recognised as a cutting-edge framework that is revolutionising the way learning environments instruct, assist, and motivate students. Educational institutions are reevaluating how they can incorporate technology within their didactic models in order to improve the procedure of instruction and education for learners . Consequently, teachers must employ this instrument in their classrooms and incorporate it as a curricular supplement. But it's important to stress that this tool doesn't replace other sources of information, like publications, blogs, and social gatherings, or the mental processes involved in learning.

CHATGPT'S FUNCTION AND INFLUENCE IN THE TRANSFORMATION OF ONLINE EDUCATION

In the dynamic field of online learning, AI is still at the forefront of innovation. Assessment design and language learning are two fields that are undergoing a dramatic change thanks to technologies like ChatGPT. Numerous online learning environments, such as NPTL, use AI to find common blunders in assignments. With ChatGPT, educators can produce unique assessments and educational resources, and businesses (such as Course Hero) might discover that the AI's reasonably priced adaptability poses a threat to their paid homework assistance models. Through personalised questioning and feedback on responses, AI chatbots can assist students in improving their text comprehension. It can also be used to enhance one's capacity for analysis and critical thought. Another key component of ChatGPT is its ability to assist students in language exploration.

They are able to comprehend sentence structure, practise correctly pronouncing words, modify sentences, and offer perspectives in real time. Persisting in writing responses to essay or exam questions is perhaps the least significant along with controversial utilisation of ChatGPT. Teachers and students can use this software to create articles upon any topic by entering prompts. Furthermore, ChatGPT can provide advice on how to make multiple rewrites of the exact same essay more grammatically sound, concise, or clear. This aids users in overcoming writing challenges and presents fresh viewpoints on the subject they have selected. There are significant ramifications for morality and trade. Content creators may reconsider paying high cost for membership for AI-powered imaginative instruments such as Grammarly after utilising ChatGPT. According to the Gartner Hype Cycle, ChatGPT users are currently in a "trough of disillusionment," meaning they have no hope. The technology arrives at the "plateau of productivity" while people and businesses embrace, accept, and use it after research and development.

Nevertheless, OpenAI hopes to expand its skill set, boost productivity, and commercialise innovative discoveries by partnering with Microsoft. When ChatGPT4 was released in March 2023, it generated a lot of talk because it seemed to be more responsive, accurate, and dependable. Adoption will increase as a result of these enhancements and better interoperability with other productivity applications like Zoom as well as Slack via smartphones along with Internet of Things devices. The launch of ChatGPT4 emphasises how important it is to accept and understand the application of AI-powered learning resources as they develop, opening the door for more precise, dependable, as well as responsive technology.

Utilizing ChatGPT to Teach

For educators, Employing ChatGPT can be beneficial as a basis for developing lesson plans, teaching materials, and assessment tasks. Nonetheless, there are concerns about the generated content's legitimacy that must be addressed. A potential fix would be to use ChatGPT to generate course-specific instructional materials for bots. For instance, ChatGPT may be utilised to help students learn the language by pretending to be a "native speaker" that they can converse with.

After confirming the accuracy of the content, educators can ask ChatGPT to transform the content into a layout that is compatible with AI-based chatbots. Students will benefit from a unique and engaging learning experience as a result. ChatGPT can also improve active learning techniques. One possible approach is switched education, in which students are expected to read the content in advance. This type of instruction may enable more interactive learning activities, such as group discussions in the classroom. However, in traditional flipped classrooms, students may find it challenging to learn before class.

This problem was highlighted by the COVID-19 pandemic, as students who completed their coursework entirely online underperformed in the classroom and demonstrated little interest in helping their peers share knowledge. As a virtual instructor, ChatGPT can help students conduct their autonomous research online by responding to their inquiries, and it can improve teamwork by offering suggestions for a framework for debate and a timely answer.

IoT AND CHATGPT: ENTWINED IN CONTEMPORARY LEARNING

The use of contemporary technologies in the classroom, such as ChatGPT and Internet of Things-IoT by K K(2023), Liyakat(2023), has become essential in today's society. Students now have unprecedented information at their disposal thanks to the Internet of Things, which facilitates self-directed learning. Teachers and students should make use of the IoT to develop an environment that promotes learning and exploration as information becomes more and more readily available.

A natural language processing method called ChatGPT, or Chat-based Generative Pre-trained Transformer, enables computers to comprehend and reply to human dialogues. Customers can now speak with bots directly rather than waiting on the phone for a customer support agent thanks to the widespread usage of this technology in customer service applications. These days, ChatGPT is utilised in the classroom to aid students in comprehending and learning new ideas. By giving students rapid accessibility to information, ChatGPT turned into a vital resource for teachers.

Teachers can now create a more dynamic and engaging atmosphere for learning thanks to ChatGPT's integration with the Internet of Things. Teachers can track students' progress with IoT devices, giving them immediate feedback on what needs more focus. Rather than waiting for an instructor to answer, students may pose questions and get responses via a chatbot with ChatGPT. Students are encouraged to think independently and critically as a result of this increased engagement.

Additionally, virtual tutors can be made with ChatGPT. These online tutors can be configured to offer each student individualised assistance, assisting in the comprehension of challenging ideas and the improvement of problem-solving techniques.

Teachers can design a learning environment that is specific to the requirements of their pupils by integrating ChatGPT with IoT. All things considered, ChatGPT and IoT have completely changed how teachers can communicate with their students. These technologies have made it possible for teachers to establish more successful and effective learning environments by giving students more individualised support and stimulating learning opportunities. The adoption of these tools in the contemporary educational system is going to grow increasingly crucial as information becomes more widely available. Online education will be greatly benefited by the integration of ChatGPT along with IoT, thereby transforming the way teachers and students employ new learning platforms for better teaching and learning. NLP has been integrated into IoT, allowing for more informal and direct communication between devices and educators. By doing collaborative online platforms (such as video conferences as well as messaging apps) upon devices such as tablets, e-readers, and smartphones, educators and ChatGPT can have more natural, chance-based conversations. This is made possible by the complementary technologies of the Internet of Things and NLP.

Moreover, ChatGPT enables increasingly intricate and sophisticated dialogues with IoT devices, encompassing customised assignments such as providing answers to queries and generating suggestions for teachers and learners. In conclusion, ChatGPT integration into IoT devices enables natural language communication, deeper and more intelligent communication, and the elimination of remote controllers.

POSSIBILITIES FOR ChatGPT

OpenAI's successful LLM ChatGPT has the power to completely alter our relationship with technology and cause a paradigm shift. Though a review of the literature on the subject's effects revealed a range of opinions, from positive to negative, there have been many scholarly articles written about ChatGPT.

Like calculators, which are now required in science and math classes, ChatGPT is going to be a helpful tool for everyday tasks such as writing and work. Machha et al.(2022) recommend educators and students to utilise ChatGPT and other AI tools to the fullest extent possible rather than avoiding them. In this section, researchers, educators, and students discuss ChatGPT's potential and opportunities for study and instruction.

i. Possibilities for Students

With so many options, ChatGPT could be a helpful tool for students. Learners can use this tool to understand and solve difficult problems. For students who prefer experiential learning and experimentation, ChatGPT is an excellent resource. One of ChatGPT's best features is its ability to understand and respond to natural language queries. This allows students to ask ChatGPT questions in the same way they normally would ask tutors. As a result, ChatGPT has become more intuitive and user-friendly. It is applicable to all levels of learning, from elementary to postsecondary, as well as professional development. The ChatGPT model can help students improve their reading and writing skills by providing recommendations (such as syntactic and grammatical ones) and creating practice questions and tests for a variety of topics (including physics, language, literature, and mathematics). Furthermore, the ChatGPT model can produce explanations and comprehensive fixes for a particular problem; it can support the growth of critical and creative thinking in addition to problem-solving skills.

By providing each student with personalised guidance during the discussion, ChatGPT is additionally suitable for discussions and group discussions as well. ChatGPT provides speech-to-text and text-to-speech services, which can be helpful for students with disabilities. The ChatGPT model can function as an expert tutor for language skill development, computer programming, report writing, project management, and technical (IT, legal, and medical) report writing. What's even more fascinating is that students can discuss the justifications, responses, and other suggestions made using ChatGPT. Consequently, ChatGPT provides students with interactive support at any time or place. In addition, we tested the ChatGPT model to find the derivatives of various mathematical equations, and it solved every equation correctly.

ii. Possibilities for Teachers

As an LLM, ChatGPT may be a helpful tool for educators in many ways. ChatGPT can be useful for educators conducting fruitful research and providing instruction. Here are a few examples of how ChatGPT can be applied to research and teaching.

Lesson Planning: ChatGPT can be used to create effective lesson plans for classes in math, physics, computer science, electrical engineering, electronics engineering, and literature. ChatGPT provides topic-specific exercises, activities, and illustrations to help teachers teach their students more effectively. Furthermore, ChatGPT can be used to create topic-specific assessments which are compatible with the subject matter and degree of difficulty.

Tailored Learning Assistance: Educators can employ ChatGPT to provide their pupils with personalised lessons. In accordance with a student's needs and preferred learning style, ChatGPT can suggest materials and exercises that are specifically suited to their needs. For example, teachers can use ChatGPT to look at information regarding student performance and identify areas where students are struggling to understand particular concepts or algorithms. It is possible for a teacher to identify a student who struggles with sorting algorithms. In this case, the instructor can use ChatGPT to generate resources that are especially suited to the student's learning style and ability level. Figure 1 illustrates the personalized learning process.

Answering Questions from Students: ChatGPT can help teachers answer questions from students. Furthermore, if teachers are able to ask ChatGPT for explanations and examples on a particular subject, the effectiveness of their instruction will surely increase. For example, in response to a learner's question, "abstract on effect of ChatGPT in modern Education?",AI tool or ChatGPT can provide instructors with information summaries (see Figure 2). Educators can also ask ChatGPT for specific, personalized information by requesting explanations and examples on a challenging subject.

Figure 1. ChatGPT for personalized learning

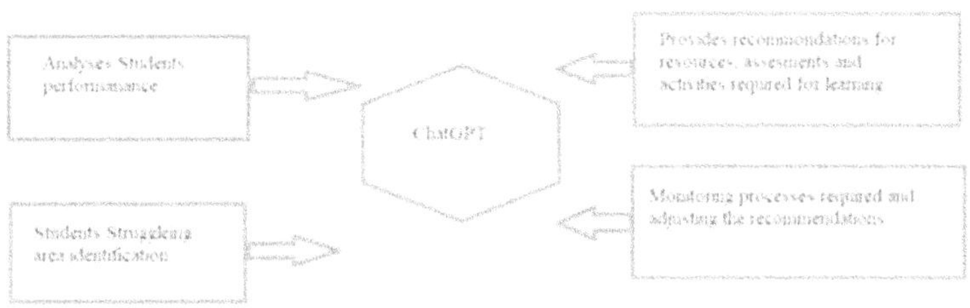

Figure 2. Answering the queries

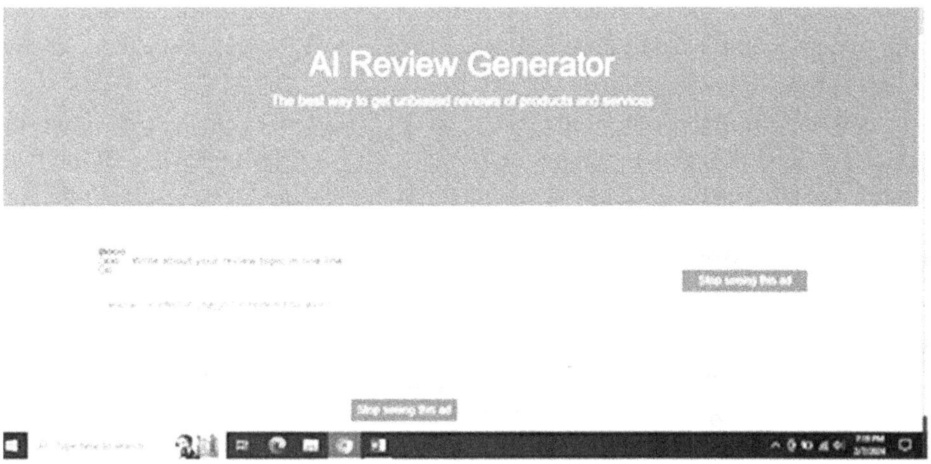

Quick Assessment and Evaluation: Instructors can also quickly assess and evaluate student assignments and tests by using ChatGPT's capabilities. You can use ChatGPT to look for plagiarism in assignments that have already been turned in. Interestingly, the model can generate quizzes on the same subject with different difficulty levels (e.g., high, medium, and easy). When the AI tool was asked to create an extremely difficult quiz on "abstract on ChatGPT in Modern Education," for example, as shown in Figure 2. When users inquired about quizzes on ChatGPT at different difficulty levels, such as medium or hard, they found that the availability of answers marked a clear difference between the two categories of quizzes. In addition, tests and homework can be graded utilising the model. This has the potential to save teachers a great deal of time.

Prospects for Scholars: There are several advantages for researchers using the ChatGPT emulate. First of all, it can be a great help when writing a research paper. In its simplest form, it can improve writing by pointing out and correcting typos, emphasising grammatical errors, providing complex vocabulary, and making improvement suggestions. This gives the researchers more time for implementation and experimentation. The model may additionally summarise the previously published research on the topic in question to help researchers understand it. It can also provide ideas and research topics by looking at a specific topic. We requested, for instance, an untested research proposal from ChatGPT on "how to develop a ML/NN Algorithm related to some resource constraints (like time/memory limits) in code (like epochs) for programmers." ChatGPT offered some intriguing and intriguing research ideas in response to this inquiry.

METHODOLOGY

i. Research Approach

The current study focused exclusively on analysing the effects of ChatGPT use in education, which filled the knowledge gap left by previous research. Gaining a comprehensive understanding of its potential benefits and challenges in the field was the aim. As AI and machine learning continue to be integrated into educational technology, it is imperative that the implications of ChatGPT be carefully considered. By tackling this problem, we can help teachers and students realise ChatGPT's greatest potential for transforming learning while also preserving the effectiveness and integrity of education. In order to learn greater depth about the subject at hand and to obtain an improved comprehension about the way this kind of equipment is employed in the educational field, the SLR was conducted with awareness of the ethical issues surrounding this topic.

Moreover, analysing the ethical questions that ChatGPT's use raises can help develop standards for the moral use of this kind of technology in educational settings. After gathering all the data from the different literature sources, it is crucial to start going through each and every result, adding or removing specific literature by using specific criteria and research questions which will make it easier to remember the exact data needed for this study. To locate literature sources for this study, the SLR was conducted by searching through the journal lists on websites such as Scopus, WoS, IEEE Xplore, ScienceDirect, and ISSN journals. This SLR has allowed for a deeper understanding of the different approaches authors have taken to address ChatGPT's educational application and its impact on the field. With the help of keywords, search filters, and criteria, the SLR was also able to focus even more on specific findings;

as a result, the analysis carried out was capable of assess the topic that hand with as much precision as possible.

ii. Keywords and Criteria Used for Research

Once the research question was established, we employed an assortment of keywords for searching the publication databases selected for the study. This allowed us to gather enough data without deviating from the study's primary focus, which was education. We also had to keep in mind that the information needed to make some sense in order to be examined further. In this study, the search results in each of the selected journal databases were filtered using the following set of keywords: (("ChatGPT" AND ("acquiring" OR "training" OR "e-learning" OR "educating") AND ("artificial intelligence" OR "AI")).

After acquiring the outcomes of the databases that were consulted, these keywords proved easier to navigate through the literature that was found and read the publications that evaluate the research topic. However, these keywords wouldn't have been sufficient if the SLR's objective during this investigation had been to obtain more specific and in-depth information. Because of this, publications which failed to satisfy the study's objectives were filtered out using specific criteria. Below are the criteria (Table 1) that were used to eliminate any unnecessary literature that did not provide any fresh perspectives for this investigation.

A number of articles were gathered after these criteria were applied. Table 2 displays the total number of articles discovered across all searched databases.

Table 1. Criteria for including and excluding an article

Sr. No.	Considered Criterion	Description for Criterion	Article Inclusion/Excision Status
1	Language required	English language is selected depends on the requirement of study (Education)	Article included
2	Publication Year	e.g year of publication is 2022 or 2021	Article included
3	Field	Select field of education or research	Article included
4	Contents of articles	ChatGPT or AI or Chatboat	Article excluded
5	Content relevance	Whether contents are relevant of your education field or not	Article excluded

Table 2. Searched database

Journal Database – Indexing	No. of Available Articles
Scopus	6
WoS	4
ScienceDirect	2
IEEE Xplore	3
Journal with ISSN Number	4
Book chapters	1

iii. Risks Associated With ChatGPT for Higher Education

These keywords made it simpler to read the publications that assess the research topic and navigate through the research which was discovered after obtaining the results of the databases that had been consulted. These keywords, however, would not have been adequate if the goal of the SLR during the investigation had been to to gather more detailed and precise information. As a result, publications that did not meet the goals of the study were excluded based on predetermined standards. The criteria (Table 1) listed below were used to weed out any unneeded literature that didn't offer any novel insights for this study. Moreover, ChatGPT may produce inaccurate or false data. In addition to impeding the educational process for students who rely on ChatGPT, such mistakes run the risk of compromising the integrity and dependability of the classroom atmosphere, which shatters the trust that is necessary for a successful education.

The problem with content created by AI being confused for creative academic work has grown in frequency. Investigations have shown that ChatGPT can produce content that appears original in order to avoid being detected as plagiarised by programmes like Turnitin. According to the literature, academics who utilised ChatGPT were under greater pressure to plagiarise than people who did not. Academic validity, credibility, and the objectivity of student learning evaluation are seriously threatened by this. Even in circumstances where using ChatGPT is permitted during exams, students who use it unfairly benefit themselves over those who do not. More importantly, using ChatGPT can make it more difficult for teachers to assess students' performance accurately, causing keeping an eye on pupils' learning problems difficult.

Chatbots have the potential to improve education, but given the technological divide and digital poverty, it is critical to recognise the risks they may present. For instance, students who are unable to use a dependable Internet connection or who do not have the means to participate in virtual classes could be denied access to chatbots or additional technological learning resources. To combat this, educational institutions need to be proactive in making sure that all students have fair access to digital tools like chatbots. Convincing students which all individuals have the same utilisation of technology as themselves may also be difficult. By including discussions about digital disparities and the need for universal access in their curricula, educators can greatly aid in the spread of this understanding. Finally, by providing themselves with free laptops and Internet access, local organisations that assist underprivileged students can work with colleges and universities.

CHATGPT'S OPPORTUNITIES AND RISKS FOR EDUCATION

Extensive language models, like ChatGPT, could be very influential in real-world instruction and learning. For example, this could involve having the ability to facilitate more tailored and adaptive learning as well as more skillfully set up the assessment and evaluation procedures. Speech-to-text technologies and automated written text generation can help people with visual impairments or partial impairments like dyslexia learn more easily.

This encourages education that is inclusive. The interactive feature of ChatGPT, which makes it possible to implement effective learning mechanisms, is what gives it its special potential for education. Feedback is one crucial element of learner support that makes learning easier, for instance. ChatGPT acts as an experienced partner or instructor's assistant, offering feedback when students give considerate cues. Companies like Khan Academy is attempting to leverage ChatGPT's learning partner potential as soon as possible by integrating the tool with encourages which are already on their platform.

These options for education contrast with the risks and disadvantages of artificial intelligence. One of the most important limitations of ChatGPT's Reinforcement Learning training is the absence of an archive of the truth. As such, there's a good chance that ChatGPT will produce texts that sound plausible but contain accurate information. Teachers and students must be capable of critical reflection in addition to having professional knowledge in order to assess the responses given.

ChatGPT might not explicitly promote critical thinking as a learning partner. However, when implemented with teacher guidance, it can offer opportunities for critical thinking (e.g., when students learn to adjust prompts based on their understanding of the genre or context). Over the next few years, a major and multidisciplinary research question will surface regarding how to maximise the educational potential of ChatGPT (and its successors) while minimising any risks that may arise.

PROSPECTS FOR THE FUTURE AND POSSIBLE OBSTACLES

Based on our thorough knowledge of AI and our experience in the field of education, we have identified the following major challenges for the near future:

- Restricting or banning ChatGPT won't make the issue go away. Accepting it and creating clear rules for its use in academic settings is preferable.
- There is a significant risk that ChatGPT poses to conventional evaluation techniques. Unquestionably, autonomous thoughts, logical deduction, reflective thought, complex problem-solving that anticipates the use of AI tools, innovative thinking, and challenging and confirming data inputs must all be given more weight in future evaluation models.
- As ChatGPT evolves, more oversight and transparency will be needed to discern between information generated by AI and humans. Although regulators are currently far behind technological advancement, legislative action is certain as a result of the conversation that all parties involved have started.
- To guarantee accurate, captivating, and pertinent responses in the context of prompt engineering, novel approaches are needed to enhance and optimise the questions asked of ChatGPT.
- When trying to operate a chatbot, students with special needs might run into more difficulties. While learners with visual impairments might find it difficult to see chatbot content, those with intellectual disabilities might need additional assistance understanding and using chatbots. Teachers must ensure that students who struggle can receive the support they require.
- The conversation goes far beyond the narrow focus of education: learning and assessment are continuous processes in today's corporate environment. When a new hire is integrated into the business and technical operations of an organisation, or when a software engineer is evaluated and hired through a coding challenge, there are parallel opportunities and challenges that present themselves. ChatGPT may prove to be very helpful if it can help developers produce more reliable software faster. Nonetheless, it is our duty as instructors to instruct the software engineer in the management and evaluation of technology for the best outcomes, which calls for an open and transparent action log.

- IoT and ChatGPT both have a lot of room to grow and expand, and their respective fields may find applications in everything from cutting-edge medical technology to contemporary teaching methods. The combination of ChatGPT and IoT is revolutionising how educators and students interact with contemporary learning environments, and this will have a significant positive impact on online education.

DISCUSSION

Acquiring the necessary data for this SLR facilitated a more profound comprehension of the particular uses of ChatGPT for education and its influence on the field. The purpose of the study is to identify the different ways that ChatGPT is used in educational contexts and how these uses affect the quality of teaching and learning. This SLR obtained valuable insights into the advantages, difficulties, and consequences of integrating ChatGPT into teaching methods through a comprehensive review of the literature. The study aims to address the research questions by closely examining the results of the qualitative as well as quantitative content evaluations carried out in the twelve chosen studies.

Que: What's the overall status of scientific research concerning ChatGPT's application in education?

Because ChatGPT has only recently been used in educational settings—it is still in its early stages—there is a dearth of scientific research on the topic in general. Twelve relevant articles, all published in 2023, were gathered for a systematic review. This is because, as ChatGPT was only introduced at the end of 2022, it is still a relatively new practise in educational settings. As a result, meaningful data on the impact on education cannot be gathered until the first few months of the following year, which is why long-term studies have not been conducted. Regarding geographic focus, there was a higher proportion of studies from the Asian region. The rapid adoption of technology and emphasis on education in Asian countries may account for the preponderance of research from these regions. These data may also be influenced by other variables like the availability of funding for research and cooperation between academic institutions. It should be mentioned that the use of this tool in educational institutions has been outlawed in a number of nations. A notable feature of the methodology employed in the chosen articles about ChatGPT's educational impact is the high percentage of theoretical articles compared to qualitative and/or quantitative research. It might be feasible given that artificial intelligence technologies, like ChatGPT, are still in the early stages of development and implementation in the field of education. Therefore, investigating the opportunities and difficulties first requires a primarily theoretical approach before undertaking empirical research.

Que:- Which are the advantages and difficulties of using ChatGPT in a classroom setting?

Technological advancement has become essential to our existence in a society that is constantly changing, and it has inevitably had an impact on education. ChatGPT, an inventive product of OpenAI, is completely changing how teachers and students approach teaching and learning in the classroom. To raise the standard of instruction in the classroom, educational agents must be aware of the advantages and difficulties associated with implementing ChatGPT in schools. It is recommended that teachers use it within the classroom as a promising tool that has several educational advantages. With the help of this tool, lessons and activities can be tailored to meet the unique needs of every student, increasing the efficiency of instruction. Stated differently, it facilitates students' ability to adjust to their own learning style and offers ongoing assistance with their process of acquiring knowledge. The culmination of all of this is more individualised and personalised instruction, which raises student motivation and commitment and is regarded as a vital educational tool for enhancing the teaching and learning process. In addition, ChatGPT encourages cooperation among students by letting them pool their resources to conduct group research projects and hone their teamwork and communication abilities while using this tool to enhance the learning process. Additionally, ChatGPT is a readily available and user-friendly tool for educators and learners, facilitating a seamless integration into the classroom. Lastly, ChatGPT frees up teachers to concentrate on other crucial facets of teaching, like customised interaction and feedback, by helping with the creation of content and activities. Nonetheless, it is important to emphasise that training that is appropriate for the current context is necessary for the effective use of this tool. It is imperative that educators receive the requisite technological training to enable them to utilise this tool efficiently within the classroom, thereby avoiding teacher resistance to its adoption. Thus, in addition to learning how to use the technology, educators also need to comprehend its potential and constraints and deal with the pedagogical and ethical issues that arise. In light of this, it is important to apply this tool thoughtfully in order to create a responsible learning environment in the classroom. To make sure that it doesn't take the place of these crucial skills, its application in the educational system needs to be closely considered. But it's important to take into account the potential educational misuse of ChatGPT that's associated from employing text generation technologies in a highly unethical or fraudulent manner. Furthermore, ChatGPT's understanding is still restricted and hasn't been revised with data after 2021 . As such, its responses might not always be trustworthy or accurate, particularly when it comes to specialised subjects and current affairs. Furthermore, ChatGPT might produce erroneous or even false information. Students who rely on ChatGPT for information during their learning process may find this to be difficult. One of these particular restrictions in this regard is the "hallucination" phenomenon. When talking about responses that seem plausible yet are false or nonsensical, chatbots like ChatGPT are said to be experiencing hallucinations. In other words, the chatbot might produce responses that seem well-written and logical but are actually inaccurate or unsupported statements. This phenomenon can present challenges in the educational setting because it may lead to students being given misleading or confusing information, which would impair their ability to learn and comprehend the material. Because of this, it's crucial to consider these constraints and thoroughly assess the chatbot's accuracy and dependability before utilising it as a teaching tool.

Que:- What new directions will ChatGPT's application in education take in terms of research and trends?

To visualize exploration trends regarding the usage of ChatGPT in learning, a bibliometric analysis was carried out following an analysis with the VOSviewer software. Through this analysis, we were able to identify 3 main emergent study areas and the guidelines that, this field of study is heading in. The analysis discovered 3 clusters that group the keywords existing in the headings and synopses of the readings institute in the databases. In the initial instance, AI is used to drive the entire discussion around the function of the teacher in the classroom. In the context of artificial intelligence use, the teacher's role is essential for advancing innovative teaching approaches and enhancing educational practise. Trainers can create curricula, assessment activities and teaching materials with the help of ChatGPT, which is a useful tool. The influence and application of AI in the teaching space are the subject of the 2nd line of exploration in the arena of education, which has piqued the interest of pedagogical experts and teachers alike. Numerous studies have been conducted and show promise in the use of AI as a supplemental tool in the teaching-learning process. In this context, it has been noted that artificial intelligence—ChatGPT in particular—has the potential to enhance academic performance and promote the growth of critical thinking in students. ChatGPT makes it easier to obtain current, pertinent information by giving prompt, precise answers to specific queries. This can be especially helpful for students as they learn about various subjects and conduct research . Furthermore, artificial intelligence adjusts to the unique learning speed of every student, letting them advance at their own speed and get individualised support according to their requirements. This increases student engagement and motivation while also giving teachers more time to work on more creative and interactive projects like one-on-one tutoring and constructive criticism. But, when using artificial intelligence in the classroom, it's also critical to keep in mind a few difficulties and moral issues. For instance, in order to prevent the spread of false or biassed information, it is crucial to guarantee the security and privacy of student data as well as to evaluate the dependability and correctness of the responses offered by AI. The final sentence is directly related to how artificial intelligence affects the procedures of teaching and learning, taking into account elements like the technological, institutional, cultural, and socioeconomic environments. In conclusion, artificial intelligence (AI) technologies like ChatGPT can assist educational institutions in managing and allocating learning resources intelligently, enhancing their use and effectiveness, significantly altering the nature of education quality and efficiency, and offering students better learning services that will better prepare them for the demands of a changing society.

CONCLUSION

ChatGPT is a cutting-edge LLM that can carry on human-like dialogues and produce nearly indistinguishable text for any NL-natural language request. This can be used to learn programming, write papers, solve puzzles, clarify difficult subjects, give virtual tutoring, practise languages, and answer questions. It can also be used to teach and assist research. In addition, the ChatGPT model can be applied to non-technical problems like language and literature as well as technical ones like computer programming and engineering. The results of surveys demonstrate the value of ChatGPT for research and education in addition to programming instruction. But even though ChatGPT is effective tool, can produce impressive answers on a wide range of subjects, it still has some drawbacks, like lack of common sense, the possibility of bias, trouble with complex reasoning, and an inability to process visual information. When using ChatGPT, it's critical to be aware of its limitations and not to rely solely on it. Furthermore, it is important to carefully consider the complex and multifaceted ethical implications of ChatGPT. Notwithstanding the many obstacles and hurdles, We believe that in order to ensure consistent and equitable access to LLMs over teaching and research, the hazards provided may be appropriately managed and should be taken into account. As a cutting-edge and promising tool to improve student-teacher interaction and the overall learning experience, ChatGPT has become a popular choice in education. The use of ChatGPT by teachers shows a significant transform towards teaching and learning schemes as its possibilities are explored and understood. When applied properly, this artificial intelligence tool greatly enhances students' academic performance and serves as a motivating tool for students by requiring them to use information and communication technologies. It is imperative to remember, though, that using it poses a number of difficulties, which educators need to be aware of in order to prevent improper use. In light of this, adequate training for educators and learners can help them utilise the programme appropriately and prevent abuse in the classroom. This technology has the potential to improve teaching and learning while creating new educational opportunities when used ethically and under close supervision. In this way, even though AI is nothing new, ChatGPT's introduction has sparked discussion in the field of education, raising concerns about established tasks, methods, and assessment. As a result, it's critical to keep investigating these tools' potential and effects, taking into account scientific and didactic factors, and advocating for the moral and responsible incorporation of artificial intelligence into education. The primary constraint of this assessment is the restricted quantity of literature incorporated into the examination. This is due to the fact that there haven't been sufficient studies done thus far that specifically address ChatGPT's use in higher education institutions. Compared to other educational levels, the use of educational technology—like ChatGPT—in higher education may be more recent and has therefore received less research. This is because the subject of educational technology is always growing and changing. Notwithstanding this drawback, the review offers a summary of ChatGPT's impact at the tertiary level. It will prove helpful to extend the study to obtain a more thorough grasp of its impact and benefits at this particular educational level as more research is done and knowledge about the use of ChatGPT in higher education grows. Future research could incorporate additional databases, like Dialnet or ERIC, to guarantee a thorough and thorough search for pertinent studies.

REFERENCES

AlshaterM. M. (2022). Exploring the role of artificial intelligence in enhancing academic performance: A case study of ChatGPT. SSRN 2022. doi:10.2139/ssrn.4312358

Frieder, S., Pinchetti, L., Griffiths, R. R., Salvatori, T., Lukasiewicz, T., Petersen, P. C., Chevalier, A., & Berner, J. (2023). Mathematical capabilities of chatgpt. *arXiv* arXiv:2301.13867.

Fütterer, T., Fischer, C., Alekseeva, A., Chen, X., Tate, T., Warschauer, M., & Gerjets, P. (2023). ChatGPT in education: Global reactions to AI innovations. *Scientific Reports*, *13*(1), 15310. doi:10.1038/s41598-023-42227-6 PMID:37714915

Gill, S. S., Xu, M., Patros, P., Wu, H., Kaur, R., Kaur, K., Fuller, S., Singh, M., Arora, P., Parlikad, A. K., Stankovski, V., Abraham, A., Ghosh, S. K., Lutfiyya, H., Kanhere, S. S., Bahsoon, R., Rana, O., Dustdar, S., Sakellariou, R., ... Buyya, R. (2024). Transformative effects of ChatGPT on modern education: Emerging Era of AI Chatbots. *Internet of Things and Cyber-Physical Systems*, *4*, 19–23. doi:10.1016/j.iotcps.2023.06.002

GilsonA.SafranekC.HuangT.SocratesV.ChiL.TaylorR. A.ChartashD. (2022). How Well Does ChatGPT Do When Taking the Medical Licensing Exams? The Implications of Large Language Models for Medical Education and Knowledge Assessment. medRxiv.

Jalil, S., Rafi, S., LaToza, T. D., Moran, K., & Lam, W. (2023). ChatGPT and Software Testing Education: Promises & Perils. *arXiv* 2023, arXiv:2302.03287. doi:10.1109/ICSTW58534.2023.00078

Kazi, K. S. (2023). Detection of Malicious Nodes in IoT Networks based on Throughput and ML. *Journal of Electrical and Power System Engineering*, *9*(1), 22–29.

Kazi, V., & ... . (2023). Deep Learning, YOLO and RFID based smart Billing Handcart. *Journal of Communication Engineering & Systems*, *13*(1), 1–8.

Kung, T. H., Cheatham, M., Medenilla, A., Sillos, C., De Leon, L., Elepaño, C., Madriaga, M., Aggabao, R., Diaz-Candido, G., Maningo, J., & Tseng, V. (2023). Performance of ChatGPT on USMLE: Potential for AI-assisted medical education using large language models. *PLOS Digital Health*, *2*(2), e0000198. doi:10.1371/journal.pdig.0000198 PMID:36812645

Kutubuddin, K. (2022). Big data and HR Analytics in Talent Management: A Study. *Recent Trends in Parallel Computing*, *9*(3), 16–26.

Liyakat, K. K. S. (2023). Machine Learning Approach Using Artificial Neural Networks to Detect Malicious Nodes in IoT Networks. In P. K. Shukla, H. Mittal, & A. Engelbrecht (Eds.), *Computer Vision and Robotics. CVR 2023. Algorithms for Intelligent Systems*. Springer. doi:10.1007/978-981-99-4577-1_3

Liyakat, K. K. S. (2023). Detecting Malicious Nodes in IoT Networks Using Machine Learning and Artificial Neural Networks. *2023 International Conference on Emerging Smart Computing and Informatics (ESCI)*, 1-5, 10.1109/ESCI56872.2023.10099544

Liyakat, K. K. S. (2024). Machine Learning Approach Using Artificial Neural Networks to Detect Malicious Nodes in IoT Networks. In S. K. Udgata, S. Sethi, & X. Z. Gao (Eds.), *Intelligent Systems. ICMIB 2023. Lecture Notes in Networks and Systems* (Vol. 728). Springer. doi:10.1007/978-981-99-3932-9_12

Machha Babitha, Ms., C Sushma, et al. (2022). Trends of Artificial Intelligence for online exams in education. *International Journal of Early Childhood Special Education*, *14*(01), 2457–2463.

Malinka, K., Perešíni, M., Firc, A., Hujňák, O., & Januš, F. (2023). On the educational impact of ChatGPT: Is Artificial Intelligence ready to obtain a university degree? *arXiv* 2023, arXiv:2303.11146. doi:10.1145/3587102.3588827

Montenegro-Rueda, M., Fernández-Cerero, J., Fernández-Batanero, J. M., & López-Meneses, E. (2023). Impact of the Implementation of ChatGPT in Education: A Systematic Review. *Computers*, *12*(8), 153. doi:10.3390/computers12080153

Rahman, M. M., & Watanobe, Y. (2023). ChatGPT for Education and Research: Opportunities, Threats, and Strategies. *Applied Sciences (Basel, Switzerland)*, *13*(9), 5783. doi:10.3390/app13095783

Vargas-Murillo, A. R., Pari-Bedoya, I. N. M. A., & Guevara-Soto, F. J. (2023). Challenges and Opportunities of AI-Assisted Learning: A Systematic Literature Review on the Impact of ChatGPT Usage in Higher Education. *International Journal of Learning. Teaching and Educational Research*, *22*(7), 122–135. doi:10.26803/ijlter.22.7.7

Chapter 2
Artificial Intelligence-Based Deep Learning Approach to Identify the Web-Based Attack

Kavi Chelvy
Mother Theresa Post Graduate and Research Institute of Health Sciences Educational Institution, India

Ch. Srividhya
Institute of Aeronautical Engineering, Hyderabad, India

B. Swathi
New Horizon College of Engineering, Bangalore, India

Amandeep Nagpal
Lovely Professional University, Phagwara, India

Q. Mohammad
Hilla University College, Babylon, Iraq

ABSTRACT

The use of cutting-edge technologies like computerised material arrangements, artificial intelligence (AI), and the internet of things (IoT) raises the possibility of netting-located attacks in industrial manufacturing. In industrial settings, instances of cyberattacks may corrupt data, disrupt operations, and even inflict bodily injury. To identify manufacturing web-based attacks, this study proposes novel deep-learning strategies. It examines the effectiveness of deep learning models, including convolutional neural networks impacting animate nerve organ systems (CNNs or CNN), reiterating impacting animate nerve organ systems (RNNs), and change models in classifying attacks and identifying the typical attack attribute. Regarding manufacturing detection, the anticipated engineer-based structure exhibits superior performance in veracity, precision, and recall compared to conventional artificial intelligence systems and existing deep knowledge methods.

DOI: 10.4018/979-8-3693-4268-8.ch002

1. INTRODUCTION

In industries, the pinnacle of contemporary technological defiance, emphasises the integration of automated physical plans, artificial intelligence, and the Net to create a dynamic, informed, and interconnected manufacturing environment. This model shift has increased the skill, productivity, and customisation of the manufacturing sector. Money optimisation is accelerated by energy conservation and pollution minimization. Logistics, healthcare, automotive, and agriculture are all being transformed by Industry 5.0 (Awuor, 2023). New cybersecurity vulnerabilities have made Industry structures more susceptible to netting-located attacks as they become more linked and complicated. IoT, cloud, and expanding dossiers boost Industry 5.0's attack surface, indicating hackers may exploit (Pillai & Sharma, 2023). Functioning technology (OT) along with IT enhances the risk of high-tech-material occurrences that affect security, protection, and confidence (Tekerek & Bay, 2019).

Web-located attacks to a degree distributed dismissal influential, SQL inoculation, and cross-station create writing position thoughtful risks to Industry foundation and outcome in the deficit of secret data, movements being upset, and economic misfortunes (Salam et al., 2023). These occurrences can likewise challenge community count on arising skills, impeding their extensive Web-based assaults counting DDoS, injection of SQL, and cross-station write-ups threaten Industry 5.0 basis and cause data loss, transaction disruption, and financial losses. (Hearst et al., 1998) By developing efficient and dependable attack discovery methods, Industry 5.0 structures may maintain their flexibility and assets (Shahid et al., 2022). Machine intelligence is used to identify net-located attacks. (Arafat & Moh, 2019) These methods often fail to keep up with cyber threats' growing sophistication and culture. (Narsimhulu et al., 2022b)

Deep education approaches have shown extraordinary effectiveness in representation acknowledgement, natural language understanding, and conversation acknowledgement, promising cybersecurity reconstruction in Industry 5.0 (Biradar & Hosalli, 2024). Inexperienced dossiers may be automatically analyzed using CNNs, RNNs, and machine model-driving devices to uncover intricate patterns and representations (Eisenhardt & Martin, 2000). Because of this feature, deep-education models may identify sophisticated assaults that are difficult for traditional gadget-learning models to spot. Deep teaching approaches can also handle cybersecurity dataset issues including noise, inequality, and non-stationarity. They may be used with supporting expertise and hostile education to generate more healthy and adaptive assault discovery methods. Deep knowledge approaches may use these progressive capacities to detect and prevent netting-located threats in Industry 5.0, improving the security, safety, and long-term viability of the rapidly increasing digital countryside.

Manufacturing 5.0 relies on human-machine interaction; thus, cybersecurity must benefit people. Effective attack discovery requires electronic and human data and decision-making. To improve attack discovery, humans may establish circumstances, comprehension, and domain knowledge. Cyber-attack halt manufacturing values human knowledge, situational understanding, adaptability, artistry, human-machine interaction, consumer awareness, and training.5.0. Human expertise is needed to defend against complex threats and design active defence mechanisms. Cybersecurity is seen as useful, cultural, and moral. Adaptability and innovation help the bureaucracy solve new problems. Machine cooperation can translate and automate data, but humans understand and take responsibility. User awareness and education programmers promote safety and reduce human exposure to support cybersecurity.

Combining human principles with Industry 5.0's computerised assault recognises people's unique abilities and ability to adapt to educational institution-nonlogical systems. Organisations can authorise an inclusive and solid safety foundation that efficiently protects against cyber warnings in the developing digital countryside by exploiting human expertise, understanding the situation, growing cooperation, and improving consumer knowledge. Many approaches, tests, and datasets for developing 5.0 computerized attack deterrence integrate human factors. These studies try to strengthen cybersecurity methods including consumer analytics for performance and person-in-the-middle computerized protection databases by influencing human knowledge, attitude, and interactions.

Using consumer act analytics (UBA), human performance patterns are monitored and resolved to detect cyberattacks. UBA algorithms alert customers to aberrant behaviour via digital networks. UBA can detect insider alarms, credential theft, and destructive initiatives, research finds. Misdistinguishing normal from atypical activities and addressing single concerns that justify extensive consumer monitoring remain challenges. Researchers created person-in-the-middle cybersecurity datasets to develop and test cybersecurity systems using human components. These datasets consist of confirmation from user logs, network activity, and consumer replies to simulated assaults. They help examine cyber-attack behavioural patterns and develop data-driven explanation techniques. Methods, trials, and datasets merging human components in producing cyber-attack stops have shown promise, but skills are still lacking.

Deep education approaches for cybersecurity are promising, but their use in Industry 5.0 is unclear. CNNs and RNNs have been used to discriminate attack situations in previous studies. However, manufacturing 5.0 lacks a comprehensive grasp of deep learning approaches and their suitability for different netting-located assaults. This data leak hinders effective and effective deep education-located cyber warning detection and checking in manufacturing 5.0 environments.

Considering these obstacles, new studies on the use of deep learning methods for manufacturing 5.0 netting-located attack detection are urgently required. Such studies should aim to integrate different methods, identify acceptable approaches for different attack synopses, and ultimately provide acceptable results. By trying this study breach, the current study goals are to help the progress of cybersecurity related to manufacturing 5.0, guaranteeing the definition of fault-finding foundation, delicate data, and overall count on arising electronics.

This study aims to address the increasing vulnerability of Industry 5.0 systems to web-based assaults, which are caused by their more sophisticated and interconnected nature. Because of the failure of conventional AI patterns to adequately address these concerns, it is essential to investigate other, more effective approaches, such as deep learning.

This study seeks to better comprehend deep education approaches' ability to identify netting-based threats connected to manufacturing 5.0 and assist create more secure, robust, and dependable industrialised arrangements. Despite its potential to detect web-based attacks, deep learning algorithms in Industry 5.0 research are scarce. Additionally, earlier research focused on specific deep-learning methods like CNNs or RNNs without comparing their performance. This work compares CNNs (RNNs) with transformer models to establish a deep learning-based method for identifying online-based attacks in the trade.

The Goals are:

- Examine deep learning methods for the detection of web-based attacks in the industry
- Assess deep learning algorithms' accuracy, precision, and recall.
- Identify the ideal DL method for identifying online-based attacks in the industry.

Industry 5.0 study seeks the finest deep-learning web-based threat detection system. Compare the CNN, RNN, and transformers model accuracy, precision, and recall. Modern industrial systems may be secured by understanding this scientific challenge. Four parts make up the paper. Industry 5.0, internet-based assaults, and advanced learning attack-finding methods are examined in Section 2 to identify research needs. The approach, dataset, neural network deep learning system, and finding metrics are described in Section 3. Section 4 analyses experimental outcomes, including method comparison, implications and performance. Section 5 concludes with an overview of the results, implications, and research goals.

2. METHODOLOGY

This section explains the methods for creating and assessing neural network models for detecting intrusions. The course covers dataset definition, preprocessing, feature selection, extraction, and several deep-learning approaches. Transformer, CNN, and RNN models. The assessment measures used to evaluate model performance are also provided. The suggested technique is shown in Figure 1.

Figure 1. Anticipated deep learning web outbreak detection system

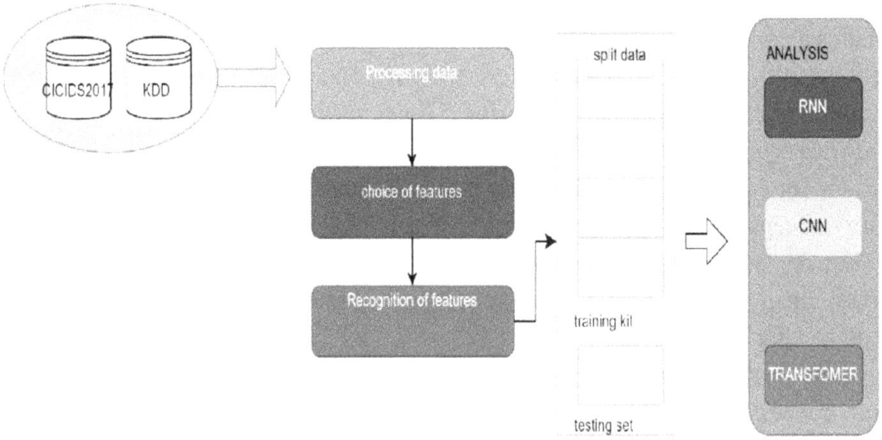

2.1 Preprocessing and Dataset

The KDD Cup 1999 data and the CICIDS2017 data were combined for this study, providing a complete collection of web-based assaults like SQL injection, DDoS attacks, and cross-site scripting. To simulate various assaults, these datasets (see Table 1) were constructed by capturing the Transmission Control Protocol/ traffic in a monitored net environment.

Table 1. Dataset descriptions

Dataset	No. of Illustrations	Occurrence Sorts
KDD Cup 2000	6 million	U2R, DoS, R2L, probe
CICIDS2016	3.8 million	Web attack, physical force, botnet, access, DDoS

About five million connection records in the KDDCup2000 dataset are characterised by 41 characteristics and classified as 'attack' or 'normal', with the latter categorised into four broad types: DDoS, R2L, U2R, and probe. CICIDS2016 is a popular cybersecurity dataset for evaluating and researching intrusion detection systems (IDS). It has roughly 3.8 million instances with 79 characteristics. Although the dataset mainly emphasises internet traffic and scheme events, it also includes human components, like real-world network traffic reflecting user behaviour and activities. The human factor in assault situations is represented by the diversification of attacker motives and techniques. Additionally, CICIDS2017 sources and ends IP, ports, and protocol types reveal individual-network interactions, allowing researchers to study and simulate human behaviour in cyber-attacks. Attack payloads may reveal attacker strategies for exploiting vulnerabilities and deceiving users. This feature enhances human engagement by analysing the influence on people's systems and data. Data pre-processing included eliminating duplicate entries and addressing missing values. Normalising the data ensures consistent scale across characteristics, decreasing bias towards high-magnitude ones. Normalisation used min-max scaling to scale features too.

2.2 Selecting and Extracting Features

Overfitting and computational complexity may arise from large dimensionality datasets, making machine learning models difficult to handle. To decrease dimensionality and keep the most important features, feature selection was conducted. The feature selection procedure used the mutual information criteria, which measures the amount of knowledge gained by seeing one random variable via another. Researchers prioritised characteristics built on their significance for the output mutable and selected the top-ranked features.

Features were extracted after collection to minimise dimensionality and increase model generalisation. Principle component analysis (PCA) was used to extract features, resulting in uncorrelated, maximum variance-capturing principal components. Figure 2 depicts the data pre-treatment, choosing features, and extraction flow.

Figure 2. Choice and extraction of features

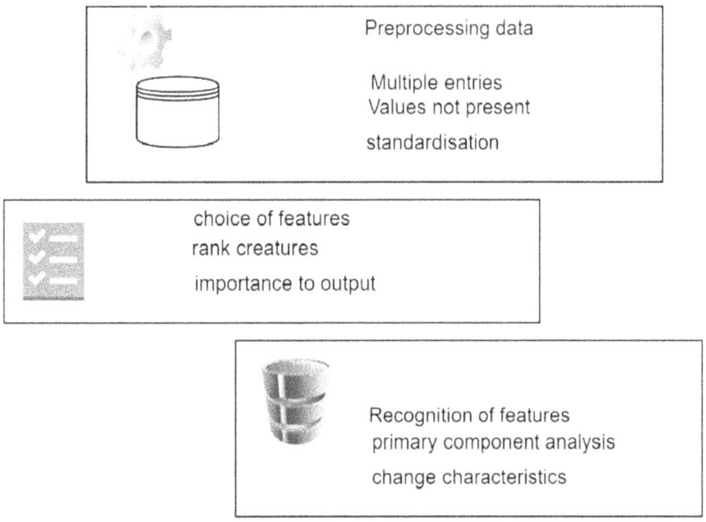

2.3 Models Deep Learning

This study employs RNNs, CNNs, and transformer models for deep learning. These models were chosen for their demonstrated performance in numerous sectors, including cyber security.

2.3.1 A CNNS Model

CNNs excel in image processing by capturing regional trends and spatial hierarchies. However, its use in cyber security, particularly web-based threat detection, is gaining popularity. This work uses CNNs to detect possible attack flags by learning patterns in input feature space. CNN model architecture includes convolutional, pooling, and fully linked layers. Convolutional layers identify local patterns, pooling layers minimise spatial dimensions, and fully linked layers classify. The CNN model architecture is shown in Figure 3.

Figure 3. CNN models architecture

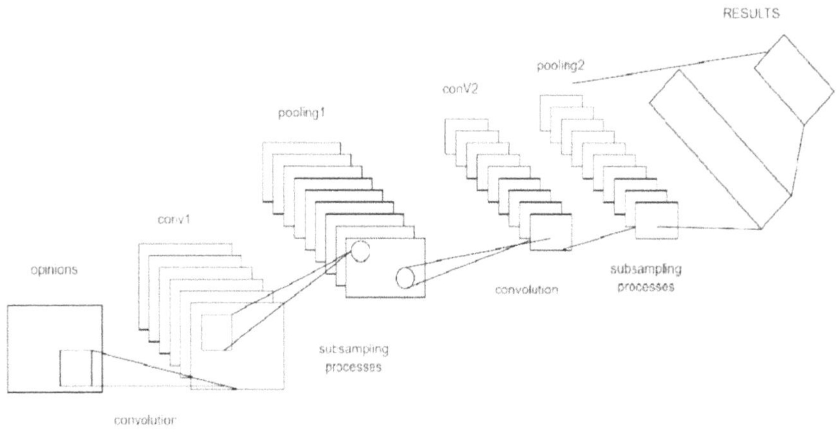

2.3.2 An RNN Model

RNNs are effective at temporal dependencies since they handle sequential data. When detecting web-based attacks, the sequence of network packets might reveal traffic characteristics. The RNN model architecture incorporates LSTM cells, a type of RNN that successfully manages long-term information addictions. A completely linked layer conducts classification after the LSTM layer, as seen in Figure 4.

2.4 Model Transformers

Transformer models inspired by the 'attention' mechanism have revolutionised natural language processing. They excel at interpreting complicated data patterns by focusing on certain elements of the input sequence while creating output. This work uses a transformer model to identify web-based attacks. Encoders process input sequences and decoders create output in the model. The encoder uses numerous self-attention layers to concentrate on specific sections of an input sequence, improving its capacity to detect possible assaults.

Table 2 summarises several topologies and characteristics utilised in transformer models. The design has four layers and 257 hidden dimensions. Eight attention heads capture distinct input features in the model. Set the feed-forward dimension to 1025 to accommodate non-linear modifications in the model. We set the positional encoder length to 1000 to educate the model around the comparative placements of characters in the input data order. Collectively, these characteristics characterise the framework and actions of the research modifier models.

Figure 4. Model architecture of RNN

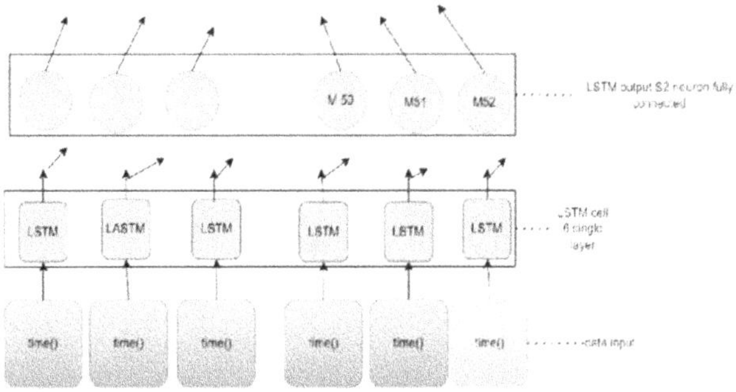

Table 2. Transformer model designs and parameters

Construction	Limitations
Quantity of layers	7
Concealed dimension	257
Q1'	9
Feed-Forward measurement	1025
Input terminology size	10,000
Positional programming distance	10,000
Target terminology size	1000

2.5 Models Evaluation Metric

When validating studies, it is important to consider potential biases or limitations that may affect the study's conclusions. The investigation of deep learning algorithms for the discovery of intrusions in Industry 5.0 identifies vulnerabilities such as confusing factors, sample bias, generalizability, model overfitting, choosing features and measurement bias.

This study used two diverse datasets, KDD 2000 and CI CIDS 2016, to minimise sampling bias, model overfitting, and generalisation. CICIDS2016 is a popular Industry 5.0 dataset Additionally, PCA, transform, rank, and relevance to output algorithms are used to minimise bias and limitations in feature selection and extraction. Table 3 shows feature sizes.

Table 3. Feature sizes

Data	Dimensions After Characteristics Abstraction	Dimensions After Characteristics Collection	Dimensions Next Pre-Processing
KDD Cup 2000	80,000	90,000	76,000
CICIDS2016	170,000	150,000	160,000

2.5.1 Accuracy

This performance metric is the most obvious. Accuracy is the ratio of accurately anticipated negative and positive cases to several occurrences. Method for calculating precision:

$$accuracy = \frac{[tp + tn]}{[tp + tn + fp + fn]}$$

Where TP stands for the total number of accurately detected attacks, TN for the total number of correctly classified normal behaviours, FP for the total number of incorrectly detected attacks, and FN for the total number of wrongly classified attacks.

2.5.2 The Precision

The proportion of accurately anticipated positive cases to total expected positive instances is precision, often known as positive predictive value. It is calculated as follows:

$$precision = \frac{(tp)}{(tp + fp)}$$

A classifier's precision indicates how well it can avoid false positives.

2.5.3 Recall

Recall is the ratio of the total number of properly predicted positive cases to the total number of actual positive instances; it is also called hit rate, sensitivity, or true positive (TP). Here is how it is computed:

$$recall = \frac{(tp)}{(tp + fn)}$$

The recall of a classifier is defined as its capacity to identify all positive samples.

2.5.4 F1 Score

Accuracy and recall are weighted to get the F1 score. Hence, this score considers both the good and negative outcomes. When dealing with a distribution of classes that is not uniform, it is often more helpful than precision. The F1 score is determined below:

$$f1\ score = \frac{2\times(precision\times recall}{(precision+recall}$$

The following paper presents the results of judging the models' depictions utilizing these measures. Using these four tests together gives an all-encompassing judgment of the models' potential and forms it smooth to equate bureaucracy reasonably.

3. RESULTS AS WELL AS DISCUSSION

CNN, RNN, and transformer system testing are shown here. After validation and training, each model detected web-based attacks on the test set. Use the four metrics from the previous chapter—accuracy, remember, accuracy, and F1 score—to evaluate each model.

3.1 Assessing Model Performance

Cross-site scripting, SQL injection, and DDoS are common online assaults. All three systems detect varied attacks, with the transformer model scoring the highest again. Thus, the modifier of the model's self-attention mechanism improves web-based threat detection and recognises particular attacks.

3.2 Compared to Modern Technique

Besides evaluating new deep learning approaches, it is important to compare them to current state-of-the-art methods. This contrast helps assess the level of development obtained by the offered models. Traditional web assault uncovering approaches include signature-based, anomaly-based, and artificial intelligence methods including support vector machines, decision trees, and ensembles. Recent approaches use deep learning methods but tend to concentrate on specialised models like CNNs or RNNs, neglecting transformer models. evaluates suggested models against many state-of-the-art methodologies based on F1 scores.

Demonstrates that suggested models outperform current methodologies. For example, the transformer model has an F1 score of 0.04 points greater than the finest state-of-the-art methodology (collaborative techniques). This shows that deep learning, particularly transformer models, may enhance web-based threat discovery in Industrial 5.0. The tests show that deep learning approaches may be used for web-based threat detection in Industrial 5.0. All three models performed well, indicating that these strategies may identify and differentiate web-based assaults from regular conduct.

Transformer performed best of the three models. Its self-attention device, which lets it concentrate on various sections of the input order while creating output, may be especially good for this job. A recent study supports the efficacy of the transformers model in the sequential data processing. Despite not beating the engine model, RNNs and CNNs revealed outstanding accomplishments, indicating their potential as practicable finishes for this task. RNNs granted permission to beat CNNs in judgment patterns in network packets owing to their competency to analyse subsequent dossier. Note that these verdicts cannot relate to all web-located assaults or Industry 5.0 wholes. More study is necessary to decide the adeptness of these approaches in miscellaneous circumstances and against miscellaneous attackers. Although these models function well, still have the potential for bettering. Future research abilities advance depiction by incorporating supplementary approaches or designing refined deep-education models.

4. CONCLUSION

This paper analyses the use of CNNs, which are RNNs, and generator models for web-located discovery of warnings related to manufacturing 5. All models acted well, suggesting that deep knowledge can identify netting-located warnings. Transformer models acted best with the three models, suggesting their potential for this purpose. The study has strong associations for embellishing Industry 5.0 protection. The study plans that deep knowledge approaches may efficiently recognize netting-located interruptions, a hazard to Industry 5.0. The findings display that engine models, although underutilised in this place's background, grant permission to be very beneficial. This power educates the concoction of more complex and reliable freedom solutions for Industry 5.0, embellishing elasticity and sustainability. Although valuable, the study includes limitations that suggest future research topics. The research first examined three distinct deep-learning models and three distinct assaults. Further study might investigate various models and assaults to better understand the possibility of deep learning for web-based threat detection. The models outperform established procedures; however, they do not include hybrid methods that integrate these techniques.

Future studies might explore hybrid approaches that combine the benefits of classical and advanced learning techniques. The models' interpretability was not examined in the research. Future studies might enhance the interpretation of deep neural network models for web-based threat detection since it is crucial in many security applications.

REFERENCES

Allam, Z., Dey, G., & Jones, D. S. (2020). Artificial intelligence (AI) provided early detection of the coronavirus (COVID-19) in China and will influence future urban health policy internationally. *AI*, *1*(2), 156–165. doi:10.3390/ai1020009

Arafat, M. Y., & Moh, S. (2019). Routing Protocols for Unmanned aerial vehicle networks: A survey. *IEEE Access : Practical Innovations, Open Solutions*, *7*, 99694–99720. doi:10.1109/ACCESS.2019.2930813

Awuor, O. G. (2023). Assessment of existing cyber-attack detection models for web-based systems. *Global Journal of Engineering and Technology Advances, 15*(1), 70–89. doi:10.30574/gjeta.2023.15.1.0075

Biradar, N., & Hosalli, G. (2024). Segmentation and Detection of Crop Pests using Novel U-Net with Hybrid Deep Learning Mechanism. *Pest Management Science*, ps.8083. Advance online publication. doi:10.1002/ps.8083 PMID:38506377

Eisenhardt, K. M., & Martin, J. A. (2000). Dynamic capabilities: What are they? *Strategic Management Journal*, *21*(10–11), 1105–1121. doi:10.1002/1097-0266(200010/11)21:10/11<1105::AID-SMJ133>3.0.CO;2-E

Hearst, M. A., Dumais, S. T., Osuna, E., Platt, J., & Schölkopf, B. (1998). Support vector machines. *IEEE Intelligent Systems & their Applications*, *13*(4), 18–28. doi:10.1109/5254.708428

Narsimhulu, K., Ramchander, N., & Swathi, A. (2022). *An AI-enabled Framework With Feature Selection for Efficient Heart Disease Prediction*. https://doi.org/ doi:10.1109/IC3I56241.2022.10073155

Pillai, S., & Sharma, A. (2023). Hybrid unsupervised web-attack detection and classification – A deep learning approach. *Computer Standards & Interfaces*, *86*, 103738. doi:10.1016/j.csi.2023.103738

Salam, A., Ullah, F., Amin, F., & Abrar, M. (2023). Deep Learning Techniques for Web-Based Attack Detection in Industry 5.0: A Novel approach. *Technologies*, *11*(4), 107. doi:10.3390/technologies11040107

Shahid, W. B., Aslam, B., Abbas, H., Khalid, S. B., & Afzal, H. (2022). An enhanced deep learning based framework for web attacks detection, mitigation and attacker profiling. *Journal of Network and Computer Applications*, *198*, 103270. doi:10.1016/j.jnca.2021.103270

Sharma, S., Zavarsky, P., & Butakov, S. (2020b). *Machine Learning based Intrusion Detection System for Web-Based Attacks*. doi:10.1109/BigDataSecurity-HPSC-IDS49724.2020.00048

Tekerek, A., & Bay, Ö. F. (2019). Design and implementation of an artificial intelligence-based web application firewall model. *Neural Network World*, *29*(4), 189–206. doi:10.14311/NNW.2019.29.013

Chapter 3
ChatGPT and Virtual Experience:
Student Engagement in Online Script Writing – An Experimental Investigation Among Media Students

Biju Kunnumpurath
https://orcid.org/0000-0003-3204-6559
Christ University, India

Vishnu Achutha Menon
Central University of Tamil Nadu, India

Ajith Paul
Christ University, India

ABSTRACT

To study and assess the immersive virtual environment experience of ChatGPT on student engagement in online script writing among media students, an experiment was conducted at the VR Experiential Lab, Christ University, between September 2023 and January 2024. The media students were tasked with writing a script for a short film within a VR environment, with ChatGPT displayed using an Oculus HMD (head-mounted display). A total of 180 students were recruited for the study through purposive sampling, and experiment photos are provided in the appendix. The data collection tool utilized was the virtual experience questionnaire developed by Tcha-Tokey.

INTRODUCTION

Virtual Reality (VR) is an immersive technology that simulates a realistic environment, allowing users to interact with and experience a computer-generated world. It typically involves the use of a head-mounted display (HMD) along with other peripherals to create a sense of presence and immersion. ChatGPT, short for Generative Pre-trained Transformer, is an artificial intelligence language model developed by

DOI: 10.4018/979-8-3693-4268-8.ch003

OpenAI. It is trained on vast amounts of text data and capable of generating human-like text based on the input it receives. ChatGPT can engage in conversations, answer questions, and assist with various language tasks. ChatGPT is utilized for online brainstorming sessions to generate creative ideas and assist with scripting. By interacting with ChatGPT, users can explore different concepts, brainstorm plotlines, and refine their scripts in collaboration with the AI. Experiencing ChatGPT in a VR environment takes this interaction to a new level of immersion. Users can engage with ChatGPT as if it were a virtual character or guide within the VR space. This integration enhances the brainstorming process by providing a more immersive and interactive experience, allowing users to explore their ideas in a visually stimulating environment. The objective of this study is to investigate the impact of integrating ChatGPT, an AI language model, with virtual reality (VR) technology on student engagement in online script writing among media students. Specifically, the study aims to assess how the combination of ChatGPT and VR enhances the brainstorming process, facilitates idea generation, and improves the quality of scriptwriting outcomes. Through an experimental investigation, the study seeks to evaluate the effectiveness of this innovative approach in fostering creativity, collaboration, and immersion in the scriptwriting process within an online learning environment.

Objective

To assess the immersive virtual environment experience of ChatGPT on student engagement in online script writing among media students.

REVIEW OF LITERATURE

Virtual worlds offer a platform that fosters heightened levels of collaboration, engagement, and deeper cognitive processing among students compared to conventional Web 2.0 tools. According to Gallini and Barron (2001), online communication tools were utilized by a minimum of 50% of faculty members and nearly all students, indicating a widespread adoption. Moreover, the orientation process has been identified as a positive contributor to students' seamless integration, leading to meaningful and interactive engagements (Christopoulos et al., 2018). Notably, virtual role-play experiences have garnered significant favour among students (Rogers et al., 2022). Studies by Hernández-Lara and Serradell-López (2018) highlight the positive impact of both generic and specific managerial skills on learning outcomes. Wang (2014) suggests that employing instant messaging techniques can enhance dialogue and reduce transactional distance, particularly beneficial in online course environments. Alabbasi (2022) underscores the importance of behavioural and learning-experience design in driving student engagement, as observed from both instructors' and students' perspectives. Lee (2013) found that students adopting deep learning approaches and scoring high on perception scales outperformed their counterparts. Tcha-Tokey et al. (2018) identified the influence of experience consequences on flow as a novel pathway in user experience dynamics. Hughes and Daykin (2002) argue for heightened attention to design and facilitator skills in the transition to online delivery. Looi (2005) emphasizes the significance of text chat in synchronous communication among students and other learning partners, such as teachers and experts, in online distributed learning environments. Swan (2001) asserts that design clarity, instructor interaction, and active participant discussions significantly impact student satisfaction and perceived learning in asynchronous online learning settings. Avatars serve as conduits for personal narratives and facilitate participation in immersive virtual learning environments (Wan et al., 2011). Tanrıkulu (2022) suggests that collaborative digital storytelling enhances students' writing skills. Chakraborty and Nafukho (2015) posit that teaching presence and immediacy influence learners' cognitive and affective experiences in online class environments. Moreover, Schuster et al. (2014) found that Virtual Theatre enhances spatial presence and flow. Blaine (2019) notes significant discrepancies in the perception of interaction between teachers and students within online courses. Robertson and Despa (2006) highlight the role of social presence in influencing the success of role-playing experiences. Lowell and Alshammari (2019) argue that role-playing simulations offer experiential learning opportunities for students to develop interviewing and diagnosis skills. Molesworth (2004) found mixed attitudes among campus-based students towards computer-mediated communication.

During times of crisis, higher education institutions must adopt approaches that cater to the specific needs of different student groups (Sim & Rahmat, 2022). The asynchronous nature of online conferences provides an interactive textual environment conducive to both social interaction and cognitive meaning construction (Lapadat, 2006). Educators must meticulously plan their in-world learning activities to ensure engaging experiences for their students (Christopoulos et al., 2016). Utilizing a combination of data mining and text mining techniques on large sets of online learning data can unveil valuable patterns in students' learning behaviours (He W, 2013). Online discussions foster active learning behaviours and improve learner outcomes (Williams & Lahman, 2011), with forums being the preferred tool among students (Hampel & Pleines, 2013). Well-designed online discussions among linguistically diverse upper elementary students can contribute to language and literacy development (Zheng & Warschauer, 2015). Comparatively, text-based discussions tend to be more engaging and interactive than video-based discussions (Swartzwelder et al., 2019). The interplay between students' self-reported use of interactive functions, their perceptions of usefulness, and actual usage logs directly influences online learning performance (Wei et al., 2015). Feelings of isolation may arise among students due to the lack of face-to-face interaction with peers and instructors (Gibbs, 1998). The learners' frequency and duration of course access significantly correlate with their academic achievement (Manou et al., 2021). Pre-exposure to a virtual marine environment enhances both argumentative and summative writing outcomes (Lamb et al., 2019), while virtual interaction boosts learner satisfaction with conceptual knowledge acquisition (Cao et al., 2008). Effective teaching strategies involve implementing guided writing alongside virtual reality videos as teaching aids to improve writing achievement and classroom dynamics (Virgiawan et al., 2020). Instructors' demand for tools supporting their analyses is crucial for effective course design (Damasceno et al., 2019). Virtual worlds are fundamentally reshaping the design and delivery of learning experiences (De Freitas et al., 2010). Moreover, constructivism's implications for online adult learning programs encompass interactive, experiential, self-directed, collaborative, and authentic learning (Khanal, 2013).

Perceptions of immersive virtual experiences vary across age, gender, and locality, as noted by Falloon (2010). Immersion in future workplaces provides students with an initial glimpse into their prospective projects and professions (Tham et al., 2018). Moreover, virtual storytelling draws upon research findings from diverse fields such as artificial intelligence and groupware (Schfer, 2003). The emergence of new interactive technologies prompts questions that resonate with literary and artistic traditions predating the electronic era (Abbas & Ryan, 2004). Despite the proliferation of communication methods, email remains the preferred mode of interaction, especially among younger students (Chang, 2009). Offering students, a choice of discussion formats for online discourse proves to be an effective instructional strategy, enhancing both learning outcomes and satisfaction (Lin & Overbaugh, 2007). In the educational landscape of the United States, there's a growing trend of graduate programs in games, simulations, and virtual environments within educational technology programs (Ritzhaupt et al., 2016). The integration of virtual reality (VR) technology in flipped classrooms has shown promise in enhancing student engagement (Lyu, 2020). Incorporating game-like content can positively impact student engagement and learning outcomes. Students have demonstrated improved learning outcomes through engaging in online activities, with tools like ChatGPT proving advantageous for exploring relevant information (Kiy, 2023).

Following a VR experiment, Menon et al. (2022) observed a significant difference in immersive virtual experiences regarding skill, judgement, and technology adoption between males and females. Females tended to immerse more in skill-based experiences, while males exhibited higher levels of judgement and technology adoption. In the realm of asynchronous online discussions, forums serve as environments conducive to fostering a sense of community and engaging students in collaborative dialogues, thus transforming them into meaningful learning activities (Krasnova & Ananjev, 2015). Comparatively, the engagement level within virtual learning environments surpasses that of traditional learning settings (Halili et al., 2018). Features like video and text chat in virtual classrooms offer avenues for continuous interaction, thereby enhancing student engagement and fostering a sense of community (Berry, 2019). Moreover, learner perceptions in critical thinking group tasks within virtual environments are influenced by their perceptions of user difficulty and the collaborative activity's nature (Ghosh et al., 2012).

The integration of interactive communication tools in online learning facilitates robust student-instructor interactions, thereby enhancing perceptions of instructor presence, student engagement, and overall satisfaction with online classes (Park & Kim, 2020). Emphasizing the utility of ChatGPT in learning contexts, Shoufan (2023) advocates for its effective use in educational settings. During online peer review activities, students exhibit interest in identifying grammatical errors, providing additional explanations, paraphrasing sentences, commenting on writing styles, suggesting colloquial expressions, self-repairing, self-clarifying, and incorporating post-interaction. Additionally, they engage in translating words into English. Both students and educators appreciate the incorporation of virtual simulations and serious games in classroom settings, recognizing their value in enhancing learning experiences (Kapralos et al., 2011).

Students derive enjoyment from crafting their digital stories, and the provision of purely online environments fosters student engagement within immersive spaces, thereby enhancing their sense of presence and community (Cheney et al., 2019). In the domains of active learning and autonomy, students perceive online education as offering greater benefits compared to face-to-face education (Carver, 2014). Virtual learning environments are characterized as interactive, narrative spaces wherein participants collaborate, strategize, plan, and interact with various elements such as objects, resources, and other individuals (D'Alba et al., 2011). Across numerous universities worldwide, virtual worlds have been seamlessly integrated into regular academic curricula (Banerjee et al., 2013). Utilizing online discussions is a prevalent method to enhance student understanding of topics and foster social interaction within online learning environments, either among students or between students and instructors (Cho & Tobias, 2016). The utilization of ChatGPT has been shown to enhance performance in functionality, user flow, and content comprehension among students, surpassing the outcomes of relying solely on traditional search engines (Elkhodr et al., 2023). Moreover, tools facilitating communication between instructors and students are deemed more crucial and satisfying by students compared to tools enabling student-student interactions (Small et al., 2012). However, there exist both strengths and weaknesses in employing VR-based English learning activities, impacting the quantitative data regarding students' English learning achievements, particularly in writing skills within public secondary schools in North Bali (Sepang et al., 2021).

Research Questions

1. What is the relationship between different components of immersive virtual experience?
2. Is there any difference in the perception of immersive virtual experience with respect to age, gender, and locality?
3. What influences do participants' prior experiences have on their perception and engagement with various components of immersive virtual experiences?

METHODOLOGY

The experiment took place at the VR Experiential Lab, Christ University, between September 2023 and January 2024. The media students were tasked with writing a script for a short film in a VR environment. ChatGPT was displayed using an Oculus HMD (Head-Mounted Display) with two controllers and accessories, including a Link cable as provided. The HMD features a resolution of 1832 x 1920 and supports refresh rates of 60, 72, and 90 Hz. A total of 180 students were recruited for the study through purposive sampling. Experiment photos are attached in the appendix.

The data collection tool utilized was the Virtual Experience Questionnaire developed by Tcha-Tokey et al. (2016).

The study focused on several key variables:

1. Presence: This variable assesses the extent to which participants feel as though they are physically and socially present within the virtual environment. Presence is defined as the subjective feeling of being elsewhere than one's actual physical location due to the influence of a computer-generated simulation.
2. Engagement: This variable measures the level of involvement and energy exerted by participants while experiencing Virtual Reality. Engagement encompasses emotional, cognitive, and behavioural aspects of interaction.
3. Immersion: Immersion refers to the illusion created by VR technology, wherein the user's sensory stimuli are replaced by virtual sensory stimuli, leading to a heightened sense of presence within the virtual environment.
4. Flow: Flow is characterized as a positive psychological state wherein users feel a sense of control and deep engagement while interacting with VR content.
5. Emotion: Emotion encompasses the range of feelings experienced by users during VR interaction, including satisfaction, joy, disappointment, anxiety, pleasure, and frustration.
6. Skill: Skill represents the knowledge and proficiency gained through VR interaction. This variable provides insight into users' attitudes toward technology and their comfort level with computer-based activities.
7. Judgment: Judgment refers to users' overall evaluation of their experience within the virtual environment, encompassing factors such as enjoyment, usability, and satisfaction
8. Experience: This variable explores physiological reactions experienced by users during VR interaction, including motion sickness, stress, dizziness, and headaches.
9. Technology Adoption: Technology adoption assesses users' intentions and actions regarding future use or adoption of VR technology based on their experience within the virtual environment.

RESULTS

RQ1: What is the relationship between different components of immersive virtual experience?

Table 1. Correlation between components of immersive virtual experience

	1	2	3	4	5	6	7	8	9
Presence (1)	1	.739**	.848**	.781**	.524**	.076	-.477**	.387**	.153*
Engagement (2)		1	.582**	.559**	.463**	.114	-.354**	.275**	.189*
Immersion (3)			1	.709**	.457**	.156*	-.401**	.313**	.209**
Flow (4)				1	.384**	.070	-.503**	.549**	.194**
Emotion (5)					1	.371**	-.785**	.613**	.579**
Skill (6)						1	-.023	-.118	.766**
Judgement (7)							1	-.942**	-.318**
Experience Consequence (8)								1	190*
Technology Adoption (9)									1

*p<0.05 **p<.001

Table 1 presents the correlations among various components of immersive virtual experience, as indicated by the Pearson correlation coefficient (r). Presence, denoting the feeling of being present in the virtual environment, exhibits strong positive correlations with Engagement ($r = 0.739, p < 0.001$), Immersion ($r = 0.848, p < 0.001$), and Flow ($r = 0.781, p < 0.001$), suggesting that a higher sense of presence aligns with increased engagement, immersion, and flow. Engagement also correlates positively with Immersion ($r = 0.582, p < 0.001$) and Flow ($r = 0.559, p < 0.001$), indicating that heightened engagement relates to deeper immersion and better flow. Immersion further correlates positively with Flow ($r = 0.384, p < 0.001$) and Emotion ($r = 0.371, p < 0.001$), emphasizing a connection between enhanced immersion, improved flow, and stronger emotional responses. Flow correlates positively with Emotion ($r = 0.613, p < 0.001$), suggesting that individuals experiencing better flow tend to have stronger emotional reactions. Skill in navigating virtual environments shows a moderate positive correlation with Emotion ($r = 0.579, p < 0.001$), indicating that individuals with higher skill levels often experience more intense emotional responses. Conversely, Judgement negatively correlates with Experience Consequence ($r = -0.942, p < 0.001$), suggesting that individuals who exhibit more judgmental tendencies perceive fewer consequences from their virtual experiences. Experience Consequence shows a moderate positive correlation with Technology Adoption ($r = 0.190, p < 0.05$), implying that individuals perceiving more consequences from virtual experiences are more inclined to adopt associated technologies.

RQ 2: Is there any difference in the perception of immersive virtual experience with respect to age, gender, and locality?

Table 2 displays the results of one-way ANOVA tests conducted to compare immersive virtual experience scores across different age groups. For Presence, Engagement, and Immersion, there were statistically significant differences observed between age groups. Specifically, Presence ($F = 2.991$, p =

0.053), Engagement (F = 3.810, p = 0.024), and Immersion (F = 3.712, p = 0.026) showed significant variations across age categories, suggesting that age may influence these aspects of immersive virtual experiences. However, for Flow, Skill, Experience Consequence, and Technology Adoption, the ANOVA tests did not reveal statistically significant differences between age groups. Flow (F = 0.674, p = 0.511), Skill (F = 1.279, p = 0.281), Experience Consequence (F = 2.703, p = 0.070), and Technology Adoption (F = 2.556, p = 0.080) exhibited non-significant p-values, indicating that age may not play a significant role in determining these components of immersive virtual experiences. Interestingly, significant differences were found in Emotion (F = 10.454, p < 0.001) and Judgement (F = 4.824, p = 0.009) across age groups. These findings suggest that age has a notable impact on emotional responses and judgment within immersive virtual environments.

Table 2. One-way ANOVA comparing immersive virtual experience based on age

		Sum of Squares	Mean Square	F	Sig.
Presence	Between Groups	114.048	57.024	2.991	.053
	Within Groups	3354.936	19.062		
Engagement	Between Groups	17.736	8.868	3.810	.024
	Within Groups	409.705	2.328		
Immersion	Between Groups	54.996	27.498	3.712	.026
	Within Groups	1303.898	7.409		
Flow	Between Groups	26.569	13.285	.674	.511
	Within Groups	3468.000	19.705		
Emotion	Between Groups	1316.456	658.228	10.454	.000
	Within Groups	11082.091	62.966		
Skill	Between Groups	161.909	80.954	1.279	.281
	Within Groups	11139.287	63.291		
Judgement	Between Groups	8364.701	4182.350	4.824	.009
	Within Groups	152596.081	867.023		
Experience Consequence	Between Groups	4575.277	2287.639	2.703	.070
	Within Groups	148956.935	846.346		
Technology Adoption	Between Groups	326.089	163.045	2.556	.080
	Within Groups	11226.905	63.789		

*p<0.05

Further the post hoc tests, employing the Least Significant Difference (LSD) method, aimed to discern significant differences among age groups (15 years and below, 16 years to 45 years, and 46 years to 75 years) concerning several dependent variables: Presence, Engagement, Immersion, Flow, Emotion, Skill, Judgement, Experience Consequence, and Technology Adoption. The results unveiled various noteworthy findings across different dependent variables. In terms of Presence, significant differences were observed between the youngest age group (15 years and below) and both the middle and oldest age groups, indicating differing levels of presence experienced. Engagement exhibited significant disparities between the youngest age group and the oldest, suggesting distinct levels of engagement in activities. Similarly, Immersion displayed significant differences between the youngest age group and both older age groups, indicating varying degrees of immersion experienced. Emotion significantly differed across all age group pairs except between the middle and oldest age groups, signifying nuanced emotional responses based on age. Skill also showed significant differences between the youngest age group and both older age groups, suggesting variations in skill levels across age brackets. Judgement demonstrated significant differences between all age group pairs, indicating diverse judgment capabilities among different age groups. Experience Consequence revealed significant differences between the youngest and oldest age groups, implying differing consequences experienced as a result of various experiences. However, Technology Adoption did not display significant differences between any age group pairs at the conventional significance level of 0.05. These findings underscore the importance of considering age-related differences when examining the impact of various factors on individuals' experiences and behaviours.

Table 3. Independent sample t-test comparing immersive virtual experience based on gender

	Gender	Mean	SD	t	df	Sig.
Presence	Male	87.4815	4.48983	1.407	177	.168
	Female	86.5352	4.26558			
Engagement	Male	29.1296	1.48571	1.992	177	.003
	Female	28.6620	1.61195			
Immersion	Male	48.2685	2.70896	-.131	177	.102
	Female	48.3239	2.86244			
Flow	Male	96.0185	4.39197	-.263	177	.218
	Female	96.1972	4.51860			
Emotion	Male	75.9907	7.13880	-2.115	177	.000
	Female	78.6620	9.73938			
Skill	Male	52.3611	9.52268	-3.653	177	.000
	Female	56.6620	3.39303			
Judgement	Male	60.3704	26.30220	.825	177	.000
	Female	56.5775	35.11640			
Experience Consequence	Male	34.9722	29.07466	-.207	177	.550
	Female	35.9014	30.01055			
Technology Adoption	Male	56.1296	8.49529	-4.001	177	.839
	Female	60.8592	6.40601			

*p<0.05

Table 3 illustrates the outcomes of independent sample t-tests analyzing immersive virtual experience scores across gender lines. The study detected no statistically significant disparity in presence scores between male (M = 87.48) and female (M = 86.54) participants (t = 1.407, p = 0.168), suggesting a comparable sense of being present in the virtual environment for both genders. Male participants (M =

29.13) demonstrated significantly higher levels of engagement compared to their female counterparts (M = 28.66) (t = 1.992, p = 0.003), indicating a greater involvement and interest in the immersive experience among males. While no significant difference was observed in immersion scores between male (M = 48.27) and female (M = 48.32) participants (t = -0.131, p = 0.102), both genders experienced a similar depth of immersion within the virtual environment. Both male (M = 96.02) and female (M = 96.20) participants exhibited analogous levels of flow experience, with no significant difference noted (t = -0.263, p = 0.218), implying a comparable state of absorption and enjoyment during the immersive task. Male participants (M = 75.99) reported markedly lower emotional responses compared to female participants (M = 78.66) (t = -2.115, p < 0.001), suggesting that females may experience a stronger emotional connection or reaction to the virtual content.

Female participants (M = 56.66) showcased significantly higher skill levels than male participants (M = 52.36) (t = -3.653, p < 0.001), indicating a greater proficiency or mastery in navigating and interacting within the virtual environment among females. Male participants (M = 60.37) exhibited notably higher judgment scores compared to female participants (M = 56.58) (t = 0.825, p < 0.001), indicating differences in the assessment and decision-making processes during the immersive task. No significant difference emerged in experience consequence scores between male (M = 34.97) and female (M = 35.90) participants (t = -0.207, p = 0.550), suggesting that both genders may perceive similar consequences resulting from their immersive experiences. Female participants (M = 60.86) demonstrated significantly higher levels of technology adoption than male participants (M = 56.13) (t = -4.001, p < 0.001), indicating a greater readiness or inclination to embrace technological advancements among females. These findings underscore gender-based disparities in immersive virtual experiences, particularly in engagement, emotional response, skill level, judgment, and technology adoption. However, no significant differences were observed in presence, immersion, flow, and experience consequence between male and female participants.

Table 4 displays the results of a one-way ANOVA assessing the differences in immersive virtual experience across different localities. There was a significant difference in presence scores between different localities, as indicated by a significant F-value (F = 5.904, p = 0.003). This suggests that participants from different localities experienced varying levels of presence in immersive virtual environments. No significant difference was found in engagement scores across different localities (F = 0.907, p = 0.405), indicating that participants from different areas demonstrated similar levels of engagement during immersive tasks. The analysis revealed a significant difference in immersion scores between localities (F = 3.314, p = 0.039), suggesting that participants from different regions experienced varying degrees of immersion within the virtual environment. A highly significant difference was observed in flow scores across localities (F = 17.316, p < 0.001), indicating that participants from different areas experienced significantly different levels of flow during the immersive task. Significant differences were found in emotion scores between localities (F = 5.841, p = 0.003), suggesting that participants from different regions experienced varying emotional responses to the virtual content. The analysis revealed a significant difference in skill levels across different localities (F = 15.589, p < 0.001), indicating that participants from different areas demonstrated varying levels of proficiency in interacting within the virtual environment.

A highly significant difference was observed in judgment scores across localities (F = 33.773, p < 0.001), suggesting that participants from different regions exhibited significantly different levels of judgment during immersive tasks. Significant differences were found in experience consequence scores between localities (F = 43.708, p < 0.001), indicating that participants from different areas perceived varying consequences resulting from their immersive experiences. A significant difference was observed in technology adoption scores across localities ($F = 9.035$, $p < 0.001$), suggesting that participants from different regions demonstrated varying levels of acceptance and utilization of technology in immersive settings.

Table 4. One-way ANOVA comparing immersive virtual experience based on locality

		Sum of Squares	Mean Square	F	Sig.
Presence	Between Groups	218.113	109.057	5.904	.003
	Within Groups	3250.870	18.471		
Engagement	Between Groups	4.363	2.181	.907	.405
	Within Groups	423.079	2.404		
Immersion	Between Groups	49.310	24.655	3.314	.039
	Within Groups	1309.583	7.441		
Flow	Between Groups	574.570	287.285	17.316	.000
	Within Groups	2920.000	16.591		
Emotion	Between Groups	771.726	385.863	5.841	.003
	Within Groups	11626.822	66.061		
Skill	Between Groups	1700.727	850.364	15.589	.000
	Within Groups	9600.468	54.548		
Judgement	Between Groups	44641.533	22320.766	33.773	.000
	Within Groups	116319.249	660.905		
Experience Consequence	Between Groups	50950.722	25475.361	43.708	.000
	Within Groups	102581.490	582.849		
Technology Adoption	Between Groups	1075.726	537.863	9.035	.000
	Within Groups	10477.269	59.530		

*p<.05

Further post hoc tests conducted using the LSD (Least Significant Difference) method aimed to identify significant differences among various locations (Rural, Urban, and Semi Urban) regarding several dependent variables, including Presence, Engagement, Immersion, Flow, Emotion, Skill, Judgement, Experience Consequence, and Technology Adoption. Results indicated significant differences in Presence between Rural and Urban, Rural and Semi Urban, as well as Urban and Semi Urban locations. However, no significant differences were found in Engagement. In terms of Immersion, significant differences emerged between Rural and Semi Urban, and Semi Urban and Urban locations. Similarly, Flow exhibited significant differences across all pairs of locations. Emotion showed significant differences between Rural and Urban, Urban and Semi Urban, and Semi Urban and Rural locations. Skill varied significantly between Rural and Semi Urban, Urban and Semi Urban, and Urban and Rural locations. Judgement and Experience Consequence both demonstrated significant differences across all pairs of locations. Technology Adoption revealed significant differences between Rural and Urban, Urban and

Semi Urban, and Semi Urban and Rural locations. These findings provide valuable insights into the influence of location on participants' experiences and perceptions within the studied context.

RQ 3: What influences do participants' prior experiences have on their perception and engagement with various components of immersive virtual experiences?

Table 5 revealed notable gender differences across various dimensions of immersive virtual experiences. Male participants exhibited significantly higher levels of presence in immersive virtual environments compared to females ($t = 3.927$, $p < 0.001$), indicating a stronger sense of being within the virtual space. Similarly, males displayed significantly greater engagement ($t = 4.096$, $p < 0.001$) and immersion ($t = 3.689$, $p < 0.001$) compared to females, emphasizing their deeper involvement and connection with the virtual content. Male participants reported significantly stronger emotional responses ($t = 5.526$, $p = 0.035$) and exhibited higher skill levels ($t = 4.188$, $p < 0.001$) than their female counterparts, indicating a more intense emotional engagement and better proficiency in navigating the virtual environment.

Table 5. Independent sample t-test comparing immersive virtual experience based on participant's prior VR experience

	Gender	Mean	SD	t	df	Sig.
Presence	Male	90.0000	.00000	3.927	177	.000
	Female	86.5695	4.61232			
Engagement	Male	30.0000	.00000	4.096	177	. .000
	Female	28.7483	1.61335			
Immersion	Male	50.0000	.00000	3.689	177	.000
	Female	47.9735	2.90045			
Flow	Male	97.4286	5.01427	1.751	177	.395
	Female	95.8411	4.28656			
Emotion	Male	84.4643	8.23040	5.526	177	.035
	Female	75.6755	7.63549			
Skill	Male	59.6071	.49735	4.188	177	.000
	Female	53.0397	8.27678			
Judgement	Male	42.6071	29.16662	-3.195	177	. 551
	Female	61.8808	29.35051			
Experience Consequence	Male	45.4286	33.39930	1.995	177	.005
	Female	33.4702	28.28847			
Technology Adoption	Male	59.2500	7.09525	.889	177	.477
	Female	57.7748	8.22287			

*p<0.05

DISCUSSIONS

The examination elucidates the significant interrelations among diverse facets of immersive virtual experience through the lens of the Pearson correlation coefficient. It reveals robust positive correlations between Presence, denoting the sensation of being present in the virtual environment, and Engagement, Immersion, and Flow, indicating that an augmented sense of presence is concomitant with heightened levels of engagement, immersion, and flow, thereby facilitating a cohesive and immersive experience. The positive associations observed between Engagement and Immersion, as well as between Immersion and Flow, underscore the proposition that deeper engagement engenders enhanced immersion and superior flow, thereby contributing to a more enriching virtual encounter. The correlation between Immersion and Emotion underscores the emotional dimension of immersive experiences, suggesting that heightened immersion correlates with intensified emotional responses, thereby enhancing the overall experiential quality. Moreover, the positive correlation between Flow and Emotion reaffirms this notion, indicating that individuals experiencing optimal flow tend to manifest heightened emotional reactions, thereby augmenting their immersion. The moderate positive correlation discerned between Skill in navigating virtual environments and Emotion suggests that individuals with enhanced navigational skills may evoke more pronounced emotional responses, potentially reflecting their adeptness and comfort within virtual environments. Conversely, the negative correlation between Judgement and Experience Consequence implies that individuals demonstrating a predisposition towards judgmental attitudes perceive fewer ramifications from their virtual encounters, possibly indicating a more discerning or disengaged approach to virtual interactions. Finally, the positive correlation noted between Experience Consequence and Technology Adoption suggests that individuals perceiving greater consequences from their virtual experiences are more predisposed to embrace associated technologies, underscoring the potential influence of immersive experiences on technology adoption tendencies.

The analysis delineates noteworthy differences observed across age groups, genders, and localities concerning various components of immersive virtual experiences. The significant disparities in Presence, Engagement, and Immersion across age cohorts suggest that age may indeed exert influence over these dimensions of immersive virtual encounters. The observed discrepancies in Emotion and Judgement underscore age-related variations in emotional responses and cognitive assessments within immersive virtual environments, possibly influenced by differing life experiences and cognitive development stages. On the other hand, the gender-based differences elucidated through independent sample t-tests unveil distinct patterns in immersive virtual experiences between male and female participants. While males demonstrated higher levels of Engagement, females exhibited greater Emotion, Skill, and Technology Adoption, reflecting gender-specific tendencies in immersive engagement and technological readiness. Lastly, the significant differences revealed by one-way ANOVA tests across different localities underscore the impact of geographical context on immersive virtual experiences. While Engagement scores remained consistent, variations in other dimensions such as Presence, Immersion, and Emotion highlight the nuanced influence of locality on individuals' perceptions and experiences within virtual environments. Overall, these findings underscore the importance of considering demographic factors such as age, gender, and locality when assessing and designing immersive virtual experiences, as they can significantly shape individuals' engagement, emotions, and perceptions within virtual environments. The observed differences across age groups, genders, and localities in various components of immersive virtual experiences likely stem from a combination of factors related to individuals' backgrounds, experiences, and societal contexts. Regarding age, developmental stages, cognitive abilities, and generational differences may contribute to variations in how individuals perceive and engage with immersive virtual environments. For gender, societal norms, cultural expectations, and differences in technology use patterns may influence the ways males and females interact with and experience immersive technologies. Geographical context, socio-economic factors, and access to technology infrastructure could account for the disparities observed across different localities. Overall, these factors intersect to shape individuals' perceptions, emotions, and behaviours within immersive virtual environments, highlighting the need for nuanced considerations of demographic factors in understanding and designing immersive experiences.

The analysis highlights the significant impact of participants' prior experiences on their perception and engagement within immersive virtual environments, particularly in relation to gender differences. Male participants consistently demonstrated higher levels of presence, engagement, immersion, emotional responses, and skill compared to females. This discrepancy suggests that individuals' prior experiences, shaped by factors such as exposure to technology and gaming, may influence their engagement with immersive virtual spaces. For instance, those with extensive gaming experience or familiarity with virtual environments may feel more at ease and immersed, leading to heightened engagement and emotional responses. Individuals with greater technological proficiency may navigate virtual environments more effectively, influencing their overall engagement with immersive experiences. Consequently, the findings underscore the importance of considering participants' backgrounds and experiences when designing immersive virtual environments to ensure inclusivity and optimal engagement. However, it's essential to note that while prior experiences contribute significantly, other factors such as socio-cultural context and individual preferences may also influence participants' perceptions and engagement within immersive virtual spaces. Therefore, a holistic approach that considers a range of factors is crucial for designing immersive experiences that cater to diverse audiences effectively.

CONCLUSION

In conclusion, the findings underscore the intricate interplay between various components of immersive virtual experiences and their relationships with individual characteristics such as age, gender, and prior experiences. The Pearson correlation analysis revealed significant associations among presence, engagement, immersion, flow, emotion, skill, judgement, experience consequence, and technology adoption. These correlations shed light on the interconnected nature of these components, suggesting that a higher sense of presence tends to align with increased engagement, immersion, and flow, while deeper immersion relates to better flow and stronger emotional responses. Moreover, age-related and gender-based differences were observed, indicating disparities in aspects such as engagement, emotion, skill, judgement, and technology adoption across different demographics. Participants' prior experiences, particularly their exposure to technology and gaming, emerged as significant influencers of their perception and engagement within immersive virtual environments. Understanding these dynamics is essential for designing tailored and effective immersive experiences that cater to diverse user demographics and backgrounds. By considering individual characteristics and experiences, developers can optimize the design and implementation of immersive virtual environments to enhance user engagement, immersion, and overall experience satisfaction.

Implication

Implications of the Research Paper:

1. Enhanced Student Engagement: The findings of this research paper have significant implications for enhancing student engagement in online script writing. By leveraging ChatGPT and virtual reality (VR) technology, educators can provide students with an immersive and interactive learning experience that stimulates creativity and active participation.
2. Improved Scriptwriting Skills: This research suggests that integrating ChatGPT with VR can lead to improvements in scriptwriting skills among media students. By utilizing AI-powered tools for brainstorming and idea generation within a virtual environment, students may develop a deeper understanding of narrative structures, character development, and dialogue crafting.
3. Efficient Collaborative Work: The study highlights the potential for ChatGPT and VR to facilitate collaborative work among students in online script writing projects. By enabling real-time interactions and idea exchange within a virtual space, students can collaborate more effectively, regardless of geographical limitations or scheduling constraints.
4. Accessibility and Inclusivity: The use of ChatGPT and VR in online script writing can promote accessibility and inclusivity in media education. These technologies offer alternative avenues for learning and creative expression, accommodating diverse learning styles and preferences.
5. Future Educational Practices: The research paper underscores the importance of integrating emerging technologies into educational practices. As ChatGPT and VR continue to evolve, educators can explore innovative approaches to teaching and learning in media studies and other disciplines.
6. Implications for Pedagogy: The findings of this study may inform pedagogical strategies for incorporating AI and immersive technologies into curriculum design. Educators can adapt instructional methods to leverage the potential of ChatGPT and VR for enhancing student learning outcomes and fostering digital literacy skills.
7. Industry Relevance: The research outcomes may have implications for industry professionals in the media and entertainment sector. Understanding the benefits of ChatGPT and VR in scriptwriting education can inform industry practices and workflows, leading to the adoption of innovative tools and techniques for content creation.

Data availability

Data is available upon request.

ACKNOWLEDGMENT

We extend our gratitude to the Christ University Media Students of Yeshwanthpur Campus for their invaluable contribution. The researchers would like to express sincere appreciation to Katy Tcha-Tokey and Oliver Christmann from Arts et Métiers ParisTech, Paris, France, for generously granting permission to utilize the Virtual Experience Questionnaire.

REFERENCES

Abbas, N. B., & Ryan, M.-L. (2004). Narrative as virtual reality: Immersion and interactivity in literature and electronic media. *The Yearbook of English Studies*, *34*, 277. doi:10.2307/3509518

Alabbasi, D. (2022). Factors influencing students engagement in virtual classrooms and their impact on satisfaction. *Information Sciences Letters*, *11*(4), 1203–1215. doi:10.18576/isl/110420

Banerjee, I., Perera, I., & Choudhury, J. (2013). Introducing immersive technologies for learning: A study evaluating the readiness for using virtual worlds for learning and teaching in an Indian University. *2013 Sixth International Conference on Contemporary Computing (IC3)*. 10.1109/IC3.2013.6612202

Berry, S. (2019). The role of video and text chat in a virtual classroom: How technology impacts community. In *Educational Technology and Resources for Synchronous Learning in Higher Education* (pp. 173–187). IGI Global. doi:10.4018/978-1-5225-7567-2.ch009

Blaine, A. M. (2019). Interaction and presence in the virtual classroom: An analysis of the perceptions of students and teachers in online and blended Advanced Placement courses. *Computers & Education*, *132*, 31–43. doi:10.1016/j.compedu.2019.01.004

Cao, J., Crews, J. M., Lin, M., Burgoon, J. K., & Nunamaker, J. F. Jr. (2008). An empirical investigation of virtual Interaction in supporting learning. *The Data Base for Advances in Information Systems*, *39*(3), 51–68. doi:10.1145/1390673.1390680

Carver, D. L. (2014). *Analysis of student perceptions of the psychosocial learning environment in online and face-to-face career and technical education courses*. Old Dominion University Libraries.

Chakraborty, M., & Nafukho, F. M. (2015). *Strategies for virtual learning environments: Focusing on teaching presence and teaching immediacy*. Internet Learning. doi:10.18278/il.4.1.1

Chang, C.-W. (2009). Efficacy of interaction among college students in a web-based environment. *Journal of Educational Technology Development and Exchange*, *2*(1). Advance online publication. doi:10.18785/jetde.0201.02

Cheney, A. W., McClannon, T., Bolt, L., & Sanders, R. L. (2019). Perceptions of presence and community in immersive online learning environments. In *Emerging Technologies in Virtual Learning Environments* (pp. 116–131). IGI Global. doi:10.4018/978-1-5225-7987-8.ch006

Cho, M.-H., & Tobias, S. (2016). Should instructors require discussion in online courses? Effects of online discussion on community of inquiry, learner time, satisfaction, and achievement. *International Review of Research in Open and Distance Learning*, *17*(2). Advance online publication. doi:10.19173/irrodl.v17i2.2342

Christopoulos, A., Conrad, M., & Shukla, M. (2016). How do students 'really' interact with virtual worlds? - the influence of proper induction for virtual interactions. *Proceedings of the 8th International Conference on Computer Supported Education*. 10.5220/0005755700430054

Christopoulos, A., Conrad, M., & Shukla, M. (2018). Increasing student engagement through virtual interactions: How? *Virtual Reality (Waltham Cross)*, *22*(4), 353–369. doi:10.1007/s10055-017-0330-3

D'Alba, A., Najmi, A., Gratch, J., & Bigenho, C. (2011). Virtual learning environments. The oLTECx: A study of participant attitudes and experiences. *International Journal of Gaming and Computer-Mediated Simulations*, *3*(1), 33–50. doi:10.4018/jgcms.2011010103

Damasceno, A. L. de B., Ribeiro, D. dos S., & Barbosa, S. D. J. (2019). What the literature and instructors say about the analysis of student interaction logs on virtual learning environments. *2019 IEEE Frontiers in Education Conference (FIE).*

De Freitas, S., Rebolledo-Mendez, G., Liarokapis, F., Magoulas, G., & Poulovassilis, A. (2010). Learning as immersive experiences: Using the four-dimensional framework for designing and evaluating immersive learning experiences in a virtual world. *British Journal of Educational Technology*, *41*(1), 69–85. doi:10.1111/j.1467-8535.2009.01024.x

Elkhodr, M., Gide, E., Wu, R., & Darwish, O. (2023). ICT students' perceptions towards ChatGPT: An experimental reflective lab analysis. *STEM Education*, *3*(2), 70–88. doi:10.3934/steme.2023006

Falloon, G. (2010). Using avatars and virtual environments in learning: What do they have to offer? *British Journal of Educational Technology*, *41*(1), 108–122. doi:10.1111/j.1467-8535.2009.00991.x

Gallini, J. K., & Barron, D. (2001). Participants' perceptions of web-infused environments: A survey of teaching beliefs, learning approaches, and communication. *Journal of Research on Technology in Education*, *34*(2), 139–156. doi:10.1080/15391523.2001.10782341

Ghosh, R., Rude-Parkins, C., & Kerrick, S. A. (2012). Collaborative problem-solving in virtual environments: Effect of social interaction, social presence, and sociability on critical thinking. In *The Next Generation of Distance Education* (pp. 191–205). Springer US. doi:10.1007/978-1-4614-1785-9_13

Gibbs, W. J. (1998). Implementing on-line learning environments. *Journal of Computing in Higher Education*, *10*(1), 16–37. doi:10.1007/BF02946984

Halili, S. H., Rahman, N. H. A., & Razak, R. A. (2018). Traditional versus virtual learning: How engaged are the students in learning English literature? *Indonesian Journal of Applied Linguistics*, *8*(1). Advance online publication. doi:10.17509/ijal.v8i1.11467

He, W. (2013). Examining students' online interaction in a live video streaming environment using data mining and text mining. *Computers in Human Behavior*, *29*(1), 90–102. doi:10.1016/j.chb.2012.07.020

Hernández-Lara, A. B., & Serradell-López, E. (2018). Student interactions in online discussion forums: Their perception on learning with business simulation games. *Behaviour & Information Technology*, *37*(4), 419–429. doi:10.1080/0144929X.2018.1441326

Hughes, M., & Daykin, N. (2002). Towards constructivism: Investigating students' perceptions and learning as a result of using an online environment. *Innovations in Education and Teaching International*, *39*(3), 217–224. doi:10.1080/13558000210150036

Kapralos, B., Hogan, M., Pribetic, A. I., & Dubrowski, A. (2011). Virtual simulations and serious games in a laptop-based university: Gauging faculty and student perceptions. *Interactive Technology and Smart Education*, *8*(2), 106–120. doi:10.1108/17415651111141821

Khanal, P. (2013). Making virtual learning interactive and meaningful: Implications of constructivism for adult students. *International Journal of Research Studies in Education*, *2*(4). Advance online publication. doi:10.5861/ijrse.2013.302

Kiy, H. (2023). A study on writing experience with ChatGPT of college students. *The Korean Society of Culture and Convergence*, *45*(9), 853–868. doi:10.33645/cnc.2023.09.45.09.853

Krasnova, T., & Ananjev, A. (2015). Students' perception of learning in the online discussion environment. *Mediterranean Journal of Social Sciences*. Advance online publication. doi:10.5901/mjss.2015.v6n6s1p202

Lamb, R. L., Etopio, E., Hand, B., & Yoon, S. Y. (2019). Virtual reality simulation: Effects on academic performance within two domains of writing in science. *Journal of Science Education and Technology*, *28*(4), 371–381. doi:10.1007/s10956-019-09774-y

Lapadat, J. C. (2006). Written interaction: A key component in online learning. *Journal of Computer-Mediated Communication, 7*(4). doi:10.1111/j.1083-6101.2002.tb00158.x

Lee, S. W.-Y. (2013). Investigating students' learning approaches, perceptions of online discussions, and students' online and academic performance. *Computers & Education*, *68*, 345–352. doi:10.1016/j.compedu.2013.05.019

Lin, S. Y., & Overbaugh, R. C. (2007). The effect of student choice of online discussion format on tiered achievement and student satisfaction. *Journal of Research on Technology in Education*, *39*(4), 399–415. doi:10.1080/15391523.2007.10782489

Looi, C.-K. (2005). Exploring the affordances of online chat for learning. *International Journal of Learning Technology*, *1*(3), 322. doi:10.1504/IJLT.2005.006520

Lowell, V. L., & Alshammari, A. (2019). Experiential learning experiences in an online 3D virtual environment for mental health interviewing and diagnosis role-playing: A comparison of perceived learning across learning activities. *Educational Technology Research and Development*. *Educational Technology Research and Development*, *67*(4), 825–854. doi:10.1007/s11423-018-9632-8

Lyu, H. (2020). How are students immersed by providing virtual reality technology? The role of psychological distance in online flipped class. *International Journal of Information and Education Technology (IJIET), 10*(1), 79–83. doi:10.18178/ijiet.2020.10.1.1343

Manou, E., Lazari, E.-C., Thomopoulou, G.-E., Agrogiannis, G., Kavantzas, N., & Lazaris, A. C. (2021). Participation and interactivity in synchronous E-learning pathology course during the COVID-19 pandemic. *Advances in Medical Education and Practice*, *12*, 1081–1091. doi:10.2147/AMEP.S317854 PMID:34584484

Menon, V. A., Prasad, A., & Boobalakrishnan, N. (2022). "Kathakali" & Virtual Reality: An Experiment. *International Journal of Art & Design*, *6*(2), 118–130. doi:10.5281/ZENODO.7437385

Molesworth, M. (2004). Collaboration, reflection and selective neglect: campus-based marketing students' experiences of using a virtual learning environment. *Innovations in Education and Teaching International, 41*(1), 79–92. doi:10.1080/1470329032000172739

Park, C., & Kim, D.-G. (2020). Perception of instructor presence and its effects on learning experience in online classes. *Journal of Information Technology Education, 19*, 475–488. doi:10.28945/4611

Ritzhaupt, A. D., Poling, N., Frey, C., Kang, Y., & Johnson, M. (2016). A phenomenological study of games, simulations, and virtual environments courses: What are we teaching and How? *International Journal of Gaming and Computer-Mediated Simulations, 8*(3), 59–73. doi:10.4018/IJGCMS.2016070104

Robertson, J., & Despa, J. O. (2006). Ghostwriter: Educational drama and presence in a virtual environment. *Journal of Computer-Mediated Communication, 8*(1). doi:10.1111/j.1083-6101.2002.tb00159.x

Rogers, S. L., Hollett, R., Li, Y. R., & Speelman, C. P. (2022). An evaluation of virtual reality role-play experiences for helping-profession courses. *Teaching of Psychology, 49*(1), 78–84. doi:10.1177/0098628320983231

Schfer, L. (2003). Storytelling in virtual environments. *Virtual Reality (Waltham Cross), 7*(1), 1–1. doi:10.1007/s10055-003-0115-8

Schuster, K., Hoffmann, M., Bach, U., Richert, A., & Jeschke, S. (2014). Diving in? How users experience virtual environments using the virtual theatre. In Design, User Experience, and Usability. User Experience Design for Diverse Interaction Platforms and Environments (pp. 636–646). Springer International Publishing. doi:10.1007/978-3-319-07626-3_60

Sepang, K. M., Santosa, M. H., & Suprianti, G. A. P. (2021). Exploring influence of Virtual Reality-based English learning activities towards secondary students' English writing achievement. *The Art of Teaching English as a Foreign Language, 1*(1), 63–74. doi:10.36663/tatefl.v1i1.88

Shoufan, A. (2023). Exploring students' perceptions of ChatGPT: Thematic analysis and follow-up survey. *IEEE Access : Practical Innovations, Open Solutions, 11*, 38805–38818. doi:10.1109/ACCESS.2023.3268224

Sim, M. S., & Rahmat, N. H. (2022). Online group interactions in online classrooms: Does experience matter? *International Journal of Academic Research in Business & Social Sciences, 12*(8). Advance online publication. doi:10.6007/IJARBSS/v12-i8/13185

Small, F., Dowell, D., & Simmons, P. (2012). Teacher communication preferred over peer interaction: Student satisfaction with different tools in a virtual learning environment. *Journal of International Education in Business, 5*(2), 114–128. doi:10.1108/18363261211281735

Swan, K. (2001). Virtual interaction: Design factors affecting student satisfaction and perceived learning in asynchronous online courses. *Distance Education, 22*(2), 306–331. doi:10.1080/0158791010220208

Swartzwelder, K., Murphy, J., & Murphy, G. (2019). The impact of text-based and video discussions on student engagement and interactivity in an online course. *The Journal of Educators Online, 16*(1). Advance online publication. doi:10.9743/jeo.2019.16.1.13

Tanrıkulu, F. (2022). Students' perceptions about the effects of collaborative digital storytelling on writing skills. *Computer Assisted Language Learning, 35*(5–6), 1090–1105. doi:10.1080/09588221.2020.1774611

Tcha-Tokey, K., Christmann, O., Loup-Escande, E., Loup, G., & Richir, S. (2018). Towards a model of User eXperience in immersive virtual environments. *Advances in Human-Computer Interaction*, *2018*, 1–10. doi:10.1155/2018/7827286

Tcha-Tokey, K., Christmann, O., Loup-Escande, E., & Richir, S. (2016). Proposition and validation of a questionnaire to measure the user experience in immersive virtual environments. *The International Journal of Virtual Reality : a Multimedia Publication for Professionals*, *16*(1), 33–48. doi:10.20870/IJVR.2016.16.1.2880

Tham, J., Duin, A. H., Gee, L., Ernst, N., Abdelqader, B., & McGrath, M. (2018). Understanding virtual reality: Presence, embodiment, and professional practice. *IEEE Transactions on Professional Communication*, *61*(2), 178–195. doi:10.1109/TPC.2018.2804238

Virgiawan, M., Suryani, N., & Sutimin, L. A. (2020). The effectiveness of guided writing combined with virtual reality video as teaching media on students' writing achievement. *International Journal of Linguistics. Literature and Translation*, *3*(10), 41–47. doi:10.32996/ijllt.2020.3.10.5

Wan, J., Reddy, M., & Longman, D. (2011). Understanding student engagement in 3D virtual learning environments. *International Journal of Technology Enhanced Learning*, *3*(5), 468. doi:10.1504/IJTEL.2011.042099

Wang, L.-C. C. (2014). Student Perceptions of Using Instant Messaging Software to Facilitate Synchronous Online Class Interaction in a Graduate Teacher Education Course. *Journal of Computing in Teacher Education*, 15–21.

Wei, H.-C., Peng, H., & Chou, C. (2015). Can more interactivity improve learning achievement in an online course? Effects of college students' perception and actual use of a course-management system on their learning achievement. *Computers & Education*, *83*, 10–21. doi:10.1016/j.compedu.2014.12.013

Williams, L., & Lahman, M. (2011). Online discussion, student engagement, and critical thinking. *Journal of Political Science Education*, *7*(2), 143–162. doi:10.1080/15512169.2011.564919

Zheng, B., & Warschauer, M. (2015). Participation, interaction, and academic achievement in an online discussion environment. *Computers & Education*, *84*, 78–89. doi:10.1016/j.compedu.2015.01.008

Chapter 4
Exploring Gen Z Perspectives Toward ChatGPT in Academic Contexts

Koppala Venugopal
Aditya Institute of Technology and Management, India

ABSTRACT

This study delves into the attitudes of Generation Z (Gen Z) towards ChatGPT within academic contexts, employing a rigorous analysis. With the rise of advanced language models, understanding how the digitally native Gen Z perceives and engages with ChatGPT is crucial for shaping the future of academic technology. The research assesses various factors influencing Gen Z attitudes, including accessibility, academic pressure, time constraints, language barriers, curiosity, instant gratification, fear of missing out, and technology integration. The study utilizes a robust regression model to comprehensively analyze these factors and their impact on Gen Z's anticipation of increased ChatGPT usage in academics. The research underscores the significance of Gen Z's perspectives in shaping the integration of ChatGPT into educational landscapes. By unraveling their attitudes and perceptions, this research aims to provide valuable insights for educators, policymakers, and developers, facilitating informed decisions for optimizing the utility of ChatGPT in academic settings.

1. INTRODUCTION

The integration of advanced language models, particularly ChatGPT, into educational environments marks a paradigm shift in the way students interact with technology and access information. As "Generation Z" (Gen Z) becomes the predominant demographic in educational institutions, their attitudes towards innovative tools like ChatGPT play a pivotal role in shaping the future of academic technology.

With its ability to comprehend and generate human-like text, ChatGPT holds great promise for various academic applications, ranging from assisting in writing assignments to providing real-time support for diverse subjects (Vakamullu Gopalakrishna & Koppala Venugopal, 2023). The dynamic nature of Gen Z, characterized by a high degree of tech-savviness and digital immersion, makes them a particularly

DOI: 10.4018/979-8-3693-4268-8.ch004

interesting group to study regarding their embrace or resistance to such technological advancements in academic settings.

Crafted for swift connection and cohesive responses, ChatGPT operates akin to conversational tools such as bots and virtual assistants. This interoperability enables businesses to extend their current offerings, creating unique AI-powered chatbots capable of promptly understanding and addressing consumer demands. Additionally, ChatGPT facilitates secure and private conversations (A. Bozkurt et al., 2023).

In the realm of education, new technologies frequently surface and, over time, some fade away, with only a select few becoming integral to the structure. ChatGPT produces an excellent array of concerns for collaborative student work, and naturally, students have the option to independently develop these challenges (M. Perkins et al., 2023).

While students might have gained some understanding of probability through practical experience, engaging in activities like these enhances their comprehension by prompting collaboration on diverse approaches, testing and refining theories. These problems can be swiftly generated whenever a gulf is identified. ChatGPT empowers both teachers and students to craft a variety of materials, such as writing prompts, discussion topics, puzzles, and more. Learners have the flexibility to produce these materials as required and take charge of their own research and practice (E. A. van Dis et al., 2023).

ChatGPT offers a superior step-by-step explanation, complete with visual examples and insights into common pitfalls, surpassing Google's response. The global educational landscape was once again astonished by the emergence of ChatGPT. Acting as both an exceptional instructor and an exemplary student, ChatGPT has the potential to elevate the capabilities and opportunities of both instructors and students. This mirrors the impact of technologies like AI, akin to the transformative role that math calculators played in the past (B. Rathore et al., 2023).

This assistance proves valuable as students extend their education beyond the classroom. AI-powered learning assistants can be employed to guide and support students in their learning journey by improving search capabilities and providing personalized suggestions for materials and other resources (J. Kocon et al., 2023).

Several factors influence the usage of ChatGPT by students for academic purposes, reflecting the intricate dynamics between technology and education. Key determinants include technological proficiency, perceived utility, accessibility and ease of use, integration into curriculum, peer influence, educational institution policies, trust and reliability and privacy and security concerns. Understanding these factors is essential for educators, developers, and policymakers to effectively integrate ChatGPT into educational settings and ensure that it aligns with the needs, preferences, and expectations of students.

Although there is significant promise in integrating ChatGPT into educational settings, there exists a notable void in comprehending how Generation Z perceives and interacts with this technology, particularly in the context of academic usage. The intricacy of this challenge lies in untangling the multifaceted factors that shape the attitudes of Gen Z towards ChatGPT, understanding their potential concerns, and gauging the overall impact of incorporating this language model within the academic realm (Koppala Venugopal & Saumendra Das 2023). Bridging this knowledge gap is of paramount importance, as it is integral for educators, policymakers, and developers to gain insights that will enable them to effectively harness the full potential of ChatGPT for enhancing the educational experience. Addressing these considerations is crucial for the successful integration of ChatGPT into educational practices and ensuring that it aligns seamlessly with the needs and expectations of the tech-savvy Generation Z.

2. OBJECTIVES OF THE RESEARCH:

- To investigate the attitudes of Generation Z towards the utilization of ChatGPT in academic contexts.
- To identify the factors influencing Gen Z's acceptance or reluctance towards ChatGPT for academic tasks.
- To develop and apply a regression model and machine learning applications to analyze the correlation between different variables and Gen Z's attitude towards ChatGPT.

3. LITERATURE REVIEW

ChatGPT's capabilities may be used to identify content bias and fix problems with educational materials. Given the growing need for updated teaching materials, ChatGPT can assist the state in creating and implementing an impartial and fair curriculum. If implemented appropriately, this might act as a bridge to lessen the pressure on a stressed-out educational system (A.B. Mbakwe et al., 2023).

Education is assisted by ChatGPT with its abilities of converting and expanding the content and solve certain academic queries.

This tool allows students to promptly evaluate their writing, eliminating the need to wait for an instructor's feedback. After assessing their work, students can instruct the AI tool to perform specific editing or revision actions. Furthermore, it serves as a highly efficient word organizer for creative content. The primary focus of this paper is to explore the notable applications of ChatGPT in education (L. Bishop et al., 2023).

Irrespective of the suitability of ChatGPT for educational settings, there is unanimous consensus regarding the paramount importance of safeguarding students' online security. This imperative assumes heightened significance within platforms like ChatGPT, where stringent filters are instituted to exclude potentially harmful content. Despite the efficacy of content filters installed on school computers in thwarting access to unsafe materials, there exist occasional vulnerabilities that can be exploited to circumvent these safeguards. (W. C. H. Hong et al., 2023).

Teachers may help their students learn more effectively by utilising ChatGPT to motivate conversations, provide tailored feedback, and improve their language and literacy abilities. Individual students may get tailored feedback and coaching using ChatGPT (D.Baidoo-Anu, et al., 2023).

The application offers comprehensive feedback for student writing, boosting confidence and motivation. ChatGPT, with its text understanding, automates essay grading, providing reasoning and improved solutions. It evaluates assignments for grammar, structure, plagiarism, and content, and aids in generating ideas, summaries, and speeches. For research, it guides data organization. In language learning, it provides instant feedback on pronunciation and grammar. Facing reading and writing challenges, ChatGPT suggests improvements (T. H. Kung et al., 2023).

ChatGPT has the potential to influence various facets of education, such as writing, instructional methods, and teaching pedagogy. Writing, a longstanding practice fostering creative and critical thinking through information organization and narrative creation, remains pivotal in education despite the prevalence of AI. As such, the focus should be on providing insights that surpass the comprehension of AI (A. Haleem et al., 2023).

Indeed, while ChatGPT facilitates the acquisition of new vocabulary and comprehension of concepts, its role in education remains contentious. While it provides valuable assistance with homework and independent learning, heavy reliance on it might impede critical thinking and problem-solving skills development. Furthermore, its susceptibility to errors and potential biases necessitates caution in its educational integration. (L. J. Quintans et al., 2023).

Employing ChatGPT is an excellent method to sustain student interest in the subject matter. Trained on extensive datasets to comprehend and engage in human language, ChatGPT responds based on learned patterns. It can effectively elucidate grammar-related concepts, impart new language in context, and rectify users' errors. (V. L. Bommineni et al., 2023)

ChatGPT emulates human behavior when instructing users and delivering information. Its capabilities encompass a range of activities, such as crafting poetry, coding, responding to inquiries, composing emails and essays, and translating documents. What sets ChatGPT apart from other chatbots is its ability to provide instant responses, fostering diverse and dynamic discussions on nearly any topic (Y. K. Dwivedi et al., 2023).

ChatGPT can aid students in debate preparation by generating plausible arguments and counterarguments on specific subjects. It also offers innovative writing ideas to inspire students and help them improve their writing skills (P. A. Rospiigliosi et al., 2023)

ChatGPT is examined as a tool to enhance students' skills by cultivating their capacity to pose and articulate precise questions, broadening their knowledge through the model's responses, and instructing them in assessing the accuracy, reliability, and quality of ChatGPT's answers. Additionally, it imparts skills to filter relevant information from the provided answers. This adaptable technology is well-suited for various applications as it can adapt to diverse conditions and situations (M. Halaweh et al., 2023).

Capable of engaging in discussions resembling those between two individuals, ChatGPT proves to be a valuable tool for businesses operating in customer service, marketing, and content development. Serving as a virtual assistant, ChatGPT adeptly interacts with users, responding to inquiries in a manner akin to human conversation. The technology employs deep learning algorithms to create natural language interactions between humans and machines (F. C. Kitamura et al., 2023).

To aid students and enhance their writing skills, ChatGPT can identify grammatical and structural issues in their work, offering valuable feedback. Students can further receive personalized feedback based on their writing style to better comprehend and focus on areas requiring improvement. ChatGPT enables computers to simulate human conversations (M. Perkins et al., 2023).

ChatGPT can aid in identifying and resolving coding issues by providing clarifications, recommendations, and examples. Additionally, businesses can leverage the model to target specific individuals with personalized content. Through training the model on a dataset of user information, ChatGPT enables the generation of personalized content such as emails, social media posts, and product recommendations (S. Badini et al., 2023).

Beyond conventional assignments such as essays, showcasing a student's writing proficiency will necessitate more varied assessments. ChatGPT is already capable of tackling programming homework and generating impressive historical and philosophical writings. Given that AI can adeptly handle current tasks, the methods for evaluating students must undergo significant changes (A. Thurzo et al., 2023).

ChatGPT has the capability to understand the context and meaning of words, enabling it to provide accurate answers based on that knowledge. The creation of chatbots capable of engaging in lively and interesting conversations with users becomes achievable through ChatGPT. Tailoring it for specific domains or roles, such as customer service, by training it on relevant data allows ChatGPT to deliver more precise and relevant responses to user input (T. Yue Thomas., 2023).

Students can engage with ChatGPT by inputting a question and then evaluating the language generated by the bot, assessing its strengths and weaknesses. With minimal human input, ChatGPT is capable of composing anything from a high school essay to complex computer programs. Education leaders can leverage ChatGPT as a highly effective tool for generating website content, accelerating the creative process, and enhancing consistency (D. Singh et al., 2023).

Utilizing ChatGPT can expedite the creative process and enhance consistency. This involves providing clear and explicit directions, evaluating and adjusting the output, and using ChatGPT as a tool to maximize its potential. Leveraging ChatGPT enables cost-effective support and customer service, allowing businesses to reduce the number of customer support agents needed to address client inquiries, ultimately leading to a reduction in overhead expenses (P. Fernandez et al., 2023.

An additional potential application of generative AI-based ChatGPT in education is the development of interactive tutoring programs capable of responding to students' inquiries and offering real-time feedback and guidance. Ultimately, generative AI holds the potential to enhance learning by making it more personalized, interactive, and effective. (E. Bonsu et al., 2023)

ChatGPT possesses the ability to comprehend everyday language and offer precise responses to queries. Teachers can leverage this technology to tailor individualized learning experiences for students, taking into account their specific requirements, interests, and learning preferences. This may involve utilizing AI to generate bespoke resources or exercises and delivering real-time feedback and assistance to students during their work (Y. Tan et al., 2023).

When teachers integrate AI technology to facilitate communication and collaboration, students can collaborate on projects, exchange ideas, and learn from one another. ChatGPT, as an advanced language generation model, has the potential to revolutionize how businesses communicate with their customers. Various tasks in educational contexts make use of ChatGPT (H. Dai et al., 2023)

For a comprehensive education, online learners should actively explore diverse sources and utilize ChatGPT to complement their other learning materials. Instead of solely employing ChatGPT for risk management, numerous individuals are contemplating its use to enhance education. Many instructors are already incorporating it as a teaching tool (M. Aljanabi et al., 2023)

As a study aid, ChatGPT can assist students by generating pertinent content and sources on specific subjects. Additionally, it can offer feedback to help students enhance their understanding, ensuring they receive an appropriate level of challenge and materials that align with their interests (N. M. S. Surameery et al., 2023).

ChatGPT holds the potential to elevate students' educational experiences and has been embraced as a game-changer in the education sector. It can support personalized learning experiences, facilitate knowledge acquisition through research, and automate testing processes. Additionally, ChatGPT can be utilized to develop chatbots and virtual assistants that engage with client inquiries in a conversational manner (C. Zhou et al., 2023).

As a writing assistant, ChatGPT can aid in generating cohesive, relevant, and context-aligned content. However, educational institutions are actively addressing the potential misuse of ChatGPT by implementing measures such as plagiarism detection software, educational initiatives for students, providing resources, and enforcing strict guidelines to ensure responsible usage (Z. Han et al., 2023).

ChatGPT possesses the potential to serve as a valuable educational tool by creating course materials, offering task feedback, and responding to student inquiries. With its strong command of the English language and the ability to acquire new knowledge, ChatGPT proves to be a valuable asset for both teachers and students (Y. Li, Y. Duan et al., 2023).

ChatGPT serves as an accessible writing assistant for students of all ages. It facilitates the writing process by providing suggestions for topics, organizing ideas, suggesting sentence structures, and expanding vocabulary. The user-friendly interface of ChatGPT enables students to access comprehensive and accurate information through their search results (D. Sobania et al., 2023).

4. METHODOLOGY

The study employed a mixed-methods research design that combines quantitative and qualitative approaches. This enabled a comprehensive exploration of Generation Z's attitudes toward ChatGPT in academic contexts.

The study carried out a stratified random sampling technique to ensure representation across diverse academic disciplines, educational levels, and socio-demographic backgrounds within Generation Z. The sample size of 385 was determined through statistical considerations to achieve adequate power for the regression model.

Researchers administered structured surveys to gather quantitative data on attitudes. The survey included Likert scale questions to measure perceptions, preferences, and concerns related to ChatGPT in academic usage.

The study Identified key variables such as technological proficiency, perceived utility, accessibility, integration into curriculum, peer influence, institutional policies, trust, reliability, and privacy concerns. These will serve as the basis for regression model analysis.

The study constructed a regression model using the gathered quantitative data to assess the relationship between dependent variables (attitudes toward ChatGPT) and independent variables (identified factors). This will provide statistical insights into the significant predictors of attitudes within Generation Z. Utilized statistical software for quantitative data analysis and thematic coding for qualitative data. The integration of findings from both approaches provided a holistic understanding of Generation Z's attitudes toward ChatGPT in academic settings.

This methodology aimed to employ a robust and comprehensive approach to assess Generation Z's attitudes toward ChatGPT in academic contexts, providing valuable insights for the effective integration of this technology into educational practices.

The research commenced by conducting a comprehensive factor extraction process, aiming to identify and isolate key factors that contribute to the anticipated rise in ChatGPT usage among Generation X in academic settings. Subsequently, the investigation advanced to employ multiple regression analysis, a robust statistical technique, to evaluate the individual strength and significance of each variable in elucidating the potential escalation of ChatGPT utilization within the academic domain by Generation X in the future (D. Pranaya & Koppala Venugopal, 2023). This dual-stage approach allowed for a nuanced exploration of the multifaceted factors influencing the projected surge in ChatGPT adoption, providing a more granular understanding of the intricate interplay between variables. Through factor extraction, the study aimed to distil essential themes and patterns, while the multiple regression analysis served as a quantitative lens, quantifying the impact of each variable and contributing to a comprehensive comprehension of the dynamics driving the envisaged increase in ChatGPT usage among Generation X in academic pursuits in the future (Koppala Venugopal, et al. 2023).

5. ANALYSIS AND INTERPRETATION:

5.1. Machine Learning Applications and Modelling

Machine learning techniques have been employed to analyze the gathered data, uncover patterns, and derive insights into Gen Z attitudes and preferences regarding AI in academia. The findings from this research could inform the development and implementation of AI technologies in educational environments, catering to the specific needs and preferences of Generation Z students.

5.1.1. Classification Algorithm

Table 5.1.1shows the performance of various machine learning algorithms on a classification task. The models are evaluated using five metrics: Area Under the ROC Curve (AUC), Classification Accuracy (CA), F1 score, Precision, and Recall. Looking at the table, we can see that all the models achieved a good score on all the metrics. Amongst the above algorithms of KNN, Decision Tree, Random Forest, SVM, Naïve Bayes and Logistic Regression, the best score achieved by Random Forest (AUC: 0.998, CA: 0.987, F1: 0.987) which can be considered as a modelled algorithm for the further study.

Table 1. Classification algorithm

Model	AUC	CA	F1	Precision	Recall
kNN	0.997	0.987	0.987	0.975	1.000
Tree	0.998	0.987	0.987	0.975	1.000
SVM	0.988	0.987	0.987	0.975	1.000
Random Forest	0.998	0.987	0.987	0.975	1.000
Naive Bayes	0.795	0.732	0.721	0.764	0.682
Logistic Regression	0.950	0.945	0.949	0.903	1.000

5.1.2. Confusion Matrix and ROC Analysis

Table 2 presents the comparison between the actual and predicted values generated by the Random Forest model, assessing its classification performance on test data. The dataset comprises 29 items related to various aspects of ecological consciousness practices, categorized into five prediction classes: 'Strongly Disagree', 'Disagree', 'Neutral', 'Agree', and 'Strongly Agree'. The Classification Accuracy stands at 98.7%, calculated as (TP + TN) / (TP + FP + TN + FN), indicating the proportion of correctly classified instances. Conversely, the Misclassification Rate is 1.3%, computed as (FP + FN) / (TP + FP + TN + FN), representing the rate of incorrect predictions. Furthermore, the occurrence of Type 1 errors is minimal and Type 2 errors are null.

Table 2. Confusion matrix

Actual \ Predicted	1	2	3	4	5	Σ
1	0	3	1	2	5	11
2	0	39	0	0	0	39
3	0	0	61	0	0	61
4	0	0	0	78	0	78
5	0	0	0	0	195	195
Σ	0	42	62	80	200	384

Despite very minor misclassifications, the Random Forest model demonstrates robust performance in accurately classifying students' behavioral responses concerning the usage of ChatGPT for academic purpose. Consequently, it is deemed suitable for classification tasks, as evidenced by the analysis of the confusion matrix.

Table 3. ROC analysis

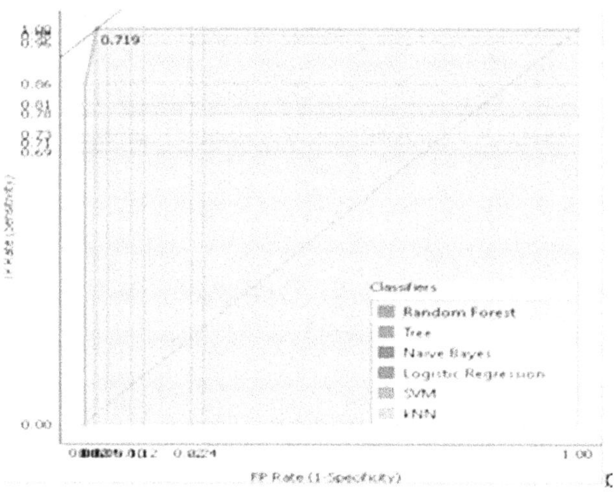

The ROC (Receiver Operating Characteristic) curve is plotted using specificity (False Positive Rate) and sensitivity (True Positive Rate) metrics, ranging from 0 to 1. Figure illustrates the ROC curves for different experimental models, focusing on the targeted class "Usage pattern of ChatGPT by students for academic purposes." In this analysis, several experimental models are employed, including kNN, C4.5

Decision Tree, Support Vector Machine (SVM), Random Forest, Naïve Bayes, and Logistic Regression. Their respective Area Under the Curve (AUC) values for predicting the targeted class "ChatGPT usage for Academic purpose" are as follows: 0.997, 0.998, 0.988, 0.998, 0.795, and 0.950. Upon examining the ROC Analysis, it's observed that the ROC curve corresponding to the Random Forest model almost touches the upper-left corner. This indicates that the Random Forest model achieves the highest AUC value of 0.998, making it the most efficient and effective in predicting the practices of ChatGPT usage, especially for unknown values within the class.

Table 4. Correlation

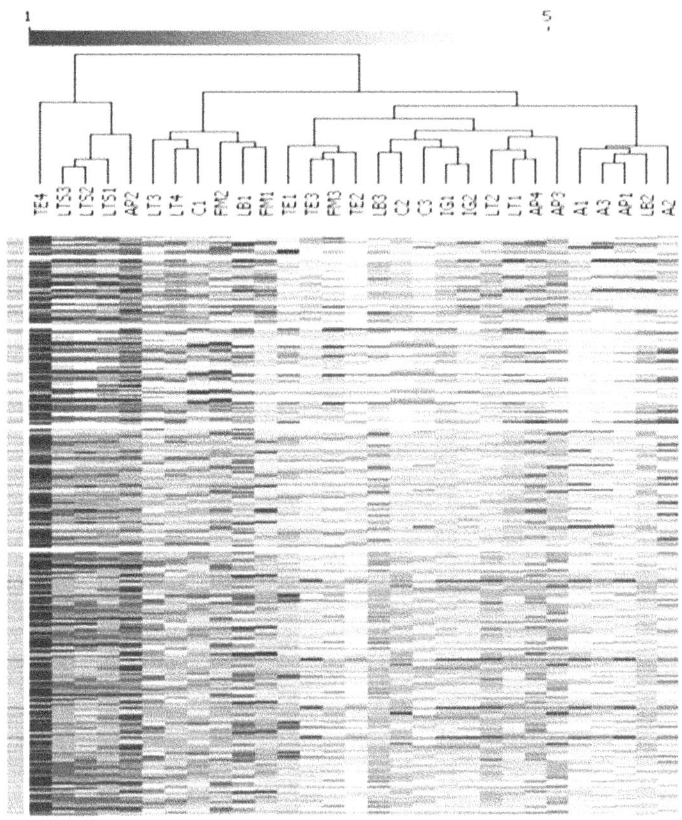

5.1.3. Correlation With Clustering Analysis

The heatmap presented visualizes the correlations and clusters existing among the variables under study. Dark blue hues represent weak correlations, while lighter shades of green signify stronger correlations. The color spectrum reflects the varying degrees of relationships, with lighter shades indicating robust correlations, particularly between the variables and the target variable. Notably, the heatmap reveals minimal multicollinearity among the three thematic variables. Additionally, the heatmap highlights clusters observed among the cross variables influenced by ChatGPT usage practices. Notable clusters include associations between "Lack of Time and Academic Pressure", "Technology Integration and Fear of Missing Out", and "Curiosity and Instant Gratification". These findings suggest a need for emphasis on factors such as time-related academic pressure, concerns about technology integration, and the allure of curiosity and instant gratification.

5.1.4. Rank

Table 4. presents a comparison of various feature selection methods, including Information Gain, Gain Ratio, Gini Importance, ANOVA results, ReliefF scores, and FCBF scores. These metrics evaluate the efficacy of each method in identifying relevant features for classification tasks. While the table offers rankings for each method (with 1 indicating the highest ranking), the optimal choice varies depending on specific application requirements and prioritized criteria.

Interestingly, the Lack of Teachers' Support (LTS) elements, specifically LTS3 ("I feel better relying on ChatGPT than my teacher"), LTS2 ("I can't get good feedback from teachers so I use ChatGPT"), and LTS3 ("I don't have adequate teacher support so I use ChatGPT"), secured the top three ranks. These findings underscore the significant influence of teacher support-related factors on students' propensity to utilize ChatGPT for academic purposes. Moreover, elements associated with Technology Integration (TE), such as TE4 ("We can rely on ChatGPT for its quality") and TE3 ("It exposes students to use AI tools effectively"), ranked 4th and 5th, respectively. This highlights the substantial impact of perceptions regarding technology integration on students' adoption of ChatGPT for academic endeavors.

Table 5. Rank

		#	Info. gain	Gain ratio	Gini	ANOVA	χ^2	ReliefF	FCBF
1	LTS3		0.120	0.065	0.035	2.264	4.863	0.085	0.069
2	LTS2		0.101	0.057	0.023	3.542	15.394	0.045	0.000
3	LTS1		0.022	0.015	NA	1.355	4.082	0.037	NA
4	TE4		0.023	0.016	0.006	0.662	2.801	0.120	0.000
5	TE3		0.027	0.018	NA	1.096	2.565	0.048	NA
6	TE2		0.085	0.018402776064478606	[illegible]	6.291	7.156	0.094	0.000
7	TE1		0.111	0.066	0.040	4.758	7.267	0.041	0.000
8	FM3		0.047	0.032	NA	2.945	10.921	0.054	NA
9	FM2		0.102	0.058	0.026	2.002	5.352	0.075	0.000
10	FM1		0.233	0.141	0.064	9.276	17.184	0.043	0.152
11	IG2		0.062	0.046	NA	3.152	10.601	0.010	NA
12	IG1		0.087	0.065	NA	0.792	5.423	0.015	NA
13	C3		0.114	0.068	0.024	3.548	5.050	0.061	0.000
14	C2		0.097	0.069	NA	10.945	37.768	0.034	NA
15	C1		0.045	0.029	0.016	0.889	2.239	0.025	0.000
16	LB3		0.114	0.065	0.042	7.840	14.007	0.062	0.000
17	LB2		0.023	0.016	NA	0.412	5.729	0.007	NA
18	LB1		0.123	0.066	0.028	1.144	6.246	0.071	0.000
19	LT4		0.142	0.084	0.035	2.649	5.438	0.079	0.000
20	LT3		0.111	0.058	0.026	1.789	6.554	0.084	0.000
21	LT2		0.157	0.099	0.047	11.254	14.761	0.047	0.000

5.2. Factor Analysis

A KMO value between 0.6 and 0.8 is generally considered good, indicating that the data is suitable for factor analysis. In this case, as shown in Table 5, the KMO value of 0.765 suggests that the sample is adequate for factor analysis. Bartlett's Test checks the null hypothesis that the correlation matrix is an identity matrix (no correlations between variables). A low p-value (in this case, 0.000) indicates that the observed correlation matrix is significantly different from an identity matrix. Therefore, the data is suitable for factor analysis.

Table 6. KMO and Bartlett's test

Kaiser-Meyer-Olkin Measure of Sampling Adequacy.		**.765**
Bartlett's Test of Sphericity	Approx. Chi-Square	6.846E3
	df	406
	Sig.	.000

The initial eigenvalues represent the amount of variance explained by each component before rotation. Component 1 has the highest initial eigenvalue (8.265), suggesting it explains a substantial portion of the variance. These values represent the variance explained by each component after rotation. Component 1 still dominates, explaining 28.499% of the variance, followed by Components 2 and 3 and so on up to 8. The cumulative variance explained by the first eight components is 70.860

Component 1 seems to capture the convenience and quick access aspect of ChatGPT. Component 2 reflects a set of statements associated with additional responsibilities and the desire for competition. Component 3 highlights the educational and learning aspects of using ChatGPT. Component 4 indicates a component associated with dissatisfaction with teacher support and feedback. Component 5 encompasses statements related to technology and the quality of ChatGPT.

The variables, namely, "I have no knowledge on my own," "Results are guaranteed," "There are no mistakes from ChatGPT, which makes task accomplishment," "I use it since it is novel," and "We can rely on ChatGPT for its quality," exhibit a low level of loading. Consequently, these variables are excluded from the subsequent stage of the multiple regression analysis.

Overall, these components provide insights into the diverse reasons and perceptions surrounding the use of ChatGPT, ranging from convenience and learning to dissatisfaction with traditional educational support.

5.3. Multiple Regression Analysis

Table 8 presents the results of an Analysis of Variance (ANOVA) for a regression model examining various predictors on the dependent variable, "There will be an increase of ChatGPT usage in academics in the future." Below is an analysis and interpretation of the key components:

Access: The F-Statistic (6.505) is highly significant ($p < 0.001$), suggesting that the predictor variable "Access" significantly contributes to the model. Hence, the access to ChatGPT significantly influences the perceived increase in its usage for academic purposes.

Table 7. Total variance explained

Component	Initial Eigenvalues			Extraction Sums of Squared Loadings			Rotation Sums of Squared Loadings		
	Total	% of Variance	Cumulative %	Total	% of Variance	Cumulative %	Total	% of Variance	Cumulative %
1	8.265	28.499	28.499	8.265	28.499	28.499	4.232	14.594	14.594
2	3.308	11.408	39.907	3.308	11.408	39.907	2.984	10.289	24.883
3	2.398	8.271	48.177	2.398	8.271	48.177	2.976	10.262	35.145
4	1.771	6.108	54.285	1.771	6.108	54.285	2.793	9.633	44.777
5	1.396	4.815	59.101	1.396	4.815	59.101	2.695	9.293	54.070
6	1.209	4.170	63.271	1.209	4.170	63.271	1.925	6.638	60.709
7	1.190	4.102	67.373	1.190	4.102	67.373	1.507	5.197	65.906
8	1.011	3.487	70.860	1.011	3.487	70.860	1.437	4.955	70.860
9	.906	3.124	73.984						
10	.876	3.020	77.004						
11	.756	2.607	79.611						
12	.715	2.467	82.078						
13	.657	2.264	84.342						
14	.592	2.040	86.382						
15	.469	1.616	87.998						
16	.454	1.564	89.562						
17	.395	1.362	90.924						
18	.365	1.259	92.183						
19	.348	1.201	93.384						
20	.309	1.067	94.450						
21	.270	.931	95.381						
22	.250	.862	96.244						
23	.225	.777	97.020						
24	.211	.727	97.747						
25	.171	.591	98.338						
26	.155	.535	98.873						
27	.129	.444	99.317						
28	.101	.349	99.666						
29	.097	.334	100.000						

Extraction Method: Principal Component Analysis.

Academic Pressure: The F-Statistic (1.035) is not significant ($p = 0.389$), indicating that "Academic Pressure" does not significantly contribute to the model. So, Academic pressure is not a significant predictor of the anticipated increase in ChatGPT usage in academics.

Table 8. Rotated component matrix[a]

	Component							
	1	2	3	4	5	6	7	8
1. I use ChatGPT because of easy access!	.648							
2. I need not afford money for the trial ChatGPT	.640							
3. Access from lap & mobile is also convenient!	.816							
4. I need quick solutions so that, I prefer ChatGPT	.844							
5. I have no knowledge on my own!						.493		
6. Results are guaranteed!		.485						
7. I follow ChatGPT since, I will meet my sir's expectations.		.651						
8. I have a multi tasks to complete.	.570							
9. I have to attend extract extracurricular activates.		.528						
10. I need to do part time job also								.792
11. I need ChatGPT since I don't have time.		.789						
12. Since, I am poor in English, I take the help of ChatGPT.							.530	
13. I can easily complete my assignments through the ChatGPT	.715							
14. There are no mistakes from ChatGPT which makes tasks accomplishment.							.403	
15. I use it since it is novel.		.497						
16. I use it since it is highly applicable			.736					
17. I learn a lot through ChatGPT.			.714					
18. I prefer ChatGPT since it provide instant assumes.			.573					
19. It appeals a lot since the results are immediate.	.624							
20. I want to compete my friends through using ChatGPT						.584		
21. I will lag beyond if, I don't use ChatGPT.						.752		
22. Many of my friends go forward through ChatGPT.					.759			
23. Technology is promoted by own institution.					.753			
24. ChatGPT is one of the learning tools useful to students.					.652			
25. It exposes students to use AI tools effectively.					.617			
26. We can rely on ChatGPT for its quality.								.173
27. I don't have adequate teacher support so I use ChatGPT.				.855				
28. I can't get good feedback from teachers so I use ChatGPT.				.890				
29. I feel better to rely on ChatGPT than my teacher				.866				
Extraction Method: Principal Component Analysis. Rotation Method: Varimax with Kaiser Normalization.								
a. Rotation converged in 11 iterations.								

Lack of Time: The F-Statistic (6.236) is highly significant ($p < 0.001$), suggesting that the predictor variable "Lack of Time" significantly contributes to the model. Hence, the perception of a lack of time is a significant predictor of the expected increase in ChatGPT usage in academics.

Table 9. ANOVA[b]

Model (Regression)	Sum of Squares	df	Mean Square	F	Sig.
Access	20.589	3	6.863	6.505	.000[a]
Academic Pressure	4.550	4	1.138	1.035	.389[a]
Lack of Time	26.030	4	6.508	6.236	.000[a]
Language Barrier	26.169	3	8.723	8.384	.000[a]
Curiosity	23.090	3	7.697	7.341	.000[a]
Instant Gratification	1.374	2	.687	.623	.537[a]
Fear of Missing Out	10.399	3	3.466	3.206	.023[a]
Technology Integration	27.932	4	6.983	6.723	.000[a]

a. Predictors: (Constant), Access, Academic Pressure, Lack of Time, Language Barrier, Curiosity, Instant Gratification, Fear of Missing Out, Technology Integration

b. Dependent Variable: There will be an increase of ChatGPT usage in academics in future

Language Barrier: The F-Statistic (8.384) is highly significant ($p < 0.001$), indicating that the predictor variable "Language Barrier" significantly contributes to the model. Hence, a perceived language barrier significantly influences the expected increase in ChatGPT usage for academic purposes.

Curiosity: The F-Statistic (7.341) is highly significant ($p < 0.001$), suggesting that "Curiosity" significantly contributes to the model. So, Curiosity is a significant predictor of the anticipated increase in ChatGPT usage in academics.

Instant Gratification: The F-Statistic (0.623) is not significant ($p = 0.537$), indicating that "Instant Gratification" does not significantly contribute to the model. So, Instant gratification is not a significant predictor of the expected increase in ChatGPT usage in academics.

Fear of Missing Out: The F-Statistic (3.206) is significant ($p = 0.023$), suggesting that the predictor variable "Fear of Missing Out" significantly contributes to the model. So, The fear of missing out is a significant predictor of the expected increase in ChatGPT usage in academics.

Technology Integration: The F-Statistic (6.723) is highly significant ($p < 0.001$), indicating that "Technology Integration" significantly contributes to the model. Hence, the perceived integration of technology significantly influences the expected increase in ChatGPT usage for academic purposes.

The regression model, incorporating predictors such as Access, Lack of Time, Language Barrier, Curiosity, Fear of Missing Out, and Technology Integration, significantly contributes to explaining the anticipated increase in ChatGPT usage in academics. So, further study of coefficients may be proceeded.

Table 5.3.2. presents the coefficients from a regression analysis, exploring the relationship between various factors (Access, Lack of Time, Language Barrier, Curiosity, Fear of Missing Out, and Technology Integration) and the dependent variable, "There will be an increase of ChatGPT usage in academics in the future."

Access: "I use ChatGPT because of easy access!" has a negative and significant relationship (Beta = -0.222) with the dependent variable, suggesting that easier access is associated with a decrease in anticipated ChatGPT usage. "I need not afford money for the trial ChatGPT!" has a positive and significant relationship (Beta = 0.173), indicating that the availability of free trials is linked to an increase in anticipated ChatGPT usage. "Access from lap & mobile is also convenient!" shows no significant relationship with the dependent variable.

Table 10. Coefficients[a]

	Access	Unstandardized Coefficients		Standardized Coefficients	t	Sig.
		B	Std. Error	Beta		
1	(Constant)	4.598	.279		16.465	.000
	I use ChatGPT because of easy access!	-.286	.082	-.222	-3.503	.001
	I need not afford money for the trial ChatGPT!	.179	.059	.173	3.036	.003
	Access from lap & mobile is also convenient!	.000	.072	.000	-.007	.995
Lack Of Time						
2	(Constant)	4.405	.296		14.888	.000
	I have a multi tasks to complete.	.111	.081	.087	1.364	.173
	I have to attend extract extra-curricular activates.	-.318	.088	-.231	-3.611	.000
	I need to do part time job also	-.113	.056	-.113	-2.040	.042
Language Barrier						
3	(Constant)	5.037	.285		17.687	.000
	Since, I am poor in English, I take the help of ChatGPT.	-.010	.052	-.010	-.190	.849
	I can easily complete my assignments through the ChatGPT	.065	.071	.049	.914	.361
Curiosity						
4	(Constant)	5.228	.307		17.013	.000
	I use it since it is highly applicable	-.312	.081	-.233	-3.867	.000
	I learn a lot through ChatGPT.	-.050	.073	-.039	-.688	.492
Fear Of Missing Out						
5	(Constant)	4.891	.307		15.923	.000
	I want to compete my friends through using ChatGPT	-.051	.066	-.041	-.765	.445
	I will be lag behind, if I don't use ChatGPT	-.159	.065	-.132	-2.449	.015
	Many of my friends go forward through ChatGPT.	-.022	.062	-.018	-.351	.726
Technology Integration						
6	(Constant)	4.953	.332		14.897	.000
	Technology is promoted by own institution.	-.347	.072	-.275	-4.831	.000
	ChatGPT is one of the learning tools useful to students.	.125	.081	.095	1.555	.121
	It exposes students to use AI tools effectively.	.004	.080	.003	.056	.955
	We can rely on ChatGPT for its quality.	-.073	.059	-.062	-1.244	.214

a. Dependent Variable: There will be an increase of ChatGPT usage in academics in future

Lack of Time: "I have a multi-tasks to complete." is not significantly related to the dependent variable. "I have to attend extract extra-curricular activates." and "I need to do part-time job also" both have negative and significant relationships, suggesting that these factors are associated with a decrease in anticipated ChatGPT usage.

Language Barrier: "Since, I am poor in English, I take the help of ChatGPT." and "I can easily complete my assignments through ChatGPT" show no significant relationships with the dependent variable.

Curiosity: "I use it since it is highly applicable" has a negative and significant relationship, suggesting that high applicability is associated with a decrease in anticipated ChatGPT usage. "I learn a lot through ChatGPT." is not significantly related to the dependent variable.

Fear of Missing Out: "I want to compete my friends through using ChatGPT," "I will be lag behind if I don't use ChatGPT," and "Many of my friends go forward through ChatGPT" all show no significant relationships with the dependent variable.

Technology Integration: "Technology is promoted by own institution" has a negative and significant relationship, indicating that institutional promotion of technology is associated with a decrease in anticipated ChatGPT usage. "ChatGPT is one of the learning tools useful to students," "It exposes students to use AI tools effectively," and "We can rely on ChatGPT for its quality" are not significantly related to the dependent variable.

The analysis suggests that factors like easy access, affordability, and engagement in extra-curricular activities or part-time jobs may influence the anticipated increase in ChatGPT usage among Generation X in academics. However, factors related to language barriers, curiosity, fear of missing out, and institutional technology promotion do not seem to significantly impact the expected rise in ChatGPT usage. The findings provide valuable insights into the nuanced relationship between different factors and the future adoption of ChatGPT in academic settings.

6. SUGGESTIONS

- Ensuring seamless access and affordability plays a pivotal role in shaping students' attitudes toward ChatGPT. Encourage usage by offering free trials and optimize the user interface for enhanced accessibility.
- Students managing multiple tasks or engaged in part-time jobs may perceive ChatGPT as a time-saving tool. Promote time-saving features through various channels and consider integrating ChatGPT into time-management workshops.
- Language proficiency has minimal impact on anticipated ChatGPT usage. Market its multilingual capabilities and provide language support for diverse academic subjects.
- While high applicability might deter expected ChatGPT usage, highlighting its diverse applications beyond academics and emphasizing curiosity-driven learning features can mitigate this perception.
- The fear of falling behind does not strongly influence expected ChatGPT usage. Position ChatGPT as a tool for personalized learning, emphasizing its supplementary role rather than a competitive one.
- Institutional technology promotion adversely affects anticipated ChatGPT usage. Collaborate with institutions to address concerns and underscore how ChatGPT enhances traditional learning methods without replacing them.
- Users do not significantly associate ChatGPT with high quality. Implement quality assurance measures and consistently communicate ongoing improvements and updates.
- Customization based on user preferences is crucial. Introduce personalized learning plans and allow users to tailor their ChatGPT interactions.
- Users may not be fully aware of ChatGPT's capabilities. Conduct educational workshops and webinars, utilizing targeted marketing to highlight its features and benefits.

- The lack of a significant correlation with learning through ChatGPT suggests the need for a robust feedback system. Encourage users to provide feedback for continuous improvement.

These suggestions aim to enhance the user experience, address concerns, and align ChatGPT with the expectations and preferences of Generation X students in academic settings. Continuous monitoring, feedback analysis, and adaptation of strategies will be essential for successful implementation.

REFERENCES

Ahmad, A., Waseem, M., Liang, P., Fahmideh, M., Aktar, M. S., & Mikkonen, T. (2023). *Towards Human-Bot Collaborative Software Architecting with ChatGPT*. 10.48550/arXiv.2302.14600.

Aljanabi, M. (2023). ChatGPT: Future directions and open possibilities. *Mesopotamian Journal of Cybersecurity*, 16-17.

Badini, S., Regondi, S., Frontoni, E., & Pugliese, R. (2023). *Assessing the capabilities of ChatGPT to improve additive manufacturing troubleshooting*. Advanced Industrial and Engineering Polymer Research. doi:10.1016/j.aiepr.2023.03.003

Baidoo-AnuD.AnsahO. (2023). *Education in the Era of Generative Artificial Intelligence (AI): Understanding the Potential Benefits of ChatGPT in Promoting Teaching and Learning*. doi:10.2139/ssrn.4337484

Bishop, L. (2023). A computer wrote this paper: What chatgpt means for education, research, and writing. *Research and Writing*.

Bommineni, V. L., Bhagwagar, S., Balcarcel, D., Davatzikos, C., & Boyer, D. (2023). Performance of ChatGPT on the MCAT: the road to personalized and equitable premedical learning. MedRxiv, 2023-03. doi:10.1101/2023.03.05.23286533

BonsuE.Baffour-KoduahD. (2023). *From the consumers' side: Determining students' perception and intention to use ChatGPT in Ghanaian higher education*. doi:10.2139/ssrn.4387107

Bozkurt, Xiao, Lambert, Pazurek, Crompton, Koseoglu, & Jandrić. (2023). Speculative futures on ChatGPT and generative artificial intelligence (AI): A collective reflection from the educational landscape. *Asian J. Distance Educ.*

Dai, H., Liu, Z., Liao, W., Huang, X., Wu, Z., Zhao, L., . . . Li, X. (2023). Chataug: Leveraging chatgpt for text data augmentation. arXiv preprint arXiv:2302.13007.

Dwivedi, Y. K., Kshetri, N., Hughes, L., Slade, E. L., Jeyaraj, A., Kar, A. K., & Wright, R. (2023). So what if ChatGPT wrote it? Multidisciplinary perspectives on opportunities, challenges and implications of generative conversational AI for research, practice and policy. *International Journal of Information Management*, *71*, 102642. doi:10.1016/j.ijinfomgt.2023.102642

Fernandez, P. (2023). Through the looking glass: Envisioning new library technologies AI-text generators as explained by ChatGPT. *Library Hi Tech News*, *40*(3), 11–14. doi:10.1108/LHTN-02-2023-0017

Gopalakrishna & Venugopal. (2023). Assessment on the Intricacies of English Speaking Abilities by Rural Students in India. In *English Language Competence in Rural Youth: Improving Job Readiness.* Current Publications.

Halaweh. (2023). ChatGPT in education: Strategies for responsible implementation. *Contemp. Educ. Technol., 15*(2).

Haleem, A., Javaid, M., & Singh, R. P. (2022). An era of ChatGPT as a significant futuristic support tool: A study on features, abilities, and challenges. *BenchCouncil Transactions on Benchmarks, Standards and Evaluations, 2*(4), 100089.

Hong, W. C. H. (2023). The impact of ChatGPT on foreign language teaching and learning: Opportunities in education and research. *Journal of Educational Technology and Innovation*, *5*(1).

Kitamura, F. C. (2023). ChatGPT is shaping the future of medical writing but still requires human judgment. *Radiology*, *307*(2), e230171. doi:10.1148/radiol.230171 PMID:36728749

Koppala Venugopal, Vital, Das, Jena, & Mohapatro. (2023). Usage Determinants of Mobile Applications Impelling Students Group: Assessment through Machine Learning Models and Regression. *Vytapeni, Vetrani, Instalace Journal, 11*(11), 151-178. https://vvijournal.com/volume-11-issue-112023/

Kung, T. H., Cheatham, M., Medenilla, A., Sillos, C., De Leon, L., Elepaño, C., & Tseng, V. (2023). Performance of ChatGPT on USMLE: Potential for AI-assisted medical education using large language models. *PLOS Digital Health*, *2*(2), e0000198. doi:10.1371/journal.pdig.0000198 PMID:36812645

LiY.DuanY. (2023). The ethical performance of artificial general intelligence models based on DIKWP. doi:10.13140/RG.2.2.36224.10242

Mbakwe, A. B., Lourentzou, I., Celi, L. A., Mechanic, O. J., & Dagan, A. (2023). ChatGPT passing USMLE shines a spotlight on the flaws of medical education. *PLOS Digital Health*, *2*(2), e0000205. doi:10.1371/journal.pdig.0000205 PMID:36812618

Perkins. (2023). Academic integrity considerations of AI Large Language Models in the post-pandemic era: ChatGPT and beyond. *J. Univ. Teach. Learn. Pract., 20*(2).

Pranaya & Venugopal. (2023). Impact of Mother Tongue on Students' speaking Abilities in English Language at Rural Places. In *English Language Competence in Rural Youth: Improving Job Readiness.* Current Publications.

Rathore, B. (2023). Future of AI & generation alpha: ChatGPT beyond boundaries. *Eduzone: Int. Peer Rev. Refer. Multidiscip. J.*, *12*(1), 63–68.

Singh, D. (2023). ChatGPT: A new approach to revolutionise organisations. *Int. J. New Media Stud.*, *10*(1), 57–63.

Sobania, D., Briesch, M., Hanna, C., & Petke, J. (2023). An analysis of the automatic bug fixing performance of chatgpt. arXiv preprint arXiv:2301.08653. doi:10.1109/APR59189.2023.00012

Surameery, N. M. S., & Shakor, M. Y. (2023). Use ChatGPT to solve programming bugs. *Int. J. Inf. Technol. Comput. Eng.*, *3*(01), 17–22.

Tan, Y., Min, D., Li, Y., Li, W., Hu, N., Chen, Y., & Qi, G. (2023). Evaluation of ChatGPT as a question answering system for answering complex questions. arXiv preprint arXiv:2303.07992.

Thurzo, M., Strunga, M., Urban, R., Surovková, J., & Afrashtehfar, K. I. (2023). Impact of artificial intelligence on dental education: A review and guide for curriculum update. *Education Sciences*, *13*(2), 150. doi:10.3390/educsci13020150

van Dis, E. A., Bollen, J., Zuidema, W., van Rooij, R., & Bockting, C. L. (2023). ChatGPT: Five priorities for research. *Nature*, *614*(7947), 224–226. doi:10.1038/d41586-023-00288-7 PMID:36737653

Venugopal, K., & Das, S. (2023). Prediction Analysis of Gen Zers' Attitudes on Ecological Consciousness. In *Sustainable Science and Intelligent Technologies for Societal Development*. IGI Global.

Yue, T. (2023). Democratizing Financial Knowledge with ChatGPT by OpenAI: Unleashing the Power of Technology. SSRN *Electronic Journal*. doi:10.2139/ssrn.4346152

Zhou, C., Li, Q., Li, C., Yu, J., Liu, Y., & Wang, G. (2023). *A comprehensive survey on pre-trained foundation models: A history from bard to ChatGPT.* arXiv preprint arXiv:2302.09419.

Chapter 5
Artificial Intelligence-Supported Teacher Tools to Increase Participation in Online Courses

Ayşin Gaye Üstün
Sinop University, Turkey

Mehmet Yavuz
https://orcid.org/0000-0001-6218-232X
Bingöl University, Turkey

ABSTRACT

The aim of the study is to examine AI tools that will increase student engagement in online courses and provide support to teachers. In this context, AI tools were examined as a result of the literature review. These tools were examined under six headings: adaptive learning platforms, customized material creation tools, feedback and guidance tools, exam and test creation tools, student engagement monitoring tools, and classroom management tools. Some of the tools analyzed are ALEKS, SlidesAI, Squirrel, MagicForm, Quizbot, Nearpod, and Knewton Alta. It can be argued that these tools provide a range of benefits such as improving learning outcomes by increasing student engagement in online courses, personalizing learning experiences, improving teaching quality, providing tailored courses for students, and improving assessment. However, concerns such as unethical use of student data, limitations in measuring and assessing the learning process, and the inability of automated assessment systems to adequately assess emotion and creativity should be taken into account when using these tools.

INTRODUCTION

Artificial Intelligence (AI) is defined as the art of producing machines that can fulfil tasks using human intelligence (Kurzweil et al., 1990). AI, which has become indispensable in our lives, affects many fields such as health, trade, transport and education. It is thought that its widespread use especially in education will provide a significant development (İşler & Kılıç, 2021). AI applications in online education as

DOI: 10.4018/979-8-3693-4268-8.ch005

well as in traditional education are used by students and teachers today. AI in online education includes various tools and applications such as intelligent tutoring systems, human-computer interactions, learning analytics, teaching robots, and adaptive learning systems (Chen et al., 2020; Hinojo et al., 2019; Roll et al., 2018). These tools are needed to make the lessons more professional, interesting and fun, to select the most appropriate teaching material for a specific student population, and to make learning permanent by making learning processes easier (Nabiyev & Erümit, 2020). In addition, integrating these technologies into the education process will make learning more individualised, provide effective learning experiences, enable students to discover their talents, develop their creativity and reduce the workload of teachers (Haseski, 2019).

According to the Community of Inquiry theory developed by Garrison et al. (2003), the distance education process prioritises the interaction and collaboration between learners and the teacher, and encourages learners to have learning experiences together. The three basic elements of the community of enquiry are cognitive, social and instructional presence (Garrison et al., 2003). Instructional embeddedness refers to the role and influence of the teacher in a learning environment. According to instructional embeddedness, the teacher assumes a leadership role that manages the structure and process of the learning environment, supports learners to receive regular feedback and achieve their learning goals (Polat et al., 2013). Therefore, the use of AI in online education makes the role of the teacher even more important. Baker et al. (2019) state that if teachers use AI tools that perform tasks such as administration, assessment, feedback and plagiarism detection in their lessons, they can track students' learning progress, help them prepare lessons customised to students' needs, and focus on more creative activities with students, reducing the burden on teachers. Similarly, Pedro et al. (2019) state that teachers spend a lot of time on routine and other administrative tasks such as frequent repetition and answering questions about many subjects. Therefore, they argue that if AI-supported tools perform these routine tasks that teachers perform during the educational process, teachers can spend much more time on student guidance and one-to-one communication with their students.

The Role and Potential of Artificial Intelligence in Online Education

AI is increasingly being integrated into various fields of education, including distance education, to enhance learning experiences and outcomes. Although it has a long history in the field of education, there is still not enough information about its effects on teaching and learning, especially in higher education. Although it has the potential for greater usability, especially in online courses, it is still not used at the desired level (Yu et al., 2017). Higher education institutions should be mentally and strategically prepared to understand the revolution AI can bring and its ethical limitations. AI can offer benefits in increasing student success, facilitating student enrolment, and better managing resources (Taşçı & Çelebi, 2020).

AI applications in online courses contribute to more efficient and effective learning environments by covering personalisation, exam and homework assessment, educational planning and management, quality assessment, tutoring and evaluation (Zawacki-Richter et al., 2019; Lainjo & Tsmouche, 2023; González-Calatayud et al., 2021). Moreover, AI is seen as a key factor in the development of learning strategies, especially in distance education, which is expected to become mainstream due to its potential to address the shortcomings of traditional education methods (de Oliveira Durso, 2022; Wang, 2023). The process of incorporating AI into education systems has accelerated with the transition to online education, especially during the COVID-19 pandemic. This has emphasised the importance of AI in adapting to new educational paradigms (Ng et al., 2023). In particular, artificial intelligence, machine learning and deep learning applications enable educators to monitor students' progress, identify areas of struggle and customize teaching methods to improve learning outcomes (Shafique et al., 2023). In addition, artificial intelligence technologies can be used to provide the necessary support services by analysing learners' online learning behaviours, learning needs and preferences, and personal characteristics such as performance and cognitive styles (Hwang & Chien, 2022).

The literature shows that AI in distance education offers a range of benefits such as improved efficiency, personalized learning experiences, rich content delivery, and more effective educational management (Chen et al., 2020). Goel and Polepeddi (2016) stated that tools such as teacher assistants can improve teachers' performance. Hua (2022) stated that it can improve students' educational outcomes. Especially in the context of distance education, it has been emphasized that it increases students' awareness and its importance in shaping the future of education (Tawafak et al., 2022). It is also stated that using AI can provide personalized learning experiences, optimize educational processes, and encourage autonomous and personalized learning modes (Wang et al., 2023). These technologies have the potential to improve teaching and learning practices, support educators in designing effective learning strategies, and improve student performance (Sari & Purwanta, 2021). Finally, Tang et al. (2023) examined the capacity of intelligent learning systems to provide feedback to students, while Casas-Roma and Conesa (2021) emphasized that the integration of artificial intelligence into online learning provides fairness and accessibility for society.

For teachers, it contributes to the fast and easy realisation of student follow-up, measurement and evaluation activities, and the creation of course content. In this way, teachers' workload is reduced, classroom management is facilitated and time is saved (Cunningham-Nelson et al., 2019; Khan et al., 2021; Kim et al., 2021). It can be said that there is a need for applications based on AI technology to support this whole learning process, to create personalised learning environments that are suitable for the needs and wishes of learners, and to ensure the sustainability of learning. In order to meet this need, the opportunities offered especially to distance education are discussed under four headings. These are profiling and prediction, measurement and evaluation, adaptive systems and personalisation, smart teaching systems (Şenocak, 2020). de Oliveira Durso and Arruda (2022) stated that AI is used in distance education for reasons such as smart tutoring systems, adaptive systems and personalisation and measurement-evaluation.

In contrast to the potential and opportunities offered by AI in distance education, there are various challenges and concerns. For example, there are challenges in effectively utilising big data and AI for policy-making and industry applications (Luan et al., 2020). In addition, low motivation and inability to benefit from the opportunities of face-to-face communication for students; job loss and increased expectations of professional competence for teachers; ethical concerns, technical failures, inability to evaluate student creativity and concerns about classroom discipline for the educational organisation (Osetskyi et al., 2020). The prominent opportunities and concerns in this regard are given in Table 1.

Table 1. Opportunities and concerns offered by AI technology in distance education environments (Şenocak, 2020)

Opportunities Offered by AI to Distance Education	Concerns Raised by AI in Distance Education
• Identification of the learner profile with a high probability of leaving the system and prediction of academic success/performance • Providing immediate and personalised feedback in the evaluation of assignments and exams, evaluating and improving the programme or teaching • Making the individual's learning experience suitable for individual needs and creating flexible, adaptable, personalised learning environments suitable for the learner profile in line with the objectives and standards of the course • Facilitating the educational experiences of teachers and learners with special needs by taking into account their needs • The use of virtual smart assistants that provide instant feedback to learners on issues such as admission, registration processes, financial support, new learner orientation, campus life, health services and programme content, and the advantages of smart teaching systems for learners, teachers and institutions in terms of workload, time and economy	• Ethical issues ✓ Unethical use of demographic information and past performance of learners, thus creating labelling and prejudice against learners ✓ The use of learners' digital personal information without their notification and consent may cause problems in terms of privacy and security of this information ✓ The use of learner data by organisations without the knowledge of learners affects the freedom of thought and expression of learners ✓ Intelligent automated assessment systems cannot adequately assess the emotions, thoughts and creativity of learners • Concern that AI could replace teachers in the future • AI technology requires high investment in terms of time, cost and resources, which may be reflected to learners as high course fees

Artificial Intelligence Tools to Increase Student Engagement

When the communication between teachers and students is not sufficient, students tend to drop online courses (Peng, 2017). Student engagement is especially important for students to continue their learning in an online environment where they may feel isolated (Dixson, 2015). Traditional e-learning systems often lack the ability to personalise content delivery and adapt to students' needs. This reduces student engagement in online courses. Therefore, AI-supported adaptive online tools can provide better student engagement (El-Sabagh, 2021). These tools can help teachers with important tasks such as understanding students' individual learning needs, personalising content and providing effective feedback. For example, they can identify students' learning levels and provide them with appropriate content, allowing each student to progress at their own pace. AI-enabled analytical tools provide teachers with valuable information to monitor students' progress and intervene when necessary. These tools empower the teacher's role and help provide a more effective and personalised learning experience for students. However, teachers can benefit from AI tools to complete classroom management such as lesson plans, student attendance lists, reporting student learning outcomes, creating learning media and learning resources. However, Timms (2016) states that teachers' use of AI is insufficient. For this reason, it is important to provide information about the usage areas and benefits of AI in education in order for teachers to keep themselves up to date on the subject and adapt themselves to new technologies. In addition, the study is important in providing up-to-date information and being a resource for those who want to work on AI-based education. In this direction, the study will examine the AI-supported tools in Figure 1, which are thought to support teachers and increase students' participation in online education.

As seen in Figure 1, AI-supported teacher tools were handled with 19 tools under six categories. These tools are given below in order.

Figure 1. Artificial intelligence-supported teacher tools

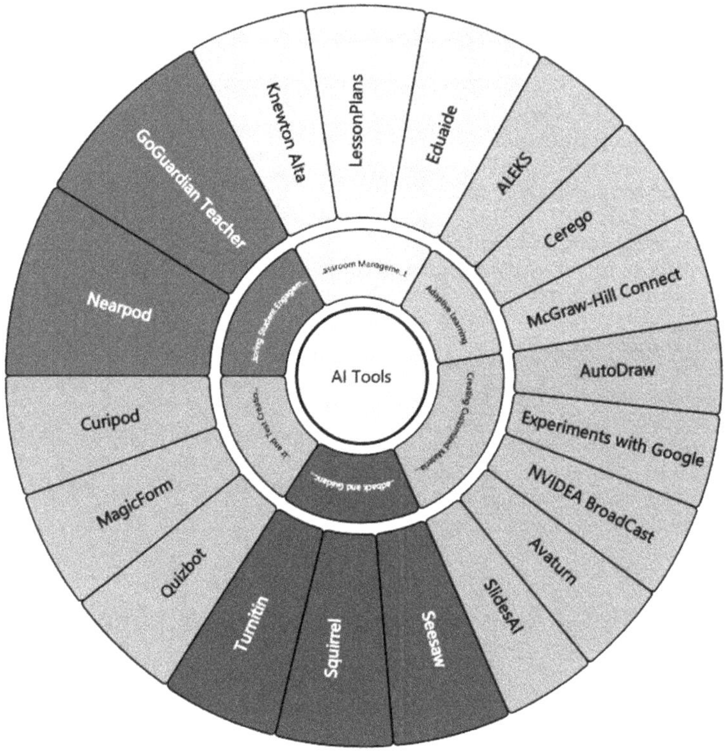

Adaptive Learning Platforms

Adaptive learning systems are personalised learning platforms that adapt to students' learning strategies, the order and difficulty of task skills, the timing of feedback, and students' preferences (Pliakos et al., 2019). Data-driven algorithms and artificial intelligence are utilised to dynamically adjust content, delivery, and pace of instruction based on student performance and engagement (Gligorea et al., 2023). Adaptive online learning platforms allow students to progress on their own, encouraging them to follow their learning processes independently of teachers and helping teachers to better manage and support their students' learning processes (Burgos et al., 2007).

Assessment and Learning in Knowledge Spaces (ALEKS). ALEKS is an AI-powered platform designed by McGraw Hill that provides teachers with adaptive educational materials in accordance with the individual learning needs of students. This platform assesses the knowledge level of students and determines the appropriate learning topics and questions for each student (Harati et al., 2021). Teachers can track the progress of their students with the detailed reports and analyses provided by ALEKS and determine in which areas their students need support. This adaptive AI-supported platform allows students to learn at their own pace and offers teachers the opportunity to manage their students' learning processes more effectively (Hill, 2024). (https://www.aleks.com/)

Cerego. Cerego is an AI-enabled adaptive learning platform based on the principles of neuroscience and cognitive science. It supports instructional design with Open Educational Resources (OER), real-time media, standards-aligned content, lesson plans, and student-generated materials (Shellenbarger, 2019).

It allows teachers to create personalised learning experiences that adapt to students' individual learning styles and paces. Through the detailed progress reports and analyses provided by Cerego, teachers can see where students are strong or weak and adjust their teaching strategies accordingly. (https://www.cerego.com/)

McGraw-Hill Connect. McGraw-Hill Education (MGHE) has developed an AI-powered course management system called "Connect", which is widely used in higher education institutions around the world to enhance traditional teaching methods and improve students' performance (Ahmed & Mesonovich, 2019). MGHE defines Connect as "a digital learning environment that integrates assignments, grading, and course content, making the entire course experience seamless while delivering better outcomes for students and educators" (McGraw-Hill Education). LearnSmart, part of the MGHE Connect platform, is an adaptive learning tool that can be used on top of fully online or on-campus courses at any university (Sun et al., 2017; White, 2020). Students can study every part of the course using LearnSmart, which is designed to improve understanding of course content through its online interactive platform (Babtain, 2021). The system monitors students' performance, identifies in which areas they need additional support and provides feedback to teachers based on this information. (https://www.mheducation.ca/higher-education/learning-solutions/connect).

Customised Material Creation Tools

AI-supported learning material creation tools help teachers to customise and personalise course content. They create materials suitable for students' learning needs and learning styles.

SlidesAI.io. This AI-supported platform allows teachers to convert text-based content into professional-looking presentation slides. This platform provides visual support to teachers when explaining complex topics to students. Teachers can automatically create visually rich slides by uploading lecture notes or teaching plans to the platform. SlidesAI.io can also be used to create interactive course materials. Teachers can create slides with interactive elements such as questionnaires, quizzes or discussion topics to encourage students' active participation in lessons. This platform helps teachers to enrich their lesson content with the ability to automatically integrate visual aids such as graphs, diagrams and infographics. (https://www.slidesai.io/tr)

Avaturn.me. In online courses, teachers can create unique avatars using Avaturn.me and use these avatars as presenters in their course presentations. Thus, they can increase students' participation in the lessons. In addition, by asking students to create their own avatars, they can encourage them to use these avatars in class discussions. This approach encourages students' active participation in the lessons while helping students to develop their creativity and digital skills. (https://avaturn.me/)

NVIDEA BroadCast. Thanks to its AI-powered audio and video enhancement features, this platform makes lessons more professional and interactive. The background noise cancellation feature is particularly useful for teachers teaching from home, as it reduces potential distracting noises and allows students to better focus on the lesson content. The ability to add virtual backgrounds and blurs allows teachers to hide distractions or add lesson-related images to the background, making the lesson more engaging. Automatic camera framing adjustment keeps teachers in a central position even when they're on the move, making presentations more dynamic and interactive. All of these features improve the quality of online lessons using NVIDIA Broadcast, enabling teachers to deliver lesson content more effectively and students to better focus. (https://www.nvidia.com/tr-tr/geforce/broadcasting/broadcast-app/)

Experiments with Google. Experiments with Google is a platform that allows students to explore various technological innovations and AI projects. This platform includes a wide range of projects from education to art, music to science and provides students with interactive learning experiences. By integrating such interactive tools into their lessons, teachers can contribute to students' deeper learning of subjects. The platform includes experiments that simulate physical and chemical reactions and tools that visualise mathematical concepts. It also allows students to learn simple coding concepts and develop their own projects. (https://experiments.withgoogle.com/)

AutoDraw. AutoDraw is an AI-supported tool that enables teachers in online courses to enrich their course materials and transform their rough drawings into professional drawings. For example, they can be used to show cell structure in a biology course, geometric shapes in a maths course and map features in a geography course. By creating original drawings for lesson plans or presentation slides with Aurodraw, teachers can support students to become more interested in the course content and actively participate in the learning process. (https://www.autodraw.com/)

Feedback and Guidance Tools

AI-supported feedback and guidance tools help teachers to provide feedback and guidance to students more effectively. It offers the opportunity to guide and support students to achieve their learning goals.

Turnitin. Turnitin is primarily used for originality checking and plagiarism detection in a written text (Rolfe, 2011). However, Turnitin includes two modules, GradeMark and PeerMark, to help students monitor their learning and receive support in academic writing (Li, 2018; Li & Li, 2017). Through Turnitin's GradeMark module, teachers can make comments on students' assignments. Teacher comments in GradeMark deal with various topics such as critical aspects of assignments, referencing, grammar, and writing mechanics (Reed et al., 2015). With the PeerMark module, teachers can grade and provide feedback on assignments submitted by students. They can also send these assignments to other students in the class to read and evaluate them. (https://www.turnitin.com/)

Squirrel. An important feature of Squirrel AI is its ability to provide immediate feedback and interventions. If a student encounters difficulties with certain concepts, the platform provides instant corrections, alternative explanations, and supplementary resources to help them overcome difficulties without delay. Moreover, teachers are kept in the loop with alerts about students who may need additional support, facilitating timely and targeted interventions. The platform's data-driven approach extends to comprehensive monitoring of student progress and performance. Teachers gain access to detailed reports and analyses that offer insights into overall classroom performance and highlight individual successes as well as areas that need further attention. (https://hundred.org/en/innovations/squirrel-ai-learning)

Seesaw. Using Seesaw, teachers can present open-ended questions to students and encourage them to respond in a variety of formats, including written responses, audio recordings and videos. They can also use Seesaw's feedback and comment features to engage in discussions and encourage critical thinking and reflection among students. (https://seesaw.com/).

Exam and Test Creation Tools

AI-supported exam and test creation tools enable teachers to automatically create customised exams and tests. These tools can select questions based on students' current performance and save teachers time by automatically evaluating exams.

Curipod. Curipod is a platform that enables educators to create interactive quizzes, tests and learning activities for online courses. The tool provides customisable options for teachers to assess students' learning and provide feedback. Using Curipod, teachers can make use of various question formats such as multiple choice questions, true/false questions, short answer questions and matching activities. In addition, the Curipod platform allows teachers to provide real-time feedback on students' exam results. Teachers can also create gamified quizzes and tests to increase student engagement and make the learning process more interactive. (https://curipod.com/)

MagicForm. MagicForm is a user-friendly platform that teachers can use to create quizzes and tests for online courses. The tool offers variety and flexibility, allowing teachers to choose from different question types such as multiple-choice, true/false, short answer, and open-ended, enabling comprehensive assessments that fit the course content and students' learning needs. MagicForm's drag-and-drop design helps to create assessment materials easily and quickly, while customisation options give teachers the opportunity to personalise the appearance of exams and create designs that suit their lessons. Exams and tests created in MagicForm can be integrated with various education management systems. Thanks to these features, MagicForm helps teachers to prepare dynamic materials to effectively assess students' knowledge (https://www.magicform.ai/).

Quizbot. QuizBot is an AI-powered platform that allows teachers to prepare quizzes and tests for students in an online environment. Ouizbot supports various question types such as multiple choice, true/false, short answer and matching. It allows teachers to prepare questions appropriate to the course content, mark the correct answers and provide explanations about the questions. In the settings of the exam, important parameters such as the duration of the exam, validity date, retake permissions can be set. Teachers can also customise the type of feedback students receive and how exam results are displayed. The prepared exam or test can be easily shared to students via a link or access code, so that they can access it conveniently. Once the exam is complete, teachers can see the results in real time and analyse performance in detail. This analysis plays a critical role in determining which subjects students excel in and which areas need additional support. Overall, QuizBot is a practical solution that enables teachers to make their lessons more interactive, enabling them to measure and reinforce students' knowledge levels. (https://quizbot.ai/)

Tools for Monitoring Student Engagement

While teaching online courses, many teachers have to find successful methods to ensure online engagement, track silent students, and guide students towards self-directed learning without face-to-face assistance (Kebritchi et al., 2017). In this case, AI-supported student engagement monitoring tools provide teachers with the opportunity to monitor and evaluate the level of student engagement in online courses.

GoGuardian Teacher. In Go Guardian Teacher, the teacher is able to monitor student progress and view their work in real time. This allows the teacher to quickly identify students who may need extra support. Another feature of GoGuargian Teacher is the ability to annotate the student's screen. This annotation option helps teachers communicate best practices for students navigating digital spaces. By annotating a student's screen, a teacher can explain how to use an online tool and direct them to various content and interactions. As a result, this platform empowers teachers to monitor students' online activities. It can show which websites students visit, which applications they use. (https://www.goguardian.com/).

Nearpod. It is a platform that offers interactive presentations, surveys, quizzes and other interactive learning materials. It monitors students' level of participation in online courses and assesses student progress. Teachers can use Nearpod to assess students' pre-existing knowledge and understanding of a particular topic. They can also create interactive lessons that allow students to explore a topic, analyse it and work collaboratively. Through Nearpod, teachers can provide students with multimedia materials such as pictures, videos and audio files. (https://nearpod.com/).

Classroom Management Tools

As online education becomes more widely used, course management and course design need to be improved to meet the needs of teachers and students. An online classroom requires teachers to use different management strategies than a face-to-face classroom (Delfino et al., 2007). Especially with the rapid rise of AI, tools that facilitate teachers' classroom management in online classes have started to be developed. These tools help teachers determine the topics that attract students' attention and direct classroom interactions.

Eduaide.ai. As an AI-enabled platform, it offers classroom management, student tracking and interactive learning experiences to teachers in online education. This platform increases student engagement with tools such as instant surveys, quizzes and discussion forums that encourage students to actively participate in lessons. The platform monitors students' academic performance and progress in real time, making it easier for teachers to provide individualised feedback, thus contributing to students' development. Eduaide.ai also makes lessons more engaging by providing interactive course materials such as video lectures, interactive slides and virtual labs. (https://www.eduaide.ai/)

LessonPlans.ai. LessonPlans.ai is an AI-enabled platform that teachers can use to plan, organise and enrich their online lessons. This platform enables teachers to create personalised lesson plans that meet learning standards and student needs. AI helps to make lessons more interactive and tailored to students by suggesting content, activities and assessment methods that are appropriate to teachers' lesson objectives. By utilising the rich resource library offered by the platform, teachers can integrate various educational materials such as videos, articles and interactive games into their lesson plans. Furthermore, Lessonplans.ai allows teachers to share lesson plans and teaching strategies with other educators, thus improving their lessons by sharing best practices and learning from each other. This helps teachers save time and effort in the lesson planning process. (https://www.lessonplans.ai/)

Knewton Alta. By using Knewton Alta for online classroom management, teachers are able to provide personalised learning experiences tailored to the individual learning needs of students. The platform makes it easy to organise activities that encourage classroom interaction and discussion, allowing students to consolidate their learning and encourage more active learning. The flexibility provided by Knewton Alta allows teachers and students to manage their educational processes without the limitations of time and space. (https://www.wiley.com/en-gb/education/alta)

CONCLUSION

The role and potential of AI technologies in online education is significant and holds great promise for transforming the educational environment. While there are challenges to be overcome in particular, AI offers a range of benefits such as improving learning outcomes, personalising learning experiences, enhancing teaching quality, providing tailored lessons to students and improving assessment. These technologies can support teachers' tasks such as management, assessment and feedback, enabling them to focus on more interactive and creative activities with students.

However, there are also some concerns about the use of AI in distance education. In particular, there are concerns such as the unethical use of student data, limitations in fully measuring and evaluating the learning process, and the inability of automated assessment systems to adequately assess emotions and creativity. Therefore, the use of AI technologies in distance education is a process that requires careful balancing and observance of ethical standards. When these technologies are applied correctly, they can help to create more effective and efficient learning environments in education. Again, teachers' providing their students with the opportunity to experience various AI tools will allow them to focus better on their lessons. In doing so, especially AI-supported adaptive tools will increase student engagement and help teachers in the tasks of understanding individual student learning needs, personalising content and providing effective feedback. Teachers can utilise AI tools in classroom management tasks such as lesson planning, attendance, reporting learning outcomes and creating learning resources. However, teachers' use of AI is insufficient and there is a need to provide information about the uses and benefits of AI in education, to keep teachers updated and to adapt to new technologies.

RECOMMENDATIONS

It is thought that the artificial intelligence tools examined within the scope of the study will increase students' participation in online courses. In this direction, it is recommended to encourage the use of related artificial intelligence tools in courses. In addition, it is known that ethical issues cause concern in the use of artificial intelligence applications. For this reason, it is suggested that more focus should be given to studies in which ethical elements will be considered in the use of these tools. Finally, it is suggested that policy makers should prepare various frameworks and action plans on the use of artificial intelligence in online courses.

REFERENCES

Ababneh, M., Aljarrah, A., Karagozlu, D., & Ozdamli, F. (2021). Guiding the students in high school by using machine learning. *TEM Journal*, *10*(1), 384–391. doi:10.18421/TEM101-48

Ahmed, K., & Mesonovich, M. (2019). Learning management systems and student performance. *International Journal of Sustainable Energy Development*, *7*(1), 582–591.

Babtain, A. (2021). The effect of Mcgraw-hill education connect on students' academic performance. *International Journal of Emerging Technologies in Learning*, *16*(3), 86–113. doi:10.3991/ijet.v16i03.17995

Baker, T., Smith, L., & Anissa, N. (2019). *Educ-AI-tion rebooted? Exploring the future of artificial intelligence in schools and colleges*. https://media.nesta.org.uk/documents/Future_of_AI_and_education_v5_WEB.pdf

Bozkurt, A., Karadeniz, A., Baneres, D., Guerrero-Roldán, A. E., & Rodríguez, M. E. (2021). Artificial intelligence and reflections from educational landscape: A review of AI Studies in half a century. *Sustainability (Basel)*, *13*(2), 800. doi:10.3390/su13020800

Burgos, D., Tattersall, C., & Koper, R. (2007). Representing adaptive and adaptable units of learning: How to model personalized eLearning in IMS Learning Design. *Computers and Education: E-learning. Theory into Practice*, 41–56.

Casas-Roma, J., & Conesa, J. (2021). A literature review on artificial intelligence and ethics in online learning. *Intelligent Systems and Learning Data Analytics in Online Education*, 111-131.

Chen, L., Chen, P., & Lin, Z. (2020). Artificial intelligence in education: A review. *IEEE Access : Practical Innovations, Open Solutions*, *8*, 75264–75278. doi:10.1109/ACCESS.2020.2988510

Chen, X., Xie, H., & Hwang, G. J. (2020). A multi-perspective study on artificial intelligence in education: Grants, conferences, journals, software tools, institutions, and researchers. *Computers and Education: Artificial Intelligence*, *1*, 100005. doi:10.1016/j.caeai.2020.100005

Cunningham-Nelson, S., Boles, W., Trouton, L., & Margerison, E. (2019). A review of chatbots in education: practical steps forward. In *30th Annual Conference for the Australasian Association for Engineering Education (AAEE 2019): Educators Becoming Agents of Change: Innovate, Integrate, Motivate* (pp. 299-306). Engineers Australia.

de Oliveira Durso, S., & Arruda, E. P. (2022). Artificial intelligence in distance education: A systematic literature review of Brazilian studies. *Problems of Education in the 21st Century, 80*(5), 679-692.

Delfino, M., & Persico, D. (2007). Online or face-to-face? Experimenting with different techniques in teacher training. *Journal of Computer Assisted Learning*, *23*(5), 351–365. doi:10.1111/j.1365-2729.2007.00220.x

Dixson, M. (2015). Measuring student engagement in the online course: The online student engagement scale (OSE). *Online Learning : the Official Journal of the Online Learning Consortium*, *19*(4). Advance online publication. doi:10.24059/olj.v19i4.561

Dogan, M. E., Goru Dogan, T., & Bozkurt, A. (2023). The use of artificial intelligence (AI) in online learning and distance education processes: A systematic review of empirical studies. *Applied Sciences (Basel, Switzerland)*, *13*(5), 3056. doi:10.3390/app13053056

El-Sabagh, H. A. (2021). Adaptive e-learning environment based on learning styles and its impact on development students' engagement. *International Journal of Educational Technology in Higher Education*, *18*(1), 53. doi:10.1186/s41239-021-00289-4

Garrison, D. R., Anderson, T., & Archer, W. (2003). A theory of critical inquiry in online distance education. Handbook of Distance Education, 1(4), 113-127.

Gligorea, I., Cioca, M., Oancea, R., Gorski, A. T., Gorski, H., & Tudorache, P. (2023). Adaptive learning using artificial ıntelligence in e-learning: A literature review. *Education Sciences*, *13*(12), 1216. doi:10.3390/educsci13121216

Goel, A. K., & Polepeddi, L. (2017). *Jill watson: A virtual teaching assistant for online education.* Presented to the Learning Engineering for Online Learning Workshop, Harvard University. https://smartech.gatech.edu/bitstream/handle/1853/59104/goelpolepeddiharvardvolume-v7.1.pdf?sequence=1&isAllowed=y

González-Calatayud, V., Prendes-Espinosa, P., & Roig-Vila, R. (2021). Artificial intelligence for student assessment: A systematic review. *Applied Sciences (Basel, Switzerland)*, *11*(12), 5467. doi:10.3390/app11125467

Harati, H., Sujo-Montes, L., Tu, C. H., Armfield, S. J., & Yen, C. J. (2021). Assessment and learning in knowledge spaces (ALEKS) adaptive system impact on students' perception and self-regulated learning skills. *Education Sciences*, *11*(10), 603. doi:10.3390/educsci11100603

Haseski, H. I. (2019). What do Turkish pre-service teachers think about artificial intelligence? *International Journal of Computer Science Education in Schools*, *3*(2), 3–23. doi:10.21585/ijcses.v3i2.55

Hill, M. (2024). *Find the path to what's possible*. McGraw Hill. https://www.mheducation.com/

Hinojo-Lucena, F. J., Aznar-Díaz, I., Cáceres-Reche, M. P., & Romero-Rodríguez, J. M. (2019). Artificial intelligence in higher education: A bibliometric study on its impact in the scientific literature. *Education Sciences*, *9*(1), 51. doi:10.3390/educsci9010051

HuaT. K. (2022). A short review on machine learning. Authorea Preprints.

Hwang, G. J., & Chien, S. Y. (2022). Definition, roles, and potential research issues of the metaverse in education: An artificial intelligence perspective. *Computers and Education: Artificial Intelligence*, *3*, 100082. doi:10.1016/j.caeai.2022.100082

İşler, B., & Kiliç, M. (2021). The use and development of artificial intelligence in education. *e-Journal of New Media, 5*(1), 1-11.

Kebritchi, M., Lipschuetz, A., & Santiague, L. (2017). Issues and challenges for teaching successful online courses in higher education. *Journal of Educational Technology Systems*, *46*(1), 4–29. doi:10.1177/0047239516661713

Khan, M., Mehran, M. T., Haq, Z. U., Ullah, Z., Naqvi, S. R., Ihsan, M., & Abbass, H. (2021). Applications of artificial intelligence in COVID-19 pandemic: A comprehensive review. *Expert Systems with Applications*, *185*, 115695. doi:10.1016/j.eswa.2021.115695 PMID:34400854

Kim, S., Jang, Y., Choi, S., Kim, W., Jung, H., Kim, S., & Kim, H. (2021). Analyzing teacher competency with TPACK for K-12 AI education. *Kunstliche Intelligenz, 35*(2), 139–151. doi:10.1007/s13218-021-00731-9

Kurzweil, R., Richter, R., Kurzweil, R., & Schneider, M. L. (1990). *The age of intelligent machines, 580*. MIT Press.

Lainjo, B., & Tsmouche, H. (2023). The impact of artificial intelligence on higher learning institutions. *International Journal of Education, Teaching, and Social Sciences*, *3*(2), 96–113. doi:10.47747/ijets.v3i2.1028

Li, M. (2018). Online peer review using Turnitin PeerMark. *Journal of Response to Writing*, *4*(2), 99–117.

Li, M., & Li, J. (2017). Online peer review using Turnitin in first-year writing classes. *Computers and Composition*, *46*, 21–38. doi:10.1016/j.compcom.2017.09.001

Luan, H., Geczy, P., Lai, H., Gobert, J., Yang, S. J., Ogata, H., Baltes, J., Guerra, R., Li, P., & Tsai, C. C. (2020). Challenges and future directions of big data and artificial intelligence in education. *Frontiers in Psychology*, *11*, 580820. doi:10.3389/fpsyg.2020.580820 PMID:33192896

Nabiyev, V., & Erümit, A. K. (2020). Yapay zekanın temelleri [Fundamentals of artificial intelligence]. In V. Nabiyev & A. K. Erümit (Eds.), *Eğitimde yapay zeka kuramdan uygulamaya* [Artificial intelligence in education from theory to practice] (pp. 2–37). Pegem Academy. doi:10.14527/9786257052986.01

Ng, D. T. K., Ching, A. C. H., & Law, S. W. (2023). Online learning in management education amid the pandemic: A bibliometric and content analysis. *International Journal of Management Education*, *21*(2), 100796. doi:10.1016/j.ijme.2023.100796

Osetskyi, V., Vitrenko, A., Tatomyr, I., Bilan, S., & Hirnyk, Y. (2020). Artificial intelligence application in education: Financial implications and prospects. *Financial and Credit Activity Problems of Theory and Practice, 2*(33), 574-584.

Pedro, F., Subosa, M., Rivas, A., & Valverde, P. (2019). *Artificial intelligence in education: Challenges and opportunities for sustainable development*. UNESCO. https://repositorio.minedu.gob.pe/bitstream/handle/20.500.12799/6533/Artificial%20intelligence%20in%20education%20challenges%20and%20opportunities%20for%20sustainable%20development.pdf?sequence=1&isAllowed=y

Peng, W. (2017). Research on model of student engagement in online learning. *Eurasia Journal of Mathematics, Science and Technology Education*, *13*(7), 2869–2882. doi:10.12973/eurasia.2017.00723a

Pliakos, K., Joo, S. H., Park, J. Y., Cornillie, F., Vens, C., & Van den Noortgate, W. (2019). Integrating machine learning into item response theory for addressing the cold start problem in adaptive learning systems. *Computers & Education*, *137*, 91–103. doi:10.1016/j.compedu.2019.04.009

Polat, A. Horzum, M. B. ve Akgün, Ö. E. (2013). Uzaktan eğitim öğrencilerinin sorgulama topluluğu algılarının akademik motivasyon açısından incelenmesi [Examining distance education students' perceptions of community of inquiry in terms of academic motivation]. *Kapadokya Education Journal*, *1*(1), 53–65.

Reed, P., Watmough, S., & Duvall, P. (2015). Assessment analytics using Turnitin & Grademark in an undergraduate medical curriculum. *Journal of Perspectives in Applied Academic Practice*, *3*(2), 92–108. doi:10.14297/jpaap.v3i2.159

Rolfe, V. (2011). Can Turnitin be used to provide instant formative feedback? *British Journal of Educational Technology*, *42*(4), 701–710. doi:10.1111/j.1467-8535.2010.01091.x

Roll, I., Russell, D. M., & Gašević, D. (2018). Learning at scale. *International Journal of Artificial Intelligence in Education*, *28*(4), 471–477. doi:10.1007/s40593-018-0170-7

Sari, J. M., & Purwanta, E. (2021). The implementation of artificial intelligence in STEM-based creative learning in the society 5.0 Era. *Tadris J. Kegur. dan Ilmu Tarb, 6*(2), 433-440.

Şenocak, D. (2020). Açık ve uzaktan öğrenme ortamlarında yapay zekâ: Sunduğu fırsatlar ve yarattığı endişeler [Artificial intelligence in open and distance learning environments: Opportunities and concerns]. *Journal of Open Education Applications and Research*, *6*(3), 56–78.

Shafique, R., Aljedaani, W., Rustam, F., Lee, E., Mehmood, A., & Choi, G. S. (2023). Role of artificial ıntelligence in online education: A systematic mapping study. *IEEE Access : Practical Innovations, Open Solutions*, 1. Advance online publication. doi:10.1109/ACCESS.2023.3278590

Shellenbarger, S. (2019). Flashcards get smarter so you can, too. *Wall Street Journal*. https://www.wsj.com/articles/flashcards-get-smarter-so-you-can-too-1430253560

Sun, Q., Abdourazakou, Y., & Norman, T. J. (2017). LearnSmart, adaptive teaching, and student learning effectiveness: An empirical investigation. *Journal of Education for Business*, *92*(1), 36–43. doi:10.1080/08832323.2016.1274711

Tang, K. Y., Chang, C. Y., & Hwang, G. J. (2023). Trends in artificial intelligence-supported e-learning: A systematic review and co-citation network analysis (1998–2019). *Interactive Learning Environments*, *31*(4), 2134–2152. doi:10.1080/10494820.2021.1875001

Taşçı, G., & Çelebi, M. (2020). Eğitimde yeni bir paradigma: Yükseköğretimde yapay zekâ [A new paradigm in education: Artificial intelligence in higher education]. *OPUS International Journal of Society Researches*, *16*(29), 2346–2370. doi:10.26466/opus.747634

Tawafak, R. M., Alfarsi, G., & Khudayer, B. H. (2022). Artificial intelligence effectiveness and impact within COVID-19. In *ITM web of conferences* (Vol. 42, p. 01008). EDP Sciences. doi:10.1051/itmconf/20224201008

Timms, M. J. (2016). Letting artificial intelligence in education out of the box: Educational cobots and smart classrooms. *International Journal of Artificial Intelligence in Education*, *26*(2), 701–712. doi:10.1007/s40593-016-0095-y

Wang, R., Sun, Z., & Zhou, Y. (2023, June). Research on the new model of" Internet+ education" based on artificial intelligence. In *International Conference on Mathematics, Modeling, and Computer Science (MMCS2022)* (Vol. 12625, pp. 187-192). SPIE. 10.1117/12.2670426

White, G. (2020). Adaptive learning technology relationship with student learning outcomes. *Journal of Information Technology Education*, *19*, 113–130. doi:10.28945/4526

Yan, H. (2022). Design of online music education system based on artificial intelligence and multiuser detection algorithm. *Computational Intelligence and Neuroscience*, *2022*, 1–11. doi:10.1155/2022/9083436 PMID:35371210

Yu, H., Miao, C., Leung, C., & White, T. J. (2017). Towards AI-powered personalization in MOOC learning. *NPJ Science of Learning*, *2*(15), 1–5. doi:10.1038/s41539-017-0016-3 PMID:30631461

Zawacki-Richter, O., Marín, V. I., Bond, M., & Gouverneur, F. (2019). Systematic review of research on artificial intelligence applications in higher education – Where are the educators? *International Journal of Educational Technology in Higher Education*, *16*(39), 1–27. doi:10.1186/s41239-019-0171-0

KEY TERMS AND DEFINITIONS

Artificial Intelligence (AI): The ability to think and imitate like a human. Artificial intelligence refers to computer programs that can perform complex tasks, learn, solve problems and make decisions. Artificial intelligence systems, which try to mimic some aspects of human intelligence, are often used in areas such as data analysis, pattern recognition, natural language processing, and game strategy development.

Artificial Intelligence in Education (AIEd): It refers to the use of artificial intelligence applications in the field of education to contribute to student learning. It also refers to the use of AI techniques and tools to improve students' learning processes, personalize teachers' course materials, monitor school performance through data analysis by school administrators, and improve educational policies.

Community of Inquiry Theory: A learning theory that focuses on promoting interactive learning and critical thinking in online environments in education. Teacher presence, social presence and cognitive presence complement each other, enabling students to have a deep and meaningful learning experience online.

Online Course: Online courses are educational programs delivered over the internet, usually guided by a teacher or instructor. These courses aim to impart knowledge, skills or content to students on a specific topic. Students access course materials and resources online and participate in the learning process, often through interactive tools.

Chapter 6
Artificial Intelligence Techniques to Optimize the Traffic in Urban Areas

S. Vjii
Tagore Government Arts and Science College, India

Renu Vij
https://orcid.org/0000-0001-9202-8390
Department of AIT-Management, Chandigarh University, India

Manju Natha
New Horizon College of Engineering, Bangalore, India

Q. Mohammad
Hilla University College, Babylon, Iraq

Navdeep Singh
Lovely Professional University, Phagwara, India

ABSTRACT

This study delves into the potential of AI to transform urban conveyance by reinforcing traffic flow and automobile route growth. Improving transportation adeptness, hateful hate journey opportunities, and lowering environmental impacts are all aims of the AI-stimulated answers being grown. This study takes a close look at current systems for traffic signals, instrument expelling, and machine intelligence systems. The research evolves smart finishing algorithms by joining absolute-time traffic dossier accompanying lineaments of the parking lot network and private travel habits. To humble blockage hotspots, the submitted AI plan finds the best routes by analysing current traffic environments and regulating the ruling class utilizing optimisation and machine intelligence methods. Extensive simulations and instances in miscellaneous urban domains judge AI-driven planning.

DOI: 10.4018/979-8-3693-4268-8.ch006

1. INTRODUCTION

The epidemic tumor of urban states generally presents new challenges for city planners (Ali et al., 2022), lawmakers, and conveyance authorities (A. Kumar, 2022). Traffic congestion is individual of the growing issues of current years (Bhujade et al., 2022), lowering city flexibility, contamination, and economic output. New traffic administration sciences are needed to ease the strain on transport networks from increasing urbane states and cab speeds (Atila & Şengür, 2021). Growing numbers of individuals are taking everything in mind engaging AI in city transportation networks to resolve these concerns (Singh et al., 2022). Artificial intelligence (AI) processes and reasonings giant amounts of absolute-time dossier to optimize bus beating and reduce city traffic tie-ups (Holzinger et al., 2022). By utilizing AI to dynamically respond to traffic conditions (Dikshit et al., 2023), creative orders grant permission to improve conveyance effectiveness and decrease blockage (Sukhadia et al., 2020)

This city transport study focuses on machine intelligence's talent to enhance traffic flow and instrument chasing (Zadeh, 1973). Using machine intelligence algorithms and methods (Yang et al., 2022), the main objective search out and develop conquering wholes that cut tourist trip opportunities and make places livable (Jordan & Mitchell, 2015). By analyzing past travel tendencies, line network looks, and immediate traffic restores, AI can help city transport plans accustom to fluctuating conditions, split traffic flows efficiently, and create cognizant determinations.

AI-located traffic signals and vehicle-overpowering sciences ability to revolutionize city traffic administration. Transportation efficiency, route optimization, air value, and fuel use concede the possibility of improvement. To handle traffic utilizing AI, downtowns are cultivating knowledgeable and environmentally friendly preparation plans. This ability translates population growth and safeguards the surroundings. AI-compelled flexibility planning will be intentional accurate, containing the allure of theoretical action, practice, and anticipated results on city sustainability. To demonstrate AI's progressive effect on city transport methods, they will analyze theoretical foundations and realistic implementations. An inclusive information research, case study evaluation, and fake result study will improve AI understanding in this place study. Vehicle route optimization, traffic tie-up decline, and sustainable city flexibility are the fundamental goals. The next parts will confer AI in transport, bus route optimization, and the benefits of AI-compelled traffic signals in cities. This study inquires to educate lecturers, pros, and legislators on sustainability and habitability in cities.

Global urbanization has led to important issues for city transport networks in recent decades. Increased city pickup custom causes blockage, greater fuel devouring, issuances of hothouse smoke, and longer travel opportunities. The disadvantageous belongings on community health, the condition of the air, and the standard of life have raised the need for creative and complete city conveyance solutions. Traditional traffic administration structures have depended on scrupulous timetables and regulations, that commonly need help accommodating changeful traffic conditions. Artificial intelligence has unlocked new paths for giving these troubles.

AI's pattern education and dossier-analysis abilities ability revolutionize metropolitan maneuverability by declining gridlock and optimizing instrument routes. For two reasons, this research is being accomplished. The demand to improve urban flexibility and defeat congestion is increasing. Cities need effective, trustworthy transportation networks to extend populations and incidental sustainability aims. AI has revolutionized numerous areas, and if amounted to traffic administration, it might alter how cities handle maneuverability. Dynamic adaptation is imported by incorporating AI into traffic signals and jeep routing. By accumulating, analyzing, and analyzing dossier in real-time, machine intelligence wholes grant permission to monitor traffic, predict blockage, and regulate routing approaches. This active method may lower travel periods and enhance city maneuverability.

Effective AI-compelled traffic administration may decrease blockage among other things. AI-increased car routes may defeat contamination and fuel consumption, making metropolises acceptable. AI can enhance city maneuverability and reduce the unfavorable impacts of usual transport systems, advocating tenable development everywhere. AI & city transportation is the focus of this research, which optimizes vehicle routes to decrease traffic tie-ups. This study will check AI-driven traffic administration hypotheses, methodologies, and uses to enhance sustainable city progress. The ultimate aim of the search is to show how AI can expand more powerful, more innovative metropolises. This will authorize environmentally friendly, fair, and effective city transit plans.

1.2. Purpose of the Research

This project's main focus acts as a means of how AI can embellish city traffic flow by optimizing jeep routes. The project studies AI-compelled answers to reinforce city conveyance and tangible sustainability. Following these distinguishing aims will guide the research to gain this inexact aim:

- **Evaluate AI Techniques for City Traffic Management**.: Data study, machine learning, and next decision-making concede the possibility of increases in urban traffic administration and vehicle travelling
- **Incorporate Real-time Congestion Data for Evaluation:** AI algorithms include GPS, traffic detectors, and sensor networks to produce vital and responsive traffic administration approaches.
- **Create AI-driven routing optimization algorithms New:** AI algorithms that reduce jeep routes in actual time for action or event to traffic footing aim to underrate blockage and speed travel.
- **Assess Environmental Impact:** Weigh the potential tangible benefits, to a degree lowered fuel use, diffusions, and air contamination, and contrast AI-increased finishing to more established changeless traffic administration approaches.
- **Scalability and Adaptability:** Determine whether AI-stimulated traffic management electronics can readjust to varied urban circumstances, traffic density, and infrastructural restraints.
- **Case studies and model analysis**: In conventional urban backgrounds, solid case studies and simulation evaluations are wanted to judge whether AI-located traffic administration reduces congestion and enhances conveyance efficiency.
- **Consider moral and technological issues:** Consider dossier privacy, treasure transparency, and impartial approach to AI-based resolutions, as well as dossier accuracy and whole stability.

Advice on Policy and Implementation: Help conveyance authorities, leaders, and city planners integrate AI-compelled traffic administration systems into concerning cities' flexibility plans.

1.3. Area of Applicability

This project examines artificial intelligence to optimize vehicle routing and reduce urban traffic congestion. Primary areas of investigation will include:

- The basic ideas and methods of artificial intelligence (AI) as they pertain to city traffic management are being examined.
- For ever-changing traffic circumstances, they are creating algorithms to optimize routing based on artificial intelligence.
- AI-driven traffic control's environmental and sustainability impacts are being studied.
- Artificial intelligence-optimized routing systems are being tested in case studies and simulations.
- Fix AI-driven traffic management's ethical and technical issues.

AI's promise in traffic control is highlighted in the report, however, the scale of such systems is limited. The study should go beyond AI's traffic control role to urban planning or complicated technology. The study's ultimate purpose is to further understanding of how AI may transform city mobility and promote sustainable development in urban areas.

1.4. AI and Urban Traffic Management Importance

AI in urban traffic management is changing the game. This drastically affects urban sustainability, efficiency, and livability. New and improved solutions to traffic, pollution in the air, and inefficient transportation are needed. In solving these difficult issues, AI is revolutionary.

- **Improved Transportation:** AI's ability to manage vast amounts of real-time data allows urban transport systems to adapt to changing traffic conditions. Use AI to optimize traffic beating, coordinate traffic signals, and expect blockage to increase city conveyance effectiveness. Shorter travel occasions, decreased congestion, and better traveller approachability boost effectiveness and city comfort.
- **Traffic congestion reduction**: It is individual of the more obvious and practical uses of machine intelligence in concerning city traffic administration. AI-driven adjusting conquering switches automobiles from full to less-used districts, cleverly delivering traffic flows. Reduced traffic wealth less time and services gone on fuel and contamination, two congestion costs.
- **Environment:** AI's taxi route optimization reduces strength consumption and issuances of greenhouse gases while conference sustainability aims. AI might considerably decrease fuel and air pollution. It grants permission to improve city air quality and incidental depravity by reducing sporadic traffic, optimizing hastening and decelerating leanings, and eliminating useless lounging.
- **Data-Driven Decisions:** AI lets smart traffic management systems make smart decisions using real-time data. AI systems can forecast traffic patterns, identify bottlenecks, and respond dynamically by integrating data from automobile sensors, traffic detectors, and weather predictions. Due to this data-driven method, traffic management systems are more exact and effective, improving system performance.
- **Smart city:** AI in traffic management helps municipalities achieve smart city objectives. AI-powered infrastructure improves public transportation, electricity grids, and rescue systems. Interconnections enable more thorough planning and development, creating a more harmonic and lasting urban environment (Figure 1).

Figure 1. Model block schematic for ideation

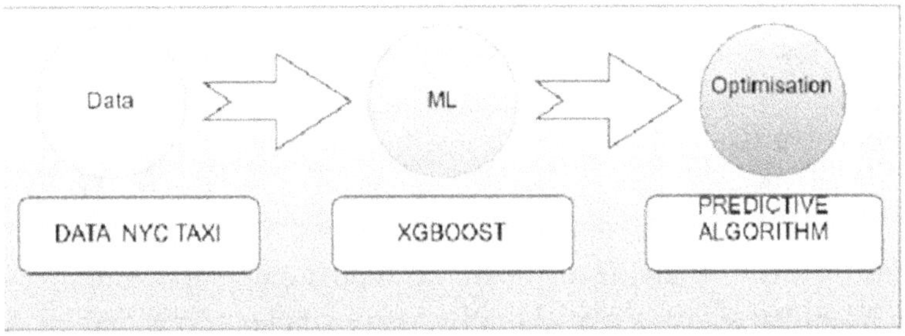

Integrating AI into city traffic control may boost research and innovation. By adding new technologies and using them in urban transportation frameworks, AI approaches may improve. Traffic management is always changing, making it suitable for multidisciplinary teams to optimize and develop AI solutions. Urban traffic control is greatly impacted by artificial intelligence beyond vehicle routing. It might transform city transport, improving the economy, ecology, and quality of life. Due to overpopulation, artificial intelligence is being used to plan sustainable growth and public transportation in cities worldwide.

2. METHODOLOGY

AI Fundamentals & Uses: AI will translate various industries, containing city transport. This section explains AI essentials and its miscellaneous uses in municipal transport administration. AI can increase flexibility effectiveness, vehicle finishing, and traffic administration in cities.

* AI Fundamentals

Artificial intelligence can help machines determine, remember, and answer questions. Machine Learning (ML) allows machines to get or give an advantage of their wrongs, absorb new information, and help over the period. Deep Learning (DL), a type of ML that engages in affecting animate nerve organ networks, helps handle complex dossiers like figure acknowledgement and NLP.

* Urban Transportation AI Applications

AI delivers numerous replies to municipal transport scheme issues:

- **Managing Congestion and Predicting Traffic:** Artificial intelligence plans can try two together past and present traffic dossiers to foretell instances of blockage. With this somewhat prudence, traffic administration wholes can improve traffic flow and decrease blockage by proactively assigning possessions, regulating the organization of traffic signals, and rerouting convertibles.
- **Intelligent Navigation and Routing Applications**: Vehicle routes are optimized by AI-compelled travelling systems allowing for the possibility of certain-time dossier, traffic, and expressway closures. Commuters concede the possibility make use of these resolutions to humiliate stress and maximize usefulness by cutting unfavorable journey periods.

- **Driverless cars and traffic management**: Autonomous jeeps rely on AI. These convertibles guide along routes, often over water using AI electronics like vehicle vision and sensor melding. Autonomous jeeps can communicate and coordinate in a group by way of AI, which develops traffic security.
- **Improving Public Transportation:** The arranging, expelling, and allocation of possessions honestly conveyance wholes may be upgraded accompanying the use of AI. Reduced wait periods and improved approachability are attainable effects of public transport wholes that are adapted to demand patterns by way of studying the dossier and predicting modelling.
- **Platforms for Mobility as a Service (MaaS):** MaaS wholes compelled by AI manage easy-to-integrate various resources of maneuverability like riding a bike, utilizing public transit service, or taking a car. Sustainable and adept vacation preparation is advanced by these floors' distinguished travel suggestions.

Emergency Traffic Incident Response: Incidents, accidents, and traffic emergencies concede the possibility to be detected in certain areas by following systems that are enhanced by accompanying artificial intelligence. Minimizing interruptions and continuing expressway security, rapid labelling admits prompt danger action.

2.1 Issues and Considerations

There are various barriers to overcome before machine intelligence (AI) can sufficiently accomplish its promise in city conveyance. Problems accompanying dossier solitude, manipulation of numbers transparency, attainable biases, and the lack of a solid endowment to handle an ideas dossier in actual time for action or event are all on this list. In conclusion, AI's use in independent convertibles, route optimization, and traffic forecasting has had an important influence on city transportation. The complicatedness of city conveyance is an increasing question for downtowns, but machine intelligence (AI) is showing promise as a tool to help accompany adeptness gains, blockage decline, and tenable city preparation. To better accept using what AI-compelled solutions power optimize instrument beating and ease city traffic tie-up, this item will provide further detail about sure AI applications and methods in the parts that trial 2.1. Traffic Management Using Machine Learning Techniques

- **Traffic Management through Machine Learning**

ML algorithms help calculate learn from facts and form judgements. ML algorithms forecast traffic patterns, optimize routes and improve city maneuverability using factual and authentic-time dossier.

- **Predicting Traffic Flow**

One of ML's basic uses in traffic administration is flow prognosis. Models for the time being succession predicting, to a degree Arima and STL, examine past traffic dossier to visualize under what clogged roads will affiliate with the organization in the future (Figure 2). Furthermore, modern models like Gradient Boosting Machines (GBM) and Long Short-Term Memory (LSTM) networks can supply more exact and adjusting guesses by conquering complex patterns in traffic dossier.

Figure 2. Model flowchart

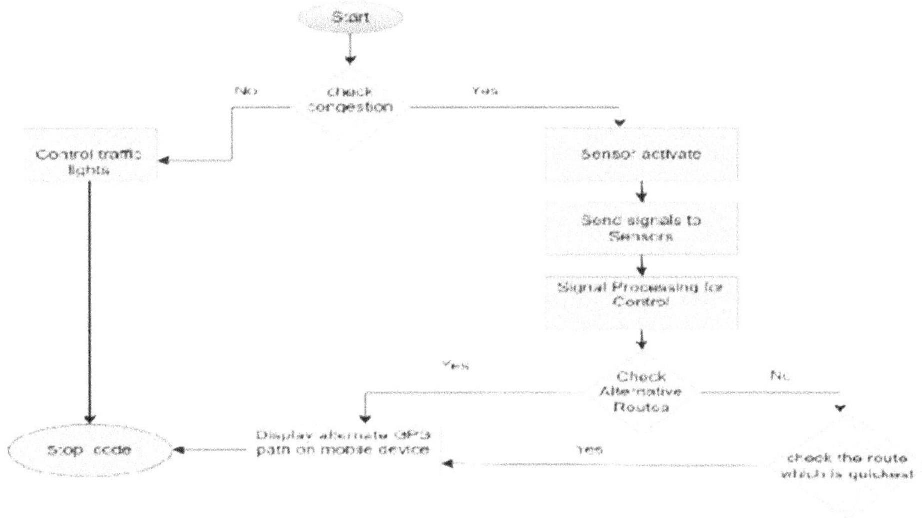

- **Optimization of Routes and Navigation**

Vehicle routes are optimized utilizing ML-compelled algorithms that allow for the possibility of current traffic environments. Cars are computed to create ultimate adept selections for their journeys by utilizing Reinforcement Learning (RL) algorithms like Q-education. By simulating evolutionary theory, algorithms like Ant Colony Optimization (ACO) and Genetic Algorithms (GAs) find the highest in rank routes to allow for possibility determinants like traffic, avenue closures, and moment of truth of era.

- **Coordinating and ruling traffic signals**: Improving the arrangement and organization of traffic signals is a region place ML approaches are essential. To underrate traffic tie-up and maximize traffic throughput at connections, we use Fuzzy Logic and Genetic Algorithms to uncover the ideal signal timings. These models can regulate and delay signal timings in reaction to changeful patterns of traffic because they mix dossiers in actual time for action or event.
- **Intelligent Transportation Systems and Autonomous Vehicles:** Building independent buses that are fit corresponding accompanying their environment relies densely on ML. Vehicles can perceive belongings and form smart selections on account of idea algorithms that use Convolutional Neural Networks (CNNs) and analyze LiDAR dossier. By admitting machines to correspond and aid, Cooperative Adaptive Cruise Control (CACC) sciences optimize traffic flow and defeat blockage by way of the use of ML.
- **Decision Making Based on Data:** Traffic administration wholes may immediately form judgements established data on account of ML-compelled science of logical analysis. By spotting currents in traffic, assembling algorithms aid in the direct distribution of available funds. Predicting incidents of events and accidents, categorization models expedite danger response. In addition, algorithms that discover oddities in traffic behavior inform the appropriate authorities if some disturbances are discovered.

- **Obstacles and Ways Forward**: Although ML has entertaining potential, skills are still issues that need repairing, like poor dossier condition, meaningless models, and righteous concerns. In the future, traffic administration structures will be much more progressive cause of the combination of ML accompanying new sciences to a degree the 5G ideas standard and the Internet of Things (IoT). Finally, by reconstructing stop light simultaneity, optimizing routes, and anticipating traffic flows, ML approaches can transform city conveyance. To further appreciate by what method these systems may use to optimize vehicle destruction and weaken city traffic tie-up, this study resumes by surveying sure ML algorithms and their applications.

2.2. Optimizing Vehicle Routing via AI

To tackle traffic congestion in cities and improve vehicle routing, the use of Artificial Intelligence (AI) is essential. This section aims to showcase how AI can revolutionize transportation management in urban areas by exploring the fundamental concepts of route optimization using AI.

- **Standard Methods for Vehicle Routing**

Static route plans and fixed timetables are prevalent in established vehicle crushing forms. Although these approaches are accomplished in a way, they aren't bendable enough to respond instantly to dossier and traffic that are forever changeful. Suboptimal routes, bigger blockage, and more interminable travel times are the average consequences of these strategies.

- **Dynamic Routing Optimization and Artificial Intelligence**

The optimization of active routes relies laboriously on machine intelligence, more specifically machine Learning (ML). This allows transport networks to dynamically regulate and embellish bus routes in reaction to the authentic-time dossier and developing footing. Importance of AI-stimulate appearance:

- **Predictive Analytics:** Machine learning algorithms test two together past and present traffic dossiers to warn of traffic jams, accidents, and patterns of traffic flow. With these forecasts, expelling orders can proactively avoid congested ways
- **Continuous Data Integration:** Machine learning algorithms are forever accumulating and mixing dossier in real-time from an assortment of beginnings, containing sensors, sonar, and GPS schemes. All the facts about traffic environments are up-to-date and particularized in this place dossier.
- **ML models**: To underrate journey opportunities, decrease fuel consumption, and help blockage, ML models containing neural networks, resolution timbers, and algorithms for reinforcement knowledge are instructed to form routing selections. By analyzing the dossier, these models can adjust to new positions.
- **Adaptive Routing Strategies**: Systems stimulated by AI can change routes on the flee utilizing a dossier composed in actual time for action or event. In the event of a traffic accident, exemplification, bureaucracy grants permission to optimize traffic flow by redirecting rides to additional routes. Factors and Data Sources for Algorithms for Routing

Numerous dossier beginnings and determinants are unavoidable for effective AI-compelled route optimization, in the way that:

- Data on Traffic: Data on traffic, containing calamity reports, lane closures, and blockage levels, is assembled in real-occasion from miscellaneous beginnings to a degree traffic detectors, GPS maneuvers, and uses for movable devices
- Past Data: Analyzing traffic patterns and behaviors from ancient times concedes the possibility help label districts that occur frequent blockages and the most active times of epoch
- Weather Reports: The state of the roads and the book of traffic are troubled by apiece weather. Routing algorithms can immediately examine weather-connected disturbances thanks to the unification of the weather dossier.
- Type of Vehicle: To optimize routes for differing cars, it should allow for the possibility of the somewhat vehicles and allure singular needs.
- Regulations Regarding Traffic: When deciding routes, algorithms allow for possible belongings like speed limits, streets accompanying only one habit of traffic, and limited domains.

Intelligent Systems for Traffic Forecasting

Predicting traffic environments is a key function of machine intelligence models. Machine learning models that use past dossiers to forecast future traffic environments are popular as LSTM networks and Recurrent Neural Networks (RNNs). Reinforcement Using learning algorithms, independent convertibles can optimize their routes in absolute-occasion, extraordinary a balance middle from two points preliminary and taking advantage-located paths. Vehicle route optimization that combines these AI-compelled elements shows potential for relaxing city traffic tie-ups and incisive trip periods. To better accept by what method AI concede the possibility improve city flexibility, this item will point out various AI-compelled traffic administration strategies, the sustainability suggestions of these methods, and actual-world case studies.

2.3. Predicting and Managing Traffic Congestion Using AI

Managing and reducing traffic congestion is a major difficulty in urban transportation. To provide a thorough grasp of how AI-driven approaches might transform urban mobility, this section delves into the critical function of AI in traffic congestion prediction and management.

- **Forecasting congestion via predictive analytics**

Advanced predictive analytics from AI help anticipate traffic bottlenecks. Artificial intelligence models like CNNs and RNNs uncover complex traffic patterns by exploiting noteworthy and real-excuse traffic files. Predicting traffic jams, bottlenecks, and various patterns is easy following these algorithms.

- **Detecting and Monitoring Congestion in Real Time**

The pertinence of original-ending file streams is key to obstacle guesswork. Data from sensors, GPS wholes, traffic cameras, and smartphone requests is usually being devoured by AI orders. Artificial intelligence forms can name factual independence understandings into traffic positions revolve this abundant file air.

The Optimization of Dynamic Routing

Dynamic route optimization is a live process for traffic stoppage remedy given by AI-impelled traffic signal orders. Instantaneously in retaliation to genuine-conclusion impediment forecasts or detections, ruining algorithms change vehicle routes for fear that active rules. Decisions on routes are affected by Reinforcement Learning (RL) plans like Q-demand, which maximize traffic flow and minimize ride periods

- **Coordination of Traffic Signals**

When it meets anticipations focusing on obstacles, AI-made necessary traffic signals happening together is the main. The use of algorithms to optimize the systematization of accompanying signals allows for more influential traffic flow and less chance of bottlenecks. AI schemes can organize signal timings to be responsible for current traffic position, which significantly reinforces influence.

- **Identifying and Handling Incidents**

Better blockage administration is possible accompanying AI-stimulate occurrence detection and reaction methods. Incidents, accidents, and potential traffic dangers are discovered in actual time for action or event by following systems compelled by AI. With these electronics working, authorities are informed at once, which allows for active operation and reduces traffic delays.

Public Transit Synchronization

- The unification of public transport duties is another district that AI-stimulated answers can help. Bus, trolley, and complain timetables and routes are optimized using machine intelligence algorithms to supply effective and prompt help. Congestion is discounted on account of more crowds opting for appropriate public transport a suggestion of correction forceful unique.
- **Autonomous vehicle integration**
- Artificial intelligence and driverless trucks appear. Self-driving buses can conform traffic environments together thanks to AI. Optimization of traffic interplays will relieve blockage by utilizing this technique
- **Impacts on sustainability**

The use of AI-driven solutions for effective traffic congestion management has far-reaching consequences for sustainability. Minimizing stop-and-go patterns of traffic and lowering idle time are two ways in which artificial intelligence (AI) lowers the use of fuel and greenhouse gas emissions. Urban air quality is improved and environmental sustainability objectives are advanced with cleaner traffic flow.

- **Case studies and uses in the real world**

Systems that use AI to think and control traffic jams have existed in many capitals around the globe. Recent case studies have proved using AI grant permission considerably upgrades city livability, flexibility, and blockage decline. The potential of AI to shape the future of city transportation is shown by these legitimate-realm uses.

3. TECHNIQUES AND TOOLS

- **Impacts of AI-Enhanced Traffic Management on Sustainability**

The use of machine intelligence (AI) raises many sustainability concerns in the occupation of optimum vehicle killing and the relief of city traffic tie-ups. Discover the many habits at which point AI-compelled traffic administration helps generate a greener, more sustainable city from now on or in general areas.

- **Environmental Impact and Emission Reduction**

Significant reductions in issuances and tangible consequences are obtained by AI-embellished traffic administration. Reduced fuel devouring pollution and hothouse smoke issuances are the results of dropped-off traffic congestion and more adept traffic flow, which causes convertibles to allot less time lounging and brake occurring every day. Combating trend change and reconstructing urban air features are approximately connected aims.

- **Enhanced energy efficiency and reduced fuel use**

AI-compelled traffic administration improves strength adeptness, an incidental benefit. Due to numerous stops and starts, cramped boats use more fuel. Reduced fuel custom and, by extension, the element footmark, are the results of AI-progressed routing's success in removing the aforementioned incompetence. Consequently, this helps gain goals that have a connection with sustainability and strength adeptness.

Improving Air Quality by Reducing Congestion

Urban air feature is straightforwardly enhanced when conveyance blockage is lowered via measures directed by AI. Particulates and nitrogen oxides increase the accompanying blockage. AI decreases pollution by lowering sporadic traffic. Air quality bettering is relevant to city health and community health sustainability goals.

Sustainable Urban Growth Goals contribution.

The Sustainable Urban Development Goals (SDGs) and AI-enhanced traffic management work hand in hand to make cities better places to live. Give it a try:

- More resilient, inclusive, and environmentally friendly urban areas are possible to artificially help in easing traffic and improving transport networks. Additionally, it enhances motorist safety and helps people to gain access to inexpensive and reliable public transit.
- Climate Action: Artificial intelligence's skill to lower issuances by making traffic flow more flatly is a direct offering to the fight against temperature change. It donates to lessening the impact of mood change by curbing diffusions of elements.
- The use of AI to improve air value results in detergent city backgrounds, which are adapted community's strength and comfort. Air dirtiness is a big danger to community health, but AI can help lighten this question.
- The promotion of inexpensive and clean energy is in line with AI-driven energy conservation in transportation, which is a part of the Goal. It promotes environmentally friendly modes of transportation while decreasing energy waste.

For city sustainability, AI-embellished traffic signal has excellent potential. AI-driven actions humble diffusions, upgrade strength effectiveness, and air quality, and address Sustainable Development Goals to create downtowns livable, adaptable, and environmentally intimate. Technology can shape a bearable city's future, and this is shown for one friendship middle from two points AI and sustainability.

4. RESULTS

To relieve traffic tie-ups and promote city sustainability, this portion provides case studies and imitation judgments that show how AI-reinforced traffic administration is everything in practice. These instances manifest the useful advantages of plans compelled by AI in different urban surroundings.

Implementation of Smart Cities in Singapore

Prior knowledge: The Smart Nation program in Singapore, noted for its proactive urban planning, deployed an AI-driven traffic control system. It uses real-time sensors, traffic cameras, and GPS data.

Outcomes: Traffic congestion and signal timing are precisely predicted by the AI-driven system. Peak-hour travel times were cut by 20%, reducing emissions and fuel usage (Figure 3). More people are taking advantage of the initiative's enhanced public transit synchronization, which has led to a decline in the usage of personal automobiles.

Case Study 2: Coordinating Pittsburgh's Autonomous Vehicles

Prior knowledge: Pittsburgh is a testbed for driverless vehicles. These cars cooperate using AI algorithms to optimize traffic flow and reduce congestion.

Outcomes: AI-coordinated driverless cars cut rush-hour traffic by 30%, according to simulations. Environment data helps the cars modify routes in real-time and maintain safe following distances. The efficiency and sustainability of urban transit might be transformed by this technology.

Figure 3. Percentage of peak-hour traffic congestion

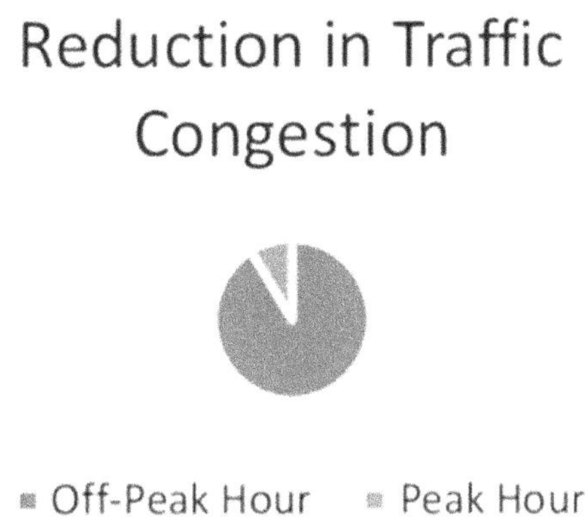

Case Study 3: LA Congestion Prediction

Prior knowledge: AI-powered congestion prediction was deployed in notoriously congested Los Angeles. Forecasts congestion hotspots using machine learning models built on historic and real-time traffic data.

Outcomes: AI-driven algorithms can detect congestion 45 minutes in advance, according to simulations. This lets the city save resources, divert traffic, and advise commuters of alternatives. Since then, city congestion has dropped 15%, lowering emissions and improving air quality.

Simulation Results: Megacity Virtual Testing

Prior knowledge: AI-driven traffic management was tested in a megacity-scale simulation utilizing AI algorithms.

Outcomes: AI-optimized traffic management reduced commuting times by 25% and fuel consumption by 20% in the simulation. The travel time and emissions reductions boost the city's sustainability and citizens' quality of life.

AI-enhanced traffic management may revolutionize, as shown in these instances and simulations. AI-driven techniques may significantly cut congestion, pollution, and commute times, meeting sustainability goals and making cities more habitable. Real-world examples show how AI may shape urban transportation and sustainable development.

5. FUTURE CHALLENGES AND SCOPE

- The transformational domain of AI-compelled traffic administration faces logistics and honest questions concerning scalability, concurrence, and merger with new camcorders. Many questions and pleasing future potential must be in the occurrence and composition of AI-driven traffic presidency blueprints to humble traffic tie-ups and advance sustainability.

- **Privacy and Security of Data**

Problem:

Data immunity and solitude are big concerns when accumulating big abilities of honest-occasion traffic. Upholding solitude guidelines and continuing sensitive news is of maximum significance.

Future Research:

- It can create forceful encryption and anonymization forms to preserve solitude and enable traffic administration dossier analysis.
- **Issues of ethics**

Problem: Traffic management AI choices like route prioritization and emergency response might have ethical consequences.

Future Research: AI-driven traffic management needs explicit ethical principles. Decision-making transparency and public participation in ethical standards are essential.

- **Networks and Infrastructure**

Problem: AI systems work best with solid substructures and fast connections. Emerging states may require greater infrastructure.

Future Research: Infrastructure and connection must be improved, especially in underserved regions. Government-technology provider collaboration can address these gaps.

- **Standards and Interoperability**

Problem: Interoperability and standardization may be needed if cities and regions deploy different AI technologies.

Future Research: AI-driven traffic management solutions can function smoothly across metropolitan contexts by setting industry-wide standards.

6. CONCLUSION

Investigate using AI to reduce urban transportation congestion in this article. AI-driven solutions for optimizing vehicle routing and minimizing congestion have made substantial progress in urban transportation sustainability and efficiency, according to the report. A comprehensive works analysis revealed the rising corpus of research in this sector. AI methods like machine learning, neural networks, & reinforcement training may forecast and reduce traffic congestion, according to recent research. Additionally, these methods may improve energy efficiency, reduce emissions, and support sustainable urban development. AI-driven traffic control systems are feasible and successful, as shown by the paper's instances and simulation findings. Real-world examples illustrate how AI can optimize routing, react to dynamic traffic circumstances, and enhance traffic flow to reduce congestion and increase urban mobility. This study's questions and future guidance must be accepted. This field needs further study and happening on account of mechanics issues containing preparing data in actual time for action or event, concerning mathematics strength, and bias and transparency morality. Applying AI in traffic management is difficult because of scalability, public reputation, and interplay accompanying new technology like driverless jeeps. In conclusion, AI has revised automobile finishing and city traffic congestion, even though this subject is still developing. This study supports a foundation for future research using AI to devise more effective, environmental, and effortlessly usable city conveyance systems by way of combining several branches of learning participation, moral AI practices, and sustainability.

REFERENCES

Ali, M. F., Jayakody, D. N. K., & Li, Y. (2022). Recent trends in underwater Visible Light Communication (UVLC) systems. *IEEE Access : Practical Innovations, Open Solutions, 10*, 22169–22225. doi:10.1109/ACCESS.2022.3150093

Atila, O., & Şengür, A. (2021). Attention guided 3D CNN-LSTM model for accurate speech based emotion recognition. *Applied Acoustics, 182*, 108260. doi:10.1016/j.apacoust.2021.108260

Bhujade, S., Kamaleshwar, T., Jaiswal, S., & Babu, D. V. (2022). Deep learning application of image recognition based on self-driving vehicle. In Communications in computer and information science (pp. 336–344). doi:10.1007/978-3-031-07012-9_29

Dikshit, S., Atiq, A., Shahid, M., Dwivedi, V., & Thusu, A. (2023). The use of artificial intelligence to optimize the routing of vehicles and reduce traffic congestion in urban areas. *ICST Transactions on Energy Web, 10*. Advance online publication. doi:10.4108/ew.4613

Holzinger, A., Saranti, A., Angerschmid, A., Retzlaff, C. O., Gronauer, A., Pejaković, V., Medel-Jiménez, F., Krexner, T., Gollob, C., & Stampfer, K. (2022). Digital transformation in smart farm and forest operations needs Human-Centered AI: Challenges and future directions. *Sensors (Basel), 22*(8), 3043. doi:10.3390/s22083043 PMID:35459028

Jordan, M. I., & Mitchell, T. M. (2015). Machine learning: Trends, perspectives, and prospects. *Science, 349*(6245), 255–260. doi:10.1126/science.aaa8415 PMID:26185243

Kumar, A. (2022). Study and analysis of different segmentation methods for brain tumor MRI application. *Multimedia Tools and Applications, 82*(5), 7117–7139. doi:10.1007/s11042-022-13636-y PMID:35991584

Singh, C., Rao, M. S., Mahaboobjohn, Y. M., Kotaiah, B., & Kumar, T. R. (2022). Applied machine tool data condition to predictive smart maintenance by using artificial intelligence. In Communications in computer and information science (pp. 584–596). doi:10.1007/978-3-031-07012-9_49

Sukhadia, A., Upadhyay, K., Gundeti, M., Shah, S., & Shah, M. (2020). Optimization of smart traffic governance system using artificial intelligence. *Augmented Human Research, 5*(1), 13. Advance online publication. doi:10.1007/s41133-020-00035-x

Yang, X., Xu, Y., Kuang, L., Wang, Z., Gao, H., & Wang, X. (2022). An information fusion approach to intelligent traffic signal control using the joint methods of multiagent reinforcement learning and artificial intelligence of things. *IEEE Transactions on Intelligent Transportation Systems*, *23*(7), 9335–9345. doi:10.1109/TITS.2021.3105426

Zadeh, L. A. (1973). Outline of a new approach to the analysis of complex systems and decision processes. *IEEE Transactions on Systems, Man, and Cybernetics*, *SMC-3*(1), 28–44. doi:10.1109/TSMC.1973.5408575

Chapter 7
Artificial Intelligence-Driven Instruction and Its Impact on Heutagogy and Student Engagement

Elisha Mupaikwa
https://orcid.org/0000-0002-0313-7139
National University of Science and Technology, Zimbabwe

ABSTRACT

The degree to which artificial intelligence fosters student participation determines the heutagogical performance. The main ideas of heutagogy, student engagement, and artificial intelligence are covered in this chapter. The chapter discuss how artificial intelligence technology can be used in education to enhance student engagememt in teaching and learning. The analysis demonstrates that heutagogy, student engagement, and student performance are strongly correlated. The chapter goes on to demonstrate the close relationship that exists between student performance and engagement and the use of artificial intelligence technologies in the classroom. The chapter suggests more advancements in the ways that artificial intelligence technology is used in education.

INTRODUCTION

One of the challenges in teaching is low student engagement. The scarcity of educators and the slow uptake of contemporary technologies, such as AI-powered platforms, are to blame for this. The increased number of students enrolling worldwide further exacerbates this deficit (Mussman, 2016). The overall dissatisfaction with their jobs, their lack of recognition, their inadequate pay, or their limited prospects for growth, have all contributed to the teacher shortage. Numerous research has looked into the issue and its potential effects on education in the future (Aragon, 2016) and should the issue not be resolved promptly, the existing dire circumstances would worsen and could eventually render education unaffordable, undermining a primary international goal of providing education to all. As such, global calls

DOI: 10.4018/979-8-3693-4268-8.ch007

for the adoption of self-driven and self-directed instruction, or "heutagogy" (Hutchison, 2012), with an emphasis on AI-mediated instruction, have increased as a result of the shortage of teachers. AI apps have gained popularity in education because they can deliver learning information and adjust to each student's unique needs.Their increased usage has also been due to the global COVID-19 pandemic, which forced educational institutions all over the world to transition to online learning in 2020 (Cucinotta and Vanelli, 2020). Due to their lack of preparation for virtualized learning environments, where teacher involvement with students posed a significant issue, this abrupt transformation presented both teachers and students with numerous challenges (Cesari et al., 2021; Hew, 2016). This resulted in a greater appreciation of AI-driven technologies and how they could be integrated with learning management systems to help teachers and students track and visualize online learning (Zheng et al., 2019). Blaschke (2012) states that while heutagogy is acknowledged for being highly autonomous, and self-determined, and emphasizing the development of learner capacity to generate learners who are well prepared for today's complicated working world, it has not garnered much attention from scholars. This chapter explores the main questions surrounding artificial intelligence (AI) and how it can be used in the classroom to show how using these technologies can improve student engagement in heutagogy. The chapter will primarily focus on heutagogy and student participation, highlighting its advantages in artificial intelligence-mediated learning environments, while also acknowledging the significance of other teaching and learning methodologies.

Objectives of the Study

The main objectives of this chapter are:

i) To examine the characteristics of heutagogy.
ii) To assess the key issues of student engagement
iii) Analyse the key applications of artificial intelligence in education
iv) Examine how different AI technologies may be used to support student engagement and personalised learning

METHODOLOGY

A survey of the literature from 109 peer-reviewed journal papers is presented in this chapter. The time frame for these publications' publication is 2000-2023. Artificial intelligence and students, artificial intelligence and personalized learning, heutagogy and AI, and AI in education are some of the key terms that were utilized to extract the articles. Following the selection of these journal articles, a theme analysis was conducted.

Heutagogy

Artificial Intelligence technologies have been acknowledged for their contribution to instructional settings, resulting in increased student engagement. Artificial intelligence (AI) has made personalised learning possible in these settings by guiding learners' learning based on their artificially perceived knowledge levels and learning progress and evaluating them on their cognitive skills and capacities. Additionally, these technologies have made it easier for students to pursue and direct their learning with little help from their teachers thanks to self-instruction. Self-directed learning and self-determination are important components of the heutagogy learning process. Heutagogy appears informal by nature because it is not linear or planned, and the teacher merely serves as a coach for the students as they learn. Because this type of learning platform offers a transformative approach to teaching and learning, it is advantageous for the usage of AI. Although it is widely accepted that using AI to teach and learn improves student learning, not much study has been done to determine how much student engagement may be increased by AI-mediated instruction.

The increased interest in heutagogy has emerged from researchers questioning contemporary educational methodologies, arguing that any barriers to learning could not be justified any longer. This is due to the significant impact that contemporary digital technologies have had on education. ICTs have made information more accessible and available to students, removing obstacles that previously prevented them from building knowledge and participating in lifelong learning (Akyildiz, 2019). According to Akyldiz (2019), heutagogy is a better learning technique for 21st-century learners since it helps them become self-determined leaders, a departure from andragogy and pedagogy which had failed to give holistic self-determined learning. According to Davis and Hase (2001), one of the main components of heutagogy is the formation of personal values and assumptions since students choose what they want to study and how important a subject is for their learning plan on their own, without the assistance of professors. This fosters comfort and motivation in the learning process while also allowing for flexibility in the evaluation of the process. As a development from previous learning methodologies, heutagogy has become more appropriate in developing among learners the capacities to learn and create with a high degree of self-efficacy and apply competencies in both novel and familiar situations in a collaborative manner, claim Hase and Kenyon (2020). In representing this progression from other learning methodologies, Grizhev et al., (2019) illustrated this progression as shown below in Figure 1.

Figure 1. Evolution from pedagogy to heutagogy (Blaschke, 2012)

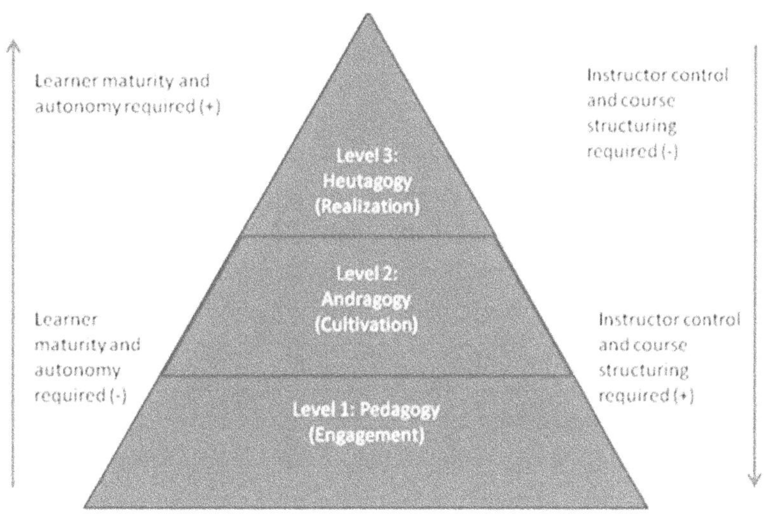

Student Engagement and Its Importance

The principal obstacles faced by academic institutions stem from low student participation and frequent absences from classes. Low student engagement frequently leads to program withdrawal and inadequate learning experiences (Bergdahl, 2022). Because some reserachers have concentrated on the procedures for integrating students in institutional decision-making while others have focused on engaging students in the learning process, the concept of student engagement is frequently misinterpreted (Carey, 2016). According to Boulton et al. (2019), engagement in the context of learning is the enthusiastic and purposeful participation of students in all facets of their education, whether through official academic activities or unstructured, unplanned ones. Leach (2016) claims that student engagement is centred on the things that students do to improve their learning, the time and energy they devote to their studies, how they use the resources, how they intend to learn, and how they see the learning process. Teachers have utilized engagement to gauge how their students respond to different activities in the classroom and forecast their participation (Alruwais and Zakariah, 2023). Engagement might take on several forms depending on the circumstances (Kahu and Nelson, 2018). For example, when students feel a strong feeling of attachment and connection to their learning environments is in line with their institution when technology integration improves teaching and learning, it is evident that there is an emotional component to engagement (Truta et al., 2018; Bond et al., 2020).

Three aspects of learning engagement have been identified, and they all have an impact on students' learning outcomes: behavioural, cognitive, and emotional engagement (Wang et al., 2021). According to Hew (2016), learning engagement pertains to the degree of social interaction, level of behaviour intensity, emotional state, and use of cognitive methods by students during learning activities. According to Furrer and Skinner (2003), learning engagement is defined as follows: from the perspective of psychology, it consists of behavioural engagement (BE), cognitive engagement (CE), and emotional engagement (EM); from the perspective of sociology, it is the sum of BE, social engagement, CE, and concept-effect engagement (Sinha et al., 2004). According to the literature, the traditional structural components of learning engagement are BE, CE, and EE (Fredricks et al., 2015). Scholars have carried out several investigations, concentrating on these three interactions. BE is the effort that students put forth in the classroom to learn, including paying close attention in class, actively responding to questions, engaging in group projects, and persevering through challenging material (Kindermann, 1993). More important than the association between emotions and CE, is the one between BE and academic achievements (Furrer and Skinner, 2003). However, basic BE might not be sufficient. While not cognitively engaged, students may be behaviorally engaged. According to Berman and Artino (2018), CE measures how willing and capable students are to tackle the current learning challenge. Online learners must construct meaning and create knowledge through interaction and reflection with learning objects, dialogue, and collaboration with the learning community. This is evident in both the 4C learning hierarchy classification of "consumption", "connection", "creation", and "contribution" proposed by Littlejohn, Milligan, and Margaryan (2011) and the four online learning activities of "aggregation", "association", "creation", and "sharing" proposed by Kop (2011). This suggests that CE is crucial to online education. According to Connell (1990), EE stands for students' curiosity, value experience, and emotional experience throughout learning activities. Students' optimism about learning and involvement is a substantial predictor of their meaningful usage of online learning tools, even while negative emotions are not a predictor of learning (Marchand and Gutierrez, 2012). High-quality teaching is accomplished through student engagement in the learning process because this approach promotes students' active participation in their education, which is necessary for student accomplishment, retention, academic motivation, performance, and satisfaction (Leach, 2016; Kahu et al., 2019). To increase student engagement, new ideas have been incorporated, such as community, motivation, and belongingness (Coates, 2006). Heagney and Benson (2017) suggest that promoting online student participation as a means of fostering social ties between mature students and their instructors and classmates can effectively mitigate feelings of isolation. For this relationship to be successful, it must incorporate informal components like approachability, curiosity, and passion in addition to formal components like evaluation guidance and lecture organisation (Peel, 2000). Furthermore, online peer contact provides a means of overcoming social isolation and a means of exchanging personal and course-related assistance for people who are studying remotely or lack the time to attend in-person activities (Heagney and Benson, 2017).

Artificial Intelligence

Because there are so many advantages to using AI technologies, a wide range of fields are adopting them. Creating computers that act intelligently and perform tasks that people would consider intelligent is the general aim of artificial intelligence. AI, according to Ertel (2017), is the study of programming computers to perform tasks at which humans are currently superior. Despite these attempts to compare robots to humans, it is widely acknowledged that computers can only perform extremely basic jobs since they exhibit very low levels of intelligence. However, it is possible to program robots to exhibit intelligent behaviours that are on par with or even better than those of humans. According to Beqiri (2016), machine learning (ML), natural language processing (NLP), speech processing, expert systems, robotics, vision processing, planning, scheduling, and optimization are the main domains and application areas of AI. As seen in Figure 2 below, these topics are further separated into various disciplines.

Figure 2. Fields of artificial intelligence

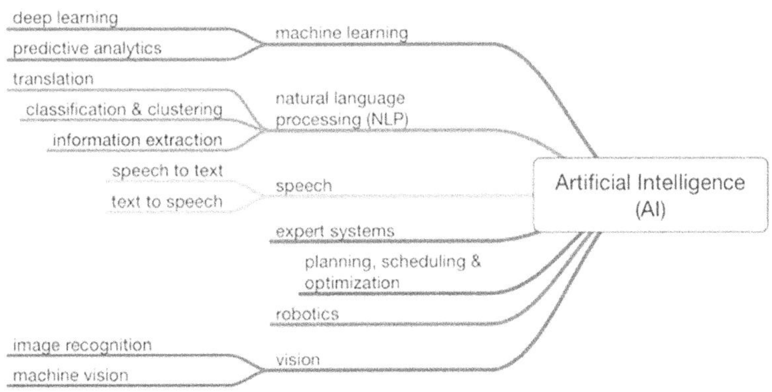

As seen in Figure 2, the several fields of artificial intelligence are gradually becoming more well-known in a variety of industries, including engineering, production and manufacturing, education, and agriculture, to name just a few.

MACHINE LEARNING

Algorithms that use vast amounts of data to make intelligent predictions are referred to as machine learning. Creating computer algorithms that can learn from their experiences utilising domain data to become more intelligent is the aim of machine learning. These programs use massive datasets to find hidden patterns that allow them to make forecasts and predictions. As seen in Figure 3 below, machine learning (ML) can be categorized as supervised learning, unsupervised learning, or reinforcement learning. These categories include a variety of methods and algorithms. Algorithms for machine learning that automate decision-making by extrapolating from well-known examples are the most effective. The user gives the algorithm pairs of inputs and intended outputs in this situation, which is referred to as supervised learning. The algorithm then figures out how to create the desired output given an input. Using supervised learning is more common in problems involving picture categorization. While supervised learning techniques are well understood and their performance is straightforward to quantify, generating a dataset of inputs and outputs is typically a tedious manual task.

Figure 3. Categories of machine learning

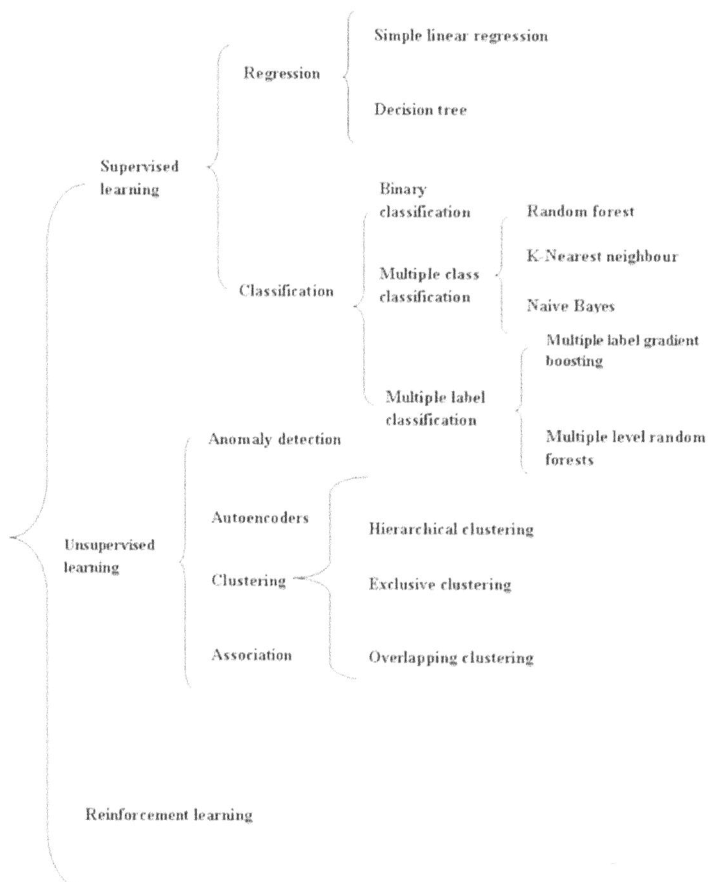

Classification and regression are the two main categories of supervised issues shown in Figure 3. Predicting a class label-a selection from a predetermined set of options-is the aim of classification. Binary classification, which is the unique situation of differentiating between precisely two classes, and multiclass classification, which is a classification between more than two classes, are two categories into which classification can occasionally be divided. Predicting a continuous or floating-point value is the aim of regression problems. In unsupervised learning, the model learns on its own using only the input data, with the algorithm not receiving any known output data. Usually, this could include activities like different types of pattern recognition or cluster identification (Nicholas et al., 2019). This method involves presenting the input data to the algorithm and asking it to derive information from it. Dimensionality reduction, which takes a high-dimensional representation of the data with many features and finds a new way to describe the data that summarizes the main properties with fewer features, is a popular application of unsupervised transformations. Reducing to two dimensions for visual aids is a typical use case for dimensionality reduction. Unsupervised transformations can also be used to identify the elements or portions that "make up" the data. Topic extraction from collections of text documents is one instance of this. Finding the unidentified subjects that are discussed in each document and discovering which themes are covered in each document are the tasks at hand. This can help monitor the subjects being discussed. Unsupervised learning techniques are typically used on data that lacks label information, making it impossible to determine what the intended result should be. As a result, determining whether a model "did well" is extremely difficult. Consequently, rather than being a component of a broader automatic system, unsupervised algorithms are frequently utilized in an exploratory setting by data scientists seeking to get a deeper understanding of the data (Müller and Guido, 2017). Reward learning, a third kind of machine learning, is applied with somewhat less regularity. Learning how to respond or behave when occasionally given reward or punishment signals can benefit from this.

Artificial Intelligence in Education

The use of AI technology to support teaching, learning, or decision-making in the educational setting is known as Artificial Intelligence in Education (AIED) (Hwang et al., 2020). The primary goal of AIED is to create computers that are capable of cognitive tasks that are typically performed by human minds in learning and teaching (Chen et al., 2020). Computer systems can use artificial intelligence (AI) to give students individualised advice, support, or feedback as well as to help educators and policymakers make decisions. As seen in Figure 4 below, computer science, statistics, and education are the three main subjects that makeup AIED, making it an interdisciplinary field. Other subfields that are closely related to AIED are also produced by the intersection of the three main domains, such as Computer-Based Education (CBE), Learning Analytics (LA), and Educational Data Mining (EDM) (Chen et al., 2020).

According to Altrabshe (2016), the main areas of application for AI in education have been student evaluation, sentiment analysis performance prediction and monitoring, reading resource recommendation, and personalized learning. These applications have opened up possibilities for better heutagogy. Artificial intelligence-driven technologies, such as intelligent robots and adaptive learning systems, are examples of AIED technologies that are being used more frequently.

Challenges with learner independence and individual differences in learning styles, needs, and talents have prompted AIED advances since it has been hard for teachers to meet the needs of every student using standard teaching approaches. This has made it possible for students to satisfy their unique requirements and have helped educators deal with difficulties relating to individual differences (Della-Ventura,

2017). Instructors can thus provide training that is tailored to each student's needs-including those with learning disabilities utilizing AI technology on an individual basis. AI-directed, learner-as-recipient; AI-supported, learner-as-collaborator; and AI-empowered, learner-as-leader are the three paradigm shifts that AIED has experienced (Ouyang and Jiao, 2021).

Figure 4. Disciplines influencing AIED (Chen et al., 2020)

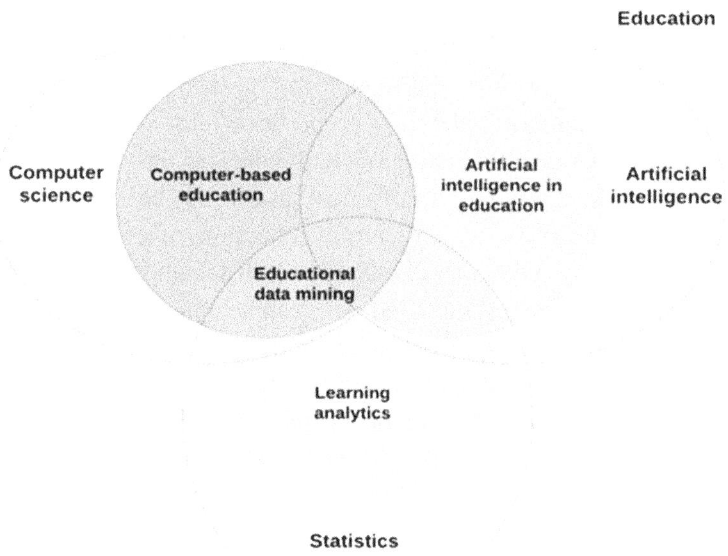

"Learner-as-recipient, AI-directed" learning involves the learner acting as a recipient of an AI service and following predetermined learning routes, while the domain knowledge is represented and learning processes are guided by the learner. This paradigm's theoretical foundation is behaviourism, which emphasizes the creation of well-planned content sequences that result in the learner doing correctly. According to the paradigm, learning is the process of reinforcing knowledge acquisition through pre-programmed instructions that present new ideas logically and incrementally, provide instant feedback on wrong answers, and maximize positive reinforcement. The learner performs the role of a recipient in response to pre-established knowledge sequences, adheres to learning protocols and paths, and carries out learning tasks assigned by AI to meet predetermined objectives. According to Burton et al. (2004), "AI-directed, learner-as-recipient" environments inherit the traits of teaching machines, such as the ability to convey subject knowledge logically, ask for the learner's overt replies, and provide instantaneous knowledge of correctness. These AI systems don't adapt their feedback to the learner as an individual or as a representative of a class of individuals; they also don't model the learner's evolving, incoming knowledge and skills. The least learner-centred approach is "AI-directed, learner-as-recipient."

"AI-supported, learner-as-collaborator" refers to a model in which the learner collaborates with the AI system to focus on their learning process, while the AI system gives up control to operate as a supporting tool. The paradigm's foundation is a cognitive and social constructivist understanding of learning, which highlights the idea that learning happens when students engage in socially situated environments involving people, information, and technology (Liu and Matthews, 2005). Accordingly, to maximize student-centred, individualized learning, the AI system and the learner should have active, reciprocal interactions in "AI-supported, learner-as-collaborator." In particular, the learner collaborates with the AI system to communicate with it to accomplish more effective learning, and the AI system gathers the learners' emergent, personalized information as input to adaptively enhance the student model. To accomplish mutual interactions between the system and the learner, various AI implementations have been developed in this paradigm, such as Exploratory Learning Environments (ELEs) and Dialogue-Based Tutoring Systems (DTSs).

The concept of "AI-empowered, learner-as-leader" emphasizes the importance of learner agency in AIED and sees AI as a means of enhancing human intelligence (Law, 2019). This paradigm is based on the complexity theory, which sees education as a complex adaptive system (Mason, 2008), where the learner's increased intelligence depends on the cooperative efforts of several system elements. AIED must be developed and implemented in this complex system with the understanding that AI methods are components of a bigger system that includes students, teachers, and other humans (Riedl, 2019). Concepts like human-computer cooperation (Hoc, 2000), human-centred artificial intelligence and machine learning systems (Riedl, 2019), human-AI collaboration (Hwang et al., 2020), and human-centred artificial intelligence in education (Yang et al., 2021) are proposed to achieve synergetic collaboration in the complex system. These concepts approach AI from a human perspective by taking human conditions, expectations, and contexts into consideration. AI helps students and teachers get enhanced intelligence in the context of "AI-empowered, learner-as-leader" by offering a high degree of transparency, accuracy, and efficacy (Riedl, 2019; Yang et al., 2021). AI technologies provide the instructor with personalized, comprehensible, and interpretable support to promote learner-centred learning. By taking on the role of the activity's leader, the learner controls the risks associated with AI decision automation and creates more effective or superior learning. The overall developing tendency of AIED, "AI-empowered, learner-as-leader," reflects the ultimate objective of using AI in education, which is to increase human potential, intelligence, and capability (Law, 2019). Another AIED classification model was created by Hwang et al. (2020), who created four categories: AI as intelligent tutees, AI as intelligent tutors, AI as intelligent learning partners, and AI as advisors for policy-making. This classification can according to the roles is shown in Figure 5 down below:

Figure 5. Categories of AIED according to roles (Hwang et al., 2020)

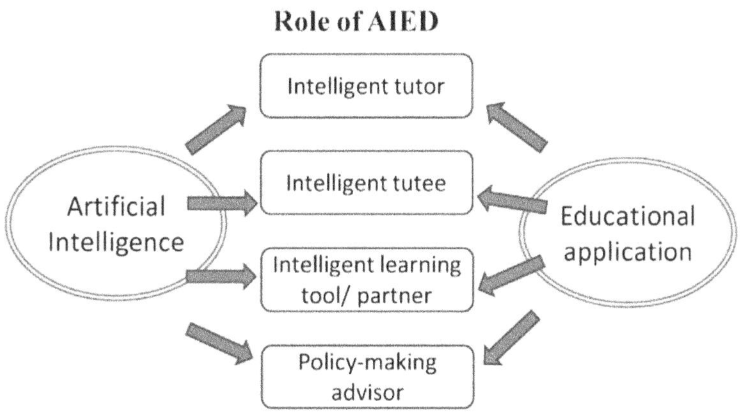

The majority of AI-based technologies used in educational settings to create individualized and adaptive learning platforms are known as AIED or intelligent tutors. ICT-enabled adaptive learning is a crucial field of study for academic institutions looking to enhance student performance (Hwang et al., 2013; Gomede et al., 2018). With the help of this method, educational components including control flow, enrollment, attention, and sequencing can be examined and appropriate recommendations may be given to students, instructors, administrators, parents, or other authorities. Additionally, learning is monitored for formatting and content adaption to optimize each student's cognitive abilities and prevent information overload. Hwang et al. (2020) define intelligent tutors as cognitive tutors and recommender systems, which were both created to aid in the teaching and learning of science and math. Because of the lack of study on intelligent tutees-mostly because the main goal of creating AI-driven educational tools is to enhance learners' learning experiences and support instructional delivery-intelligent tutees are rarely used. These AI-based technologies serve as intelligent learning partners or tools, assisting students in efficiently collecting and analyzing data so they may concentrate on crucial higher-order thinking concepts like inference and prediction. AI-based policy advisory tools have been utilized in the creation of legislation governing educational activities, giving policymakers the ability to forecast future developments and create educational regulations.

Artificial Intelligence and Student Engagement

Learning motivation and engagement are essential for effective learning. Large datasets with human labelling are typically used to train engagement detection systems to track and classify aspects like eye movements and facial expressions. Thus, to improve instruction, educational professionals are embracing strategies like video recommendation systems and game-based learning more frequently (Huang et al., 2022). Another tool that encourages communication and teamwork and raises student interest in learning is video conferencing. Zoom, Microsoft Teams, and Skype are some of the platforms that are utilized for this (Verma et al., 2023). These systems facilitate real-time audio and video communication between educators and students. Real-time connectivity improves interpersonal relationships and makes it possible for teachers and students to participate in online learning (Burke et al., 2022). Teachers can overcome the psychological and communication gap with students and give them rapid feedback by using video conferencing efficiently (Torrato et al., 2021). Wireless screen-sharing, whiteboard sharing, interactive chat rooms, opinion polls, and debate platforms can all be accessed through video conferencing. By doing this, educators can employ actions and behaviours that increase student involvement. These behaviours include supporting students' autonomy, providing a framework to increase their sense of competence, and providing relatedness support (De Meester et al., 2020). These actions and behaviours improve teachers' presence and raise student engagement, according to earlier research.

Moreover, computer vision techniques for voice, video, and facial recognition have been applied to recognize a specific user's voice and to extract pertinent data from digital photos, videos, and other visual inputs (Xu et al., 2023). To measure student engagement, computer vision examines facial expressions, posture, and hand movements (Sharma et al., 2020). When it comes to identifying the emotions and level of engagement of adult learners during online instruction, Krithika and Lakshmi Priya's (2016) study demonstrated the significance of eye and head movement. Meanwhile, Ramakrishnan et al. (2019) trained a smiling facial recognition model specifically for young learners to analyze the classroom climate. According to their findings, smiles from both teachers and students were a reliable indicator of the dynamics of a supportive learning environment. Teachers use smiling to direct, validate, and correct students' responses, according to a different study that examined video data. In a different study, Dewan et al. (2018) suggested using deep learning to identify students' levels of involvement by observing their facial expressions. They used Local Directional Pattern (LDP) and Kernel Principal Component (KPC) analysis to create a two-level (not engaged and engaged) and three-level (not engaged, normally engaged, and very engaged) classification. The study's findings were shown to have accurately determined levels of engagement.

MACHINE LEARNING AND STUDENT ENGAGEMENT

The only way for instructors to evaluate student involvement in online learning is through student data. However, online systems have certain drawbacks as a result of the lack of in-person interactions. The primary one being course dropout (Simpson, 2010). Lack of involvement is the primary cause of online course abandonment, followed closely by students' incapacity to find the necessary assignments and resources for the next test (Kuzilek et al., 2016). The answer to improving student engagement and personalization appears to lie in machine learning algorithms. Both of these learning approaches-classification and recommendation, have drawn a lot of interest from academics and educators, who acknowledge that these are the two primary tasks required for e-learning personalization. Classification, which groups comparable points within the dataset, is a crucial stage in the process of personalizing e-learning. Classifying questions and tasks as well as student status is one task that requires classification (Barata et al., 2016). Recommendation, the second stage of e-learning personalization, offers well-informed advice on suitable actions based on the outcomes of the categorization step. Researchers such as Hew, Qiao, and Tang (2018) have tested a set of five ML automatic classification models (k-nearest Neighbors, Gradient Boosting Trees, Support Vector Machines, Logistic Regression, and Naïve Bayesian), researching student engagement and its impact on performance and the likelihood of discontinuing learning programs. According to the study's findings, a large number of online course participants stated that the inclusion of somewhat difficult projects that asked them to apply the ideas they had learned as opposed to just asking them to memorize facts helped them retain the information more effectively. Additionally, participants mentioned that the course material was highly relevant because it used resources and content that focused on real-world issues. This gave the concepts being taught concrete implications, which maintained students' interest and made it easier for them to remember the information because they could see how the lessons might be used in everyday situations. Convolutional Neural Networks are another technique that has been used to research learner engagement (CNN). Murshed et al. (2019) presented an engagement detection method for digital learning environments, and they are among many who have employed CNN-based techniques to enhance engagement detection. Additionally, Bhardwaj et al. (2021) presented a method that teachers might use to determine whether or not students are actively engaged. This system uses deep learning to monitor the student's emotions in real time, including anger, disgust, fear, happiness, sadness, and surprise. This was suggested as a way to support professors in providing better student assessments in live classes, which are analogous to traditional offline classroom settings.

Sentiment Analysis and Student Engagement

Given that humans are sociable, emotions constitute a basic kind of communication (Chung et al., 2021). Positive or negative emotions are felt by people, and they must be expressed. Sentiment analysis, sometimes referred to as opinion mining, is the process of evaluating and classifying textual information to ascertain people's general emotional states. Sentiment analysis conveys learners' feelings through the use of physical characteristics like facial expressions. This process classifies natural language utterances according to their emotional mood and automatically analyzes them to identify important assertions or thoughts. Determining the sentiment's polarity- positive, negative, or neutral as well as its intensity are the main goals. Sentiment analysis used to be a tedious and time-consuming process that required reading and analyzing enormous volumes of text. However, sentiment analysis has changed since AI and NLP tools became available. Large amounts of text data may be processed quickly and effectively, and insightful information on public mood can be extracted by utilizing ML and NLP approaches. Opinion mining gives educators the ability to create sentiment insights based on trends they have seen. Sentiment analysis in online education has historically depended on student feedback to assist instructors in understanding the learning styles of their students. By giving feedback, students can let the lecturer know when they do not comprehend what the lecturer is attempting to communicate. This allows the lecturer to determine whether the teaching needs to be improved. A model for applying AI to analyze student feedback was presented by Altrabsheh et al. (2016). The model was successful in analyzing the pre-processed student feedback using Naive Bayes and SVM. Deep learning based on pre-trained data has been utilized by SVMs to create interactions based on facial expressions to identify students' subject comprehension (Maqableh, Alzyoud, and Zraqou, 2023).

ChatGPT and Student Engagement

The most basic and common type of intelligent AI system for human-computer interaction is a chatbot, sometimes referred to as smart bots, interactive agents, digital assistants, or artificial conversation entities (Bansal, and Khan, 2018). A chatbot is characterized as a software application that imitates human behaviour when communicating online by voice or message (Xu et al., 2017; Benotti et al., 2014). Applications like e-commerce, business, education, and information retrieval can all benefit from them (Shawar and Atwell, 2007). It is intended to be the best virtual assistant, assisting with everything from simple question-answering to more difficult jobs. Chatbots are increasingly being used in learning environments to improve student connection in a world where tech-savvy students mainly rely on social media and instant messaging systems. This is due to their ability to instantly deliver standardized information to students (Nelson, et al., 2019). Chatbots have the potential to improve student assistance and engagement while also greatly reducing lecturers' administrative strain, freeing them up to focus on research and course development (Singh, 2018). Additionally, chatbots can serve as virtual teaching assistants, assisting teachers in a variety of ways, such as by providing instantaneous explanations and questioning answers. The majority of chatbots were of two categories. First off, because it matches pre-programmed responses with text messages or voice input, a chatbot with pre-programmed responses is referred to as a rule-based chatbot (Vanichvasin, 2022). Second, as it uses deep learning and natural language processing (NLP) to extract appropriate responses from user input, a chatbot that generates appropriate responses is referred to as an ML-based chatbot. Thanks to machine learning algorithms and deep learning approaches, it produces responses based on user communications more accurately than the first kind (Hien et al., 2018). Chatbots have primarily been utilized in education to assist with language acquisition (Fryer, Nakao, and Thompson, 2019).

The pinnacle of chatbot technology is ChatGPT, an advanced natural language processing (NLP) model created by OpenAI. Since 2019, it has grown to incorporate features such as speech recognition and detection, emotional state detection, and the ability to converse with humans and other chatbots as if they were real people (Zemčík, 2019). One benefit of utilizing chatbots in education is that they may be used around the clock and possess traits like tenacity, integrity, responsiveness, and friendliness (Zoroayka, 2018). ChatGPT can support self-directed learners by providing them with personalized, interactive assistance that fosters their freedom and self-directed learning. In addition to promoting student autonomy, Chat GPT can enhance the educational process by providing tailored recommendations for books and other resources, as well as interactive assignments and activities that are tailored to each student's specific needs and learning goals. Personalized support, real-time feedback and guidance, increased accessibility, convenient and flexible learning, improving the use of open educational resources, and self-assessment and reflection are the six ways that Chat GPT could change e-learning encounters, according to Firat (2023). Yakin et al. (2023) conducted a study to examine the impact of ChatGPT on student engagement. The findings indicated that students' use of the technology led to a high degree of enthusiasm and engagement, promoting idea exchange, discussions, analysis, and motivation. According to additional research by Al-Obaydi et al. (2023), using ChatGPT repeatedly may offer an experience that boosts motivation and engagement. Furthermore, according to Baido-Anu and Ansah (2023), ChatGPT's advantages include fostering individualized and interactive learning and producing prompts for formative assessment exercises that offer continuous feedback to improve instruction. Labadze, Grigolia, and Machaidze (2023) discovered in another review that students benefited from AI-powered chatbots in three main areas: help with homework and studies, individualized learning, and skill development. The two biggest benefits for teachers are enhanced pedagogy and time-saving help. Peer-to-peer communication habits among learners are lacking in the Chabot application, despite the app's favourable impression stemming from the creation of a more casual and approachable communication channel with professors (Čižmešija, Horvat, and Vukovac, 2021).

Natural Language Processing and Personalised Learning

Fundamentally, natural language processing (NLP) is an approach that uses computers to automatically interpret human language (Bird et al. 2009). This analysis has a wide range of specific real-world applications, from text translation to virtual assistant development. NLP techniques are relevant to learning analytics and offer several benefits over alternative approaches to language data analysis. In particular, NLP can analyze massive amounts of text data at extremely fast speeds because it doesn't rely on human raters. Additionally, NLP is capable of handling spoken and written text data with ease. The optimum approach for figuring out how to employ natural language processing (NLP) for learning analytics is to take into account and analyze languages from a variety of angles. Afterwards, by using this data to create predictive models of student outcomes, specific feedback and interventions can be made. When used by instructors, this offers a potent tool for customized instruction.

According to Rickabaugh (2016), personalised learning (PL) is a pedagogical strategy that is gaining popularity. It is a generic instructional design or method that involves delivering content and activities to students while prioritising their autonomy and agency. The ultimate goal of PL is to improve learning outcomes. This encourages students to choose their learning objectives and fosters a reflective process along the way. It also provides a flexible enough setting for students to continue their education outside of the traditional classroom. Personalized learning can take many different forms, such as software that suggests curriculum and tools for students to self-direct their education (Lu, 2004); educational institutions that provide students with a variety of class and learning style options (Headden, 2013); or settings where students and instructors collaborate to create individualized lesson plans for each student that are based on shared standards or goals (Friend et al., 2017). Self-regulated learning, a conceptual framework for understanding the cognitive, motivational, and emotional elements of learning, is the foundation of PL. Socially shared regulation, on the other hand, refers to the mechanisms by which members of a group control their collective behaviour (Panadero & Jarvela, 2015). AI uses machine learning (ML) techniques such as natural language processing (NLP) and deep learning in PL to personalize the learning experience for students by applying pre-trained concepts to solve issues that are similar to each other. It also collects and analyzes student feedback to produce predictions about the students' opinions regarding the learning process. According to Shaik et al. (2022), these capabilities enhance teaching techniques by gathering enormous amounts of data on each student's past knowledge, emotional state, or socioeconomic background and modifying the teaching strategy through Adaptive Learning Platforms.

Robots and Student Engagement

There are several ways that educational robots can improve learning outcomes. As tools for active learning, they can encourage student cooperation, problem-solving, and active engagement. Mubin et al. (2013) claim that the function of educational robots in the classroom can be compared to that of a peer or tutor, which in turn affects the function of the instructor working in the same educational environment. Learning about robots in the classroom helps students become more creative and critical thinkers. Because engaging with robots can be less daunting and more predictable than interacting with classmates, robots can also operate as a scaffold for the development of social skills, particularly for shy youngsters or those with special needs. This can help cultivate confidence in social situations. Furthermore, children can teach concepts to robots or use them as co-learners, which helps the robot learn from the children and reinforces their comprehension. Human-robot interaction has emerged as a cutting-edge advancement in robotics research and development in recent years, and it has been used in educational settings to improve student engagement and learning. The first four have garnered the greatest attention from researchers. Pandey and Gelin (2017) outline six categories of roles for robots in educational robotics education: (1) teaching helper, (2) peer and co-learner, (3) companion, (4) entertainment, (5) telepresence, and (6) as a teaching platform. The lack of teachers worldwide is a common defence used to support the employment of educational robots (Morita et al. 2018). The potential for individualization and adaption to various student demands in teaching and learning scenarios is another justification for the usage of educational robots (Hrastinski et al., 2019). A robot-based model for predicting student involvement was created by Cui et al. in 2022. The experimental findings demonstrate that the suggested model can be used with an expected prediction accuracy of 98.78% in a real-time scenario.

CONCLUSION

Heutagogy promotes autonomous and self-directed learning. This method appears to be popular at higher education institutions because mature students frequently try to create their learning environments and figure out the learning process on their own. Such endeavours are difficult in a setting where the teachers are not very good. There is a chance to include AI in the curriculum through the use of AI technologies including machine learning, natural language processing, chatbots, voice recognition, and vision processing. The productivity of teaching and learning activities in educational settings is positively impacted by the integration of AI technology, which also has a notable positive impact on heutagogy and student engagement.

Recommendations

The chapter then offered the following suggestions after outlining the advantages of utilizing AI technologies to improve teaching and learning in pedagogical environments and the numerous applications of AI technologies in teaching and learning:

a) Educator training on the use of AI technologies and their potential to enhance training and education in heterogeneous environments.
b) Including AI in the curriculum is one of the instructional strategies that teachers at all teaching and learning levels may choose to use.
c) The advancement of artificial intelligence breakthroughs to assist instruction at all levels of instruction.
d) More investigation into the creation of AI tools for educational purposes.

REFERENCES

Akyıldız, S. T. (2019). Do 21st Century Teachers Know about Heutagogy or Do They Still Adhere to Traditional Pedagogy and Andragogy? *International Journal of Progressive Education*, *15*(6).

Al-Obaydi, L. H., Pikhart, M., & Klimova, B. (2023). ChatGPT and the General Concepts of Education: Can Artificial Intelligence-Driven Chatbots Support the Process of Language Learning? *International Journal of Emerging Technologies in Learning*, *18*(21), 39–50. doi:10.3991/ijet.v18i21.42593

Alberola, J. M., del Val, E., Sanchez-Angui, V., Palomares, A., & Dolores, T. M. (2016). An artificial intelligence tool for heterogeneous team formation in the classroom. *Knowledge-Based Systems*, *101*, 1–14. doi:10.1016/j.knosys.2016.02.010

Alruwais, N., & Zakariah, M. (2023). Student-Engagement Detection in Classroom Using Machine Learning Algorithm. *Electronics (Basel)*, *12*(731), 731. doi:10.3390/electronics12030731

Altrabsheh, N., Gaber, M. M., & Cocea, M. (2016). *SA-E: Sentiment Analysis for Education. Portsmouth University Research Portal*. Pure.

Aragon, S. (2016). *Teacher Shortages: What We Know*. Teacher Shortage Series.

Artificial Intelligence in education. (2021). Using heart rate variability (HRV) as a biomarker to assess emotions objectively. *Computers and Education: Artificial Intelligence*, *2*, 100011.

Bansal, H. and Khan, R. (2018). A review paper on human-computer interaction. *Int. J. Adv. Res. Comput. Sci. Softw.* *8*(53). . doi:10.23956/ijarcsse.v8i4.630

Barata, G., Gama, S., Jorge, J., & Gonçalves, D. (2016). Early prediction of student profiles based on performance and gaming preferences. *IEEE Transactions on Learning Technologies*, *9*(3), 272–284. doi:10.1109/TLT.2016.2541664

Benotti, L., Martínez, M. C., & Schapachnik, F. (2014). Engaging high school students using chatbots. In *Proceedings of the 2014 Innovation and Technology in Computer Science Education Conference*. ACM. 10.1145/2591708.2591728

Bergdahl, N. (2022). Engagement and disengagement in online learning. *Computers & Education*, *188*, 104561. Advance online publication. doi:10.1016/j.compedu.2022.104561

Berman, N. B., & Artino, A. R. Jr. (2018). Development and initial validation of an online engagement metric using virtual patients. *BMC Medical Education*, *18*(1), 213. doi:10.1186/s12909-018-1322-z PMID:30223825

Bhardwaj, P. K., Gupta, P., Panwar, H., Siddiqui, M. K., Morales-Menendez, R., & Bhaik, A. (2021). Application of Deep Learning on Student Engagement in E-learning Environments. *Computers & Electrical Engineering*, *93*, 93. doi:10.1016/j.compeleceng.2021.107277 PMID:36567679

Bird, S., Klein, E., & Loper, E. (2009). *Natural language processing with Python: Analyzing text with the natural language toolkit*. O'Reilly Media, Inc.

Blaschke, L. M. (2012). *Heutagogy and Lifelong Learning: A Review of Heutagogical Practice and Self-Determined Learning*. . doi:10.19173/irrodl.v13i1.1076

Bond, M., Buntins, K., Bedenlier, S., Zawacki-Richter, O., & Kerres, M. (2020). Mapping Research in Student Engagement and Educational Technology in Higher Education: A systematic evidence map. *International Journal of Educational Technology in Higher Education*, *17*(1), 2. doi:10.1186/s41239-019-0176-8

Boulton, C. A., Hughes, E., Kent, C., Smith, J. R., & Williams, H. T. P. (2019). Student engagement and well-being over time at a higher education institution. *PLoS One*, *14*(11), e0225770. Advance online publication. doi:10.1371/journal.pone.0225770 PMID:31774878

Burke, K., Fanshawe, M., & Tualaulelei, E. (2022). We can't always measure what matters: Revealing opportunities to enhance online student engagement through pedagogical care. *Journal of Further and Higher Education*, *46*(3), 287–300. doi:10.1080/0309877X.2021.1909712

Burton, J. K., Moore, D. M. M., & Magliaro, S. G. (2004). Behaviorism and instructional cancers. *The Lancet. Oncology*, *21*(1).

Carey, P. (2018). The impact of institutional culture, policy and process on student engagement in university decision-making. *Perspectives*, *22*(1), 11–18. doi:10.1080/13603108.2016.1168754

Cents-Boonstra, M., Lichtwarck-Aschoff, A., Lara, M. M., & Denessen, E. (2021). Patterns of motivating teaching behaviour and student engagement: A microanalytic approach. *European Journal of Psychology of Education*, *5*(1), 1–5. doi:10.1007/s10212-021-00543-3

Cesari, V., Galgani, B., Gemignani, A., & Menicucci, D. (2021). Enhancing qualities of consciousness during online learning via multisensory interactions. *Behavioral Sciences (Basel, Switzerland), 11*(5), 57. doi:10.3390/bs11050057 PMID:33919379

Chen, K., & Li, S. (2021). Sequential, typological, and academic dynamics of self-regulated learners: Learning analytics of an undergraduate chemistry online course. *Computers and Education: Artificial Intelligence*, *2*, 100024. doi:10.1016/j.caeai.2021.100024

Chen, W. (2020). Knowledge-aware learning analytics for smart learning. *Procedia Computer Science*, *159*, 1957–1965. doi:10.1016/j.procs.2019.09.368

Chen, X., Xie, H., Zou, D., & Hwang, G. (2020). Application and theory gaps during the rise of Artificial Intelligence in Education. Computers and Education. *Artificial Intelligence*, *1*, 100002.

Čižmešija, A., Horvat, D., & Vukovac, P. (2021). Improving student engagement and course completion using chatbot application. *INTED2021 Proceedings*, 8346-8354.

Coates, H. (2016). *Student Engagement in Campus-Based and Online Education*. Routledge.

Connell, J. P. (1990). *Context, self, and action: A motivational analysis of self-system processes across the life span*. University of Chicago Press.

Cucinotta, D., & Vanelli, M. (2020). WHO declares COVID-19 a pandemic. *Acta Biomedica*, *91*(1), 157. doi:10.23750/abm.v91i1.9397 PMID:32191675

Cui, Y., Song, X., Hu, Q., Li, Y., Sharma, P., & Khapre, S. (2022). Human-robot interaction in higher education for predicting student engagement. *Computers & Electrical Engineering*, *99*, 99. doi:10.1016/j.compeleceng.2022.107827

Davis, L., & Hase, S. (2001). *The River of Learning in the Workplace. Proceedings of Research to reality: Putting VET research to Work: Australian Vocational Education and Training Research Association (AVETRA)*.

De Meester, A., van Duyse, F., Aelterman, N., de Muynck, G. J., & Haerens, L. (2020). An experimental, video-based investigation into the motivating impact of choice and positive feedback among students with different motor competence levels. *Physical Education and Sport Pedagogy*, *25*(4), 361–378. doi:10.1080/17408989.2020.1725456

Della-Ventura, V. M. (2017). Creating inspiring learning environments employing digital technologies: A case study of the effectiveness of WhatsApp in music education. Springer.

Dewan, M. A. A., Lin, F., Wen, D., Murshed, M., and Uddin, Z. (2018). *IEEE smart world, ubiquitous intelligence & computing, advanced & trusted computing, scalable computing & communications, cloud & big data computing, internet of people and smart city innovation SmartWorld/SCALCOM/UIC/ATC/CBDCom/IOP/SCI)*. IEEE.

Dewan, M. A. A., Murshed, M., & Lin, F. (2019). Engagement detection in online learning: A review. *Smart Learning Environments*, *6*(1), 2–8. doi:10.1186/s40561-018-0080-z

Ertel, W. (2017). *Introduction to artificial intelligence. Undergraduate topics in Computer Science* (2nd ed.). Springer. doi:10.1007/978-3-319-58487-4

Firat, M. (2023). *How ChatGPT can transform autodidactic experiences and open education.* OSF-PREPRINTS.

Fredricks, J. A., Blumenfeld, P. C., & Paris, A. H. (2015). School engagement: Potential of the concept, state of the evidence. *Review of Educational Research*, *74*(1), 59–109. doi:10.3102/00346543074001059

Friend, B., Patrick, S., Schneider, C., & Vander Ark, T. (2017). *What's possible with personalized learning? An overview of personalized learning for schools, families & communities.* iNACOL.

Fryer, L. K., Nakao, K., & Thompson, A. (2019). Chatbot learning partners: Connecting learning experiences, interest and competence. *Computers in Human Behavior*, *93*, 279–289. doi:10.1016/j.chb.2018.12.023

Furrer, C., & Skinner, E. (2003). Sense of relatedness as a factor in children's academic engagement and performance. *Journal of Educational Psychology*, *95*(1), 148–162. doi:10.1037/0022-0663.95.1.148

Gomede, E., Gaffo, F. H., Briganó, G., de Barros, R., & Mendes, L. (2018). Application of computational intelligence to improve education in smart cities. *Sensors (Basel)*, *18*(1), 267. Advance online publication. doi:10.3390/s18010267 PMID:29346288

Headden, S. (2013). The promise of personalized learning: Blending the human touch with technological firepower. *Education Next*, *13*(4), 14–21.

Heagney, M., & Benson, R. (2017). How mature-age students succeed in higher education: Implications for institutional support. *Journal of Higher Education Policy and Management*, *39*(3), 216–234. doi:10.1080/1360080X.2017.1300986

Hew, K. F. (2016). Promoting engagement in online courses: What strategies can we learn from three highly rated MOOCS? *British Journal of Educational Technology*, *47*(2), 320–341. doi:10.1111/bjet.12235

Hew, K. F, Chen, Q, & Tang.Y. (2018). Understanding Student Engagement in Large-Scale Open Online Courses: A Machine Learning Facilitated Analysis of Student's Reflections in 18 Highly Rated MOOCs. *International Review of Research in Open and Distributed Learning, 193.*

Hien, H. T., Cuong, P.-N., Nam, L. N. H., Nhung, H. L. T. K., & Thang, L. D. (2018). Intelligent assistants in higher-education environments: the FIT-EBot, A chatbot for administrative and learning Support. In *Proceedings of the 9th International Symposium on Information and Communication Technology.* ACM. 10.1145/3287921.3287937

Hoc, J. M. (2000). From human-machine interaction to human-machine cooperation. *Ergonomics*, *43*(7), 833–843. doi:10.1080/001401300409044 PMID:10929820

Hrastinski, S., Olofsson, A. D., Arkenback, C., Ekström, S., Ericsson, E., Fransson, G., Jaldemark, J., Ryberg, T., Öberg, L., Fuentes, A., Gustafsson, U., Humble, N., Mozelius, P., Sundgren, M., & Utterberg, M. (2019). Critical Imaginaries and Reflections on Artificial Intelligence and Robots in Postdigital K-12 Education. *Postdigital Science and Education*, *2019*(1), 427–445. doi:10.1007/s42438-019-00046-x

Huang, A. Y. Q., Lub, O. H. T., Yan, S. J. H. (2022). Effects of Artificial Intelligence–Enabled personalized recommendations on learners' learning engagement, motivation, and outcomes in a flipped classroom. *Computers & Education, 194.*

Hutchison, L. F. (2012). Addressing the STEM teacher shortage in American schools: Ways to recruit and retain effective STEM teachers. *Action in Teacher Education*, *34*(5–6), 541–550. doi:10.1080/01626620.2012.729483

Hwang, G., Xie, H., Wah, B. W., & Gašević, D. (2020). Vision, challenges, roles and research issues of Artificial Intelligence in Education. *Computers and Education. Artificial Intelligence*, *1*, 100001.

Hwang, G., Yang, L., & Wang, S. (2013). A concept map-embedded educational computer game for improving students' learning performance in natural science courses. *Computers & Education*, *69*, 121–130. doi:10.1016/j.compedu.2013.07.008

Jackson, P. C. (1985). *Introduction to artificial intelligence* (2nd ed.). Dover Publications, Inc.

Jarvela, S., Kirschner, P. A., Hadwin, A., Jarvenoja, H., Malmberg, J., Miller, M., & Laru, J. (2016). Socially shared regulation of learning in CSCL: Understanding and prompting individual and group-level shared regulatory activities. *International Journal of Computer-Supported Collaborative Learning*, *11*(3), 263–280. doi:10.1007/s11412-016-9238-2

Kahu, E. R., & Nelson, K. (2018). Student engagement in the educational interface: Understanding the mechanisms of student success. *Higher Education Research & Development*, *37*(1), 58–71. doi:10.1080/07294360.2017.1344197

Kahu, E. R., Picton, C., & Nelson, K. (2019). Pathways to engagement: A longitudinal study of the first-year student experience in the educational interface. *Higher Education*, *79*(4), 657–673. doi:10.1007/s10734-019-00429-w

Karabchuk, T., & Roshchina, Y. (2023). Predictors of student engagement: The role of universities' or importance of students' background? *European Journal of Higher Education*, *13*(3), 327–346. doi:10.1080/21568235.2022.2035240

Kindermann, T. A. (1993). Natural peer groups as contexts for individual development: The case of children's motivation in school. *Developmental Psychology*, *29*(6), 970–977. doi:10.1037/0012-1649.29.6.970

Kop, R. (2011). The challenges to connective learning on open online networks: Learning experiences during a massive open online course. *International Review of Research in Open and Distance Learning*, *12*(3), 19–38. doi:10.19173/irrodl.v12i3.882

Krithika, L. B., & Lakshmi, P. G. G. (2016). Student Emotion Recognition System (SERS) for e-learning improvement based on learner concentration metric. *Procedia Computer Science*, *85*, 767–776. doi:10.1016/j.procs.2016.05.264

Kuzilek, J., Hlosta, M., Herrmannova, D., Zdrahal, Z., & Wolff, A., A. (2015). OU analysis: analysing at-risk students at the Open University. *Proceedings of First International Workshop on Visual Aspects of Learning Analytics and Knowledge Conference (LAK 2015)*, 1–16.

Labadze, L., Grigolia, M., & Machaidze, L. (2023). Role of AI chatbots in education: Systematic literature review. *International Journal of Educational Technology in Higher Education*, *20*(1), 56. doi:10.1186/s41239-023-00426-1

Lathuililere, S., Masse, B., Mesejo, P., & Horaud, R. (2019). Neural network-based reinforcement learning for audio-visual gaze control in human-robot interaction. *Pattern Recognition Letters*, *118*, 61–71. doi:10.1016/j.patrec.2018.05.023

Law, N. W. Y. (2019). Human development and augmented intelligence. In *The 20th International conference on artificial intelligence in education (AIED 2019).* Springer.

Leach, L. (2016). Enhancing student engagement in one institution. *Journal of Further and Higher Education*, *40*(1), 23–47. doi:10.1080/0309877X.2013.869565

Li, J., Li, P., & Niu, W. (2020). Artificial intelligence applications in upper gastrointestinal cancers. *The Lancet. Oncology*, *21*(1), e4. doi:10.1016/S1470-2045(19)30721-1 PMID:31908305

Littlejohn, A., Milligan, C., & Margaryan, A. (2011). Collective learning in the workplace: Important knowledge-sharing behaviours. *International Journal of Advanced Corporate Learning*, *4*(4), 26–31. doi:10.3991/ijac.v4i4.1801

Liu, C. H., & Matthews, R. (2005). Vygotsky's philosophy: Constructivism and its criticisms examined. *International Education Journal*, *6*(3), 386–399.

Lu, J. (2004). *A personalized e-learning material recommender system* [Paper presentation]. *2nd International Conference on Information Technology and Applications (ICITA).*

Maqableh, W., Alzyoud, F. Y., & Zraqou, J. (2023). The use of facial expressions in measuring students' interaction with distance learning environments during the COVID-19 crisis. *Visual Informatics*, *7*(1), 1–17. doi:10.1016/j.visinf.2022.10.001 PMID:36312746

Marchand, G. C., & Gutierrez, A. P. (2012). The role of emotion in the learning process: Comparisons between online and face-to-face learning settings. *The Internet and Higher Education*, *15*(3), 150–160. doi:10.1016/j.iheduc.2011.10.001

Mason, M. (2008). What is complexity theory and what are its implications for educational change? *Educational Philosophy and Theory*, *40*(1), 35–49. doi:10.1111/j.1469-5812.2007.00413.x

Müller, A. C., & Guido, S. (2017). *Introduction to Machine Learning with Python, A Guide for Data Scientists*. O'Reilly.

Murshed, M., Dewan, M. A. A., Lin, F., & Wen, D. (2019). *Engagement detection in e-learning environments using convolutional neural networks. In 2019 IEEE Intl Confon Dependable, autonomic and Secure Computing, Intl Conf on pervasive intelligence and computing, Intl Conf on cloud and big data computing, intl Confon Cyber Science and Technology Congress*. IEEE. doi:10.1109/DASC/PiCom/CBDCom/CyberSciTech.2019.00028

Mussman, K. (2016). *Prior Lake-Savage Area Schools: U.S. Department of Education Green Ribbon Schools.Prior Lake-Savage Area*. U.S. Department of Education.

Nelson, C., Boles, W., Trouton, L., & Margerison, E. (2019). A review of chatbots in education: Practical steps forward. In *30th Annual Conference for the Australasian Association for Engineering Education (AAEE 2019): Educators Becoming Agents of Change: Innovate, Integrate, Motivate*. Engineers Australia.

Nicholas, J. A., Chan, H. W., & Baker, M. A. B. (2019, February). Machine learning: Applications of artificial intelligence to imaging and diagnosis. *Biophysical Reviews*, *11*(1), 111–118. doi:10.1007/s12551-018-0449-9 PMID:30182201

Okuno, H. G., Nakadai, K., & Kitano, H. (2002). Social interaction of humanoid robot based on audio-visual tracking. *The International conference on industrial, engineering and other applications of applied intelligent systems*, 725-735.

Ouyang, F., & Jiao, P. (2021) Artificial intelligence in education: The three paradigms. *Computers and Education: Artificial Intelligence, 2.*

Panadero, E., & Jarvela, S. (2015). Socially shared regulation of learning: A review. *European Psychologist*, *20*(3), 190–203. doi:10.1027/1016-9040/a000226

Pandey, A. K., & Gelin, R. (2017). Humanoid robots in education: a short review. In A. Goswami & P. Vadakkepat (Eds.), *Humanoid robotics: a reference* (pp. 1–16). Springer. doi:10.1007/978-94-007-7194-9_113-1

Peel, M. (2000). "Nobody Cares": The challenge of isolation in school to university transition. *Journal of Institutional Research*, *9*(1), 22–34.

Ramakrishnan, A., Ottmar, E., LoCasale-Crouch, J., & Whitehill, J. (2019). Toward automated classroom observation: Predicting positive and negative climate. *14th IEEE International Conference on Automatic Face & Gesture Recognition (FG 2019),* 1-8. 10.1109/FG.2019.8756529

Rickabaugh, J. (2016). *Tapping the power of personalized learning: A roadmap for school leaders*. ASCD.

Riedl, M. O. (2019). Human-centered artificial intelligence and machine learning. *Human Behavior and Emerging Technologies*, *1*(1), 33–36. doi:10.1002/hbe2.117

Riedl, M. O. (2019). Human-centered artificial intelligence and machine learning. *Human Sciences*, *11*(5), 57. doi:10.3390/bs11050057

Shaik, T., Tao, X., Li, Y., Dann, C., Mcdonald, J., Redmond, P., & Galligan, L. (2022). A Review of the Trends and Challenges in Adopting Natural Language Processing Methods for Education Feedback Analysis. *IEEE Access : Practical Innovations, Open Solutions*, *10*, 56720–56739. doi:10.1109/ACCESS.2022.3177752

Sharma, K., Giannakos, M., & Dillenbourg, P. (2020). Eye-tracking and artificial intelligence to enhance motivation and learning. *Smart Learning Environments*, *7*(1), 13. Advance online publication. doi:10.1186/s40561-020-00122-x

SharmaP.JoshiS.GautamS.FilipeV.ReisM. J. (2019). Student engagement detection using emotion analysis, eye tracking and head movement with machine learning. *ARXIV preprint arxiv:1909.12913*.

Shawar, B. A., & Atwell, E. S. (2007). Chatbots: Are they really useful? *J. Lang. Technol Comput. Linguist.*, *22*(1), 29–29. doi:10.21248/jlcl.22.2007.88

Simpson, O. (2010). Can we do better? CWP Retention Literature Review, Report to the Centre for Widening Participation, Open University.

Sinha, S., Rogat, T. K., Adams-Wiggins, K. R., & Hmelo-silver, C. E. (2004). Collaborative group engagement in a computer-supported inquiry learning environment. *International Journal of Computer-Supported Collaborative Learning*, *10*(3), 273–307. doi:10.1007/s11412-015-9218-y

Torrato, J. B., Aguja, S. E., & Prudente, M. S. (2021). Using web video conferencing to conduct a program as a proposed model for teacher leadership and academic vitality in the Philippines. *Education Sciences*, *11*(658), 1–30. doi:10.3390/educsci11110658

Truta, C., Parv, L., & Topala, I. (2018). Academic Engagement and Intention to Drop Out: Levers for Sustainability in Higher Education. *Sustainability (Basel)*, *10*(12), 4637. Advance online publication. doi:10.3390/su10124637

Vanichvasin, P. (2022). Impact of Chatbots on Student Learning and Satisfaction in the Entrepreneurship Education Programme in Higher Education Context. *International Education Studies*, *15*(6), 15. doi:10.5539/ies.v15n6p15

Verma, N., Getenet, S., Dann, C., & Shaik, T. (2023). Designing an artificial intelligence tool to understand student engagement based on teacher's behaviours and movements in video conferencing. *Computers and Education: Artificial Intelligence*, *5*, 100187. doi:10.1016/j.caeai.2023.100187

Wang, K., Zuo, M., Yu, S., Luo, H., Yan, Y., & Ouyang, H. (2021). Use Machine Learning to Predict Primary School Students' Level of Learning Engagement. *ICETM'21: 2021 4th International Conference on Education Technology Management*. 10.1145/3510309.3510313

Whitehill, J., Serpell, Z., Lin, Y., Foster, A., & Movellan, J. R. (2014). The faces of engagement: Automatic recognition of student engagement from facial expressions. *IEEE Transactions on Affective Computing*, *5*(1), 86–98. doi:10.1109/TAFFC.2014.2316163

Xu, A., Liu, Z., Guo, Y., Sinha, V., & Akkiraju, R. (2017). A new chatbot for customer service on social media. In *Proceedings of the 2017 CHI Conference on Human Factors in Computing Systems*. ACM. 10.1145/3025453.3025496

Xu, X., Dugdale, D. M., Wei, X., & Mi, W. (2023). Leveraging Artificial Intelligence to Predict Young Learner Online Learning Engagement. *American Journal of Distance Education*, *37*(3), 185–198. doi: 10.1080/08923647.2022.2044663

Yakin, A. A., Apriani, E., Obaid, A. J., & Elngar, A. A. (2023). Transforming online learning management: Generative models on ChatGPT to enhance Online Student Engagement Scale. [Jurnal Pendidikan dan Kependidikan]. *IDARAH*, *7*(2), 135–148. doi:10.47766/idarah.v7i2.1514

Yang, S. J., Ogata, H., Matsui, T., & Chen, N. S. (2021). Human-centered artificial intelligence in education: Seeing the invisible through the visible. *Computers & Education: Artificial Intelligence*, *2*, 100008.

Zemčík, M. T. (2019). A brief history of chatbots. *DEStech Transactions on Computer Science and Engineering*. . doi:10.12783/dtcse/aicae2019/31439

Zheng, J., Xing, W., & Zhu, G. (2019). Examining sequential patterns of self- and socially shared regulation of STEM learning in a CSCL environment. *Computers & Education*, *136*, 34–48. doi:10.1016/j.compedu.2019.03.005

Zhu, H. (2020). Big data and artificial intelligence modelling for drug discovery. *Annual Review of Pharmacology and Toxicology*, *60*(1), 573–589. doi:10.1146/annurev-pharmtox-010919-023324 PMID:31518513

Zoroayka, V. S. (2018). Design and implementation of a chatbot in online higher education settings. *Issues in Information Systems*, *19*(4).

KEY TERMS AND DEFINITIONS

AIED: The application of artificial intelligence tools in education.

Artificial Intelligence: The ability of machines to perform tasks that require human reasoning.

Chatbot: A conversational agent used to simulate human conversations.

Heutagogy: Autonomous learning.

Machine Learning: A set of algorithms that allow machines to learn from data.

Natural Language Processing: Ability of computers to analyse human languages in text or multimedia.

Personalised Learning: Learning that is tailored to the specific needs of individuals.

Student Engagement: Involvement of learners in the learning process.

Chapter 8
Assessment, Evaluation, and Feedback in Online Education With Artificial Intelligence-Supported Tools

Bünyami Kayalı
https://orcid.org/0000-0001-6419-9088
Bayburt University, Turkey

Şener Balat
https://orcid.org/0000-0002-9683-1778
Bingöl University, Turkey

ABSTRACT

The increasing role of Artificial Intelligence (AI) applications in educational activities is also evident in online education. By providing personalised and adaptive learning experiences and offering support for teachers by tracking student behaviours to make inferences about student success and performance, AI reduces teachers' workload, allowing them to focus more on educational activities. AI applications especially enable the rapid and easy completion of assessment and evaluation activities, which teachers often spend significant time and effort on. Within this scope, AI-supported tools are used in online education activities to perform automatic assessments, provide real-time feedback, and conduct data analysis and performance evaluation activities. In this context, the aim of the study is determined as the examination of measurement, evaluation, and feedback activities in online education with AI-supported tools.

INTRODUCTION: ARTIFICIAL INTELLIGENCE AND ITS ROLE IN EDUCATION

Artificial intelligence (AI) was first introduced in a proposal letter presented at the Dartmouth Conference in 1956, with John McCarthy being considered the father of the concept (Zawacki-Richter et al., 2019). AI is a system that mimics the human brain to perform specific tasks and can self-improve through

DOI: 10.4018/979-8-3693-4268-8.ch008

acquired experiences (Kurzweil et al., 1990). Numerous researchers have conducted studies in this field since introducing the concept of AI. The investments and studies have increased the performance and visibility of AI technologies while reducing their costs. This has integrated AI technologies into our lives (Russell & Norvig, 2016). Today, AI technology is utilised in various fields ranging from Siri to digital journalism, predicting stock movements, predicting crime, and medical diagnostics without facial recognition (Komalavalli et al., 2020).

Just as in all aspects of our lives, AI technologies increasingly make their presence felt in education. This was highlighted as a significant development in the education sector in the 2018 Horizon Report, with AI and adaptive learning technologies emerging as significant advancements (Becker et al., 2018). AI technologies used in education can be categorised into three main types: expert systems, intelligent tutoring systems, and dialogue-based systems. Expert systems possess capabilities similar to those of experts in a particular field and are widely used in distance education. Intelligent tutoring systems are more advanced versions of expert and computer-aided systems. These systems have different databases for instructional content and strategies, making inferences based on the student's current level. They are mainly utilised in personalised and individualised learning activities (Alkhatlan & Kalita, 2018). Dialogue-based systems, on the other hand, aim to present topics through dialogue rather than providing only personalised educational activities. They are used to create suitable educational programs for students and correct deficiencies with instant feedback (Arslan, 2020).

These systems are generally used to support teaching activities. Chassignol et al. (2018) categorised the purposes of using these systems under personalised learning opportunities, innovative teaching approaches, technology-supported assessment activities, and student-teacher interaction. Moreover, mention can be made of applications that support educational institutions administratively. Innovative systems for creating lesson and exam schedules, cybersecurity, and facility management are AI applications that indirectly contribute to learning activities (Holmes et al., 2023).

Undoubtedly, the increasing use of AI technologies in educational activities is primarily due to the advantages these technologies offer to educational environments. A review of the literature indicates that AI technologies offer various benefits for students, including the ability to progress at their own pace, access to quality and lifelong learning opportunities, the creation of personalised learning environments, meeting individual needs, supporting different learning styles, enhancing collaboration, improving academic performance, and providing continuous feedback (Karsenti, 2019; Popenici & Kerr, 2017). From the perspective of teachers, AI contributes to the rapid and easy tracking of student progress, assessment and evaluation activities, and the creation of course content, thus reducing the workload, simplifying classroom management, and saving time (Cunningham-Nelson et al., 2019; Khan et al., 2021; Kim et al., 2021). Furthermore, they support teachers in creating interactive and flexible learning environments with distance learning opportunities (Tate et al., 2023). From the viewpoint of administrators, the use of intelligent assistants facilitates the easy and rapid implementation of services such as budgeting, procurement, course registration, data-driven decision-making, and facility management, thus reducing administrative burdens and allowing more time for educational activities (Çetin & Aktaş, 2021; Holmes et al., 2023). For educational institutions, using AI-supported systems contributes to increased institutional efficiency, reduced operating costs, and improved overall responsiveness (Lin & Chang, 2020; Xia et al., 2022) and expands access to education to broader audiences.

Despite all these positive contributions of AI technologies to educational activities, some criticisms have been raised regarding their use. For students, these include low motivation and the inability to benefit from face-to-face communication opportunities; for teachers, concerns about job loss and increased expectations in terms of professional competence; and for educational organisations, ethical concerns, technical glitches, inability to assess student creativity, and concerns about classroom discipline (Osetskyi et al., 2020).

In conclusion, although the impact of AI technologies on educational activities is still uncertain (Holmes et al., 2021), they have the potential to contribute to learning processes significantly (Chen et al., 2020). This necessitates further efforts towards adapting AI technologies to educational activities, not only for students (Cox et al., 2019), but also for teachers (Matthew et al., 2021), administrators, and educational institutions (Zawacki-Richter et al., 2019).

ONLINE EDUCATION AND ARTIFICIAL INTELLIGENCE

In recent years, especially with the advancements in internet technology, the shape of online education activities has changed. This technology allows educators to reach wider audiences through platforms, particularly Massive Open Online Courses (MOOCs). Millions of students and adults worldwide can learn from experts on any topic (Pelletier, 2021). Furthermore, many online programs are being offered within formal education, especially in higher education institutions, to increase student numbers without being confined to physical campuses. Despite these developments in distance education and the widespread use of online platforms, many issues remain to be addressed regarding improving student completion rates, presentation techniques, and feedback (Lin et al., 2018).

Both the problems above and the availability of data obtained from educational and exam activities conducted in online environments have made AI an essential tool for enhancing the quality of online learning activities. Notably, the ease and speed of generating, recording, and processing data in virtual classrooms compared to traditional classrooms increase the significance of this approach (Esten, 2019). In virtual classrooms, data can be converted by tracking metrics such as the time students spend on a page, navigation between contents, response times, and even eye movements. This data can be used to predict student performance, detect unwanted behaviours, provide individualised solutions, and evaluate conducted activities (Hwang et al., 2022).

Considering both the potential benefits of AI in educational settings mentioned in the first section and the contributions expressed in this paragraph, the use of AI technologies in online education environments can be evaluated under six headings. These headings are briefly explained below.

Providing Personalized Learning Experiences: AI-supported platforms can provide personalised learning experiences to all students (Fernandes et al., 2023). Educational content can be tailored to individual student needs, thereby establishing individual learning models (Rivers & Holland, 2022). Additionally, automatic learning paths can be created to adapt to each student's pace and preferences, thus ensuring a more effective and efficient learning experience.

Adaptive Learning and Assessment: AI-supported assessments can dynamically determine the difficulty level and question type based on student performance (Singh, 2023), thus providing personalised and responsive learning experiences. Past interactions and learning processes can also be analysed to recommend relevant content (Anuyahong et al., 2023). Continuous feedback can be provided to students for timely and informative feedback on their progress.

Automation of Routine Tasks: With the assistance of AI technology, administrative tasks such as grading, attendance tracking, and organising materials can be performed automatically (He & Yin, 2022).

This allows educators to focus more on the learning process. Furthermore, it helps educators create lesson plans, evaluate assignments, develop course content, and set objectives (Coglianese & Lai, 2022).

Virtual Assistance and Private Tutoring: Virtual teachers and chatbots equipped with natural language processing technology can understand student questions and provide guidance (Chae et al., 2023). Students can interact with these tools anytime and receive instant support services and feedback.

Accessibility and Inclusivity: AI-supported voice and translation applications can make online educational content more accessible and eliminate problems related to foreign language sources (Motta & Quaresma, 2023). Additionally, AI-generated images and drawings can enhance the understanding and retention of complex concepts, meeting various learning needs.

Predictive Analytics and Analysis: AI algorithms collect and analyse data from various sources to predict student performance and behaviours, providing educators with deep insights for timely intervention and support (Adane et al., 2023).

In conclusion, while AI is increasingly utilised in various tasks across different domains, educational institutions promise to enrich online education activities, enhance the efficiency and effectiveness of learning, and provide students with access to quality education. Integrating AI technologies into online education environments is still in its early stages and requires further research for successful implementation. Ethical principles must be followed when using AI technology in online education environments, ensuring the secure storage of personal and institutional data. Additionally, despite AI technologies' comprehensive and human-like responses, students should not overly rely on these responses. Valid concerns exist regarding the widening gaps in justice, access, and learning caused by this technology.

MEASUREMENT AND EVALUATION IN ONLINE EDUCATION

Since online education has become an integral part of the global education landscape, robust methods are required to measure and evaluate its effectiveness. Measuring and assessing online learning presents various challenges for both educators and students (Uzun et al., 2023). The assessment and evaluation of online education is a complex and multifaceted process. Various models, frameworks, and methodologies are being explored to ensure quality in online education environments and evaluate learning outcomes. McGorry (2003) emphasised reliability and validity in assessing the quality of online programs, proposing a model that addresses flexibility, responsiveness, interaction, student learning, technical support, technology, and student satisfaction in online courses. Balula and Moreira (2014) proposed a three-dimensional model focusing on learning, interaction, and technology for evaluating online activities in higher education. Both models provide comprehensive frameworks for evaluating the effectiveness of online education. However, educational institutions are increasingly focusing on the need for various online assessment components and tools to ensure accountability and comprehensive evaluation of student learning outcomes (Khan et al., 2023). Recently, one of the most prominent methods for measuring and evaluating the impact of online education is through AI applications or tools.

Various studies have examined the role of AI tools in online education's assessment and evaluation processes. Hooda (2022) emphasised the importance of instant and valid feedback in enhancing student achievement, suggesting the use of AI in assessment and feedback applications. Chsignol (2018) provided a broader perspective on the impact of AI in education, discussing the potential for reshaping the educational environment through customised content, innovative teaching methods, and technology-enhanced assessment. Bantugan et al. (2024) highlighted the potential of AI-supported assessment platforms to automate tasks such as grading and monitoring, allowing educators to allocate time for more creative interventions. González-Calatayud et al. (2021) utilised AI for formative assessment and automatic grading, emphasising the need to reflect pedagogical principles in AI applications. These studies indicate that AI tools can play a significant role in online education's assessment and evaluation processes.

MEASUREMENT STRATEGIES SUPPORTED BY ARTIFICIAL INTELLIGENCE

AI in education, supported by various measurement strategies, can contribute significantly. Research in this field focuses on the functions of AI, such as providing personalised feedback, enhancing assessment accuracy, and assisting in test item creation and analysis (Owan et al., 2023; Fang et al., 2023). AI facilitates the implementation of evidence-based teaching strategies, such as addressing misconceptions, low-risk testing, and evaluating learning, by supporting multiple sample strategies in material creation processes (Mollick & Mollick, 2023). Additionally, AI applications in education can effectively predict academic performance and improve student outcomes and decision-making in academic institutions (Tariq et al., 2022). Therefore, the role of AI-supported measurement strategies in education is becoming increasingly important.

Various strategies and methods can be employed to make learning processes more effective and enhance student success using AI-supported tools in education. Among these are providing personalised feedback to improve learning processes. For example, the most suitable learning materials and strategies can be recommended by analysing a student's learning style. Additionally, AI can create and analyze tests to measure students' knowledge levels. Furthermore, it can automatically generate customised tests to identify students' strengths and weaknesses and quickly analyse the results. AI-based teaching systems can be used to provide individual learning experiences to students. For instance, by analyzing students' incorrect answers, appropriate instructional materials and activities can be provided to them. Moreover, AI-supported autonomous learning tools can help students manage their learning processes. For example, these tools can guide students in setting learning goals, monitoring their progress, and exploring learning materials. AI can also be used to create test questions and assignments. For instance, it can automatically generate questions that address different difficulty levels or analyse the difficulty level of existing questions to make appropriate revisions. Furthermore, AI can adjust assessment processes automatically based on students' performance. For example, dynamically adjusting the difficulty level of questions according to students' abilities can provide a fairer assessment.

In summary, AI-supported tools or applications can be used in various ways to support measurement and assessment processes. These applications and tools enrich students' learning experiences while helping teachers optimise measurement and assessment processes of student progress.

ARTIFICIAL INTELLIGENCE-SUPPORTED DATA ANALYSIS AND PERFORMANCE EVALUATION

Performance assessment in online education holds critical importance in evaluating students' achievements, monitoring progress, and enhancing the learning experience. Unlike traditional classroom settings, different strategies and tools are required in online education to track and effectively assess students' progress. In this context, AI tools and applications offer significant potential for performance assessment in online education. AI applications such as machine learning and deep learning can contribute significantly to solving complex problems, monitoring student progress, analysing performance data, and fostering flexibility and creativity (Shafique et al., 2023). González-Calatayud et al. (2021) emphasised the frequent use of AI for formative assessment and automatic grading. Additionally, models achieving high accuracy classification rates effectively analyse student behaviours and develop interventions for struggling students (Zacharias, 2016). Big data also plays a significant role in AI educational systems by providing rich learning resources and tools for autonomous learning, prediction-based assessment modelling, and personalised guidance (Xu, 2021). AI tools such as neural networks and natural language processing enhance student assessment by predicting performance, automating evaluations, and identifying factors that increase class participation (de Souza Zanirato Maia et al., 2023).

AI can be utilised in various ways for performance assessment in online education, aiming to measure students' achievements, improve learning processes, and provide more effective feedback to teachers. AI can automatically assess evaluation materials such as tests and quizzes by analysing students' responses. For example, with an AI-supported language learning platform, students' written responses can be analysed for accuracy, grammar, and vocabulary, providing instant feedback. Additionally, monitoring students' online interactions can be used for learning analytics. Analysing how often students access course materials, which topics they struggle with the most, and which materials they prefer can guide teachers in understanding student progress. Alternatively, AI can be employed for metacognitive analysis, analysing text and other media sources to gain deeper insights into students' learning processes. Natural language processing techniques can also determine the tone, emotional states, or conceptual understanding reflected in students' language in their assignments or forum discussions.

ARTIFICIAL INTELLIGENCE-SUPPORTED FEEDBACK SYSTEMS

AI-supported feedback systems provide personalised and rapid student feedback, monitor and analyse their performance while working with educational materials, and offer instant feedback. Research on AI-based assessment systems consistently indicates that they can support personalised education by providing feedback and helping students, teachers, and parents understand the learning process and needs (Luckin, 2017). Dynamic feedback mechanisms in online learning communities, such as rating blog posts, can promote higher learning and social interaction (Thoms, 2011). Generating adaptable feedback using student data obtained from learning management systems can provide instructors with recommendations for resolving student issues, enhancing understanding of student needs, and tailoring feedback (Kosba et al., 2007). AI systems in online learning can enhance student-teacher interaction by personalising communication and support (Seo et al., 2021). Providing feedback based on collaborative processes and learning analytics can significantly improve student performance (Xu, 2021). Feedback generation through AI utilising natural language processing, educational data mining, and learning analytics can predict learning outcomes (Bulut & Wongvorachan, 2022). AI can automate various educational tasks by providing benefits such as grading and feedback on course quality, thus enhancing the overall learning experience (Singh & Mishra, 2021). Machine learning and natural language processing integrated into online learning management systems can analyse student feedback to assess teacher performance and improve teaching efficiency (Das et al., 2022).

In summary, relevant research indicates that feedback systems in online learning environments have many positive effects. For example, an AI-based application can analyse a student's grammar and vocabulary, providing appropriate exercises and instant feedback on their performance. AI algorithms can determine areas where students struggle or excel, providing additional exercises or explanations tailored to individual needs. They can also suggest materials or activities based on student's learning styles and preferences and enhance communication between students and teachers. Analysing student feedback to provide recommendations for improving lesson plans can assist teachers in evaluating the effectiveness of instructional materials.

CONCLUSION

In conclusion, the emergence of AI technologies has led to a paradigm shift in online education. The potential of AI to mimic human cognitive functions is being leveraged to enhance teaching and learning experiences in the digital realm. The role of AI in providing personalised education, automating routine tasks, and offering predictive analytics is instrumental in transforming the landscape of online education.

However, online education's complexity and multidimensionality necessitate robust measurement and assessment methods. In this context, AI tools have emerged as significant assets, offering features such as personalised feedback, improving the accuracy of assessments, and assisting in creating and analysing test items. The ability of AI to support various assessment strategies, such as creating tests based on student abilities and predicting future performance, demonstrates its transformative potential. The role of AI extends beyond measurement and assessment to encompass data analysis and performance evaluation. AI tools enable the analysis of student performance, monitoring of student interactions, and immediate feedback provision, thereby fostering a deeper understanding of student learning processes. Additionally, AI-supported feedback systems possess features for monitoring student performance, analysing student responses, and providing recommendations for improving lesson plans.

While the impact of AI technologies on educational activities remains a subject of ongoing research, their potential benefits cannot be overlooked. However, it is essential to approach the integration of AI in education carefully, ensuring that it enhances the human element in teaching and learning. As we continue to explore and understand the potential of AI in online education, it is evident that AI will play an increasingly prominent role in shaping the future of education.

REFERENCES

Adane, M. D., Deku, J. K., & Asare, E. K. (2023). Performance Analysis of Machine Learning Algorithms in Prediction of Student Academic Performance. *Journal of Advances in Mathematics and Computer Science*, *38*(5), 74–86. doi:10.9734/jamcs/2023/v38i51762

Alkhatlan, A., & Kalita, J. (2018). Intelligent tutoring systems: A comprehensive historical survey with recent developments. *arXiv preprint arXiv:1812.09628*. https://doi.org/ doi:10.5120/ijca2019918451

Anuyahong, B., Rattanapong, C., & Patcha, I. (2023). Analyzing the Impact of Artificial Intelligence in Personalized Learning and Adaptive Assessment in Higher Education. *International Journal of Innovation and Scientific Research*, *10*(4), 88–93. Advance online publication. doi:10.51244/IJRSI.2023.10412

Arslan, K. (2020). Eğitimde yapay zekâ ve uygulamaları [Artificial intelligence and applications in education]. *Batı Anadolu Eğitim Bilimleri Dergisi*, *11*(1), 71–88.

Balula, A., & Moreira, A. (2014). *Evaluation of online higher education: Learning, interaction and technology*. Springer., doi:10.1007/978-3-319-05425-4

Bantugan, B. S., Li, X., Liu, L., Liu, Y., Wang, X., Yang, M., & Zhang, X. (2024). The Adoption of Artificial Intelligence of Selected International Chinese Educators Enrolled as Graduate Students in the College of Education of St. Paul University Manila. *International Journal of Innovation and Scientific Research*, *11*(2), 133–146. doi:10.51244/IJRSI.2024.1102011

Becker, S. A., Brown, M., Dahlstrom, E., Davis, A., DePaul, K., Diaz, V., & Pomerantz, J. (2018). *NMC horizon report: 2018 higher education edition*. Educause.

Bulut, O., & Wongvorachan, T. (2022). Feedback Generation through Artificial Intelligence. In The Open/Technology in Education, Society, and Scholarship Association Conference (Vol. 2, No. 1, pp. 1-9). doi:10.18357/otessac.2022.2.1.125

Çetin, M., & Aktaş, A. (2021). Yapay zeka ve eğitimde gelecek senaryoları [Artificial intelligence and future scenarios in education]. *OPUS International Journal of Society Researches, 18*, 4225-4268. doi:10.26466/opus.911444

Chae, H., Kim, M., Kim, C., Jeong, W., Kim, H., Lee, J., & Yeo, J. (2023). TUTORING: instruction-grounded conversational agent for language learners. In *Proceedings of the AAAI Conference on Artificial Intelligence* (Vol. 37, No. 13, pp. 16413–16415). 10.1609/aaai.v37i13.27063

Chassignol, M., Khoroshavin, A., Klimova, A., & Bilyatdinova, A. (2018). Artificial Intelligence trends in education: A narrative overview. *Procedia Computer Science*, *136*, 16–24. doi:10.1016/j.procs.2018.08.233

Coglianese, C., & Lai, A. (2022). Assessing Automated Administration. *U of Penn Law School, Public Law Research Paper*, (22-28). doi:10.1093/oxfordhb/9780197579329.013.30

Cunningham-Nelson, S., Boles, W., Trouton, L., & Margerison, E. (2019). A review of chatbots in education: Practical steps forward. *30th annual conference for the Australasian association for engineering education (AAEE 2019): Educators becoming agents of change: Innovate, integrate.* Motivate: Engineers Australia.

Das, S., Roy, S., Bose, R., Acharjya, P. P., & Mondal, H. (2022). Analysis of Student Sentiment Dynamics to Evaluate Teachers Performance in Online Course using Machine Learning. In *2022 International Conference on Applied Artificial Intelligence and Computing (ICAAIC)* (pp. 668-673). IEEE. 10.1109/ICAAIC53929.2022.9792958

de Souza Zanirato Maia, J., Bueno, A. P. A., & Sato, J. R. (2023). Applications of Artificial Intelligence Models in Educational Analytics and Decision Making: A Systematic Review. *WORLD (Oakland, Calif.)*, *4*(2), 288–313. doi:10.3390/world4020019

Esten. (2019). *"Uzaktan Öğretimde Yapay Zekâ" Başlıklı Eğitimde Yapay Zekâ Çalıştayı Sonuç Raporu* [Final Report of Artificial Intelligence in Education Workshop titled "Artificial Intelligence in Distance Education"]. https://tasam.org/tr-TR/Icerik/51444/uzaktan_ogretimde_yapay_zekâ_ egitimde_yapay_zekâ_calistayi_-_5_sonuc_raporu

Fang, Y., Roscoe, R. D., & McNamara, D. S. (2023). Artificial intelligence-based assessment in education. In *Handbook of artificial intelligence in education* (pp. 485–504). Edward Elgar Publishing. doi:10.4337/9781800375413.00033

Fernandes, C. W., Rafatirad, S., & Sayadi, H. (2023). Advancing personalized and adaptive learning experience in education with artificial intelligence. In *2023 32nd Annual Conference of the European Association for Education in Electrical and Information Engineering (EAEEIE)* (pp. 1-6). IEEE. 10.23919/EAEEIE55804.2023.10181336

González-Calatayud, V., Prendes-Espinosa, P., & Roig-Vila, R. (2021). Artificial intelligence for student assessment: A systematic review. *Applied Sciences (Basel, Switzerland)*, *11*(12), 5467. doi:10.3390/app11125467

He, X., & Yin, J. (2022). Research on application of artificial intelligence technology in administrative innovation smart management system. In *2022 International Conference on Education, Network and Information Technology (ICENIT)* (pp. 379-382). IEEE. 10.1109/ICENIT57306.2022.00093

Holmes, W., Bialik, M., & Fadel, C. (2023). *Artificial intelligence in education*. Globethics Publications., doi:10.58863/20.500.12424/4276068

Holmes, W., Porayska-Pomsta, K., Holstein, K., Sutherland, E., Baker, T., Shum, S. B., Santos, O. C., Rodrigo, M. T., Cukurova, M., Bittencourt, I. I., & Koedinger, K. R. (2021). Ethics of AI in education: Towards a community-wide framework. *International Journal of Artificial Intelligence in Education*, 1–23. doi:10.1007/s40593-021-00239-1

Hooda, M., Rana, C., Dahiya, O., Rizwan, A., & Hossain, M. S. (2022). Artificial intelligence for assessment and feedback to enhance student success in higher education. *Mathematical Problems in Engineering*, 1–19. doi:10.1155/2022/5215722

Hwang, G.-J., Tu, Y.-F., & Tang, K.-Y. (2022). AI in Online-Learning Research: Visualizing and Interpreting the Journal Publications from 1997 to 2019. *International Review of Research in Open and Distance Learning*, *23*(1), 104–130. doi:10.19173/irrodl.v23i1.6319

Karlgren, K. (2005). *Intelligent tutoring systems (its)*. Academic Press.

Karsenti, T. (2019). Artificial intelligence in education: The urgent need to prepare teachers for tomorrow's schools. *Formation et Profession*, *27*(1), 112–116. doi:10.18162/fp.2019.a167

Khan, H., Kushwah, K. K., Khare, K., Mahobia, S. K., & Thakur, J. S. (2023). Methods of Evaluation and Assessment in Digital Learning. In *Mobile and Sensor-Based Technologies in Higher Education* (pp. 83–110). IGI Global. doi:10.4018/978-1-6684-5400-8.ch004

Khan, I., Ahmad, A. R., Jabeur, N., & Mahdi, M. N. (2021). An artificial intelligence approach to monitor student performance and devise preventive measures. *Smart Learning Environments*, *8*(1), 1–18. doi:10.1186/s40561-021-00161-y

Kim, H. S., Kim, N. Y., & Cha, Y. (2021). Is it beneficial to use AI chatbots to improve learners' speaking performance? *Journal of ASIA TEFL*, *18*(1), 161–178. doi:10.18823/asiatefl.2021.18.1.10.161

Komalavalli, K., Hemalatha, R., & Dhanalakshmi, S. (2020). A survey of artificial intelligence in smart phones and its applications among the students of higher education in and around Chennai City. *Shanlax International Journal of Education*, *8*(3), 89–95. doi:10.34293/education.v8i3.2379

Kosba, E., Dimitrova, V., & Boyle, R. (2007). Adaptive feedback generation to support teachers in web-based distance education. *User Modeling and User-Adapted Interaction*, *17*(4), 379–413. doi:10.1007/s11257-007-9031-z

Kurzweil, R., Richter, R., Kurzweil, R., & Schneider, M. L. (1990). *The age of intelligent machines* (Vol. 580). MIT Press.

Lin, M. P.-C., & Chang, D. (2020). Enhancing post-secondary writers' writing skills with a chatbot. *Journal of Educational Technology & Society*, *23*(1), 78–92. https://www.jstor.org/stable/26915408

Lin, P. H., Wooders, A., Wang, J. T. Y., & Yuan, W. M. (2018). Artificial intelligence, the missing piece of online education? *IEEE Engineering Management Review*, *46*(3), 25–28. doi:10.1109/EMR.2018.2868068

Luckin, R. (2017). Towards artificial intelligence-based assessment systems. *Nature Human Behaviour, 1*(3), 28. doi:10.1038/s41562-016-0028

Matthew, N. O. S., Tolulope, J. A., Abayomi, A. A., & Sarhan, M. M. (2021). Artificial intelligence in education. *International Journal of Scientific Advances*, *2*(1), 5–11. doi:10.51542/ijscia.v2i1.2

McGorry, S. Y. (2003). Measuring quality in online programs. *The Internet and Higher Education*, *6*(2), 159–177. doi:10.1016/S1096-7516(03)00022-8

MollickE. R.MollickL. (2023). Using AI to implement effective teaching strategies in classrooms: Five strategies, including prompts. Including Prompts (March 17, 2023). https://doi.org/doi:10.2139/ssrn.4391243

Motta, I., & Quaresma, M. (2023). Increasing Transparency to Design Inclusive Conversational Agents (CAs): Perspectives and Open Issues. In *Proceedings of the 5th International Conference on Conversational User Interfaces* (pp. 1-4). 10.1145/3571884.3604304

Osetskyi, V., Vitrenko, A., Tatomyr, I., Bilan, S., & Hirnyk, Y. (2020). Artificial intelligence application in education: Financial implications and prospects. *Financial and Credit Activity Problems of Theory and Practice, 2*(33), 574-584. doi:10.18371/fcaptp.v2i33.207246

Owan, V. J., Abang, K. B., Idika, D. O., Etta, E. O., & Bassey, B. A. (2023). Exploring the potential of artificial intelligence tools in educational measurement and assessment. *Eurasia Journal of Mathematics, Science and Technology Education*, *19*(8), em2307. Advance online publication. doi:10.29333/ejmste/13428

Pelletier, K., Brown, M., Brooks, D. C., McCormack, M., Reeves, J., Arbino, N., Bozkurt, A., Crawford, S., Czerniewicz, L., Gibson, R., Linder, K., Mason, J., & Mondelli, V. (2021). *2021 EDUCAUSE horizon report teaching and learning edition*. EDUCAUSE.

Popenici, S. A., & Kerr, S. (2017). Exploring the impact of artificial intelligence on teaching and learning in higher education. *Research and Practice in Technology Enhanced Learning*, *12*(1), 22. doi:10.1186/s41039-017-0062-8 PMID:30595727

Rivers, C., & Holland, A. (2022). Management education and artificial intelligence: Toward personalized learning. In *The future of management education* (pp. 184–204). Routledge. doi:10.4324/9781003095903-14

Russell, S. J., & Norvig, P. (2016). *Artificial intelligence: a modern approach*. Pearson.

Seo, K., Tang, J., Roll, I., Fels, S., & Yoon, D. (2021). The impact of artificial intelligence on learner–instructor interaction in online learning. *International Journal of Educational Technology in Higher Education*, *18*(1), 1–23. doi:10.1186/s41239-021-00292-9 PMID:34778540

Shafique, R., Aljedaani, W., Rustam, F., Lee, E., Mehmood, A., & Choi, G. S. (2023). *Role of Artificial Intelligence in Online Education: A Systematic Mapping Study*. IEEE. doi:10.1109/ACCESS.2023.3278590

Singh, S. V. (2023). *The Prospects for Advancing Adaptive Learning Technology through AI Methods. In 2023 Future of Educational Innovation-Workshop Series Data in Action*. IEEE. doi:10.1109/IEEECONF56852.2023.10105111

Singh, T., & Mishra, J. (2021). Learning with artificial intelligence systems: application, challenges, and opportunities. *Impact of AI technologies on teaching, learning, and research in higher education*, 236–253. doi:10.4018/978-1-7998-4763-2.ch015

Tariq, A., Awan, M. J., Alshudukhi, J., Alam, T. M., Alhamazani, K. T., & Meraf, Z. (2022). Software measurement by using artificial intelligence. *Journal of Nanomaterials*, *2022*, 1–10. doi:10.1155/2022/7283171

TateT. P.DoroudiS.RitchieD.XuY.UciM. W. (2023). Educational research and AI-generated writing: Confronting the coming tsunami. EdArXiv. doi:10.35542/osf.io/4mec3

Thoms, B. (2011). A dynamic social feedback system to support learning and social interaction in higher education. *IEEE Transactions on Learning Technologies*, *4*(4), 340–352. doi:10.1109/TLT.2011.9

Uzun, N. B., Aktaş, M., & Akay, C. (2023). Measurement and Evaluation Challenges in Distance Education: Systematic Review and Qualitative Meta-Synthesis. *Journal of Educational Technology*, *19*(4). Advance online publication. doi:10.26634/jet.19.4.19368

Xia, Q., Chiu, T. K. F., Lee, M., Temitayo, I., Dai, Y., & Chai, C. S. (2022). A self-determination theory design approach for inclusive and diverse artificial intelligence (AI) K-12 education. *Computers & Education*, *189*, 104582. Advance online publication. doi:10.1016/j.compedu.2022.104582

Xu, B. (2021). Artificial intelligence teaching system and data processing method based on big data. *Complexity*, *2021*, 1–11. doi:10.1155/2021/1961061

Xu, W., Meng, J., Raja, S. K. S., Priya, M. P., & Kiruthiga Devi, M. (2023). Artificial intelligence in constructing personalized and accurate feedback systems for students. *International Journal of Modeling, Simulation, and Scientific Computing*, *14*(01), 2341001. doi:10.1142/S1793962323410015

Zacharis, N. Z. (2016). Predicting student academic performance in blended learning using artificial neural networks. *International Journal of Artificial Intelligence & Applications*, *7*(5), 17–29. doi:10.5121/ijaia.2016.7502

Zawacki-Richter, O., Marín, V. I., Bond, M., & Gouverneur, F. (2019). Systematic review of research on artificial intelligence applications in higher education–where are the educators? *International Journal of Educational Technology in Higher Education*, *16*(1), 1–27. doi:10.1186/s41239-019-0171-0

KEY TERMS AND DEFINITIONS

Evaluation: The process of interpreting and making sense of concrete indicators obtained through measurement according to specific criteria. Evaluation refers to what is being measured.

Feedback: All activities are conducted to provide information about the behaviour's outcome to the individual performing a behaviour.

Measurement: Collecting concrete indicators related to students' learning outcomes. Measurement concerns what and how we measure.

Performance Assessment: The systematic measuring and evaluating of students' achievements and developments. This process determines what students have learned, how much they have learned, and how they apply it.

Predictive Analytics: A branch of data science that aims to extrapolate the future by analysing past data. In education, it is used for various purposes such as identifying critical behaviors and risks, such as future student performance, disciplinary issues, or dropout rates, based on students' previous behaviors.

Chapter 9
Monitoring, Operations, and Performance Assessment Through AI and Cloud-Based Plants

K. Mayuri
Institute of Aeronautical Engineering, Hyderabad, India

Rakesh Chandrashekar
Department of Mechanical Engineering, New Horizon College of Engineering, Bangalore, India

Ginni Nijhawan
Lovely Professional University, Phagwara, India

Q. Mohammad
Hilla University College, Babylon, Iraq

Arthi Arthii
Independent Researcher, India

ABSTRACT

This work outlines the steps necessary to build a cloud-based control-loop performance monitoring system that can centrally monitor data from several industrial facilities in different parts of the world. Given the high expenses associated with on-premises installations (including systems, human resources, maintenance, and upgrades), this is an attractive option for many businesses, and it's all made possible by current Industry 4.0 technology.

DOI: 10.4018/979-8-3693-4268-8.ch009

1. INTRODUCTION

Many academic and business groups have been working hard over the last few years to demonstrate and capitalise on the advantages of Industry 4.0. The nine KETs range from Progressive Industrial Solutions to Big Data and analytics, but remembering their features and advantages would be difficult (Dwivedi et al., 2023). Despite what would seem to be primarily benefits for the manufacturing sector at first look, the truth is that the whole process industry stands to gain from robust and integrated industrial automation (Nath et al., 2023b). As a result, whole industrial units may benefit greatly from implementing new approaches and procedures linked to the Industry 4.0 paradigm; for many, this is a necessary evil in an increasingly cutthroat business environment (Javaid et al., 2021).

Accessibility, reproducible, distributable, and adaptability are some of the inherent appealing qualities of cloud computing (Matheri et al., 2022). High computational power, the capacity to handle huge data storage and analytics, and the possibility of centralised monitoring are just a few of the many real-world benefits of this technology (Ananth et al., 2021). The other key qualities are flexibility, multitenancy, and pay-by-means of use, on-demand consumption, low prices, and no capital investment (Ramesh et al., 2019). Cloud estimating demands cyber security, reliability, palpable-occasion movement, configuration description, network construction, and the whole design, but it has several challenges (K. Kumar & Saini, 2022). (Santiteerakul et al., 2020)These apps contain data writers, examining forms, alarm administration, asset administration, accomplishment administration, training simulators, and detached disease programmes (Liu et al., 2022). Reputable research checked cloud feedback control's challenges and benefits. Commercial answers and electronics are convenient for building a platform for mechanical process dossier data leveraging Industry 4.0 concepts and cloud calculating. (Ampatzidis et al., 2020) However, there is a lack of common instances in the scientific literature of data analytics being comprehensively implemented within the framework of Industry 4.0(Livera et al., 2022). Among the rare instances, automated electric induction motors, power plant machinery, and waste-to-energy (WTE) facilities have all made use of intriguing cloud-based systems for remote monitoring and control (Hao et al., 2019). When it comes to CLPM/CLPA, one major perk of cloud computing is how easy it is to set up, manage, and update centralised systems (Jain et al., 2022). With only one monitoring system, information from many industrial locations can be easily uploaded and analysed in the cloud (Kumar et al., 2022). Operators may find this approach especially appealing when they are tasked with monitoring a large number of identical units or plants, which means they will inevitably encounter common problems and errors (Narsimhulu et al., 2022). It may also be useful when assets are geographically spread, such as in the case of energy or water supply facilities. (Kumar et al. (Patuzzi et al., 2016) There is a significant probability of mistakes and omissions and a clear time and resource drain while implementing, maintaining, and upgrading on-site solutions ((Bulgakova, 2023). As a result, the future will certainly be filled with cloud-based solutions for process evaluation and monitoring (Utama et al., 2023). (Al-Rasheedi et al., 2020) The main challenge is in getting operators' years of experience in specific facilities to another facility. Consider the difficulty to generalise and automate process and equipment-specific information transmission. This work introduces a new cloud-based performance monitoring system for control loops by describing the cloud architecture and implementation issues, demonstrating basic techniques and features in the updated analytics tool, and presenting significant case studies. A subsequent outline of the paper is as follows: The CLPM system has progressed from using standalone dispersed units to relying on the cloud, as shown in Section 2. In addition to reporting on the innovative cloud-based architecture, the article illustrates the key elements of the fundamental methods that carry out performance analysis and malfunction diagnoses. Section 3 provides examples of the several features included within the web interface that allow for remote system administration. The complete cloud-based system was tested in a pilot plant, which is described in Section 4, and some instances of its use are shown in Section 5. In conclusion, Section 6 reports the results with the future actions.

2. AN ONLINE CLPM (CONTROL LOOP PERFORMANCE MONITORING) SYSTEM

In recent years, prominent control engineering firms have put forth their own "conventional," or on-premises, software suite for evaluating and monitoring control loop performance, to be integrated into the local computer control systems of manufacturing facilities. The many commercial solutions have been updated in several surveys published in the literature. A review article on valve stiction contains the most up-to-date comparison. The University of Alberta's smart processes data analytics platform and its own Plant Check-Up (PCU) system are two instances of software packages developed inside academia.

2.1 Progress In PCU

The PCU tool, created at the University of Pisa's Chemical Process Control Laboratory's MATLAB environment, has been around for a while and is used for performance monitoring. The first full version of the system, which saw widespread use in industry, was shown in reference. Then, new versions with even more extensive use in large-scale settings were announced. As described in this article, a new version of the system is now being created specifically for use in the cloud. The PCU system can identify and fix malfunctions in the basic SISO proportional-integral-derivative (PID) control loops. Malfunctions create process variable oscillations, therefore identifying them is essential for proper repair. The main causes include external disturbances, poorly tuned controllers, defective valves and sensors, and neighbouring loop interactions. Multivariable control, controller return, instrument maintenance, and upstream intervention address these four top difficulties. Before now, field measurements could tell whether the program's basic version (PCU) or an improved edition (PCU+) was utilised, with the latter performing better. PID controllers may extract SISO feedback loop variables, as seen in Figure 1. The basic version (PCU) uses just the set point, control variable, and controller output from traditional industrial plants. ENI refineries have used these systems for years to monitor over 1,000 control loops and dozens of units. The latter version (PCU+) uses field bus and smart device communication protocols to measure more. These measures include valve position (VP), electro-pneumatic (I/P) converter output pressure (P), valve positioner drive signal (DS), and instrument and actuator safety and status characteristics.

In the flow rate control loops, PV corresponds to the operated variable (MV), which is usually linked to VP. The computation of TD, which stands for travel deviation, may be done with the availability of VP. This is the alteration between the authentic and intended valve place, calculated as TD = VP – OP.

Researchers have shown that by analysing various TD patterns and ranges, it is possible to identify friction and other potential issues with the valve actuator, such as air leakage, I/P faults, and general malfunctions. Consequently, this upgraded version enables a more precise evaluation of loops and actuators; it has been disseminated to members of the Computerization and Composition Italian End Users Club for testing and has already been implemented in many power plants in Italy (owned by ENEL). In the wake of Industry 4.0, this research provides a cloud-based control loop presentation monitoring and evaluation system. According to the following two sections, a new cloud-based analytics tool (PCU-Cloud) contains updated analytical modules from the on-premises versions. Multiple industrial facilities may use the unique technology by transmitting information to the internet and examining it with a single steering unit.

Figure 1. PID controllers may extract SISO feedback loop variables

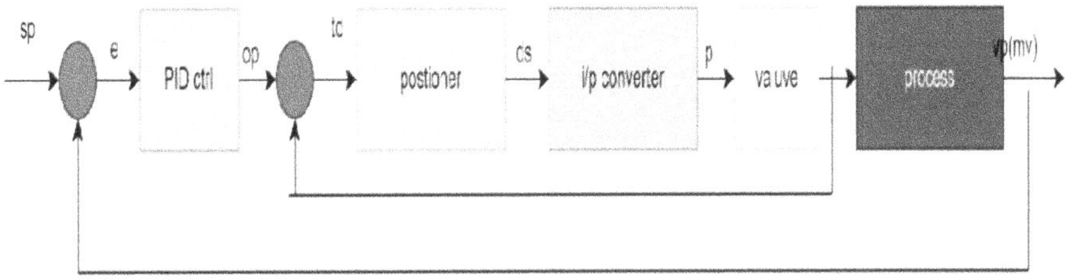

2.2 The Organisational Framework

This section describes the unique cloud-based control loop performance monitoring technology. DCS is at the bottom, PMN is in the mid, and commercial LAN is on top. This is the standard architecture of an industrial computer control system. Traditional on-premises CLPM/CLPA systems are designed with many interconnected modules that are physically placed inside the local computer control system. Each part falls into one of three broad types: interface, assistance, or application components, according to their overall usefulness. The two new on-premises CLPM systems are no different in this regard.

2.2.1 Localised Infrastructure

One design makes use of PCU as a tool for analytics (Figure 2,). At its heart, each operation is guided by a Scheduling Module (SM). Operators may build up loops, monitor the current state, and inspect and create reports from the relational SQL database using the User Module (UM). After being switched on by UM, SM tells to get OPC server data live. The SM transmits AM data files to the database after acquisition. The analytical Causes Identification Module software, which incorporates the PCU tool, surveys databases, collects input data and gives verdicts. Another on-premises system employs the improved PCU+. Figure 3 shows the same architecture in action: a Scheduler controls the processing and acquisition of data; various OPC clients retrieve data in real-time from different servers; and the Viewer app handles the analysis, plots, and verdicts. To configure a loop, one must access the database using an interface.

Figure 2. Construction of CLPM systems on-premises

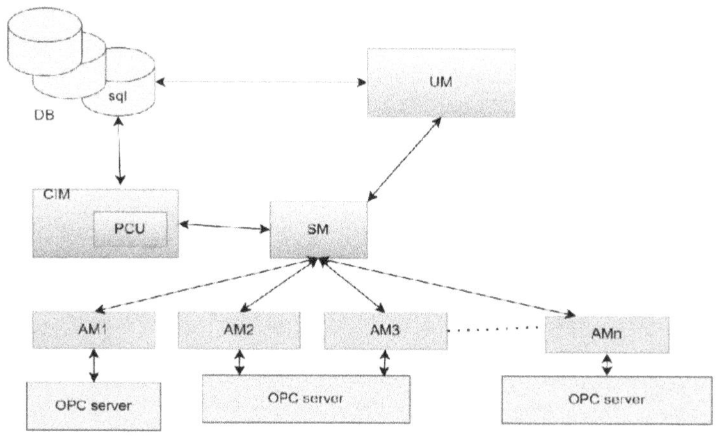

2.2.2 The System Hosted on the Cloud

As seen in Figure 4, the innovative cloud-based process monitoring solution has an entirely new architectural style. Everything is housed on a solitary distant Linux cloud server in Pisa; not a single module is deployed on-premises, meaning within the processer control systems of the several supervised manufacturing locations. The cloud database (DB) is the nerve centre of the network; it receives data over the Internet and writes and stores it. In addition to visualising results from database queries, a web interface makes it easy to control all stages of analysis, set up various loops, and more. When the quirks of industrial locations prohibit full remotization, it may be necessary to finish leftover setup processes inside local computer systems. A lightweight scheduler module activates the upgraded investigation package, which operates as a single feasible program. No matter the kind of field element— MQTT brokers in creative central cloud systems may collect messages from DCS, PLC, or simply a single smart device—sensor or actuator immediately broadcast by them (see Figure 3). Thus, as it pertains to on-premises systems conventional acquisition modules are unnecessary for this solution. Cloud computing features like MQTT and JSON are used in the system. JavaScript makes JSON data transport easier, making it more popular. MQTT, is the most popular and interoperable IoT messaging technology ISO-standard, TCP/IP-based, and secure. For limited-band lightweight machine-to-machine communications, MQTT uses a publish/subscribe system. A client/server model connects each smart field equipment to a broker. Clients who subscribe to a topic will get all communications on that topic. Any message posted to a subject reaches all subscribers, like an address. A condition monitoring system may monitor motors, compressors, and pumps for predictive and preventive maintenance by detecting and sending field variables including vibrations, rotation velocities, temperatures, and power absorption. According to Section 4, the test facility IdroLab (Figure 3) employs a PLC to collect all control loop data and send it to the cloud using a specified JSON string while protected by a local firewall.

Figure 3. Novel cloud-based field element monitoring system architecture

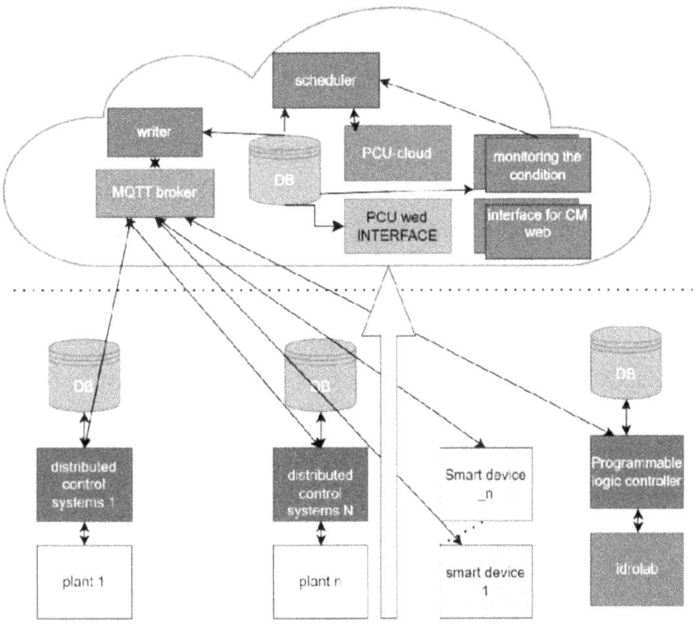

The solution's three-tiered security architecture uses a broker alias and unique usernames and passwords to identify customers, ensuring strong cybersecurity. The server supplier ensures cloud platform safety. An additional straightforward method of securing the MQTT protocol is to employ a server-side certificate throughout the Transportation Layer Security negotiation to prevent "man-in-the-middle" attacks.

. Other security methods including firewalls, ports, etc. within individual company networks are still the responsibility of industrial enterprises. Please take note that the suggested platform is industry-specific and designed to be completely scalable. For instance, there aren't any software-related problems since the basic algorithms are generic and may be simply exported to other monitoring programs. When there are many messages published into the cloud, it may be necessary to monitor numerous sites with thousands of pieces to increase the transmit band, CPU, and RAM (physical architecture limits). Lowering transmission frequency while setting local client systems saves cloud capacity. This reduces traffic and subsequent data size. Figure 3 depicts a centralised cloud structure; this section provides a quick overview of some potential future enhancements in this architecture. Using fog computing for things like data checking and filtering, alarms management, crucial and secret analytics, and building a preliminary layer near plants and smart devices, that's a good idea. To get beyond the limitations of the Internet and make the system more versatile and scalable, other communication protocols (such Web of Things using CoAP) might be used. Big data analytics may also be managed using data mining algorithms, with an eye towards predictive maintenance. Once identify any issues with their implementation or more efficient alternatives, will include these features in future industrial applications.

3. A WEBSITE APP

A Java web app interfaces with the cloud-based analytics tool (PCU-Cloud) for CLPM. The development has been carried out using Eclipse, an environmental tool, and Spring, an open-s
ce framework. The application may be managed by any interested guest reader with a reader level after they have the login and password. This section provides a concise overview of the primary features. The reader is welcome to request the user guide for more detailed information. A user-friendly, fast, and straightforward design characterises the software. On the site, find the plants that are being watched in a cascade list the parts and control loops that belong to a plant are shown after it has been chosen. The plants and sections to which a loop belongs may also be used to filter and show it. Inside a box with two coloured fields, one for the Loop Status and one for the Actuator Status, see each loop. These fields are linked to the latest tool problem. To show the current state, utilise the following colour legend: the colour red for bad, the colour yellow for alert, the colour green for good, the colour blue for manual mode, the colour white for loop not yet analysed, and the colour grey for disabled.

3.1 Execution Modes

The system supports manual and automatic execution. Actual online analysis is done at pre-set intervals in automated mode. User-defined data intervals and start and end dates/hours allow offline manual control loop analysis.

3.2 Results

Trends, cycles, and output are the several levels at which the analysis's results are shown.

3.2.1 Current Flow

The "trends" section showed loop readings over time. The primary plot illustrates the set fact and control variables, the following one displays the parametric input-output controller with planned and actual valve positions, and the third shows the travel variation or valve position error.

3.2.2 The Life Cycle

In "Cycles," polar graphs showed process and valve. Limit cycles are circular or elliptical routes that oscillate regularly and consistently around a predetermined set point on the PV diagram, which links the regulating variables to the output organizer. Sticky valves create nonlinear retro limit cycles, which have rectangular or parallelogram paths, as illustrated in the MV (OP) graph, which compares valve positions. Healthy valves do not cycle.

3.3 Output

The "output" refers to the analysis's primary findings. This is an excerpt from the PCU-Cloud output file that includes all of the detailed fields. Part 5 provides three major case studies of implementation.

3.4 Controlling the Loop

See Figure 6 for an illustration of how the web app allows for a broad configuration of analysis settings. The input records must be in.csv format, and the investigation must be executed at a certain frequency, both of which are controlled by the Frequency Execution parameter. The Time Interval specifies how long individual acquisitions will last, which is the amount of data stored in the input files. All data during the previous several minutes between two successive execution times is included in this period. To mitigate the risk of transmission interruptions that may occur during cloud storage, the maximum vacancy in data sets constrains the duration of the interval that separates consecutive data sets. The original data file is consequently partitioned into two sub-acquisitions. User privileges restrict modification of the threshold parameters for the performance indices of the various analysis methods to administrators. As stated previously, such an operation is critical and requires specialised knowledge and expertise. An online monitoring system is therefore the only viable solution for a single individual to perform the calibration of all control circuits and plants situated at any number of locations. This could be a viable alternative.

A few examples of what may be done are:

TDlim, when a 2% default operating range for the valve

- is considered acceptable for Travel Deviation;
- SATlim, the threshold for evaluating valve saturation, expressed as a proportion of the total information length;
- Oscillation detection methods' ABr, which is the percentage of ALERT status threshold values to BAD status threshold values;
- In Hagglund's ODT, the variable stands for the amplitude of oscillation used to calculate IAElim.
- cutoffs and higher bounds for the EPV and ESP indices, that are type-depend
- The system proposes controller retuning, and the user interface (UI) is the upgrading index (UI ↓).

3.5 Data Analysis

- These attributes can be utilised to estimate the complete efficiency of a segment, a plant, within a specified time. It is feasible to examine two tables that present the consolidated results.
- It is also feasible to evaluate the frequency of a combined verdict by crossing rows and columns, and the states that represent this are GOOD, MANUAL, BAD and ALERT, for the loop and actuator.
- Reasons, where many factors contributing to undesirable conduct are enumerated, including the quantity of functional actuators and loops: troubles with the controller, problems with the valves, disruptions, etc.

4. THE IDROLAB PLANT

As part of a scheme created by, the pilot plant IdroLab has recently undergone renovations to transform it into a demonstration facility for Industry 4.0 technology (see Figure 4). The plant is also meant to be used for user demonstrations and training. A new programmable logic controller (PLC) from Siemens, the Simatic S7- 1500, has been set up and programmed using the Simatic Step7 TIA Portal software to manage processes. the plant's two hydraulic circuits, one of which has an inverter-controlled centrifugal pump. Process operation and variable measurement (level, flow rate, and pressure) are made possible by an existing set of state-of-the-art actuators and sensors. As described in Section 2.3, the Profibus protocol allows smart devices to communicate with PLCs via Fieldbus, whereas the MQTT protocol allows PLCs to communicate with cloud servers. The PLC has five PID control loops pre-programmed; Table 1 details the characteristics and settings of each. While running each loop, the PLC takes a 1-second sample, adds it to its local database, and then uploads it to the server in the cloud.

A specified string is used to store the data, which is represented in JSON format using key-value notation. At each time sampling, the JSON string comprises the following information: name, moments mark, loop measures (SP, PV, OP, which are required), MV (i.e., VP), DS, and P, which are optional; controller parameter values was), control system manner (PID mode), and high and low restricts on the OP and PV, respectively; filter stable, essential stable, derivatives, and high and low restricts on OH and photovoltaic (respectively; and As said, the primary sources of malfunction may be replicated using specific physical modular components. The use of specialised software blocks is another potential source of errors.

Figure 4. IdroLab pilot plant photo

Table 1. IdroLab plant control loops

Regulator (Tag Within PCU)	Actuator Type	Type of PV	PV Variety	Device
12FK056	air-filled	compression	0–5 bar	12PT063
12FF019	air-filled	compression	0–5 bar	12PT064
12FF053	electronic	flow amount	0–5 L/s	12LP034
12FK021	air-filled	compression	0–5 bar	12PT123
12FK018	air-filled	compression	0–5 bar	12PT12

5. EXAMPLES OF USAGE

This section provides three case studies that showcase the analytics tool PCU-Cloud in action. Detailed below are the results of the IdroLab pilot plant's loop and actuator 12FK020. All major forms of malfunction have been satisfactorily examined; however, these instances do show a synthesis of certain usual behaviours.

5.1 Reward Loop

The first batch of data shows perfect behaviour, devoid of any kind of error (refer to Figure 5 A to C). The set point SP undergoes two-step alterations, the PID controller is fine-tuned, and the valve is not subjected to stiction. When comparing the loop and actuator, the PCU-Cloud correctly indicates a GOOD condition which shows no variation in PV data was detected when all six oscillation detection methods (ODT) were assessed. Since TD does not display any noticeable sticky motions and is within its acceptable range TDlim, all six of the actuator status KPIs are below their respective criteria.

Figure 5. (A to C) Case time trends: Good conduct

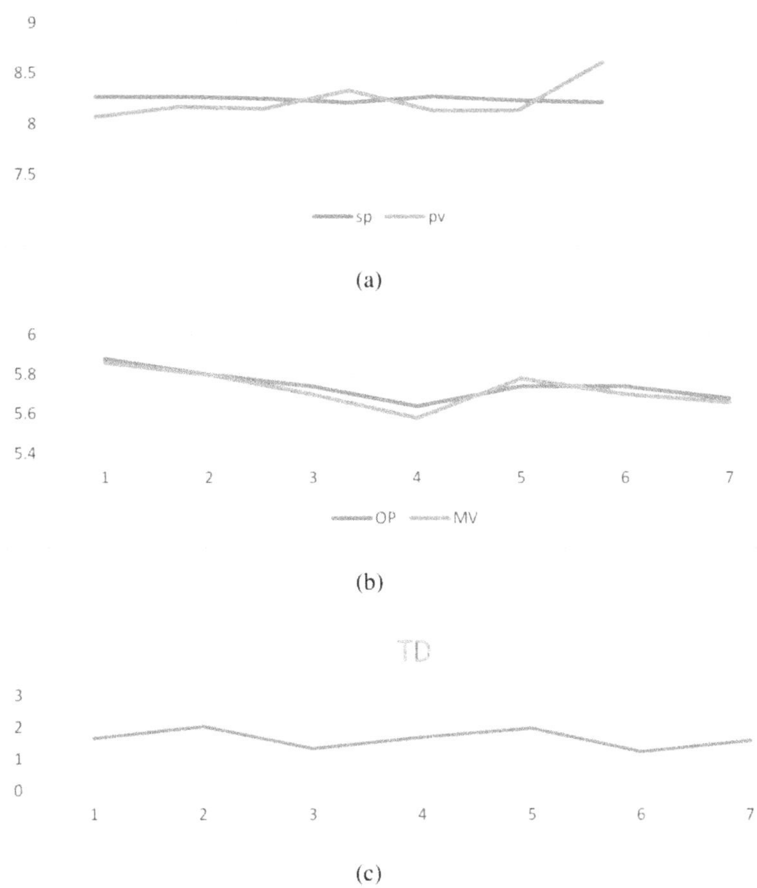

5.2 Valve Interference

The specialised software block is turned on to make valve 12FK020 imitate stiction. The parameters that follow have been defined: There is a cycle where the output signal (MV) is used as input again, with S = 4 and J = 2. Figure 6 displays typical waveforms: In contrast to OP's triangle wave shape, PV and MV's are squared. Accurate evaluation of loop and actuator status is provided by the cloud-based monitoring system. Outside of TDlim, there is a clear stick-slip pattern in travel deviation, which causes the associated KPI18 to surpass its threshold and makes stiction easy to see. Discreet fluctuations in PV statistics may also be caused by faulty valves. The different ODTs provide distinct results. Both the loop status and the averaged verdict of oscillation are ALERT.

Figure 6. Typical waveforms

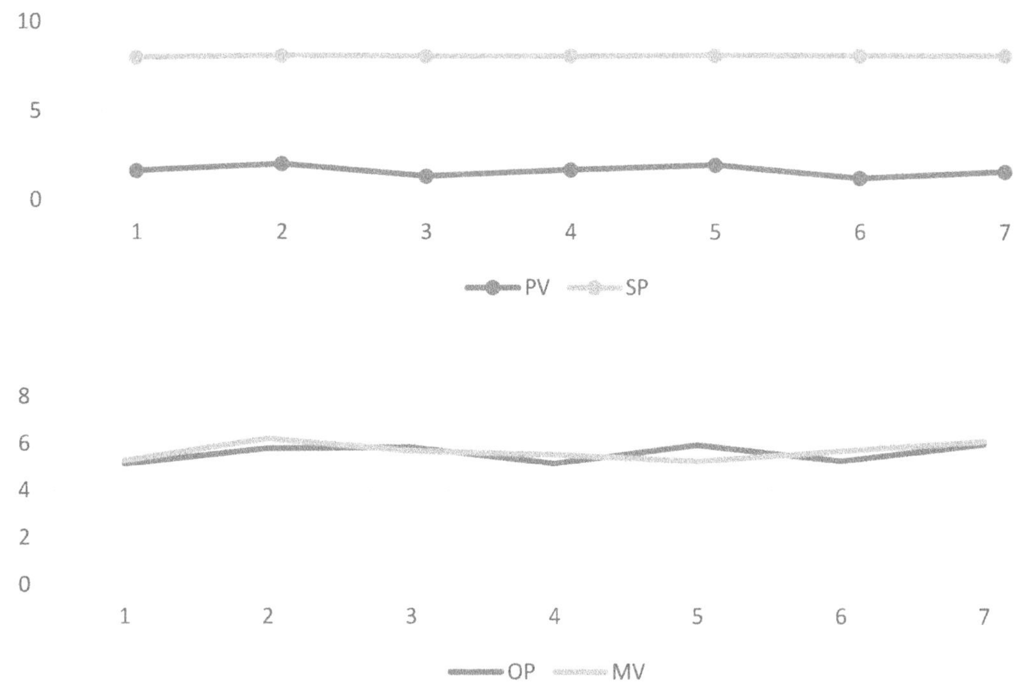

5.3 Unexpected Event

As an example, steady oscillations may be achieved by perturbing the set-point velocity of the pump inverter using software. The inputted sinusoidal disturbance has an amplitude (A) of 5% and a frequency (f) of 1/240 Hz. Its effects are most noticeable in the OP data. The PCU-Cloud correctly determines that the actuator is in a GOOD state and that the loop is in ALERT condition. Since TD is within its permissible range TDlim, all six-actuator status KPIs are below their criteria. The loop condition is assessed as ALERT in this case as well, with an average verdict of 2.5/6 for oscillation.

6. CONCLUSION

An effective cloud-based platform for monitoring and assessing process plant performance, with a focus on PID control loops, is shown by the system in this research. Global monitoring of plant performance and equipment efficiency may be readily accomplished using the same technique. For the particular use case of a pilot-scale plant, the implementation details have been shown in terms of the system's global architecture and modules inside the analytics tool (PCU-Cloud). The system may be created using affordable investments to complete the necessary automation and instrumentation, with much of it already present in the plant. It utilises technology from Industry 4.0. The savings and benefits in the requirement for a unique monitoring system will more than makeup for the increased expenses of the cloud. As a result, there will be less need to develop expertise and maintain resources in each plant. Problems with scheduling analyses and setting up the system, as well as more theoretical ones like cyber security, data traffic, and message size, will need a collaborative effort between the industrial business and the outside firm. The efficiency of cloud-based monitoring is confirmed by the results of the application of many large control loops. These loops constitute a synthesis of different kinds of malfunctions and conditions of good operation. Moving forward, the cloud-based architecture will be expanded to include more features, including condition monitoring, to oversee various plant equipment. This will help with predictive and preventative maintenance of things like motors, compressors, and pumps.

REFERENCES

Al-Rasheedi, M., Gueymard, C. A., Al-Khayat, M., Ismail, A., Lee, J. A., & Al-Duaj, H. (2020). Performance evaluation of a utility-scale dual-technology photovoltaic power plant at the Shagaya Renewable Energy Park in Kuwait. *Renewable & Sustainable Energy Reviews, 133*, 110139. doi:10.1016/j.rser.2020.110139

Ampatzidis, Y., Partel, V., & Costa, L. (2020). Agroview: Cloud-based application to process, analyze and visualize UAV-collected data for precision agriculture applications utilizing artificial intelligence. *Computers and Electronics in Agriculture, 174*, 105457. doi:10.1016/j.compag.2020.105457

Ananth, P. V. K., Muralikrishnan, K., & Chatterjee, A. (2021). Asset performance monitoring and maintenance management in cement manufacturing. In CRC Press eBooks (pp. 225–261). doi:10.1201/9781003106791-7

Bulgakova, D. (2023). The prohibited artificial intelligence practice. *Teorìâ Ta Praktika Sudovoï Ekspertizi Ì Krimìnalìstiki, 32*(3), 89–112. https://doi.org/ doi:10.32353/khrife.3.2023.06

Dwivedi, Y. K., Kshetri, N., Hughes, L., Slade, E., Jeyaraj, A., Kar, A. K., Baabdullah, A. M., Koohang, A., Raghavan, V., Ahuja, M., Albanna, H., Albashrawi, M. A., Al-Busaidi, A. S., Balakrishnan, J., Barlette, Y., Basu, S., Bose, I., Brooks, L., Buhalis, D., ... Wright, R. (2023). Opinion Paper: "So what if ChatGPT wrote it?" Multidisciplinary perspectives on opportunities, challenges and implications of generative conversational AI for research, practice and policy. *International Journal of Information Management, 71*, 102642. doi:10.1016/j.ijinfomgt.2023.102642

Hao, Y., Helo, P., & Gunasekaran, A. (2019). Cloud platforms for remote monitoring system: A comparative case study. *Production Planning and Control, 31*(2–3), 186–202. doi:10.1080/09537287.2019.1631459

Jain, J., Jain, A., Srivastava, S. K., Verma, C., Răboacă, M. S., & Illés, Z. (2022). Improved Security of E-Healthcare Images Using Hybridized Robust Zero-Watermarking and Hyper-Chaotic System along with RSA. *Mathematics*, *10*(7), 1071. doi:10.3390/math10071071

Javaid, M., Haleem, A., Singh, R. P., & Suman, R. (2021). Artificial Intelligence Applications for Industry 4.0: A Literature-Based Study. *Journal of Industrial Integration and Management*, *07*(01), 83–111. doi:10.1142/S2424862221300040

Kumar, K., & Saini, R. (2022). Data-driven internet of things and cloud computing enabled hydropower plant monitoring system. *Sustainable Computing : Informatics and Systems*, *36*, 100823. doi:10.1016/j.suscom.2022.100823

Kumar, S., Gudiseva, K., Iswarya, A., Rani, S., Prasad, K., & Sharma, Y. (2022). Automatic Music Generation System based on RNN Architecture. *2022 2nd International Conference on Technological Advancements in Computational Sciences (ICTACS)*. 10.1109/ICTACS56270.2022.9988652

Kumar, S., Singh, S., & Kumar, J. (2019). *Gender Classification Using Machine Learning with Multi-Feature Method*. doi:10.1109/CCWC.2019.8666601

Liu, Y., Yu, W., Dillon, T. S., Rahayu, W., & Li, M. (2022). Empowering IoT predictive maintenance solutions with AI: A distributed system for manufacturing Plant-Wide monitoring. *IEEE Transactions on Industrial Informatics*, *18*(2), 1345–1354. doi:10.1109/TII.2021.3091774

Livera, A., Paphitis, G., Pikolos, L., Papadopoulos, I., Montes-Romero, J., Lopez-Lorente, J., Makrides, G., Sutterlueti, J., & Georghiou, G. E. (2022). Intelligent Cloud-Based Monitoring and Control Digital Twin for photovoltaic power plants. *2022 IEEE 49th Photovoltaics Specialists Conference (PVSC)*. 10.1109/PVSC48317.2022.9938505

Matheri, A. N., Belaid, M., Ntuli, F., Nabadda, E., & Ngila, J. C. (2022). Sustainable circularity and intelligent data-driven operations and control of the wastewater treatment plant. *Physics and Chemistry of the Earth/Physics and Chemistry of the Earth. Parts a/B/C, 126*, 103152. doi:10.1016/j.pce.2022.103152

Narsimhulu, K., Ramchander, N., & Swathi, A. (2022). An AI Enabled Framework with Feature Selection for Efficient Heart Disease Prediction. *An AI-enabled Framework With Feature Selection for Efficient Heart Disease Prediction*. https://doi.org/ doi:10.1109/IC3I56241.2022.10073155

Nath, D., Kundu, I., Sharma, A., Shivhare, P., Afzal, A., Soudagar, M. E. M., & Park, S. G. (2023b). Internet of Things integrated with solar energy applications: A state-of-the-art review. *Environment, Development and Sustainability*. Advance online publication. doi:10.1007/s10668-023-03691-2

Patuzzi, F., Prando, D., Vakalis, S., Rizzo, A. M., Chiaramonti, D., Tirler, W., Mimmo, T., Gasparella, A., & Baratieri, M. (2016). Small-scale biomass gasification CHP systems: Comparative performance assessment and monitoring experiences in South Tyrol (Italy). *Energy*, *112*, 285–293. doi:10.1016/j.energy.2016.06.077

Ramesh, P., Dutta, S. J., Neog, S. S., Baishya, P., & Bezbaruah, I. (2019). Implementation of Predictive Maintenance Systems in Remotely Located Process Plants under Industry 4.0 Scenario. In Springer series in reliability engineering (pp. 293–326). doi:10.1007/978-3-030-36518-9_12

Santiteerakul, S., Sopadang, A., Tippayawong, K. Y., & Tamvimol, K. (2020). The role of smart technology in sustainable agriculture: A case study of Wangree Plant Factory. *Sustainability (Basel)*, *12*(11), 4640. doi:10.3390/su12114640

Utama, I. B. K. Y., Pamungkas, R. F., Faridh, M. M., & Jang, Y. M. (2023). Intelligent IoT platform for multiple PV plant monitoring. *Sensors (Basel)*, *23*(15), 6674. doi:10.3390/s23156674 PMID:37571458

Chapter 10
Cloud Computing Agent-Based Performance Evaluation of Resource Monitoring System in IaaS

P Anjaiah
https://orcid.org/0000-0003-2325-5893
Institute of Aeronautical Engineering, Hyderabad, India

Alok Jain
Lovely Professional University, Phagwara, India

Q. Mohammad
Hilla University College, Iraq

Ma Dhan
New Horizon College of Engineering, Bangalore, India

M. S. Madhan
I.K. Gujral Punjab Technical University, India

ABSTRACT

Applications now operating on virtual servers will be moved to another virtual or physical server, or perhaps to the same server altogether, to save power consumption in cloud data centres and maximize the use of computing resources. Optimizing resources is directly affected by knowing when to move an application to a virtual machine. Efficiently tracking the use of computer resources is the surest way to optimize performance. Therefore, to assess the efficiency of virtual machines, they require an all-inclusive intelligent monitoring agent. They provide an agent-based system for tracking resource use, namely CPU and memory, in this chapter. Virtual machine resource utilization data is collected and shown on a dashboard by the monitoring agent. The dashboard shows important performance indicators like memory and CPU use. In order to optimize resources, the cloud administrator might use the data provided by the dashboard's statistics report.

DOI: 10.4018/979-8-3693-4268-8.ch010

1. INTRODUCTION

In an Infrastructure as a Service (IaaS) cloud atmosphere, a power-based capability listening system refers to an arrangement dwelling where software powers are redistributed within the virtual instances (VMs) or hosts gossip the cloud foundation. These agents are the reason for accumulating various verifications and reports related to capital exercise, acting, and the health of the virtualized atmosphere. The power-based support listening system in IaaS cloud surroundings specifies real-opportunity acumens into the acting and utilization of money, permissive efficient administration, addition, and scalability of cloud infrastructure and uses.

1.1 Cloud Computing Outline

The concept of cloud computing facilitates instantaneous, accessible, and ubiquitous internet connection to a shared repository of configurable computer facilities that can be released and supplied without service provider involvement or administration. One potential approach to facilitate cloud computing is through the use of cloud computing (Dee et al., 2011). The three foundational service models utilised in cloud computing platforms are Internet as a Service, or IaaS, Platform to be a Service (PaaS), as well as Software as a Service, or SaaS for short (Sim, 2012). Anything may be rendered as a service through outsourcing; this is also known as everything as a Service (XaaS). this is causing skill to be a meaningful need for on-demand aids the cloud specifies a difference of duties apart from the fundamental cloud duties that are convenient (Aversa et al., 2013). The party is popular as Communication as a Service (CaaS), and it supports customers' accompanying trade ideas resolutions by way of sourcing exertions (Hafez & El-Gamel, 2016). Video conferencing, instant to foreshadow, combined use of several media convention calls, softphones, and description IP are all duties that the CaaS providers are administratively directing. (Al-Ayyoub et al., 2015) Database as a Service (DaaS) is a help that offers a by chance accommodated table to clients the one want the capability to share a table and imitate the range of capabilities of a local table (Kigo, 2016) . (Aversa et al., 2015) It is attainable to survive the miscellaneous cloud duties by way of the use of government as an aid

Monitoring for freedom, containing outside dangers, exposure detection, listening for especially to, listening for agreement accompanying Service Level Agreements (SLA), and listening for Quality influence (QoS), is composed of the aids that are provided by Monitoring as a Service (MaaS).(Meera & Swamynathan, 2013) (Jainani & Khan, 2021)An alone institution arranges to direct the possessions that are stocked in a private cloud (Ghulam & Abushammala, 2023). Community cloud aids are reserved and joined by things and arrangements that are indiscriminate the society (Kolli et al., 2023). The unification of as well individual public cloud, private cloud, or society cloud is what authorizes a mixture cloud.

1.2. Emphasis on Cloud Computing

(Manjakkal et al., 2023)(Walter et al., 2017)Monitoring the cloud may be approached from a variety of angles, including security monitoring, to achieve consistency, availability, and confidentiality of data (CIA). Resource management is the most important factor to consider while evaluating technological metrics (Tandel et al., 2020). A consumer may rent computer resources such as a processor, storage, and network via the Infrastructure as a Service (IaaS) cloud service. A data center that is hosted in the cloud is intended to include many racks of servers. Users of cloud computing services may access logical execution environments, also known as virtual machines, for the virtualization of these servers. The apps that users of the cloud run are executed on these instances of virtual machines. In terms of the actual infrastructure, they don't have any sort of direct influence over anything. In addition, this causes companies to be afraid of moving their apps and data to the cloud of the cloud. Nevertheless, the final user may be supplied with the essential faith and confidence for utilizing the cloud substructure if the appropriate security measures are implemented. A solution to this problem is provided by a system for performance tracking that can measure and report on the current condition of virtual infrastructure.

Traditional monitoring systems have a big flaw in that they only provide information related to a certain domain. Consider a networking tool that focuses only on packet monitoring. These performance tools, as a result, provide information about the utilization of resources and a clear picture of the components individually. However, they do not provide a comprehensive perspective of the cloud infrastructure as a whole. This makes it harder to analyze what is truly required for decision-making, which is ultimately problematic. Metrics are not valued by end users. In its place, consumers are on the lookout for smart reports that reveal when, where, and what kind of action is required. Customer confidence that they are paying for exactly what they use depends on a monitoring system that consolidates data from all parts of a cloud architecture and provides a report detailing the availability and use of resources.

The responsibility that comes with running a company is yet another obstacle that cloud users must overcome. A client may be eligible to obtain a service credit towards the payment of their bill if the value of their service falls below a specific threshold, as stated in the majority of the service level agreements offered by cloud technology providers. The service level agreement, on the other hand, is still struggling to achieve many of the requirements that are associated with the customer. Nevertheless, the consumer is not adequately reimbursed for the loss of data or company in a significant number of instances.

After taking a close look at the problems, it's easy to see that techno metric metrics like CPU, memory, and network bandwidth utilization should be displayed. This will allow the cloud administrator to forecast the virtual machines' tolerance capacity. Other important metrics for troubleshooting are metrics for technology metrics. Maintaining maximum application uptime, assisting with seasonal growth prediction, tracking utilization with the cost of service, and monitoring the fulfilment of service level agreements are all important from a business standpoint when it comes to monitoring systems. To ensure that cloud infrastructure is in good condition, it is necessary to have a monitoring agent.

An independent unit that is capable of carrying out certain activities on its own, a software agent is a self-sufficient apparatus. They can do this by either being defined or gaining information from their surroundings, and they can adjust to changes in their surroundings by updating their established knowledge. General purpose representatives, mobility agents, teaching agents, goal-based representatives, and utility-based representatives are the categories usually used to categorize software agents-based systems. Based on this, it is possible to comprehend that a monitoring system that is built on software agents can provide a superior solution in comparison to other platforms.

This is the structure that the rest of the paper follows. The relevant work that has been done by a variety of researchers about monitoring systems is outlined in Section II. Section III provides a definition of an architecture for a resource monitoring system that is controlled by agents. The discussion of the implementation and the outcomes takes place in part IV, and the conclusion is reached in section V.

2. RELATED WORKS

Performance evaluation and tracking have been the subject of various current and related research projects. It is suggested that a survey be conducted on cloud computing. The motives for cloud monitoring, as well as the platforms and services that are now available for cloud monitoring, have been examined. To enhance the effectiveness of cloud application management, they have created a framework known as Windows-based state monitoring (WISE). A method that only produces notifications when there is a continuous violation of the state within a certain time interval has been presented by them to cut down on the expense of the message. The purpose of the paper is to provide a self-adaptive hierarchical monitoring technique for the cloud. About the time intervals and tracking settings, the monitoring system makes it possible to configure the system on the fly. It is becoming more important to migrate virtual machines as load-balancing strategies in cloud services become more prevalent. In the few publications that are covered, the migration of virtual devices and the method for resource allocation are the topics of discussion. A proposal has been made for a system that may add or remove instances of virtual machines depending on the load that is being placed on those instances. The system does a comparison between the present load information and the threshold values that have been preset. Despite this, the whole of the effort that was indicated above concentrated on the dynamic adaptation of infrastructure. When it comes to cloud infrastructure, however, these systems may be improved further by forecasting future needs based on the monitoring metrics. Throughput, on the other hand, may be increased by analyzing the shared sources that are available across a variety of technologies. The virtual machinery that is badly impacted by resource-sharing contention has been migrated to a system that they have recommended. Throughput optimization in data stored in cloud computing centers has been the primary focus of their collaborative efforts. The expense of migration, on the other hand, is not created by their job. Analyses are performed on performance overhead. This includes downtime and overall migration time. The resource reservation mechanism is used to carry out live migration. When it comes to reserving assets in a target system for migration, however, the work they do fails to represent any policy. Information is provided on the use of brokering architecture for the allocation of virtual servers across several clouds. In addition, several investigations have been carried out by researchers on works based on agents. They provide a system for monitoring distributed resources in the infrastructure as a service cloud. Each host has a virtual machine agent that is responsible for reporting all metrics related to virtual machines, including the utilization of CPU, memory, and I/O bandwidth. A simulation is performed that uses a monitoring agent to simulate an adaptive resource allocation. About their allocation policy, the distance in geography between the cloud user and the data center is taken into consideration. The monitoring agent provides information on the state of the computing resources that are available in a data center. To minimize the amount of time that the network is delayed, requests from end users are assigned to an information center that is situated near the customer's location. An autonomous administration of virtualized data centers employing agents was the subject of their presentation. The worker agent that they envisioned would be responsible for monitoring the cloud's conditions and making its own decisions as necessary.

The monitoring services may be expanded to include the monitoring of vulnerabilities in addition to the monitoring of the computing resources. In this presentation, an autonomous agent is used to show a study of communication between virtual machines for intrusion detection. Their research results in the development of a design that performs analysis on certain components of IP packets to identify vulnerabilities. A framework for the integration of cellular resources with cloud computing is developed to facilitate real-time monitoring and control of traffic on the road. The results of their investigation demonstrate the significance of using cloud computing to record live data for purposes of testing. The conclusion that can be drawn from the examination of several research works is that monitoring is required to accurately measure performance in a cloud environment context.

3. ARCHITECTURE OF THE SYSTEM

Figure 1 depicts the architecture of an agent-based resource monitoring system that is designed for an infrastructure as a service cloud. Cloud computing is, in fact, a hybrid environment that may be dispersed. Managing and operating computer resources including servers, storage, and networks is the responsibility of a cloud data center, which is a centralized repository. Consider the scenario in which virtual computers are generated from real machines with the assistance of virtualization for a certain operation. Resource utilization of different virtual machines is the only topic covered by the design. In most cases, agents can act independently. The designated job is to be carried out by these agents. While future work will delve into autonomous agents about static, dynamic, and mobile agents, this study primarily focuses on static agents.

Figure 1. Agent-based monitoring architecture

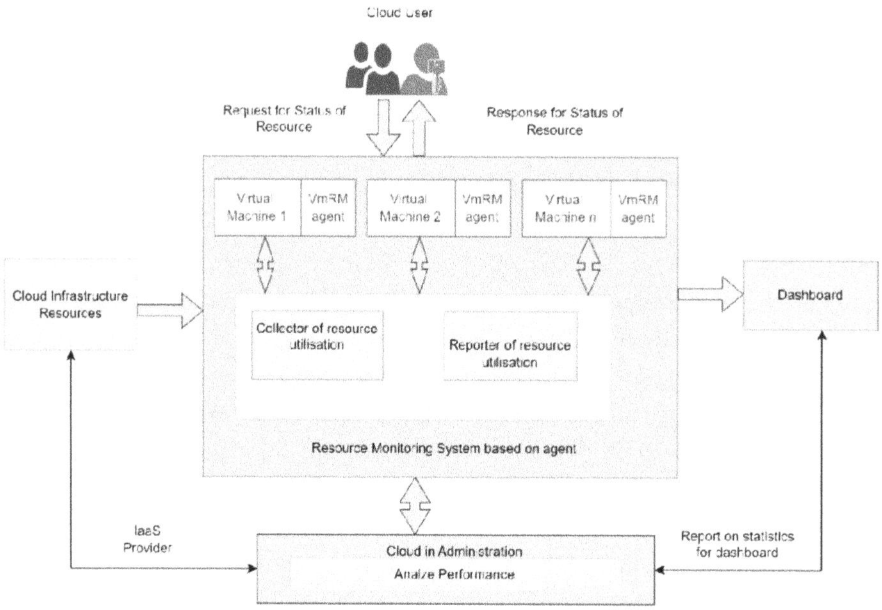

Infrastructure as a service (IaaS) cloud is intended to contain infrastructure resources that allow for the creation of virtual computers. A Virtual machine Resources Monitoring agent, also known as a VmRM agent, is installed on each virtual machine to improve the monitoring services. This VmRM agent is responsible for gathering information on the utilization of the central processing unit (CPU) and memory of each unique virtual machine that holds a variety of applications. The data on the utilization of the resources are sent to the agent-based resource monitoring system. Two components make up an agent-based resource monitoring system. To deliver the health data for each virtual machine (VM) to the resource use reporter, the resource utilization collector component gathers the information over time. To provide the cloud administrator with information on the state of virtual machines, the resource use reporter also displays this information on the dashboard. A performance analyzer module is included in the cloud administrator's toolkit. This module examines the statistics report to determine whether or not the performance is satisfactory in comparison to the service that was anticipated. In response to the cloud user's request for the resource status, the monitoring system acknowledges the request and then delivers the status as a response.

4. RESULT

A computer with a hardware configuration consisting of a central processing unit (CPU) with four 2.44 GHz processors, memory (RAM) with 3.41 GB, and a local disc with 82 GB was taken into consideration to illustrate the performance of the agent-based resource monitoring system. The executable code for the agent is written in Java. The long-term goal is to ensure efficient use of resources by deploying mobile agents for monitoring purposes. The creation of virtual machines using a CentOS image that was customized with Java & Tomcat server was accomplished with the help of Eucalyptus. Several applications that need a lot of processing power and memory, such as identifying pathways in a graph and performing factorial calculations, were implemented on top of each virtual machine to evaluate their performance. Utilization factors for the central processing unit (CPU) and memory were reviewed in Figure 2 (a to c) using an EC2 image of the small virtual machine (VM) type.

The findings make it abundantly evident that the utilization of the central processing unit (CPU) and the utilization of memory both rise as the number of virtual machines grows. Even though the utilization of the CPU is lower in comparison to the utilization of memory, the Linux cluster setup only permits the creation of two virtual machines. This is because virtual machines produce more memory than other types of machines. Ram and CPU-intensive applications continued to be executed on both the host and virtual machines via an additional web-based application. The findings of this experiment are illustrated in Figure 3. Virtual machine instances were generated utilising VMware Workstation Version 8. To evaluate the system's capability of monitoring a diverse installation, this action was taken. The hardware configuration utilised to assess the system comprised a CPU, or central processing unit, housing four 2.44 Mhz processors, 3.41 GB of memory (RAM), and an 82 GB local disc. Windows 7 was put into operation.

When compared to the amount of CPU time used, the amount of RAM used is much higher, which also restricts the creation of more virtual machines. It is possible to explore storage consolidation as a solution to this problem.

Figure 2. (a to c) Resource utilization % of Eucalyptus Compute Cloud (EC2) tiny virtual machine

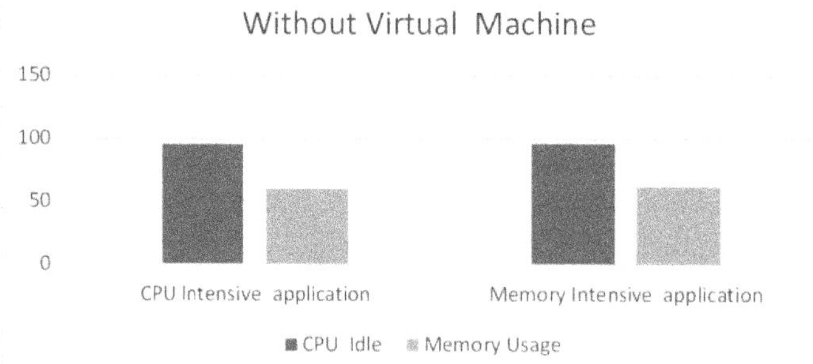

(a)

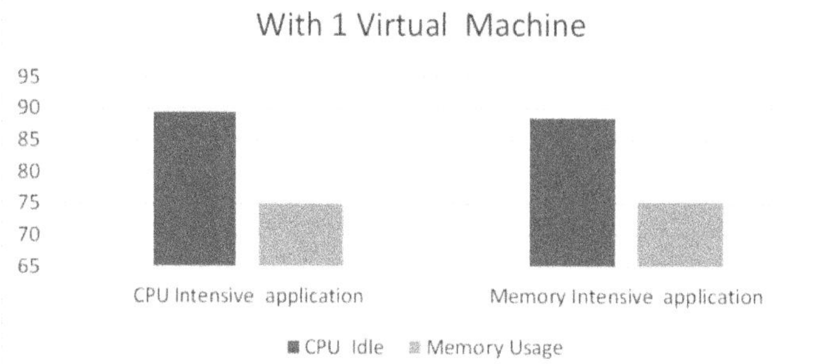

(b)

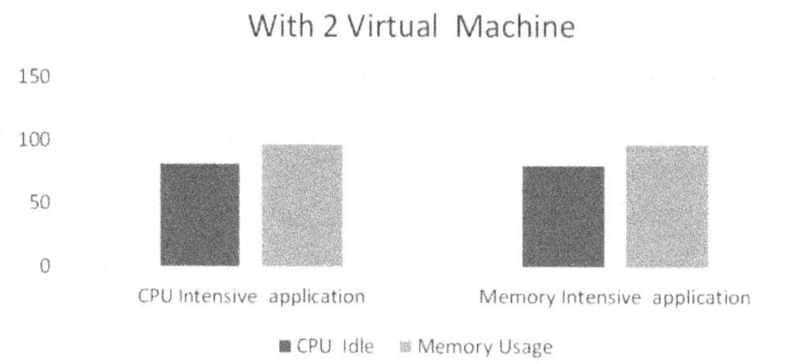

(c)

The findings make it abundantly evident that a processor with a speed of 2.50GHz for the i5 2450M CPU, 4GB of random-access memory (RAM), and a 64-bit operating system is capable of producing a maximum of three instances of virtual machines. It is possible to build a maximum of twelve virtual machines on any high-end server, such as an Intel Xeon with two processors, sixteen gigabytes of random-access memory (RAM), and a minimum of three 146 gigabytes of Raid level 5 fast discs. This is a problem that cloud researchers are still working to solve. There are a lot of physical servers in an actual data center that are hosting virtual machines. To get the most out of their CPU and memory, applications operating on those virtual machines have to be moved to a new physical server or back to the same one.

Figure 3. Workstation 8 virtual machine instances and resource utilization %

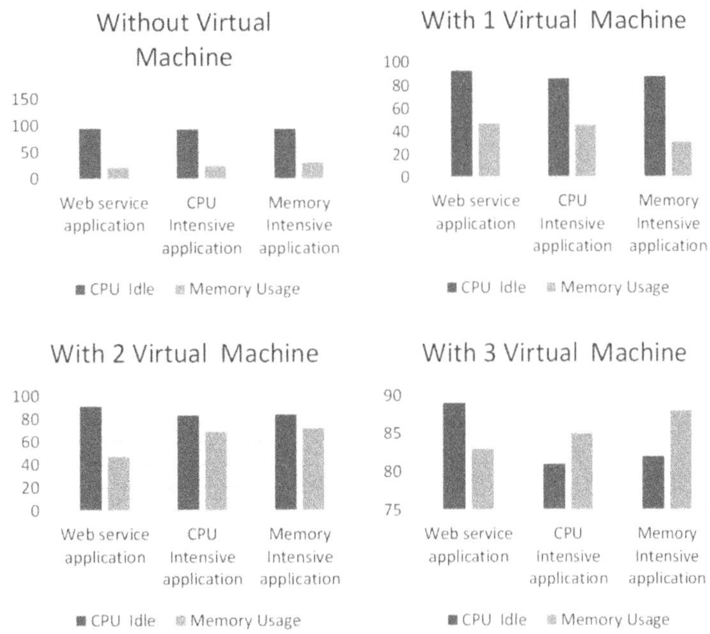

A Ganglia monitoring system is used to do an hour-long analysis of the Linux cluster utilizing virtual machine instances. The result of this analysis is a graphical representation of the total system load, memory consumption, CPU utilization, and network utilization. A single node and four processors make up the physical machine, and Fig. 4 (a) illustrates the load and processor that corresponds to each of these components. More than two virtual machines cannot be created due to the memory capacity restriction of 3.41 GB, as seen in Figure 4 (b). Network use is seen in Figure 4 (c). Near the conclusion of the graph, there is a surge in network traffic. The system is unable to generate new virtual machines due to insufficient RAM capacity, even when the CPU is used less than 26% (d). It is possible to circumvent this problem by ensuring that the monitoring system is scalable, which will be incorporated into the work that will be done in the future.

5. CONCLUSION

Cloud service providers guarantee that end users obtain services that offer a dependable and optimum business experience. Monitoring the actual utilization of resources is necessary to prevent both overestimating and underestimating the amounts of resources. Therefore, the purpose of this study is to provide an architecture for resource monitoring that makes use of an agent-based system. As a result of the fact that agents may be loaded anywhere, in a genuine cloud environment, it is simple to utilize for monitoring reasons. The researcher's goal is to develop mobile agents that can make choices automatically based on the statistics of resource utilization. This would be beneficial to both the Cloud Service and the Cloud Consumer. This would be part of the future development.

Figure 4. (a to d): CPU utilization and network utilization

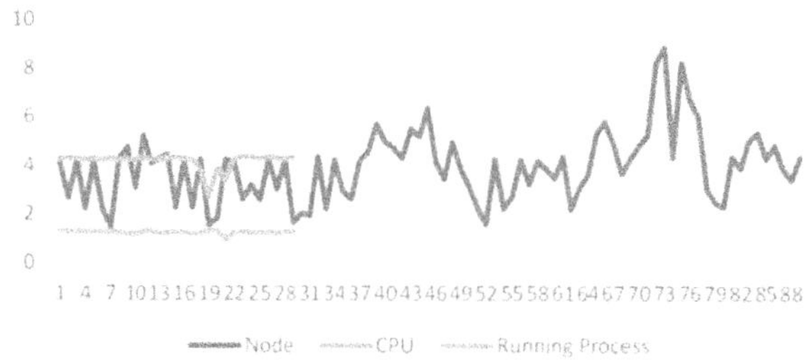

(a)

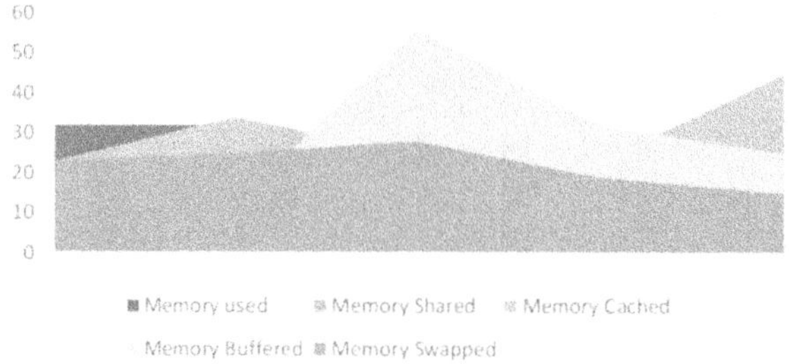

(b)

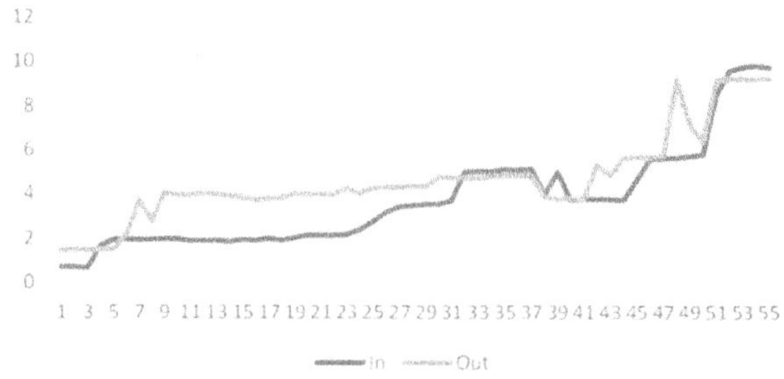

(c)

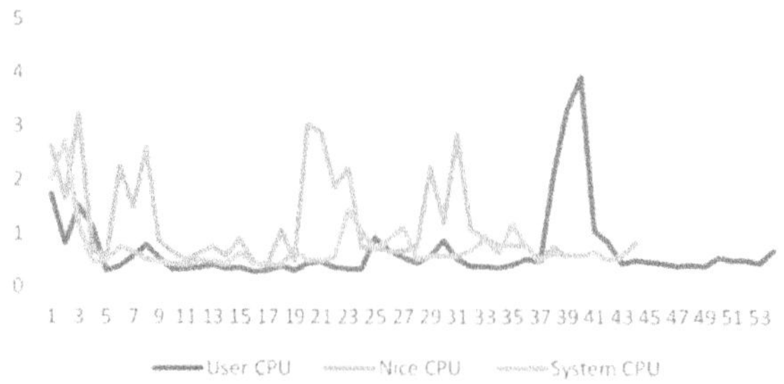

(d)

REFERENCES

Al-Ayyoub, M., Jararweh, Y., Daraghmeh, M., & Althebyan, Q. (2015). Multi-agent based dynamic resource provisioning and monitoring for cloud computing systems infrastructure. *Cluster Computing*, *18*(2), 919–932. doi:10.1007/s10586-015-0449-5

Aversa, R., Panza, N., & Tasquier, L. (2015). An Agent-Based Platform for Cloud Applications Performance Monitoring. *An Agent-based Platform for Cloud Applications Performance Monitoring.* doi:10.1109/CISIS.2015.79

Aversa, R., Tasquier, L., & Venticinque, S. (2013). *Agents Based Monitoring of Heterogeneous Cloud Infrastructures*. doi:10.1109/UIC-ATC.2013.52

Dee, D., Uppala, S., Simmons, A. J., Berrisford, P., Poli, P., Kobayashi, S., Andræ, U., Balmaseda, M., Balsamo, G., Bauer, P., Bechtold, P., Beljaars, A., Van De Berg, L., Bidlot, J., Bormann, N., Delsol, C., Dragani, R., Fuentes, M., Geer, A., ... Vitart, F. (2011). The ERA-Interim reanalysis: Configuration and performance of the data assimilation system. *Quarterly Journal of the Royal Meteorological Society*, *137*(656), 553–597. doi:10.1002/qj.828

Ghulam, S. T., & Abushammala, H. (2023). Challenges and opportunities in the management of electronic waste and its impact on human health and environment. *Sustainability (Basel)*, *15*(3), 1837. doi:10.3390/su15031837

Grzonka, D., Kołodziej, J., & Jakóbik, A. (2019). Agent–based monitoring of the task scheduling in computational clouds. *Journal of Intelligent & Fuzzy Systems*, *37*(6), 7481–7492. doi:10.3233/JIFS-179355

Hafez, M. G., & El-Gamel, M. (2016). Agent-Based Cloud Computing: A Survey. *Agent-based Cloud Computing*. *Survey (London, England)*, 285–292. Advance online publication. doi:10.1109/FiCloud.2016.48

Jainani, K., & Khan, R. (2021). *The Impact of Customer Relationship Management on Customer Satisfaction and Retention*. https://www.academia.edu/59302555/The_Impact_Of_Customer_Relationship_Management_On_Customer_Satisfaction_And_Retention_The_Mediation_Of_Service_Quality

Jung, G., & Sim, K. M. (2011). *Agent-Based Adaptive Resource Allocation on the Cloud Computing Environment*. Agent-based Adaptive Resource Allocation on the Cloud Computing Environment. doi:10.1109/ICPPW.2011.18

Kigo, N. (2016). *An agent based system for monitoring and measuring performance of public cloud applications for users*. http://erepository.uonbi.ac.ke/handle/11295/97834

Kolli, S., Ranjani, M., Kavitha, P., Daniel, D., & Chandramauli, A. (2023). *Prediction of Water Quality Parameters by IoT and Machine Learning*. doi:10.1109/ICCCI56745.2023.10128475

Manjakkal, L., Jain, A., Nandy, S., Goswami, S. K., Carvalho, J. T., Pereira, L., See, C. H., Pillai, S. C., & Hogg, R. A. (2023). Sustainable electrochemical energy storage devices using natural bast fibres. *Chemical Engineering Journal*, *465*, 142845. doi:10.1016/j.cej.2023.142845

Meera, A., & Swamynathan, S. (2013). Agent based Resource Monitoring System in IaaS Cloud Environment. *Procedia Technology*, *10*, 200–207. doi:10.1016/j.protcy.2013.12.353

Sim, K. M. (2012). Agent-Based cloud computing. *IEEE Transactions on Services Computing*, *5*(4), 564–577. doi:10.1109/TSC.2011.52

Sivakumar, S., Neeraja, B., Jamuna Rani, M., Anandaram, H., Ramya, S., Padhan, G., & Gurusamy, S. (2022). Machine learning approach on time series for PV-solar energy. *Advances in Materials Science and Engineering*, 2022.

Tandel, G. S., Balestrieri, A., Jujaray, T., Khanna, N. N., Saba, L., & Suri, J. S. (2020). Multiclass magnetic resonance imaging brain tumor classification using artificial intelligence paradigm. *Computers in Biology and Medicine*, *122*, 103804. doi:10.1016/j.compbiomed.2020.103804 PMID:32658726

Walter, A., Finger, R., Huber, R., & Buchmann, N. (2017). Smart farming is key to developing sustainable agriculture. *Proceedings of the National Academy of Sciences of the United States of America*, *114*(24), 6148–6150. doi:10.1073/pnas.1707462114 PMID:28611194

Chapter 11
Drivers and Impact of Artificial Intelligence on Student Engagement

Riya Wadhwa
IMSAR, Maharshi Dayanand University, India

Fazla Rabby
https://orcid.org/0000-0002-2683-7218
Stanford Institute of Management and Technology, Australia

Rohit Bansal
https://orcid.org/0000-0001-7072-5005
Vaish College of Engineering, India

Sheela Hundekari
MIT College of Management, MIT ADT University, India

ABSTRACT

Artificial intelligence (AI) is transforming the landscape of education by revolutionizing student engagement. Through personalized learning algorithms, AI analyzes individual student data to tailor educational content, keeping students engaged with material that suits their learning preferences and abilities. AI-driven gamification elements inject fun and motivation into the learning process, incentivizing students to progress. Analyzing engagement metrics with AI enables educators to identify struggling students early on and intervene effectively to keep them engaged. So, this research will investigate the impact of artificial intelligence on student engagement through bibliometric analysis. For the literature database, the Scopus database was examined, and the researcher got 300 research papers in total. After refining and limiting the years from 2014 to 2024, researchers selected 80 papers for the final examination. The selected papers are open-access and in the final stage. A few of the drivers of artificial intelligence on student engagement are also elaborated in this chapter.

DOI: 10.4018/979-8-3693-4268-8.ch011

INTRODUCTION

Today's higher education apprentice is progressively digitally savvy, accustomed to technology being woven into every facet of their lives. It's no wonder they hope for the same from their studying experiences. Traditional classroom models, while still crucial, are no longer the only avenue for knowledge acquisition. The growth of self-paced e-learning courses post-Covid is a testament to this shift, enabling students to grasp according to their schedules and at their own pace. AI is not just a shiny tech buzzword. It's a high-powered tool that's reshaping our approach to education, especially in the realm of self-paced learning (Fazil et al, 2024). AI authorizes educators to give students tailored learning paths, immersive experiences, and real-time feedback elements that boost engagement and facilitate deeper learning. AI brings immersion to self-paced learning. AI can modify static course materials into dynamic, interactive content. Imagine a history course where students interconnect with AI-based chatbots posing as historical figures or a literature course where AI-generated scenarios allow students to delve cavernously into a novel's context. These immersive experiences amplify engagement and can make learning more memorable and fun. AI has emerged as one of the most transformative technologies of the 21st century, revolutionizing various industries and modifying the way we live, work, and interact with machines (Parvez & Bansal, 2019). From intelligent personal assistants to self-driving cars, AI applications are rising and integrating into our daily lives, promising unparalleled efficiencies, insights, and innovations. In recent years, Artificial Intelligence (AI) has sprung up as a remarkable tool for transforming education, offering innovative solutions to enhance student engagement and learning outcomes (Ramasamy et al, 2024). By leveraging AI technologies, educators can personalize instruction, provide targeted support, and create immersive learning experiences that cater to the diverse needs of students. This article explores the various ways AI is revolutionizing student engagement in education and its potential to shape the future of learning. AI-powered adaptive learning platforms analyze students' performance data, learning styles, and interests to generate personalized learning paths. These platforms provide interactive lessons, quizzes, and activities that adapt in real-time based on student's progress, ensuring that each student receives content at their pace and level of understanding. By catering to individual learning needs, it promotes deeper engagement and fosters mastery of concepts. AI-powered educational games and simulations have revolutionized the way students engage with course material, making learning more interactive, immersive, and enjoyable. Gamification techniques, such as rewards, challenges, and progress tracking, motivate students to actively participate and persist in learning activities (Bansal, 2017). AI algorithms adapt game difficulty and content based on student's performance, ensuring an optimal level of challenge and engagement. Its technologies enable educators to create and curate high-quality educational content more efficiently and effectively. Natural language generation (NLG) algorithms can automatically generate text-based educational materials, including textbooks, quizzes, and instructional videos, based on specific learning objectives and curriculum standards. Content recommendation systems use machine learning to analyze students' preferences, learning history, and performance data to suggest relevant resources and activities. It holds tremendous promise for enhancing student engagement in education and has the potential to revolutionize student engagement in education by offering personalized learning experiences, intelligent tutoring systems, gamified learning environments, and intelligent content creation tools. By harnessing the power of AI, educators can create dynamic, interactive, and inclusive learning environments that empower students to succeed in the digital age. However, addressing ethical, privacy, and equity concerns is essential to ensure that AI-driven educational innovations benefit all students and promote lifelong learning and skill development.

Relationship Between Artificial Intelligence and Student Engagement

The relationship between Artificial Intelligence (AI) and student engagement is both reframing and innovative, transforming how education is delivered and experienced. AI makes easier personalized learning experiences by adapting content to meet individual student needs, interests, and learning speeds, thereby raising engagement through tailored instruction. It extends the boundaries of the classroom through interactive and immersive tools, such as educational games and virtual reality, making learning more appealing and enjoyable. Furthermore, AI provides immediate feedback and support, vital for maintaining student motivation and engagement by authorizing learners to understand their progress in real time. By automating administrative tasks, AI enables educators to devote more time to interactive and personalized teaching, furthermore enhancing student engagement. Moreover, AI contributes to accessibility and inclusivity, ensuring that students with diverse needs and backgrounds can fully participate in the learning process. Through advanced data analysis, AI offers insights into student engagement and performance, aiding educators in refining their teaching strategies. In essence, AI stands as a pivotal ally in education, fostering a more engaging, personalized, and efficient learning environment that can significantly benefit both students and teachers.

Drivers of Artificial Intelligence on Student Engagement

Artificial Intelligence has the potential to revolutionize student engagement in education by offering personalized learning experiences, intelligent tutoring systems, gamified learning environments, and intelligent content creation tools. By harnessing the power of AI, educators can create dynamic, interactive, and inclusive learning environments that empower students to succeed in the digital age. However, addressing ethical, privacy, and equity concerns is essential to ensure that AI-driven educational innovations benefit all students and promote lifelong learning and skill development. AI on student engagement encompasses various factors that contribute to the adoption and effectiveness of AI technologies in enhancing students' participation, motivation, and learning outcomes. Understanding these drivers provides insights into why AI is increasingly becoming a vital tool for improving student engagement in educational settings. Here are some key drivers:

1. **Personalization**: AI enables personalized learning experiences by analyzing students' learning styles, preferences, and performance data. By tailoring content, pace, and instructional methods to individual needs, AI fosters greater engagement as students receive materials that are relevant and adaptive to their unique requirements.
2. **Immediate Feedback**: AI systems provide real-time feedback on students' progress and performance, enabling them to track their understanding and address misconceptions promptly. This immediate feedback loop keeps students engaged by offering continuous support and guidance as they navigate learning activities.
3. **Adaptive Learning Paths**: AI-powered adaptive learning platforms adjust the difficulty and sequence of content based on students' mastery levels and areas of improvement. By presenting challenges that are neither too easy nor too difficult, AI keeps students appropriately challenged, promoting a state of flow and sustained engagement.

4. **Interactive and Immersive Experiences**: AI technologies such as gamification, virtual reality (VR), and augmented reality (AR) create interactive and immersive learning environments that captivate students' interest and curiosity. These engaging experiences encourage active participation and exploration, leading to deeper engagement with the material.
5. **Accessibility**: AI enhances accessibility for students with diverse needs by providing personalized accommodations and support. Through features such as text-to-speech, speech recognition, and adaptive interfaces, AI ensures that educational content is accessible to students with disabilities, thereby promoting inclusivity and engagement for all learners.
6. **Data-Driven Insights**: AI generates valuable insights from large datasets on student behavior, learning patterns, and performance metrics. Educators can leverage these insights to identify areas for improvement, tailor instruction to meet individual needs, and optimize learning experiences, leading to greater student engagement and success.
7. **Teacher Support and Efficiency**: AI assists educators by automating routine tasks, grading assessments, and providing instructional recommendations. By freeing up teachers' time and reducing administrative burdens, AI enables educators to focus more on meaningful interactions with students, fostering stronger teacher-student relationships and enhancing engagement.
8. **Continuous Improvement**: AI-driven educational technologies evolve over time through continuous iteration and improvement. By incorporating feedback from students, teachers, and educational researchers, AI systems become more effective at promoting engagement and facilitating learning outcomes, driving further adoption and utilization in educational settings.

Impact of Artificial Intelligence on Student Engagement

The impact of Artificial Intelligence (AI) on student engagement is profound and multifaceted. By harnessing AI technologies, educators can create personalized learning experiences that cater to individual students' needs, preferences, and learning styles. AI-powered adaptive learning platforms analyze students' performance data in real time, providing personalized recommendations and interventions to keep them appropriately challenged and motivated. Moreover, AI enables immediate feedback and support, addressing students' questions and misconceptions promptly, which enhances their confidence and persistence in learning tasks. Through gamification, virtual reality (VR), and augmented reality (AR), AI creates immersive and interactive learning environments that capture students' interest and foster active participation and exploration (Bachiri et al, 2023). Additionally, AI facilitates accessibility for students with diverse needs, ensuring that educational content is inclusive and engaging for all learners. Overall, AI revolutionizes student engagement by promoting personalized, interactive, and inclusive learning experiences that empower students to achieve their full potential. Many of the tools of artificial intelligence are helping them to learn in a better way. AI tools have become indispensable in the contemporary digital landscape, revolutionizing how we work, make decisions, and interact with the world around us. Their importance cannot be overstated; they enhance efficiency, accuracy, and productivity across various domains. This figure depicts the AI tools that are used by students for their learning. These 10 tools are being investigated and chart GPT is one of the tools which is used by lots of students to enhance their learning (126). The rest of the tools are also ameliorating the learning concepts and improving the performance of the students.

Figure 1. Scidirect.com

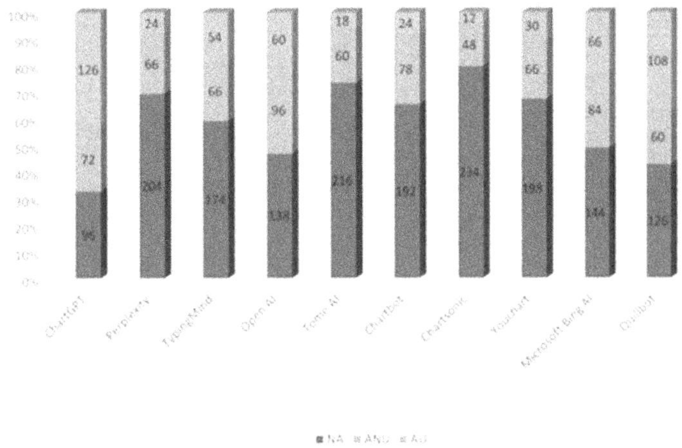

Method

The bibliometric analysis method was used in the study. This method is a content analysis method that reveals the connection of any publication, author, or cited author with other publications and authors through visual maps (Zupic & Cater, 2015). Although bibliometric studies cannot completely replace the literature reviews, they are of significance as a supplementary tool.

Data Collection

In this study, the Scopus database was used to obtain data. We tried to reach relevant studies by using Scopus's advanced search query and filtering options. Table 1 shows the codes written in the database. The search query was determined concerning previous studies (Chen et al, 2020; Song & Wang, 2020).

The documents included in this analysis contain bibliographic information obtained after a manual review of the 800 found in Scopus. 100 duplicate documents were eliminated, the names of the authors and journals were normalized, and other information like open access, the final stage, and year was limited to 2014 - 2024, which resulted in 80 documents unified in an Excel file. Biblioshiny software was used for the analysis of the data. It is a tool that analyzes all the data identified in the body of literature and identifies the main themes (Huber, 2002). The application provides a web interface for the Bibliometrix software version 3.0 (Aria & Cuccurullo, 2017) and provides the data in graphical format, if desired, to visualize the statistics. In this study, the graphs describe the information about the impact of artificial intelligence on student engagement.

Figure 2.

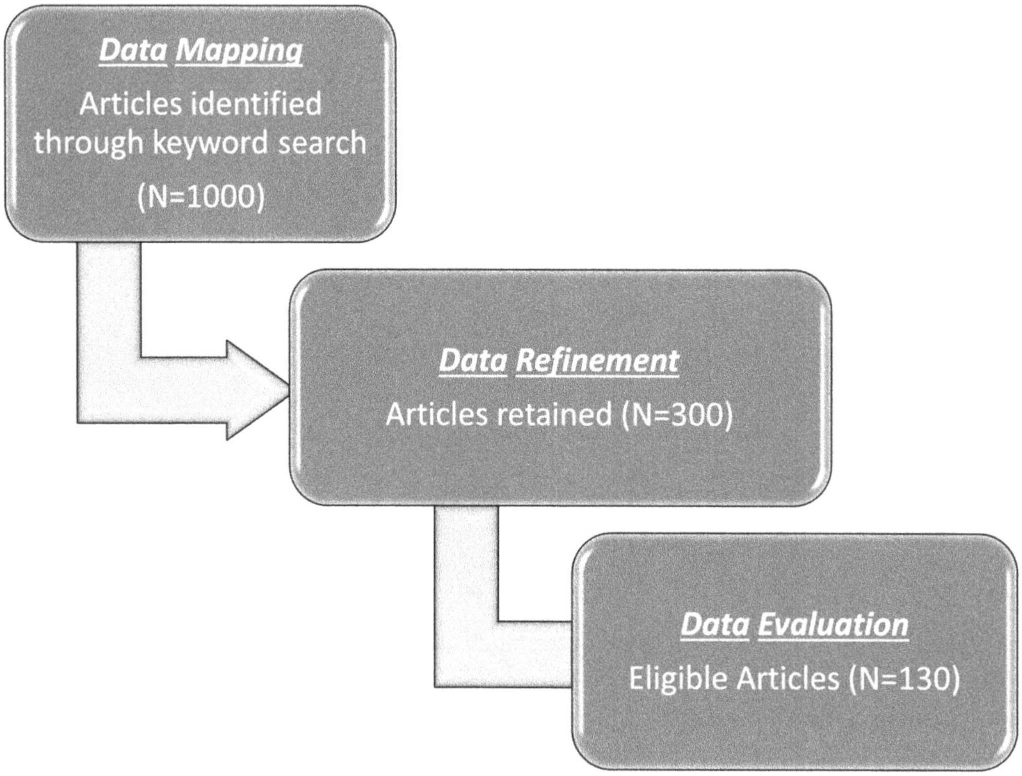

Data Analysis and Results

Three-Field Plot

The Three-Field Plot (Sankey diagram) is part of the dataset results in the form of linkages between authors, sources, and keywords. According to (Khan et al, 2023), Sankey diagrams aim to reveal and assess the flow between authors, sources, and keywords. Sankey diagrams provide a clear and intuitive way to understand complex flows of data within a system, making them valuable tools for analysis, communication, and decision-making across various fields. In this study, the correlations between the three units (the author, the author's nation, and the keywords), are depicted in Fig.3. Using the number 20 as a guide, we chose 20 different writers, 20 different nations, and 20 different keywords. The nation of the author, the writers themselves, and the top research keywords are all presented with gray relationships to illustrate the connection between one area and the one that comes after it. The extent of each rectangle in each list represents the number of items that are associated with that particular component. The middle field represents authors CR represents all the keywords and DE represents references of all the literature. from this figure, we can conclude that there is a strong flow among all the authors and their keywords and they all are helping in enhancing the impact of artificial intelligence on student engagement. As artificial intelligence is a unique strategy so, everyone is enhancing day by day and it is helping our students to enhance their learning also.

Figure 3.

Most Global Cited Documents

"Most globally cited documents" refers to academic works that have received the highest number of citations from researchers and scholars worldwide. Citation counts are often used as a measure of the impact or influence of a particular document within its field or across multiple disciplines (Maphosa & Maphosa, 2023). When a document is cited in another scholarly work, it indicates that the original work has been referenced as a source of information, data, or ideas. The more citations a document receives, the greater its perceived importance or influence within the academic community (Bansal et al, 2014). So, in this analysis, most globally cited documents were investigated and we found the top 10 documents highly cited globally by people among other 79 documents. Perkins was the best and highly cited by number 5. Rice S.'s paper got a 2 rank with a total citation of 4. Rest all papers scored low rank in number of citations.

Co-Occurrence Network

A co-occurrence network is a type of network representation used to analyze relationships or patterns of co-occurrence among elements within a dataset. These networks are particularly useful for exploring relationships in large and complex datasets where traditional statistical methods may not be sufficient. They provide a visual and analytical framework for understanding the structure and dynamics of co-occurring elements within the data. In this network, the impact of artificial intelligence on student engagement is determined and four networks are demonstrated in 4 different colors i.e. blue, green, purple, and red. Red clusters have chatbots, chatgpt, language models, computational linguistics, model, natural language processing systems, and technological development. All these are in cluster no 1 and depict the usage of lots of processing systems while using artificial intelligence. Without technology, we can enjoy the benefits. 2 clusters are represented with blue color and they include artificial intelligence, innovations, data mining, decision-making, algorithms, employment, artificial intelligence technologies, computer simulation, consumption behavior, marketing, and numerical models. All these factors narrate the effect of each other as they all are interlinked with each other. It also explains that if it is used in a better way then it can be very useful otherwise it can affect negatively. The third cluster (green) and fourth cluster (purple) explain the impact of the usage of artificial intelligence and its impact on students' lives in today's era. It also explains that it is the newer strategy to engage the students while learning and they can dive into more deeper learning. If this strategy is used in a righter way it will provide the right results and will enhance the notion of learning effectively.

Table 1.

Paper	*DOI*	*Total Citations*	*TC per Year*	*Normalized TC*
PERKINS M, 2024, J ACAD ETHICS	10.1007/s10805-023-09492-6	5	5	21.94
PERKINS M, 2024, J ACAD ETHICS-a	10.1007/s10805-023-09492-6	5	5	21.94
RICE S, 2024, TECHNOL SOC	10.1016/j.techsoc.2023.102426	4	4	17.56
REJEB A, 2024, INT J MANAGE EDUC	10.1016/j.ijme.2024.100932	2	2	8.78
POLYPORTIS A, 2024, HUM SOC SCI COMM	10.1057/s41599-023-02464-6	1	1	4.39
JIA M, 2024, HUM SOC SCI COMM	10.1057/s41599-024-02634-0	1	1	4.39
SOBOLEWSKI KM, 2024, EVAL PROGRAM PLANN	10.1016/j.evalprogplan.2024.102419	0	0	0
DARICI S, 2024, TECHNOL FORECAST SOC CHANGE	10.1016/j.techfore.2024.123327	0	0	0
HUANG Y, 2024, HUM SOC SCI COMM	10.1057/s41599-024-02869-x	0	0	0
URZEDO D, 2024, HUM SOC SCI COMM	10.1057/s41599-024-02720-3	0	0	0

Figure 4.

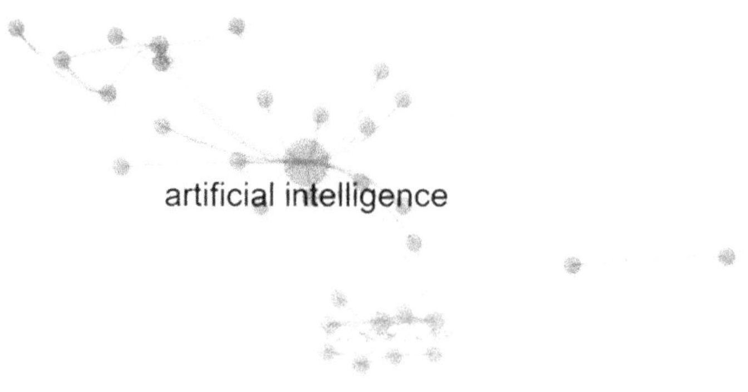

CONCLUSION

The impact of artificial intelligence (AI) on student engagement is both profound and multifaceted, signaling a seismic shift in the educational landscape. By leveraging AI, educators can now provide a more personalized, interactive, and inclusive learning experience, directly addressing the diverse needs and interests of students. Personalized learning paths created by AI algorithms cater to the unique learning pace and style of each student, making educational content more relevant and engaging. Moreover, AI-driven tools such as chatbots and virtual tutors offer round-the-clock support and feedback, ensuring students remain engaged and motivated even outside traditional classroom settings. These technologies not only facilitate a deeper interaction with the subject matter but also encourage independence and self-directed learning. Additionally, AI has the potential to democratize education, making high-quality learning experiences accessible to students regardless of geographical location or socioeconomic status. By breaking down barriers to education, AI fosters a more equitable and engaging learning environment for all. However, the true impact of AI on student engagement hinges on its thoughtful integration into educational strategies, where it complements rather than replaces the invaluable human elements of teaching and mentorship. Through bibliometric analysis, we can also conclude that artificial intelligence is coming up with outstanding results and enhancing students' learning. They provide lots of tools that can help in understanding complex projects more easily.

REFERENCES

Aria, M., & Cuccurullo, C. (2017). Bibliometrix : An R-tool for comprehensive science mapping analysis. *Journal of Informetrics*, *11*(4), 959–975. doi:10.1016/j.joi.2017.08.007

Bachiri, Y. A., Mouncif, H., & Bouikhalene, B. (2023). Artificial Intelligence Empowers Gamification: Optimizing Student Engagement and Learning Outcomes in E-learning and MOOCs. *International Journal of Engineering Pedagogy*, *13*(8), 4–19. doi:10.3991/ijep.v13i8.40853

Bansal, R. (2017). Challenges and future trends in commerce education in India. *International Journal of Techno-Management Research*, *5*(3), 25–35.

Bansal, R., Dadhich, V., & Ahmad, N. (2014). Indian commodity market–A performance review. *International Journal of Management and Commerce*, *1*(5), 19–34.

Chen, X., Xie, H., & Hwang, G.-J. (2020). A multi-perspective study on Artificial Intelligence in Education: Grants, conferences, journals, software tools, institutions, and researchers. *Computers and Education: Artificial Intelligence*, *1*, 100005. doi:10.1016/j.caeai.2020.100005

Fazil, A. W., Hakimi, M., Shahidzay, A. K., & Hasas, A. (2024). Exploring the Broad Impact of AI Technologies on Student Engagement and Academic Performance in University Settings in Afghanistan. *RIGGS: Journal of Artificial Intelligence and Digital Business*, *2*(2), 56–63. doi:10.31004/riggs.v2i2.268

Huang, A. Y., Lu, O. H., & Yang, S. J. (2023). Effects of artificial Intelligence–Enabled personalized recommendations on learners' learning engagement, motivation, and outcomes in a flipped classroom. *Computers & Education*, *194*, 104684. doi:10.1016/j.compedu.2022.104684

Khan, H. M., Ahmad, S., Javed, R., & Nasir, N. (2023). The significance of Artificial Intelligence in business and accounting: A Bibliometric analysis. *Pakistan Journal of Humanities and Social Sciences*, *11*(2). Advance online publication. doi:10.52131/pjhss.2023.1102.0417

Maphosa, V., & Maphosa, M. (2023). Artificial intelligence in higher education: A bibliometric analysis and topic modeling approach. *Applied Artificial Intelligence*, *37*(1), 2261730. doi:10.1080/08839514.2023.2261730

Pervez, A., & Bansal, R. (2019). Capital adequacy, risk and bank performance: Evidence from India. *Journal of Xi'an University of Architecture & Technology*, *XI*(XII), 199–212.

Ramasamy, V., Singsen, D., & Walia, G. S. (2024). Fostering Student Engagement and Success in STEM Education: An AI-Driven Exploration of High Impact Practices from Cross-Disciplinary General Education Courses. *Journal of Engineering Education Transformations, 37*(2).

Song, P., & Wang, X. (2020). A bibliometric analysis of worldwide educational artificial intelligence research development in recent twenty years. *Asia Pacific Education Review*, *21*(3), 473–486. doi:10.1007/s12564-020-09640-2

Chapter 12
Engaging Online Classes Through Gamification:
Leveraging Innovative Tools and Technologies

S. C. Vetrivel
https://orcid.org/0000-0003-3050-8211
Kongu Engineering College, India

K. C. Sowmiya
Sri Vasavi College, India

T. Gomathi
Gnanamani College of Technology, India

V. P. Arun
Ujjivan Small Finance Bank, India

ABSTRACT

With the advent of online education, the traditional classroom setting has undergone a significant transformation. However, one of the key challenges faced by educators in the online environment is maintaining student engagement and active participation. In this chapter, the authors explore the topic of innovative tools and technologies that have emerged to address the issue of boredom and enhance engagement in online classes. Online learning environments often suffer from a lack of face-to-face interaction, leading to diminished student engagement and increased boredom. However, educators and researchers have recognized the need to bridge this gap and have developed various tools and technologies to foster participation and interactivity. As traditional education transitions into digital platforms, the need for effective and engaging online teaching methodologies becomes paramount. This chapter explores the integration of gamification principles, innovative tools, and technologies to enhance the engagement and learning experience in online classes.

DOI: 10.4018/979-8-3693-4268-8.ch012

1. INTRODUCTION

The rapid advancement of technology has transformed the traditional classroom into a digital environment, leading to the rise of online classes. However, one challenge that educators often face in this new landscape is how to keep students engaged and motivated in a virtual setting. The study discusses the use of gamification, along with innovative tools and technologies, as a means to overcome this challenge and foster active participation in online classes.

1.1 Background

The background of the study stems from the growing significance of online education, which, while offering flexibility, often struggles to maintain student interest and participation. Recognizing the potential of gamification, the authors embark on a journey to explore how integrating game elements and mechanics into the online learning environment can transform it into a more interactive and enjoyable experience. It draws attention to the vast array of innovative tools and technologies available for gamifying educational content, highlighting their potential impact on motivating students, fostering collaboration, and ultimately improving learning outcomes, (Alsawaier,R S.,2018). As the traditional classroom paradigm undergoes a digital transformation, the chapter aims to provide educators and instructional designers with valuable insights into leveraging gamification as a powerful tool for creating dynamic and engaging online learning environments.

1.2 Purpose of the Study

It is to explore and demonstrate the effectiveness of integrating gamification techniques into the realm of online education. The overarching goal is to address the prevalent challenge of student engagement in virtual learning environments. By leveraging innovative tools and technologies, the study aims to investigate how the incorporation of game elements, such as point systems, rewards, and interactive simulations, can enhance the overall learning experience in online classes (Bai,S et al., 2020). The researchers seek to identify the impact of gamification on student motivation, participation, and knowledge retention. Additionally, the study may delve into the practical aspects of implementing gamification strategies within online educational platforms, considering the preferences and learning styles of diverse student populations (Brigham,et al., 2015). Through a comprehensive examination of the potential benefits and challenges associated with gamifying online classes, the chapter contributes valuable insights to the field of education, offering educators and instructional designers evidence-based recommendations for creating more engaging and effective virtual learning environments.

1.3 Significance of Gamification in Online Education

The significance of gamification in online education, lies in its ability to transform the learning experience, making it more engaging, motivating, and effective for a diverse range of learners. The following are the key points that highlight the significance of integrating gamification into online education:

- **Enhanced Student Engagement:** Gamification introduces elements of play, competition, and rewards into the learning process, making it more engaging for students. This can lead to increased participation, motivation, and overall interest in the educational content.
- **Motivation and Goal Achievement:** By incorporating game-like features such as challenges, levels, and rewards, gamification provides students with clear goals and objectives. This structured approach motivates learners to progress through the course, complete assignments, and achieve learning outcomes.
- **Promoting Active Learning:** Gamification encourages active participation and hands-on learning [2]. Interactive elements, simulations, and scenarios can simulate real-world situations, allowing students to apply theoretical knowledge in practical contexts, fostering a deeper understanding of the subject matter.
- **Sense of Accomplishment:** As students achieve milestones, earn badges, or progress through levels, they experience a sense of accomplishment. This positive reinforcement can boost self-esteem and confidence, creating a positive learning environment.
- **Social Interaction and Collaboration:** Gamification often includes social features such as leaderboards, team challenges, and multiplayer options. This fosters a sense of community and encourages collaboration among students, promoting peer-to-peer learning and knowledge sharing.
- **Adaptability and Personalization:** Gamified platforms can adapt to individual learning styles and pace. By providing personalized feedback and allowing learners to choose their path through the material, gamification caters to diverse learning preferences and speeds.
- **Real-time Feedback and Assessment:** Gamification allows for instant feedback on students' performance. This immediate feedback loop helps learners understand their strengths and weaknesses, enabling them to adjust their approach to learning and improving their skills in real time.
- **Long-term Retention of Knowledge:** The immersive and memorable nature of gamified experiences can enhance the retention of information. Students are more likely to remember concepts when they are presented in a context that is enjoyable and memorable.
- **Technology Integration:** Gamification often leverages innovative tools and technologies, aligning with the modern, tech-savvy nature of online education. This integration not only makes learning more enjoyable but also prepares students for a tech-driven future.
- **Addressing Challenges in Online Learning:**Online education may face challenges such as student isolation, lack of motivation, and distractions. Gamification addresses these challenges by creating a dynamic and interactive learning environment that keeps students engaged and focused.

2. THEORETICAL FRAMEWORK

The theoretical framework for gamification in online learning is rooted in principles borrowed from various fields, including education, psychology, and game design. At its core, gamification leverages the motivational and engagement aspects of games to enhance the learning experience. Self-Determination Theory (SDT) is a fundamental psychological framework often applied in this context, emphasizing the importance of autonomy, competence, and relatedness as key motivators (Brull et al.,2016). According to SDT, learners are more likely to be intrinsically motivated when they feel a sense of control over their learning, perceive their competence improving, and experience a connection with others in the learning environment. Additionally, Behaviorism contributes to the understanding of how rewards and feedback mechanisms can shape and reinforce desired behaviors, promoting a positive learning cycle. The concept of Flow, derived from positive psychology, suggests that learners are most engaged when the difficulty of a task matches their skill level. In the context of gamification, this implies designing learning activities that challenge and reward students at an optimal level, keeping them in a state of focused immersion. Furthermore, elements from game design, such as points, badges, leader boards, and narrative structures, are integrated to provide extrinsic motivators and enhance the overall user experience. This theoretical framework guides the thoughtful application of gamification principles to create an effective and enjoyable online learning environment that promotes sustained engagement and meaningful learning outcomes.

2.1 Gamification Principles

Gamification involves incorporating game elements and mechanics into non-game contexts to motivate and engage participants. The chapter likely discusses several key gamification principles, such as clear goals and objectives, meaningful rewards, and a sense of progression (Chen et al., 2012) (Dicheva et al., 2017). Clear goals and objectives in online classes provide students with a sense of purpose and direction, while meaningful rewards, such as badges or points, can reinforce positive behaviors and achievements. The concept of progression involves designing the learning experience in a way that allows students to advance and see their improvement over time. Additionally, the chapter may look into the importance of feedback and competition as motivational tools in gamified online classes. The use of innovative tools and technologies is likely explored to implement these gamification principles effectively, ensuring a dynamic and engaging online learning environment for students.

2.2 Application of Gamification in Online Learning

Gamification in online learning has emerged as a powerful tool to enhance engagement, motivation, and learning outcomes. By integrating game elements and mechanics into educational experiences, educators can create a more interactive and immersive learning environment. One significant application of gamification is the introduction of reward systems, such as badges, points, or levels, which provide immediate feedback and recognition for students' achievements. This not only fosters a sense of accomplishment but also encourages healthy competition and a desire for continuous improvement. Progress tracking is another key feature, allowing learners to visualize their advancement and identify areas for improvement. Gamification also promotes collaborative learning through multiplayer scenarios and team-based challenges, fostering communication and teamwork skills. Furthermore, the narrative aspect of gamification can make learning content more relatable and enjoyable, transforming traditionally dry subjects into engaging stories. By tapping into the intrinsic motivation that games naturally evoke, gamification in online learning creates a dynamic and enjoyable educational experience that ultimately enhances knowledge retention and student success.

2.3 Pedagogical Considerations

Gamification in online learning involves the integration of game elements and principles into educational activities to enhance engagement, motivation, and learning outcomes. Several pedagogical considerations must be taken into account to ensure the effective implementation of gamification in the online learning environment (Dicheva et al., 2015). Firstly, alignment with learning objectives is crucial. Game elements should be carefully chosen and designed to support the desired educational outcomes rather than being purely for entertainment. Secondly, the concept of flow, as proposed by psychologist Mihaly Csikszentmihalyi, is essential. Learning activities should be challenging yet achievable, maintaining a balance that keeps learners immersed and focused. Additionally, incorporating narrative and storytelling elements in gamified content can create a more meaningful and engaging learning experience, fostering a connection between the learner and the educational material (Douglas et al., 2006). It is also important to consider the diverse needs and preferences of learners, ensuring that gamification does not exclude or disadvantage any particular group. Moreover, providing timely and constructive feedback within the game framework can enhance the learning process by reinforcing positive behaviors and guiding corrective actions. Finally, continuous assessment and refinement of the gamified elements based on learner feedback and performance data contribute to the ongoing improvement of the online learning experience. Overall, effective pedagogical considerations in gamification aim to create a supportive, challenging, and enjoyable learning environment that promotes active participation and knowledge retention.

3. INNOVATIVE TOOLS FOR GAMIFICATION

Gamification in online learning involves incorporating game elements and principles to engage learners and enhance their learning experience. When implementing gamification in online learning, it's essential to align the game elements with the learning objectives and ensure that the activities enhance the educational experience rather than being mere distractions. Following are some innovative tools and strategies for gamification in online learning:

- **Kahoot!:** Kahoot! is a popular game-based learning platform that allows educators to create quizzes, surveys, and discussions. It promotes active participation and friendly competition among learners.
- **Quizizz:** Similar to Kahoot!, Quizizz is an interactive quiz platform that engages students with gamified elements. It offers features like memes, leaderboards, and avatars to make learning more enjoyable.
- **Classcraft:** Classcraft is a role-playing game (RPG) platform designed for education. It allows teachers to create a gamified classroom environment where students can earn points, level up, and collaborate on quests.
- **Duolingo:** Duolingo gamifies language learning by turning lessons into a game format. Learners earn points for completing lessons and can compete with friends, adding a competitive and fun element to language acquisition.
- **Breakout EDU:** Breakout EDU brings the escape room experience into the classroom. Educators can create digital or physical breakout challenges, requiring students to solve puzzles and work collaboratively to "escape."
- **Minecraft: Education Edition:** Minecraft is a sandbox game that has been adapted for educational purposes. It allows students to explore, create, and collaborate in a virtual environment, fostering creativity and problem-solving skills.

- **Edpuzzle:** Edpuzzle enables teachers to create interactive video lessons. Gamify the learning experience by embedding questions, quizzes, and discussions within videos, encouraging active participation and understanding.
- **BadgeOS:** BadgeOS is a WordPress plugin that enables the creation and management of badges and achievements. It's a great tool for recognizing and rewarding students' accomplishments, adding a gamified incentive to their learning journey.
- **Socrative:** Socrative is a classroom response system that can be used for quizzes, assessments, and quick polls. It provides real-time feedback and allows educators to gamify the learning process with competitive quizzes and games.
- **Escape Room Platforms:** There are various online platforms that allow educators to create virtual escape rooms, such as Breakout Games and Classtime. These platforms enable teachers to design challenging puzzles and scenarios for students to solve collaboratively.
- **PlayPosit:** Formerly known as EduCanon, PlayPosit allows educators to create interactive video lessons with quizzes and discussions. It engages learners by gamifying the video-watching experience.
- **Flipgrid:** Flipgrid is a video discussion platform that can be gamified by incorporating challenges and competitions. Students can respond to prompts with short videos, and educators can award points and badges for participation.

3.1 Virtual Reality (VR) Applications

Virtual Reality (VR) can be a powerful tool for gamification in online learning, enhancing engagement and providing immersive educational experiences. When incorporating VR into online learning, it's important to consider accessibility, technical requirements, and the learning objectives (Driskell et al., 1984) (Felszeghy et al., 2019). Additionally, regular assessment and feedback from learners can help refine and improve the gamification elements for better educational outcomes. Here are some applications of VR for gamification in online learning:

- **Simulated Environments:** Create virtual worlds that simulate real-life scenarios relevant to the learning content. For example, medical students could practice surgical procedures, or history students could explore ancient civilizations.
- **Language Learning:** VR can immerse language learners in virtual environments where they can interact with native speakers or navigate scenarios that require language skills. This makes language learning more practical and engaging.
- **Historical Reconstructions:** Take students back in time by recreating historical events or locations in VR. This allows learners to explore and understand history in a more interactive and memorable way.
- **STEM Education:** Develop VR simulations for science, technology, engineering, and mathematics (STEM) subjects. Students can experiment with virtual labs, explore physics concepts, or even visit microscopic worlds.
- **Soft Skills Training:** Use VR to simulate real-world situations that require soft skills such as teamwork, communication, and problem-solving. This is especially valuable for business and leadership training.

- **Gamified Assessments:** Turn assessments into interactive games within the VR environment. This can make the evaluation process more engaging and enjoyable for learners.
- **Virtual Field Trips:** Enable students to take virtual field trips to places they might not otherwise have access to. This could include exploring the depths of the ocean, touring famous landmarks, or visiting cultural institutions.
- **Collaborative Learning Spaces:** Create virtual classrooms or collaborative spaces where students can interact with each other and with the learning material. This fosters a sense of community and enhances the social aspect of learning.
- **Storytelling and Narrative-driven Learning:** Develop educational narratives or scenarios within VR where learners become active participants in the story. This can make learning more engaging and memorable.
- **Reward Systems and Progress Tracking:** Implement gamified elements such as point systems, badges, and rewards to motivate learners. Progress can be tracked visually within the VR environment, providing instant feedback and encouragement.
- **Problem-solving Games:** Design VR games that require critical thinking and problem-solving skills. This approach can be applied to various subjects, encouraging learners to apply their knowledge in practical scenarios.
- **Virtual Internships and Job Simulations:** Provide students with virtual internships or job simulations to gain hands-on experience in their field of study. This can be particularly beneficial for vocational and professional development.

3.2 Augmented Reality (AR) in Online Education

Augmented Reality (AR) is revolutionizing online education by seamlessly integrating digital content and information into the real-world learning environment, enhancing the overall educational experience. In the context of online education, AR overlays computer-generated perceptual information onto the physical world, providing students with interactive and immersive learning opportunities. Through the use of AR devices such as smartphones, tablets, or AR glasses, students can access a wealth of information, simulations, and interactive 3D models that bring abstract concepts to life (Figueroa-Flores et al., 2016). For instance, in science and anatomy courses, AR can enable students to explore virtual dissections or manipulate 3D models of complex biological structures, fostering a deeper understanding of the subject matter. Additionally, AR facilitates collaborative learning experiences, allowing students to interact with each other in real time, despite physical distances (Garett et al., 2019). This technology also enables educators to create engaging and dynamic content, turning traditional textbooks into interactive multimedia experiences. As online education continues to evolve, the integration of AR not only enhances comprehension and retention but also cultivates a more engaging and participatory learning environment, bridging the gap between the virtual and physical realms of education.

3.3 Gamified Learning Management Systems (LMS)

Gamified Learning Management Systems (LMS) represent a cutting-edge approach to education technology by integrating game elements into traditional learning environments. These systems leverage game design principles to enhance engagement, motivation, and knowledge retention among learners. Incorporating elements such as points, badges, levels, and leaderboards, gamified LMS platforms transform the learning experience into an interactive and competitive adventure. Learners are rewarded for completing tasks, achieving milestones, and mastering content, creating a sense of accomplishment and healthy competition. The gamification of LMS not only fosters a more enjoyable learning process but also encourages a sense of community as learners can collaborate or compete with peers. Furthermore, real-time feedback and progress tracking provide instant reinforcement and enable educators to identify areas where additional support may be needed (González et al.,2016). Gamified LMS systems can be particularly effective in corporate training, academic settings, and professional development programs, making learning more dynamic, engaging, and effective.

3.4 Case Studies on Successful Implementations

These case studies demonstrate how gamification can be effectively implemented across various domains to enhance user engagement, motivation, and the overall user experience.

- **Duolingo: Language Learning Gamification:** Duolingo is a language learning platform that incorporates gamification to make the learning process engaging and fun. Duolingo uses a point system, levels, and rewards to motivate users to learn new languages. Users earn points for completing lessons and maintaining streaks. The platform also includes a competitive element where users can compete with friends. The use of game-like elements has contributed to Duolingo's popularity and effectiveness in language education.
- **Nike+: Gamified Fitness Tracking**:Nike+ is a gamified fitness tracking system that encourages users to stay active and achieve their fitness goals. Nike+ allows users to track their runs, set goals, and compete with friends. It uses achievements, leaderboards, and challenges to keep users motivated. The gamification elements create a sense of competition and accomplishment, turning regular fitness activities into a more engaging and enjoyable experience.
- **Foldit: Citizen Science and Protein Folding**: Foldit is an online puzzle video game that enables players to contribute to scientific research on protein folding. University of Washington researchers developed Foldit to crowdsource solutions to complex scientific problems. Players manipulate protein structures to find optimal configurations, contributing valuable data for scientific research. The gamified approach has led to significant breakthroughs in understanding protein folding, showcasing the potential of gamification in citizen science.
- **LinkedIn: Professional Networking Gamification:** LinkedIn, a professional networking platform, introduced gamification elements to encourage user engagement and interaction. LinkedIn uses a profile completion progress bar, endorsements, and badges to motivate users to enhance their profiles and connect with others. The platform also incorporates notifications and personalized recommendations to keep users engaged. The gamified features contribute to increased user activity and a more dynamic professional networking experience.
- **Foldscope: Gamifying Science Education**: Foldscope is an affordable, chapter microscope designed to make science more accessible, particularly in educational settings. Foldscope incorporates gamification elements to engage students in the learning process. Teachers use challenges, competitions, and collaborative projects to make microscopy and scientific exploration more interactive and enjoyable. The gamified approach has been successful in fostering curiosity and interest in science among students.

4. TECHNOLOGICAL INTEGRATION IN GAMIFIED LEARNING

Technological integration in gamified learning represents a dynamic and innovative approach to education that leverages the power of digital tools and gaming elements to enhance the learning experience. In this context, technology serves as a facilitator for creating immersive, interactive, and engaging educational environments. Gamified learning platforms often incorporate elements such as points, badges, levels, and leaderboards to motivate and reward students, fostering a sense of competition and achievement. These platforms may also utilize virtual reality (VR), augmented reality (AR), and simulations to provide realistic and experiential learning opportunities. The integration of technology enables personalized learning experiences tailored to individual student needs, allowing for adaptive feedback and assessment. Additionally, data analytics play a crucial role, providing educators with insights into student progress and areas that may require additional attention. By merging technology and gamification, educators can create a more dynamic and effective learning environment that captures students' attention, promotes collaboration, and cultivates critical thinking skills, making the educational process not only informative but also enjoyable and memorable.

4.1 Adaptive Learning Algorithms

Adaptive learning algorithms are a class of algorithms that adjust their behavior based on the input data and feedback received. These algorithms demonstrate various approaches to adaptability, catering to different problem domains and requirements (Hamari et al.,2014). The choice of algorithm depends on the specific characteristics of the data and the learning task at hand. These are often used in machine learning and education to personalize the learning experience for individuals. Here are a few types of adaptive learning algorithms:

- **Reinforcement Learning (RL):** RL is a type of machine learning where an agent learns to make decisions by taking actions in an environment. The agent receives feedback in the form of rewards or penalties, allowing it to adapt and improve its decision-making over time.
- **Genetic Algorithms:** Genetic algorithms are optimization algorithms inspired by the process of natural selection. They use techniques such as mutation, crossover, and selection to evolve a population of candidate solutions toward an optimal solution.
- **Neural Networks with Backpropagation:** Neural networks, particularly deep learning models, use backpropagation to adjust the weights of connections between neurons during training. This iterative process allows the network to learn and adapt to the patterns in the training data.
- **Online Learning Algorithms:** These algorithms update the model continuously as new data becomes available. They are particularly useful in scenarios where the data is streaming or when there are resource constraints that prevent retraining on the entire dataset.
- **K-Nearest Neighbors (KNN):** KNN is a simple and effective algorithm for classification and regression tasks. It adapts by memorizing the training dataset and making predictions based on the majority class or average value of the k-nearest neighbors of a given data point.
- **Collaborative Filtering:** This algorithm is commonly used in recommendation systems. It makes predictions about the preferences of a user by collecting preferences from many users (collaborative) or items (item-based). The algorithm adapts as more user-item interactions are observed.

- **Decision Trees with Pruning:** Decision trees are adaptive algorithms that learn a set of rules to make decisions. Pruning involves removing parts of the tree that do not contribute significantly to its predictive accuracy, allowing it to adapt and generalize better to new data.
- **Bayesian Learning:** Bayesian methods update beliefs about parameters as new data becomes available. These algorithms provide a probabilistic framework for making predictions and are particularly useful when dealing with uncertainty.
- **Ensemble Learning (e.g., Random Forests):** Ensemble methods combine multiple models to improve predictive performance and adaptability. Random Forests, for example, train multiple decision trees on random subsets of the data and combine their predictions.

4.2 Artificial Intelligence (AI) in Gamification

Artificial Intelligence (AI) plays a significant role in enhancing gamification by adding dynamic and personalized elements to the gaming experience (Handelsman et al.,2005). Integrating AI into gamification not only enhances the gaming experience but also opens up new possibilities for creativity and innovation in game design. Following are several ways AI is utilized in gamification:

- **Personalization and Adaptation:** AI algorithms analyze player behavior and preferences to tailor the gaming experience. This includes adjusting difficulty levels, offering personalized challenges, and recommending content based on individual preferences.
- **Dynamic Difficulty Adjustment:** AI can dynamically adjust the difficulty of the game in real-time based on the player's skill level. This ensures that players are consistently challenged, leading to a more engaging and rewarding experience.
- **Procedural Content Generation:** AI can be used to generate game content dynamically, such as levels, maps, or scenarios. This not only keeps the game fresh and interesting but also allows for endless variations in gameplay.
- **Behavior Prediction:** AI can analyze player behavior to predict future actions, helping game designers create more immersive and responsive environments. This predictive analysis can be used to anticipate player choices and adjust the game accordingly.
- **Virtual Personal Assistants:** AI-driven virtual assistants within games can provide guidance, tips, or even engage in natural language conversations with players. This enhances the overall gaming experience and can assist players in overcoming challenges.
- **Adaptive Learning:** AI-powered systems can adapt and learn from a player's actions, modifying the game environment or challenges based on the player's strengths and weaknesses. This creates a more personalized learning curve for each player.
- **Emotion Recognition:** AI can be used to analyze facial expressions, voice tone, or other cues to detect player emotions. This information can be used to adjust the game environment or narrative to better match the player's emotional state.
- **Player Segmentation:** AI helps in segmenting players into different categories based on their preferences, skill levels, or playing styles. Game designers can then create targeted experiences for each segment, ensuring a more engaging and relevant game for every player.
- **Fraud Detection and Prevention:** In multiplayer or online games, AI can be employed to detect and prevent cheating, fraud, or other forms of misconduct. This helps maintain a fair and enjoyable gaming environment for all players.

- **Automated Content Moderation:** AI algorithms can assist in moderating user-generated content, filtering out inappropriate or offensive material. This ensures a safer and more enjoyable community for players.

4.3 Gamification Apps and Platforms

Gamification apps and platforms have gained significant prominence in recent years as innovative tools that leverage game mechanics to engage and motivate users in non-game contexts. These applications apply elements such as points, badges, leaderboards, and challenges to encourage desired behaviors and enhance user participation. One key aspect of gamification is its versatility, as it finds applications across various industries, including education, fitness, employee training, marketing, and customer engagement. Educational gamification platforms, for instance, transform learning experiences by incorporating game elements into lessons, making the process more interactive and enjoyable (Hung et al.,2017). Fitness apps use gamification to motivate users to achieve their health goals through challenges, rewards, and social interactions. In the business realm, employee training programs employ gamification to enhance engagement and knowledge retention. Marketing campaigns often incorporate gamified elements to captivate and retain customer interest. Popular gamification platforms provide businesses and developers with the tools to easily integrate game mechanics into their applications, allowing for customization and scalability (Krishnamurthy et al.,2022). These platforms typically offer analytics to track user engagement and performance, enabling continuous refinement of the gamification strategy. Overall, gamification apps and platforms have become powerful tools for fostering engagement, motivation, and learning in diverse fields.

4.4 Challenges in Implementing Technology in Gamification

Implementing technology in gamification can be a powerful strategy to engage users and enhance their experiences. However, there are several challenges that organizations may face when integrating technology into gamification initiatives (Landers et al., 2015). Addressing these challenges requires careful planning, user feedback, and a willingness to adapt and iterate on the gamification strategy over time. Organizations should also stay informed about emerging technologies and best practices in gamification to stay ahead of the curve. Here are some common challenges:

- **User Adoption:**
    - **Resistance to Change:** Users may resist adopting new technologies or gamified systems due to unfamiliarity or a preference for traditional methods.
    - **Lack of Motivation:** If the gamified elements are not well-designed or fail to provide meaningful incentives, users may not be motivated to participate.
- **Design Complexity:**
    - **Balancing Complexity and Simplicity:** Striking the right balance between a gamified system that is engaging and one that is not overly complex can be challenging.
    - **User Interface Design:** Creating an intuitive and user-friendly interface that encourages participation without overwhelming users can be difficult.
- **Integration with Existing Systems:**

  - **Compatibility Issues:** Integrating gamification technology with existing software or platforms can lead to compatibility issues that hinder smooth operations.
  - **Data Synchronization:** Ensuring that data is synchronized across various systems can be challenging, particularly when integrating gamification with other enterprise applications.
- **Long-Term Engagement:**
  - **Sustainability:** Maintaining user interest over the long term can be challenging. Gamification strategies need to evolve to prevent stagnation and boredom.
  - **Content Refresh:** Regularly updating and refreshing gamified content to keep it relevant and interesting requires ongoing effort.
- **Data Privacy and Security:**
  - **Data Protection:** Collecting and using user data for gamification purposes raises concerns about privacy and data security. Organizations must adhere to data protection regulations and ensure user trust.
  - **Security Risks:** Implementing gamification technology introduces potential security risks, such as vulnerabilities that could be exploited by malicious actors.
- **Scalability:**
  - **Handling Growth:** As user participation increases, the gamification system must scale to accommodate the growing user base. Scalability issues can lead to performance issues and a diminished user experience.
- **Measuring ROI and Effectiveness:**
  - **Quantifying Impact:** It can be challenging to measure the return on investment (ROI) and the overall effectiveness of gamification initiatives. Determining key performance indicators (KPIs) and evaluating their impact on business goals is crucial.
- **Cultural Fit:**
  - **Organizational Culture:** Aligning gamification with the existing organizational culture is crucial. If there is a mismatch, it may be challenging to gain employee or user buy-in.
- **Regulatory Compliance:**
  - **Legal and Compliance Issues:** Depending on the industry and geographic location, there may be legal and compliance considerations related to gamification, such as ensuring fairness, preventing discrimination, and complying with industry regulations.
- **Costs:**
  - **Development and Maintenance Costs:** Implementing and maintaining a gamification system can be costly. Organizations must carefully consider the budgetary implications and assess the long-term financial commitment.

5. BEST PRACTICES FOR EFFECTIVE LEARNING

5.1 Successful Implementation in Specific Courses

Implementing gamification in online classes can enhance engagement and improve the overall learning experience. By implementing these best practices, you can create a gamified online learning environment that enhances student engagement, motivation, and overall learning outcomes (Rivera et al., 2021)

(Rutledge et al.,2018). Given below are some best practices for engaging online classes through gamification, tailored to specific courses:

- **Understand the Audience:** Tailor gamification strategies to match the preferences and learning styles of your specific audience. Consider the age group, interests, and educational backgrounds of your students.
- **Align with Learning Objectives:** Ensure that gamified elements directly align with the course's learning objectives. Games should complement the educational content rather than distract from it.
- **Choose Relevant Game Mechanics:** Select game mechanics that enhance learning, such as points, badges, leaderboards, and challenges. Balance competition and collaboration to cater to different student preferences.
- **Create a Narrative:** Develop a compelling storyline or theme that runs through the course to create a sense of purpose and progression. Use storytelling to contextualize learning materials and activities.
- **Provide Immediate Feedback:** Implement instant feedback mechanisms to guide students in real-time. Constructive feedback can motivate students and help them understand their progress and areas for improvement.
- **Incorporate Real-World Scenarios:** Use gamification to simulate real-world scenarios and problem-solving situations relevant to the course. This approach enhances practical application and critical thinking skills.
- **Encourage Collaboration:** Include collaborative elements in games to foster teamwork and communication. Group challenges or projects can promote a sense of community and shared achievement.
- **Offer Rewards:** Introduce meaningful rewards, such as certificates, digital badges, or even tangible incentives, to motivate students. Ensure that rewards are proportional to the effort and achievement levels.
- **Flexibility and Accessibility:** Design gamified elements that are accessible to all students, including those with different learning abilities or limitations. Provide alternative ways for students to engage with the material.
- **Regularly Update and Evolve:** Keep the gamification elements fresh by regularly updating content and challenges. Introduce new levels, quests, or challenges to maintain interest and prevent monotony.
- **Integration with Learning Platforms:** Seamlessly integrate gamification features into the learning management system or online platform being used for the course. Ensure a user-friendly experience for both students and instructors.
- **Test and Gather Feedback:** Pilot gamified elements with a small group of students before full implementation. Collect feedback from students to identify what works well and areas for improvement.
- **Promote Healthy Competition:** Foster a healthy competitive spirit by balancing individual achievements with collective goals. Avoid creating an overly stressful or excessively competitive environment.

- **Technical Considerations:** Ensure that the gamified elements are compatible with various devices and browsers to accommodate diverse technical setups.Provide technical support for students who may encounter issues.
- **Training for Instructors:** Train instructors on how to effectively use and manage gamification elements. Ensure that instructors understand the educational purpose behind each gamified component.

5.2 Impact on Student Retention and Performance

Engaging online classes through gamification involves integrating game elements and principles into the educational environment to enhance student participation, motivation, and learning outcomes. Several best practices contribute to the success of this approach, significantly impacting student retention and performance (Sera et al.,2017). First and foremost, aligning game mechanics with learning objectives ensures that the gamified elements serve an educational purpose. This includes incorporating quizzes, challenges, and simulations that directly relate to the course content (Šćepanović et al.,2015). Additionally, maintaining a balance between competition and collaboration fosters a positive and inclusive learning atmosphere. By providing rewards, such as badges or points, for achievements and encouraging healthy competition, students are motivated to actively participate and strive for excellence. Regular feedback and immediate rewards for correct answers or successful completion of tasks reinforce positive behaviors and reinforce a sense of accomplishment. Moreover, incorporating a narrative or storyline into the gamified structure can make the learning experience more immersive and relatable for students. This storytelling element helps students connect with the content on a deeper level, enhancing their understanding and retention. Personalization is another crucial aspect; tailoring the gamified elements to cater to diverse learning styles and preferences ensures that all students can engage with the material effectively (Sinatra et al.,2015). Additionally, incorporating real-world applications and problem-solving scenarios within the game context helps students see the practical relevance of their learning, further increasing motivation. Fostering a sense of community through collaborative games or team-based challenges enhances social interaction and peer support. This interconnectedness can positively impact student retention by creating a supportive online learning environment. Implementing a variety of game formats and adjusting the difficulty level over time helps maintain student interest and prevents monotony (Skinnner et al., 1984). Regularly updating and refreshing the gamified elements also ensures that the learning experience remains dynamic and relevant. Adopting best practices for engaging online classes through gamification has a significant impact on student retention and performance (stoot et al.,1984). By aligning game mechanics with learning objectives, maintaining a balance between competition and collaboration, incorporating narratives, personalizing the experience, and fostering a sense of community, educators can create a compelling and effective online learning environment that motivates students to stay engaged and excel academically.

5.3 Lessons Learned From Failures

Engaging online classes through gamification is a dynamic and innovative approach to enhance the learning experience. Several best practices have emerged from lessons learned through failures in implementing gamification strategies (Tangney, et al., 2016) (Van Gaalen et al., 2021). Firstly, it is crucial to align game elements with educational objectives. Failure often occurs when the game overshadows the educational content, leading to a loss of focus on learning outcomes. Therefore, successful gamification involves careful consideration of how game elements, such as points, badges, and leaderboards, directly contribute to the mastery of the subject matter. The importance of feedback mechanisms cannot be overstated. Failures in gamified online classes often stem from inadequate or delayed feedback, hindering the immediate reinforcement of desired behaviors. Effective gamification relies on timely and constructive feedback, enabling students to understand their progress and make informed decisions to improve. Customization and adaptability are key factors in successful gamification (Zainuddin et al.,2020). Lessons learned from failures emphasize the need for flexibility in adjusting game mechanics based on student feedback and performance data. A one-size-fits-all approach is unlikely to cater to the diverse learning styles and preferences within a virtual classroom. Furthermore, the integration of collaborative elements is essential to prevent the isolation of students in gamified environments. Failed attempts often neglect the social aspect of learning, which is a crucial component of engagement. Successful gamification fosters collaboration, encouraging students to work together towards common goals and share their experiences. Best practices in engaging online classes through gamification stem from learning from past failures. It involves a careful balance between game elements and educational objectives, timely feedback, customization, and fostering collaboration. By incorporating these best practices, educators can create a dynamic and effective online learning environment that captivates students' attention and promotes meaningful learning experiences.

5.4 Recommendations for Effective Implementation

To ensure the effective implementation of gamification in online education, several best practices should be considered. First and foremost, align gamified activities with learning objectives to maintain educational relevance. Design challenges and rewards that are meaningful and contribute to the overall learning goals. Incorporate a variety of game mechanics, such as points, badges, leaderboards, and levels, to cater to diverse learner preferences (Domínguez et al., 2013). Establish clear rules and guidelines to create a fair and transparent gaming environment. Furthermore, foster a sense of competition and collaboration by encouraging healthy competition and teamwork among students. Regularly update and refresh the gamified elements to sustain interest over time. Provide timely feedback to participants, reinforcing positive behavior and correcting misconceptions. It's crucial to ensure that the gamification elements do not overshadow the educational content but rather enhance it. Lastly, consider the accessibility of gamified features to accommodate all learners, including those with diverse needs. By adhering to these best practices, educators can create a dynamic and effective online learning environment that leverages the motivational power of gamification to enhance student engagement and success.

6. EVALUATION AND ASSESSMENT

6.1 Measuring the Effectiveness of Gamification

Measuring the effectiveness of gamification involves assessing various aspects to determine the impact of gamified elements on the intended goals and objectives. Regularly reviewing these metrics and adjusting the gamification strategy based on the findings can help ensure ongoing effectiveness and user engagement. Keep in mind that the specific metrics to prioritize will depend on the nature of the gamified system and its intended goals. Given are several key metrics and methods to measure the effectiveness of gamification:

- **Define Clear Objectives:** Clearly outline the goals and objectives of implementing gamification. These could include increased engagement, learning retention, improved performance, or enhanced user satisfaction.
- **User Engagement:** Measure the level of user participation and interaction with the gamified elements. This could include tracking the number of logins, time spent on the platform, and the frequency of interactions.
- **User Retention:** Assess whether gamification has a positive impact on user retention. Analyze how long users stay engaged with the platform or application over time.
- **Performance Metrics:** Evaluate the impact of gamification on key performance indicators (KPIs) such as productivity, sales, or learning outcomes. Compare performance before and after the implementation of gamified elements.
- **Feedback and Surveys:** Collect user feedback through surveys to understand their perception of gamification. Ask specific questions about the effectiveness of game mechanics and their impact on user experience.
- **Completion Rates:** Monitor the completion rates of tasks, courses, or challenges within the gamified system. Higher completion rates may indicate increased motivation and engagement.
- **Skill Acquisition:** If the gamified system is designed for learning, assess whether users are acquiring and retaining new skills. Conduct assessments or quizzes to measure knowledge gained.
- **Social Sharing and Collaboration:** Measure the extent to which users are sharing their achievements and collaborating with others. Social interactions within the gamified system can contribute to a sense of community and engagement.
- **Time-on-Task:** Analyze the time users spend on specific tasks or challenges. This can provide insights into the level of difficulty, engagement, and interest in the gamified activities.
- **In-app Analytics:** Utilize in-app analytics tools to track user behavior, progression, and interactions within the gamified environment. Identify patterns and trends that indicate user engagement.
- **Achievement Unlocks:** Track the achievement of milestones or badges within the gamified system. Users earning rewards or progressing through levels can indicate a positive impact on engagement.
- **Cost-Benefit Analysis:** Evaluate the cost-effectiveness of implementing gamification compared to the benefits gained. Consider factors such as development costs, user acquisition, and increased revenue or productivity.
- **Adoption Rates:** Assess how quickly and widely users adopt the gamified features. Higher adoption rates suggest that users find value in the gamification elements.
- **A/B Testing:** Conduct A/B testing to compare different versions of gamified elements and identify which features or mechanics are most effective in achieving the desired outcomes.

6.2 Student Feedback and Surveys

Measuring the effectiveness of gamification in education through student feedback and surveys is a crucial aspect of understanding the impact of incorporating game elements into the learning process. Student feedback provides valuable insights into the engagement levels, motivation, and overall satisfaction of learners participating in gamified educational experiences. Surveys designed to capture these aspects typically include questions about the perceived enjoyment of gamified activities, the relevance of game elements to the learning objectives, and the impact on their overall understanding of the subject matter (Trowler et al.,2010). Moreover, students can provide feedback on specific game mechanics, such as point systems, badges, or competition elements, shedding light on what aspects of gamification are most effective in enhancing their learning experience. Additionally, surveys can assess whether gamification has positively influenced students' motivation, collaboration, and critical thinking skills. Gathering feedback on the challenges faced during gamified activities also helps educators refine and tailor the gamification approach to better suit the diverse needs of the student body. Analyzing the data from these surveys allows educators and researchers to draw correlations between gamification elements and academic performance, as well as identify areas for improvement. The feedback loop created by student input enables continuous refinement and optimization of gamification strategies, ultimately contributing to a more effective and engaging learning environment. Overall, student feedback and surveys play a pivotal role in not only assessing the current effectiveness of gamification in education but also in shaping its future implementation and development.

7. BARRIERS TO IMPLEMENTATION

Implementing engaging online classes through gamification can face several barriers, with faculty resistance being a prominent factor. Faculty members may be hesitant to adopt gamified approaches due to unfamiliarity, skepticism about its effectiveness, or concerns about diverting from traditional teaching methods. Overcoming this resistance requires effective communication, training, and showcasing successful examples of gamification in education. Technical challenges pose another significant barrier. Integrating gamification tools and platforms into existing online learning systems may be complex, requiring technical expertise and support. Inadequate infrastructure, compatibility issues, and the need for additional resources can hinder the seamless incorporation of gamified elements into online classes. Institutions need to invest in robust technical support, training programs, and infrastructure upgrades to address these challenges. Ethical considerations also play a crucial role in the implementation of gamification in online classes. Concerns may arise about the potential for student exploitation, data privacy, and the unintended consequences of using game-like incentives. Striking a balance between motivation and ethical boundaries is essential (Tu et al.,2015). Faculty and administrators must establish clear guidelines, ethical frameworks, and privacy protocols to ensure a responsible and respectful gamified learning environment. Addressing these barriers requires a holistic approach that involves collaborative efforts from faculty, administrators, and technical support teams. Overcoming resistance through effective communication, providing technical support, and establishing ethical guidelines will contribute to the successful implementation of engaging online classes through gamification, fostering a dynamic and effective learning experience for students.

8. FUTURE DIRECTIONS AND TRENDS

The future of engaging online classes through gamification is poised to be shaped by several key factors. Firstly, emerging technologies in gamification are expected to play a pivotal role. As virtual reality

(VR) and augmented reality (AR) technologies become more accessible, educators can leverage these tools to create immersive and interactive gaming experiences within the online learning environment. The incorporation of artificial intelligence (AI) can enable personalized learning experiences by adapting game content to individual student needs, providing targeted challenges and feedback. These technologies have the potential to make online classes more dynamic and engaging. Evolving pedagogical approaches will significantly impact the integration of gamification in online education. As educators continue to explore innovative teaching methodologies, gamification can be seamlessly integrated with problem-based learning, collaborative learning, and other student-centered approaches. The design of gamified activities can be aligned with educational objectives, fostering critical thinking, creativity, and collaboration (Whitton et al., 2014). The emphasis will be on creating a balance between game elements and educational content, ensuring that gamification enhances the learning experience rather than serving as a mere distraction. Finally, the role of gamification in the future of education is likely to expand beyond traditional academic subjects. Gamified elements can be employed for developing skills such as problem-solving, teamwork, and communication – skills essential in the real world. As the job market evolves, the ability to apply knowledge in practical scenarios becomes increasingly important, and gamification offers a promising avenue for honing these skills in a virtual setting. The future may witness a broader acceptance of gamification in professional development and lifelong learning, transcending the boundaries of traditional educational settings. The future of engaging online classes through gamification is an exciting frontier that will be shaped by the integration of emerging technologies, evolving pedagogical approaches, and a broader recognition of the role of gamification in cultivating essential skills for the future. As educators and technologists collaborate to harness the potential of gamification, online learning experiences are poised to become more immersive, personalized, and aligned with the dynamic needs of learners in the 21st century.

9. CONCLUSION

The incorporation of gamification in online classes presents a transformative and highly effective approach to engage learners, fostering a dynamic and interactive learning environment. The utilization of game elements, such as challenges, rewards, and competition, not only captivates students' attention but also promotes active participation and collaboration. The gamified online learning experience has proven to enhance motivation, stimulate critical thinking, and improve overall retention of information. As we navigate the ever-evolving landscape of education, embracing gamification emerges as a valuable strategy to not only meet the challenges of virtual learning but also to instill a sense of excitement and curiosity in students, making the educational journey both enjoyable and enriching. This innovative approach not only aligns with the digital era but also opens up new avenues for personalized and inclusive education, laying the groundwork for a more engaging and effective online learning future.

REFERENCES

Alsawaier, R. S. (2018). The effect of gamification on motivation and engagement. *The International Journal of Information and Learning Technology*, *35*(1), 56–79. doi:10.1108/IJILT-02-2017-0009

Bai, S., Hew, K. F., & Huang, B. (2020). Does gamification improve student learning outcome? Evidence from a meta-analysis and synthesis of qualitative data in educational contexts. *Educational Research Review*, *30*, 100322. doi:10.1016/j.edurev.2020.100322

Brigham, T. J. (2015). An introduction to gamification: Adding game elements for engagement. *Medical Reference Services Quarterly*, *34*(4), 471–480. doi:10.1080/02763869.2015.1082385 PMID:26496401

Brull, S., & Finlayson, S. (2016). Importance of gamification in increasing learning. *Journal of Continuing Education in Nursing*, *47*(8), 372–375. doi:10.3928/00220124-20160715-09 PMID:27467313

Chen, X., Siau, K., & Nah, F. F. H. (2012). Empirical comparison of 3-D virtual world and face-to-face classroom for higher education. *Journal of Database Management*, *23*(3), 30–49. doi:10.4018/jdm.2012070102

Dicheva, C., & Dicheva, D. (2017). Gamifying education: what is known, what is believed and what remains uncertain: a critical review. *International Journal of Educational Technology in Higher Education*, *14*(1), 1–36. doi:10.1186/s41239-017-0042-5

Dicheva, D., Dichev, C., Agre, G., & Angelova, G. (2015). Gamification in Education: A Systematic Mapping Study. *Journal of Educational Technology & Society*, *18*(3), 75–88. doi:10.1109/EDUCON.2014.6826129

Domínguez, A., Saenz-De-Navarrete, J., De-Marcos, L., Fernández-Sanz, L., Pagés, C., & Martínez-Herráiz, J. J. (2013). Gamifying Learning Experiences: Practical Implications and Outcomes. *Computers & Education*, *63*(1), 380–392. doi:10.1016/j.compedu.2012.12.020

Douglas, J., Douglas, A., & Barnes, B. (2006). Measuring Student Satisfaction at a UK University. *Quality Assurance in Education*, *14*(3), 251–267. doi:10.1108/09684880610678568

Driskell, J. E., & Dwyer, D. J. (1984). Microcomputer Videogame Based Training. *Technology*, *24*(2), 11–16.

Felszeghy, S., Pasonen-Seppänen, S., Koskela, A., Nieminen, P., Härkönen, K., Paldanius, K. M., Gabbouj, S., Ketola, K., Hiltunen, M., Lundin, M., Haapaniemi, T., Sointu, E., Bauman, E. B., Gilbert, G. E., Morton, D., & Mahonen, A. (2019). Using online game-based platforms to improve student performance and engagement in histology teaching. *BMC Medical Education*, *19*(1), 1–11. doi:10.1186/s12909-019-1701-0 PMID:31331319

Figueroa-Flores, J. F. (2016). Gamification and game-based learning: Two strategies for the 21st-century learner. *World Journal of Educational Research (Los Angeles, Calif.)*, *3*(2), 507–522. doi:10.22158/wjer.v3n2p507

Garett, R., & Young, S. D. (2019). Health care gamification: A study of game mechanics and elements. *Technology. Knowledge and Learning*, *24*(3), 341–353. doi:10.1007/s10758-018-9353-4

González, C. S., N. Gómez, V. Navarro, M. Cairos, C. Quirce, P. Toledo, and N. Marrero-Gordillo. (2016). Learning Healthy Lifestyles through Active Videogames, Motor Games and the Gamification of Educational Activities. *Computers in Human Behavior, 55*(Part A), 529–551. doi:10.1016/j.chb.2015.08.052

Hamari, J., Koivisto, J., & Sarsa, H. (2014). Does Gamification Work? A Literature Review of Empirical Studies on Gamification. *Proceedings of the Annual Hawaii International Conference on System Sciences*. 10.1109/HICSS.2014.377

Handelsman, M. M., Briggs, W. L., Sullivan, N., & Towler, A. (2005). A Measure of College Student Course Engagement. *The Journal of Educational Research*, *98*(3), 184–192. doi:10.3200/JOER.98.3.184-192

Hung, A. C. Y. (2017). A critique and defense of gamification. *Journal of Interactive Online Learning*, *15*(1).

Krishnamurthy, K., Selvaraj, N., Gupta, P., Cyriac, B., Dhurairaj, P., Abdullah, A., Krishnapillai, A., Lugova, H., Haque, M., Xie, S., & Ang, E. T. (2022). Benefits of gamification in medical education. *Clinical Anatomy (New York, N.Y.)*, *35*(6), 795–807. doi:10.1002/ca.23916 PMID:35637557

Landers, R. N., Bauer, K. N., Callan, R. C., & Armstrong, M. B. (2015). Psychological theory and the gamification of learning. *Gamification in education and business*, 165-186.

Rivera, E. S., & Garden, C. L. P. (2021). Gamification for student engagement: A framework. *Journal of Further and Higher Education*, *45*(7), 999–1012. doi:10.1080/0309877X.2021.1875201

Rutledge, C., Walsh, C. M., Swinger, N., Auerbach, M., Castro, D., Dewan, M., Khattab, M., Rake, A., Harwayne-Gidansky, I., Raymond, T. T., Maa, T., & Chang, T. P. (2018). Gamification in action: Theoretical and practical considerations for medical educators. *Academic Medicine*, *93*(7), 1014–1020. doi:10.1097/ACM.0000000000002183 PMID:29465450

Šćepanović, S., Žarić, N. A. Đ. A., & Matijević, T. (2015, September). Gamification in higher education learning–state of the art, challenges and opportunities. In *Proc. 6th Int. Conf. e-Learn* (pp. 128-134). Academic Press.

Sera, L., & Wheeler, E. (2017). Game on: The gamification of the pharmacy classroom. *Currents in Pharmacy Teaching & Learning*, *9*(1), 155–159. doi:10.1016/j.cptl.2016.08.046 PMID:29180148

Sinatra, G. M., Heddy, B. C., & Lombardi, D. (2015). The Challenges of Defining and Measuring Student Engagement. *Educational Psychologist*, *50*(1), 1–13. doi:10.1080/00461520.2014.1002924

Skinnner, B. F. (1984). The Shame of American Education. *The American Psychologist*, *39*(9), 947–954. doi:10.1037/0003-066X.39.9.947

Stott, A., & Neustaedter, C. (2013). Analysis of Gamification in Education. *Technical Report 2013-0422-01*.

Tangney, S. (2014). Student-centred Learning: A Humanist Perspective. *Teaching in Higher Education*, *19*(3), 266–275. doi:10.1080/13562517.2013.860099

Trowler, V. (2010). *Student Engagement Literature Review*. The Higher Education Academy. doi:10.1037/0022-0663.85.4.571

Tu, C. H., Yen, C. J., Sujo-Montes, L., & Roberts, G. A. (2015). Gaming Personality and Game Dynamics in Online Discussion Instructions. *Educational Media International*, *52*(3), 155–172. doi:10.1080/09523987.2015.1075099 van Gaalen, A. E., Brouwer, J., Schönrock-Adema, J., Bouwkamp-Timmer, T., Jaarsma, A. D. C., & Georgiadis, J. R. (2021). Gamification of health professions education: A systematic review. *Advances in Health Sciences Education : Theory and Practice*, *26*(2), 683–711. doi:10.1007/s10459-020-10000-3 PMID:33128662

Whitton, N., & Moseley, A. (2014). Deconstructing Engagement: Rethinking Involvement in Learning. *Simulation & Gaming*, *45*(4–5), 266–275. doi:10.1177/1046878114554755

Zainuddin, Z., Chu, S. K. W., Shujahat, M., & Perera, C. J. (2020). The impact of gamification on learning and instruction: A systematic review of empirical evidence. *Educational Research Review*, *30*, 100326. doi:10.1016/j.edurev.2020.100326

Chapter 13
Impact of Artificial Intelligence on Virtual Teacher Learner Engagement:
Redefining Educational Dynamics

Nidhi Goenka
Kalinga University, India

Deepti Patnaik
Kalinga University, India

Bipin Bihari Pradhan
Kalinga University, India

ABSTRACT

The study explores the transformative impact of artificial intelligence (AI) on teacher-learner engagement in virtual education settings. It uses secondary data sources to analyse the evolving landscape of virtual education facilitated by AI technologies The research explores how AI enhances personalized learning experiences, adaptive assessments, and real-time feedback mechanisms, fostering deeper engagement and understanding among learners. It also discusses the role of AI in facilitating collaboration and communication in virtual classrooms, enabling seamless interaction across geographical boundaries. The study also explores the potential of AI to address individual learning needs, promote inclusivity, and optimize learning outcomes through data-driven insights and analytics. The research emphasizes the importance of leveraging AI technologies to enhance teacher-learner engagement, promote active learning, and foster academic success in the digital age.

DOI: 10.4018/979-8-3693-4268-8.ch013

INTRODUCTION

In recent years, the integration of Artificial Intelligence (AI) into various sectors has reshaped industries, revolutionized processes, and transformed the way we interact with technology. Education, as a fundamental pillar of society, has not been immune to this wave of technological innovation. From personalized learning experiences to adaptive assessment tools, AI is increasingly being incorporated into educational systems worldwide, promising to usher in a new era of teaching and learning.

This chapter concentrates on the increasing influence of AI within the area of education, with a particular focus on its impact on virtual teacher-learner engagement. As educational institutions continue to embrace online learning platforms and virtual classrooms, understanding how AI redefines the dynamics between teachers and students in these digital environments becomes paramount (Lu & Xie., 2024). This chapter seeks to explore the multifaceted implications of AI in enhancing engagement, collaboration, and learning outcomes within virtual learning spaces.

The purpose of this chapter is twofold. Firstly, it aims to provide an overview of the growing influence of AI in education, highlighting key advancements, trends, and applications shaping the educational landscape. By examining the transformative potential of AI technologies, readers will gain insight into the evolving nature of teaching and learning in the digital age.

Secondly, this chapter underscores the importance of critically examining the impact of AI on virtual teacher-learner engagement. As online education becomes increasingly prevalent, understanding how AI-driven tools and platforms influence interactions between teachers and students is essential for educators, policymakers, and stakeholders alike. By outlining the opportunities, challenges, and considerations associated with AI in virtual teacher-learner engagement, also this chapter aims to inform discussions, inspire innovation, and guide future developments in educational practice and policy as a comprehensive exploration of AI's role in redefining educational dynamics, particularly within the context of virtual teacher-learner engagement. By unpacking the implications of AI in online education, this chapter seeks to illuminate the path forward towards more personalized, adaptive, and impactful learning experiences for all stakeholders involved.

The integration of Artificial Intelligence (AI) into education has garnered significant attention in recent years, marking a paradigm shift in teaching and learning methodologies (Sperling et al., 2024). AI's growing influence in education stems from its capacity to personalize learning experiences, optimize educational resources, and enhance both teaching and administrative processes. The growing influence of AI in education has been evident in case of personalized Learning where AI-powered adaptive learning systems analyse students' learning patterns, preferences, and performance data to deliver tailored instructional content and pathways. This approach allows educators to cater to individual student needs, pace, and learning styles, thereby maximizing engagement and improving learning outcomes. The adaptive assessment and feedback facilitates real-time assessment and feedback mechanisms, enabling educators to track student progress more accurately and provide timely interventions (Celik, 2023). Adaptive assessment tools can identify areas of strength and weakness, offer personalized feedback, and adjust instructional strategies accordingly, fostering a more effective learning environment. The AI-driven virtual assistants and chatbot's are increasingly being deployed in educational settings to support both teachers and students. These AI-based tools can provide instant responses to student queries, offer guidance on assignments and coursework, and assist with administrative tasks, thereby enhancing teacher efficiency and student engagement. Again the AI-powered intelligent tutoring systems simulate one-on-one tutoring experiences by dynamically adapting instruction based on individual student responses and performance. These systems leverage natural language processing, machine learning, and other AI techniques to provide personalized tutoring and structured support, promoting deeper learning and comprehension.

The AI-driven predictive analytics tools analyse vast amounts of educational data to identify trends, predict student outcomes, and inform data-driven decision-making processes. Educators and administrators can leverage these insights to identify at-risk students, allocate resources effectively, and design targeted interventions to support student success. Also the AI technologies facilitate the creation, curation, and customization of educational content at scale. Natural language generation algorithms can generate educational materials, quizzes, and assessments, while content recommendation systems can suggest relevant resources and learning materials based on individual student needs and interests (Takaki et al., 2022).

In toto growing influence of AI in education is reshaping traditional teaching and learning paradigms, fostering more personalized, adaptive, and engaging educational experiences (Memarian & Doleck, 2024). As AI continues to advance, its impact on education is expected to deepen, offering new opportunities to improve student outcomes, enhance teacher effectiveness, and transform the educational landscape as we know it.

Evolution of Educational Technology

The evolution of educational technology (EdTech) has been transformative, reshaping the ways in which teaching and learning are conducted (Boateng et al., 2024). Here's a chronological overview of its evolution:

Early Educational Tools: Even before the advent of modern technology, educators utilized a diverse array of tools to enrich learning experiences within classrooms. Chalkboards, textbooks, and visual aids played pivotal roles in educational settings, fostering engagement and comprehension among students (Mukul & Büyüközkan, 2023). Teachers employed chalk to inscribe diagrams, equations, and instructional content onto chalkboards, providing a visible and interactive platform for conveying information. In the absence of projectors and digital displays, educators supplemented verbal instruction with visual aids such as posters, diagrams, maps, and charts, enabling students to grasp concepts more tangibly and retain information more effectively. Printed textbooks have served as foundational educational resources for centuries, offering structured content and exercises across subjects like mathematics, languages, sciences, and humanities. These early educational tools exemplified the resourcefulness and ingenuity of educators, demonstrating their commitment to facilitating learning through accessible and impactful means, long before the dawn of modern technological advancements.

Throughout history, various tools and resources have been employed in education to facilitate learning and comprehension across different subjects. Originating in ancient times, the abacus served as a fundamental counting tool, featuring beads or stones arranged on rods. Used primarily for teaching arithmetic, this tactile and visual aid provided students with a tangible way to grasp numerical operations. In geography education, physical globes and maps played a crucial role in helping students comprehend the layout of the world, its continents, countries, and geographical features. Writing slates, compact boards typically made of slate or wood, accompanied by chalk, allowed students to practice handwriting, spelling, and arithmetic, erasing and reusing the slate as needed. Flashcards, consisting of questions or terms on one side and corresponding answers or definitions on the other, offered a simple yet effective method for memorization and review across various subjects. Additionally, three-dimensional models and manipulatives, such as geometric shapes, fraction blocks, and anatomical models, were utilized to aid students in visualizing and understanding abstract concepts in subjects like mathematics, science, and geography (Fellnhofer, 2019). These tools, ranging from the tangible to the conceptual, have long been integral components of educational practices, fostering active engagement and comprehension among learners.

Dictation and recitation were prevalent methods of instruction and assessment, wherein students would listen to the teacher read aloud or recite passages, poems, or mathematical tables. These oral exercises aimed to improve listening, memory, and verbal skills, fostering active engagement with the content. Additionally, apprenticeships and mentorship played significant roles in traditional education, particularly in societies where formal schooling was limited. Individuals learned practical skills and knowledge directly from experienced practitioners in fields such as craftsmanship, agriculture, and trade, gaining hands-on experience and guidance. These early educational tools were foundational in facilitating learning and knowledge acquisition, providing students with the means to engage with content, develop skills, and understand concepts in diverse subject areas through experiential and oral learning approaches (AlShaikh et al., 2024).

Radio and Television

During the early to mid-20th century, radio emerged as a powerful medium for educational outreach and instruction, revolutionizing the landscape of education. Radio stations produced and broadcasted a diverse array of educational programs covering subjects such as history, science, literature, and language arts, meticulously tailored to specific age groups and educational levels. This educational programming not only engaged listeners but also facilitated distance learning initiatives, enabling students in remote areas or unable to attend traditional schools to access educational content from the comfort of their homes, particularly benefiting rural communities and adult learners. Public radio stations, epitomized by institutions like the British Broadcasting Corporation (BBC) and National Public Radio (NPR), allocated significant airtime to educational content, encompassing lectures, documentaries, and cultural programming to enrich the intellectual lives of listeners. Radio programs also served as supplementary learning resources in classrooms, enhancing the overall learning experience for students by providing reinforcement of academic concepts. Moreover, radio became a valuable tool for language acquisition and proficiency enhancement, with language instruction programs utilizing audio lessons, dialogues, and pronunciation exercises to immerse listeners in foreign languages and foster linguistic competence. Overall, radio acted as a cornerstone of educational dissemination, democratizing access to knowledge and enriching learning experiences for audiences worldwide, its widespread reach and versatility as a medium continuing to underscore its enduring impact on education.

Educational Television (ETV) channels and programs emerged as influential platforms for delivering instructional content directly to viewers at home. Covering a diverse array of subjects ranging from mathematics and science to arts and humanities, these programs provided accessible avenues for learning. Television documentaries and documentary series offered in-depth explorations of historical events, scientific discoveries, and cultural phenomena, engaging viewers and providing visual context to complex topics. Children's educational programming, epitomized by shows like Sesame Street and Mister Rogers' Neighborhood, combined entertainment with learning, introducing fundamental concepts such as numbers, letters, and social skills in engaging formats. Telecourses, televised courses offered by educational institutions, allowed students to watch lectures and demonstrations on TV and complete assignments remotely, offering flexibility in learning. Television also enhanced visual learning through videos, animations, diagrams, and demonstrations, clarifying abstract concepts and fostering deeper understanding among viewers. Furthermore, educational television provided valuable resources for teacher training and professional development, offering insights into instructional techniques, classroom management strategies, and curriculum development to support educators in their professional growth. Ultimately, radio and television revolutionized education by expanding learning opportunities beyond traditional classrooms and textbooks, reaching broad audiences, promoting lifelong learning, and democratizing access to educational content on a global scale.

Computer-Based Instruction

With the rise of computers in the latter half of the 20th century, computer-based instruction (CBI) emerged as a significant development in education (Butcher & Jameson, 2016). CBI utilizes computers and software programs to deliver educational content and facilitate learning experiences. It offers numerous advantages over traditional instructional methods, including interactivity, adaptability, accessibility, cost-effectiveness, immediate feedback, and engagement. Learners can actively engage with educational material through interactive exercises, simulations, and multimedia presentations, promoting deeper understanding. CBI programs can adapt to individual learning styles, provide personalized feedback, and adjust difficulty levels based on learner progress. With widespread access to computers and the internet, educational resources become more accessible to a broader range of learners, enhancing flexibility and convenience. While there may be initial costs associated with developing CBI programs, they are ultimately more cost-effective than traditional methods, as digital materials can be easily distributed and reused. Additionally, CBI provides instant feedback, allowing students to assess their understanding in real-time and enabling instructors to monitor progress more efficiently (Khowaja and Salim, 2013). Incorporating multimedia elements such as videos and games, CBI makes learning more engaging and enjoyable, leading to higher levels of motivation and retention. Overall, CBI has revolutionized education by offering innovative ways to deliver instruction and enhance learning outcomes, with continued advancements expected to further expand its capabilities in the future.

Internet and Web-Based Learning

The proliferation of the internet in the 1990s paved the way for a revolution in education through web-based learning platforms and resources, enabling diverse forms of online learning. This transformation encompassed online courses offering flexibility for learners to study at their own pace and access educational content from anywhere with an internet connection. Virtual classrooms facilitated real-time interaction between students and instructors, fostering synchronous learning experiences despite geographical distances. The emergence of Massive Open Online Courses (MOOCs) democratized access to education by providing free or low-cost courses to a large number of participants worldwide (Harnadi, et al., 2024). Additionally, the internet offered vast educational resources, including e-books, articles, videos, and tutorials, alongside open educational resources (OER), further democratizing access to education. Web-based learning platforms leveraged data analytics and adaptive learning technologies to personalize learning experiences, while global connectivity facilitated cross-cultural exchange and collaboration among learners and educators. Moreover, web-based learning facilitated continuing education and lifelong learning opportunities, enabling professionals to update their skills and pursue advanced degrees through online programs (Shi et al., 2024). Overall, the internet and web-based learning have transformed education by expanding access, fostering collaboration, and providing innovative ways to deliver and consume educational content, with continued advancements expected to shape the future of education.

Learning Management Systems (LMS)

Learning Management Systems (LMS) like Blackboard and Moodle have emerged as indispensable tools in education, particularly from the late 20th century onward. These platforms offer centralized solutions for course management, content delivery, and student interaction, benefiting both educators and learners (Buckley et al., 2022). LMS platforms streamline administrative tasks by organizing course materials, assignments, and assessments in one accessible location. They facilitate diverse content delivery methods and foster student engagement through discussion forums and virtual classrooms. Additionally, LMS platforms simplify assessment processes and provide timely feedback, enhancing the learning experience. Offering flexibility and accessibility, they enable learners to study at their own pace and access course materials from anywhere with an internet connection. Analytics and reporting features further aid educators in tracking student progress and informing instructional decisions. As integral components of the educational landscape, LMS platforms continue to evolve, incorporating new features to meet the changing needs of educators and learners in traditional and online learning environments (Duin and Tham, 2020).

Multimedia and Interactive Learning

Advancements in multimedia technologies have revolutionized education, enabling the development of interactive educational materials like simulations, animations, and multimedia presentations. These resources have significantly enhanced engagement and understanding among learners by offering various benefits. Multimedia elements such as videos and animations captivate learners' attention, making the learning experience more engaging and immersive (Chen et al., 2021). Moreover, interactivity encourages active participation, fostering exploration, experimentation, and problem-solving for deeper comprehension. Visualizations of complex concepts through diagrams and 3D models aid in conceptualization, while personalization options cater to individual learning needs and styles. Immediate feedback mechanisms allow learners to assess their understanding in real-time, facilitating correction and progress tracking (Li et al., 2023). Accessibility across devices ensures inclusivity, while collaboration features promote teamwork and knowledge sharing. Overall, advancements in multimedia and interactive learning have transformed education, providing dynamic tools to inspire curiosity, critical thinking, and student success in the digital age.

Mobile Learning

The advent of smartphones and tablets has revolutionized EdTech, making learning more portable and accessible. Mobile apps and platforms allow learners to access educational content anytime, anywhere. Mobile learning, also known as m-learning, leverages the widespread adoption of smartphones and tablets to enhance education (Yalcinkaya and Yucel, 2023). It offers portability, enabling learning on the go without being tied to a traditional classroom or computer. Accessibility is improved, reaching learners in remote or underserved areas. Flexibility is provided, allowing learners to study at their own pace and customize their learning experiences. Interactivity is enhanced through features such as quizzes and multimedia content, improving comprehension and retention. Personalization tailors learning experiences to individual needs and preferences, while collaboration fosters community and teamwork. Multimodal learning accommodates diverse learning preferences, presenting information in various formats (Yalcinkaya and Yucel, 2023). Overall, mobile learning has transformed education, providing innovative tools and opportunities for learning anytime, anywhere, and will continue to shape the future of education as technology evolves.

Adaptive Learning and Personalization

Adaptive learning platforms have emerged as powerful tools in education, harnessing data analytics and artificial intelligence to personalize instruction for individual learners (Audureau et al., 2020). These platforms utilize algorithms to assess each learner's knowledge, skills, and learning style, dynamically adjusting content, pace, and difficulty level accordingly. Key aspects of adaptive learning and personalization include individualized instruction tailored to specific learning needs, dynamic content adaptation in real-time, continuous assessment to refine instructional strategies, timely feedback and support mechanisms, and engagement-enhancing features such as gamification and personalized learning pathways. Moreover, adaptive learning platforms offer scalability and efficiency by automating processes and accommodating diverse learner needs while minimizing the burden on educators and institutions (ZHnag et al., 2020). Overall, adaptive learning represents a significant advancement in education, providing personalized and effective learning experiences for learners of all backgrounds and abilities.

Open Educational Resources (OER)

The Open Educational Resources (OER) movement, which gained momentum in the 2000s, aims to democratize access to education by promoting the sharing and use of freely accessible educational materials. These resources, spanning textbooks, lecture notes, videos, and assessment tools, are openly licensed, allowing for their modification, redistribution, and use without financial barriers (Casanova, 2016). OER address issues of accessibility by providing learners with high-quality educational materials regardless of their financial status or location. They also alleviate financial burdens on students and institutions by eliminating the need for expensive textbooks. The flexibility of OER allows educators to customize content to suit the needs of their students, fostering engagement and relevance. Furthermore, the collaborative nature of the OER movement encourages knowledge sharing and pedagogical innovation, enhancing teaching and learning practices. Quality assurance processes ensure the credibility and excellence of OER, maintaining high educational standards. Overall, the OER movement has transformed education by facilitating collaboration, reducing costs, and expanding opportunities for lifelong learning worldwide (Vihos et al., 2023).

Gamification and Game-Based Learning

Gamification techniques and game-based learning platforms have indeed transformed the educational landscape by infusing elements of play into learning experiences, thereby increasing engagement and motivation among students (Díaz-Ramírez, 2020). Gamification strategies, such as point systems, badges, and leaderboards, incentivize participation and foster a sense of achievement. Meanwhile, game-based learning platforms leverage the intrinsic motivation inherent in games to make learning enjoyable and immersive. These platforms offer personalized experiences tailored to individual student needs, providing immediate feedback and fostering self-directed learning. Moreover, collaboration and social interaction are encouraged through multiplayer games and team-based challenges, promoting teamwork and communication skills. Ultimately, gamification and game-based learning contribute to skill development by engaging students in critical thinking, problem-solving, and creativity within interactive and enjoyable contexts, thereby enhancing the overall learning experience (Legaki, 2020).

Virtual and Augmented Reality (VR/AR)

Virtual Reality (VR) and Augmented Reality (AR) technologies have revolutionized education by offering immersive learning experiences that allow students to interact with virtual environments and objects. These technologies transport students to virtual worlds or overlay digital information onto the real world, simulating real-life scenarios, historical events, scientific phenomena, and cultural landmarks (Al-Ansi et al., 2023). Through VR/AR, students engage in experiential learning by actively exploring and interacting with educational content, such as manipulating objects, conducting experiments, and solving problems in virtual environments. Additionally, VR/AR provides visual representations of abstract concepts and spatial relationships, enhancing students' visualization skills and conceptual understanding. With interactive features, students can manipulate virtual objects and navigate environments using gestures, voice commands, or handheld controllers, fostering curiosity and inquiry-based learning. Furthermore, VR/AR technologies accommodate diverse learning needs and preferences, supporting collaboration among students through multi-user experiences and shared virtual spaces (Kim et al., 2023). Overall, VR and AR technologies offer promising opportunities to transform education, providing immersive, interactive, and accessible learning experiences that enhance student engagement, motivation, and achievement across various subjects and disciplines.

Artificial Intelligence (AI) in Education

AI technologies are indeed revolutionizing educational settings, offering a myriad of benefits such as personalized tutoring, automated grading, and adaptive learning algorithms (Perisic, 2023). Personalized tutoring systems powered by AI can tailor learning experiences to individual student needs, providing customized instruction and feedback. Furthermore, AI algorithms streamline the grading process by automating the assessment of assignments, quizzes, and exams, allowing educators to allocate their time more efficiently and providing students with immediate feedback. Additionally, adaptive learning platforms driven by AI analyze student performance data to personalize instruction, dynamically adjusting content and pacing based on individual learning needs and progress. These AI-driven innovations hold immense potential to enhance teaching and learning experiences, catering to diverse learner needs and improving educational outcomes (Ossa, 2023).

Blockchain in Education

Blockchain technology has the potential to revolutionize credentialing and verification processes in education by providing secure, tamper-proof records of academic achievements. With blockchain, digital credentials like diplomas and certificates can be cryptographically signed and stored on a decentralized ledger, ensuring their authenticity and integrity. This technology streamlines the verification of academic credentials, enabling employers, educational institutions, and other stakeholders to securely verify individuals' qualifications without relying on centralized authorities. By leveraging blockchain, the education sector can enhance the trust, transparency, and efficiency of credentialing and verification processes, paving the way for a more reliable and accessible system for validating academic achievements.

Remote and Hybrid Learning

The COVID-19 pandemic indeed accelerated the adoption of remote and hybrid learning models, leading to increased reliance on educational technology tools for online instruction, collaboration, and assessment. Remote learning refers to fully online instruction, where students participate in classes and complete assignments remotely, often using video conferencing platforms, learning management systems, and other digital tools. Hybrid learning combines online and in-person instruction, allowing students to engage in both face-to-face and remote learning experiences. This model often involves a blend of traditional classroom instruction and online activities, such as flipped classrooms and asynchronous learning modules. EdTech tools play a crucial role in supporting remote and hybrid learning environments, providing features for virtual classroom management, online collaboration, content delivery, assessment, and communication between students and educators. Overall, the evolution of educational technology reflects a continuous effort to leverage technological advancements to enhance teaching and learning outcomes, increase accessibility, and adapt to changing educational paradigms and needs.

Advantages of AI in Virtual Teacher Learning Engagement

AI has emerged as a transformative force in virtual teacher learning engagement, offering a plethora of benefits to both educators and students. One significant advantage lies in the realm of personalized learning experiences. Through sophisticated algorithms, AI can analyze vast amounts of student data to discern individual learning styles, preferences, and areas of struggle (Ferguson & Shum, 2012). By leveraging this insight, AI-powered virtual teachers can tailor educational content to meet the unique needs of each learner, thereby enhancing engagement and comprehension.

Moreover, AI facilitates adaptive feedback mechanisms that provide students with instant guidance and corrections in real-time. This immediate feedback loop not only reinforces learning but also fosters a sense of continuous improvement and mastery (VanLehn et al., 2007). The interactive nature of AI-driven virtual teachers further enriches the learning experience by simulating dynamic scenarios and simulations, making concepts come to life in ways that captivate and engage students (Johnson, 2016).

Furthermore, the 24/7 availability of AI-enabled virtual teachers ensures accessibility and flexibility in learning. Students can access educational resources and support whenever they need it, irrespective of time constraints or geographical barriers (Dede, 2010). Additionally, AI generates valuable insights for educators through data-driven analytics, enabling them to refine teaching strategies and interventions to optimize learning outcomes (Baker & Inventado, 2014).

By integrating gamification elements and natural language processing capabilities, AI fosters an immersive and interactive learning environment that captivates students' interest and motivates their participation (Hamari et al., 2014). Overall, AI's role in virtual teacher learning engagement is instrumental in fostering student success and achievement in the digital age.

Challenges of AI in Virtual Teacher Learning Engagement

While AI offers significant advantages in virtual teacher learning engagement, it also presents several challenges that need to be addressed for its effective implementation. One major challenge is the potential for exacerbating educational inequalities. AI systems may inadvertently perpetuate biases present in the data they are trained on, leading to disparities in learning opportunities for different student groups (Rajkomar et al., 2018). Furthermore, there is a risk of over-reliance on AI-driven solutions, which could undermine the role of human educators and diminish the importance of interpersonal connections in the learning process (Hill, 2019).

Another challenge lies in ensuring the privacy and security of student data. AI-powered virtual teachers collect vast amounts of sensitive information about students, raising concerns about data privacy, consent, and protection from breaches or misuse (Molnar, 2019). Additionally, the complexity of AI algorithms and their decision-making processes may pose challenges for transparency and accountability, making it difficult to understand how certain recommendations or assessments are generated (Lipton, 2016).

Moreover, the implementation of AI in virtual teacher learning engagement requires substantial infrastructure and resources, which may not be accessible to all educational institutions, particularly those in underserved or low-resource areas (Dutta et al., 2017). Furthermore, there is a need for ongoing professional development and training to ensure that educators are equipped with the necessary skills to effectively integrate AI technologies into their teaching practices (Schwartz, 2019).

Finally, ethical considerations surrounding AI in education, such as algorithmic fairness, accountability, and autonomy, must be carefully navigated to avoid unintended consequences and ensure that AI systems serve the best interests of students and society as a whole (Crawford et al., 2019).

Addressing these challenges requires a multidisciplinary approach that involves collaboration between educators, policymakers, technologists, and other stakeholders to develop ethical frameworks, policies, and practices that promote the responsible and equitable use of AI in virtual teacher learning engagement.

In addition to the challenges mentioned, there are several other complexities surrounding the integration of AI in virtual teacher learning engagement that warrant attention.

One significant challenge is the need for continuous monitoring and evaluation of AI systems to ensure their effectiveness and impact on student learning outcomes. While AI holds promise in optimizing educational experiences, its success relies on ongoing assessment and refinement to address evolving educational needs and pedagogical approaches (Bulger et al., 2016). Furthermore, the rapid pace of technological advancement means that AI systems must be adaptable and responsive to changes in educational paradigms and priorities.

Another critical issue is the potential for AI to reinforce or perpetuate existing educational inequalities. AI algorithms may inadvertently reflect and amplify societal biases, leading to disparities in educational opportunities and outcomes for marginalized groups (Dillahunt et al., 2019). Moreover, the digital divide—unequal access to technology and digital resources—can exacerbate disparities in AI-enabled learning environments, further widening the gap between privileged and underserved students.

Furthermore, the ethical implications of AI in education extend beyond issues of bias and fairness to encompass broader questions of autonomy, agency, and human dignity (Floridi et al., 2018). There is a risk that excessive reliance on AI-driven solutions could diminish students' critical thinking skills and agency, potentially undermining their ability to engage meaningfully with complex ideas and make informed decisions. Additionally, the use of AI in educational assessment raises concerns about the commodification of learning and the erosion of holistic, humanistic approaches to education.

Addressing these challenges requires a holistic and interdisciplinary approach that considers not only technical considerations but also social, ethical, and pedagogical dimensions. Educators, policymakers, technologists, and other stakeholders must collaborate to develop transparent, inclusive, and ethically sound frameworks for the design, deployment, and evaluation of AI in virtual teacher learning engagement. By prioritizing equity, transparency, and human-centered design principles, we can harness the potential of AI to enhance educational opportunities and empower learners of all backgrounds.

Emerging Trends

Artificial intelligence (AI) is enabling the customization of learning experiences for individual students based on their unique needs, preferences, and learning styles (Firlej & Ziemba, 2020). AI-powered educational platforms can analyze student data in real-time to deliver personalized recommendations, adaptive learning pathways, and targeted interventions, thereby enhancing student engagement and academic outcomes. AI-powered conversational agents and chatbots are revolutionizing virtual teacher-learner interactions by providing personalized assistance, feedback, and support to students (Alfegi et al., 2021). These virtual assistants can engage students in natural language conversations, answer questions, provide explanations, and offer guidance in real-time, enhancing learner engagement and facilitating active participation in online learning environments. AI-driven virtual reality (VR) and augmented reality (AR) technologies are reshaping virtual teacher-learner engagement by creating immersive learning environments that simulate real-world experiences (Makransky et al., 2019). These technologies enable students to interact with digital content, explore complex concepts, and collaborate with peers in dynamic and interactive virtual spaces, leading to deeper engagement and enhanced learning outcomes. AI-based intelligent tutoring systems are enhancing virtual teacher-learner engagement by providing personalized, adaptive, and responsive instructional support to students (Woolf, 2010). These systems leverage machine learning algorithms to analyze student performance data, identify learning gaps, and deliver targeted feedback, scaffolding, and remediation, thereby fostering greater learner engagement and mastery of academic content.

Gamification and Game-Based Learning: AI-powered gamification and game-based learning platforms are transforming virtual teacher-learner engagement by leveraging game mechanics, incentives, and rewards to motivate and engage students in educational activities (Deterding et al., 2011). By integrating elements of competition, collaboration, and exploration into online learning experiences, these platforms enhance student motivation, participation, and enjoyment, leading to improved learning outcomes. AI-driven tools and applications are providing virtual teacher-learner engagement by supporting social and emotional learning (SEL) skills such as empathy, communication, and self-regulation (Pekrun & Linnenbrink-Garcia, 2012). These tools analyze student behavior, sentiment, and affective states to provide personalized feedback, encouragement, and emotional support, fostering positive relationships between teachers and learners in virtual learning environments. As AI technologies continue to proliferate in educational settings, there is a growing emphasis on promoting ethical and responsible AI use to ensure equitable access, privacy protection, and algorithmic transparency (Holstein & Glas, 2020). Educators, policymakers, and technology developers are collaborating to establish guidelines, frameworks, and best practices for integrating AI into teaching and learning practices while addressing potential risks and ethical considerations.

Implication of Educational Practices and Policies

Educational institutions need to adopt personalized learning approaches that leverage AI technologies to tailor instruction and support to individual student needs. This requires a shift away from traditional one-size-fits-all teaching methods towards more flexible and adaptive instructional strategies that accommodate diverse learning styles, abilities, and interests. Schools and universities should invest in the integration of AI-powered tools and platforms into their teaching and learning environments. This includes implementing AI-driven learning management systems, virtual tutoring programs, and adaptive learning software that enhance student engagement, promote active learning, and facilitate data-driven decision-making by educators. Educators need training and professional development opportunities to effectively integrate AI technologies into their teaching practices. This includes developing skills in data analysis, instructional design, and technology integration, as well as cultivating a pedagogical mindset that embraces innovation, experimentation, and lifelong learning.

Educational policies and guidelines should prioritize the ethical and responsible use of AI in teaching and learning contexts. This requires establishing clear standards and protocols for data privacy, algorithmic transparency, and equity in access to AI-powered educational resources. Educators, policymakers, and technology developers must collaborate to ensure that AI technologies are deployed in ways that promote social justice, diversity, and inclusion. Traditional methods of assessment and evaluation may need to be reimagined in light of AI-driven learning environments. Educators should explore alternative assessment approaches that leverage AI technologies to provide real-time feedback, assess higher-order thinking skills, and measure learning outcomes more holistically. This includes incorporating performance-based assessments, authentic tasks, and self-assessment opportunities into instructional practices.

Educational institutions should allocate resources and invest in infrastructure development to support the integration of AI technologies into teaching and learning. This may involve upgrading IT systems, expanding broadband access, and providing professional development opportunities for educators to build capacity in AI literacy and pedagogy. There is a need for ongoing research and evaluation of the impact of AI on educational practices and outcomes. Educational policymakers and researchers should collaborate to conduct empirical studies, longitudinal evaluations, and comparative analyses to assess the effectiveness, scalability, and sustainability of AI-driven educational interventions. This evidence-based approach will inform decision-making and guide the development of evidence-based policies and practices in the field of education.

CONCLUSION

The transformative impact of artificial intelligence (AI) on virtual teacher-learner engagement is reshaping educational dynamics, ushering in a new era of personalized, adaptive, and immersive learning experiences. As AI technologies continue to evolve and proliferate in educational settings, educators, policymakers, and stakeholders must navigate the opportunities and challenges presented by this rapidly changing landscape. The emerging trends discussed in this paper highlight the potential of AI to revolutionize virtual teacher-learner engagement by providing personalized learning experiences, leveraging conversational agents and chatbots, creating immersive virtual reality environments, and enhancing intelligent tutoring systems. These advancements have the potential to empower students, improve learning outcomes, and promote greater equity and inclusion in education.

However, realizing the full potential of AI in education requires careful consideration of ethical, social, and pedagogical implications. Educators must balance the benefits of AI-driven technologies with concerns about data privacy, algorithmic bias, and digital divide. Policymakers need to develop regulatory frameworks and guidelines that promote ethical and responsible AI use while fostering innovation and experimentation in educational practices. Moreover, the integration of AI into educational practices necessitates ongoing professional development for educators, investment in infrastructure and resources, and collaboration among stakeholders. By embracing a collaborative, evidence-based approach, educational institutions can harness the transformative power of AI to redefine educational dynamics, foster student engagement, and prepare learners for success in the digital age.

REFERENCES

Abdullah, Al-Ansi, Jaboob, Garad, & Al-Ansi. (2023). Analyzing augmented reality (AR) and virtual reality (VR) recent development in education. *Social Sciences & Humanities Open, 8*(1). doi:10.1016/j.ssaho.2023.100532

AlShaikh, R., Al-Malki, N., & Almasre, M. (2024). The implementation of the cognitive theory of multimedia learning in the design and evaluation of an AI educational video assistant utilizing large language models. *Heliyon, 10*(3). doi:10.1016/j.heliyon.2024.e25361

Audureau, E., Carrat, F., Layese, R., Cagnot, C., Asselah, T., Guyader, D., Larrey, D., De Lédinghen, V., Ouzan, D., Zoulim, F., Roulot, D., Tran, A., Bronowicki, J.-P., Zarski, J.-P., Riachi, G., Calès, P., Péron, J.-M., Alric, L., Bourlière, M., . . . Nahon, P. (2020). Personalized surveillance for hepatocellular carcinoma in cirrhosis – using machine learning adapted to HCV status. *Journal of Hepatology, 73*(6), 1434-1445. doi:10.1016/j.jhep.2020.05.052

Baker, R. S., & Inventado, P. S. (2014). Educational data mining and learning analytics. In J. Larusson & B. White (Eds.), *Learning analytics: From research to practice* (pp. 61–75). Springer. doi:10.1007/978-1-4614-3305-7_4

Boateng, S. L., Obed, K. A. P., Boateng, R., Budu, J., Marfo, J. S., & Asamoah, P. (2024). Educational technologies and elementary level education – A bibliometric review of scopus indexed journal articles. *Heliyon, 10*(7). doi:10.1016/j.heliyon.2024.e28101

Buckley, K., Fairman, K., Pogge, E., & Raney, E. (2022). Use of Learning Management System Data to Predict Student Success in a Pharmacy Capstone Course. *American Journal of Pharmaceutical Education, 86*(4). doi:10.5688/ajpe8594

Bulger, M., Mayer-Schönberger, V., & Padilla, N. (2016). Principled artificial intelligence: Mapping consensus in ethical and rights-based approaches to principles for AI. SSRN *Electronic Journal.* doi:10.2139/ssrn.2903242

Casanova, Vicente Vicente, Prieto, Pescador, Hernández Sánchez, Almaraz Menéndez, & Morales. (2016). Toxicology learning through the use of open educational resources: The European "TOX-OER" Project. *Toxicology Letters, 258*, S302-S303. . doi:10.1016/j.toxlet.2016.06.2111

Celik, I. (2023). Towards Intelligent-TPACK: An empirical study on teachers' professional knowledge to ethically integrate artificial intelligence (AI)-based tools into education. *Computers in Human Behavior, 138*. doi:10.1016/j.chb.2022.107468

Chen, L., Zeng, S., & Wang, W. (2021). The influence of emotion and learner control on multimedia learning. *Learning and Motivation, 76*. doi:10.1016/j.lmot.2021.101762

Crawford, K., Dobbe, R., Dryer, T., Fried, G., Green, B., Kaziunas, E., ... Salehi, N. (2019). *AI now report 2019*. Academic Press.

Dede, C. (2010). Comparing frameworks for 21st century skills. 21st Century Skills. *Rethinking How Students Learn*, *51*, 51–76.

Dillahunt, T., Wang, B., Teasley, S., West, R., & Zhang, P. (2019). *Confronting Bias in AI: Practical considerations for educators*. Retrieved from https://edtechbooks.org/ai/bias

Duin, A. H., & Tham, J. (2020). The Current State of Analytics: Implications for Learning Management System (LMS) Use in Writing Pedagogy. *Computers and Composition, 55*. doi:10.1016/j.compcom.2020.102544

Dutta, S., Mia, I., & Azad, M. A. K. (2017). Artificial Intelligence in Education: Challenges and Opportunities for Sustainable Development. In *2017 4th International Conference on Electrical Engineering and Information & Communication Technology (ICEEICT)* (pp. 1-6). IEEE.

Fellnhofer, K. (2019). Toward a taxonomy of entrepreneurship education research literature: A bibliometric mapping and visualization. *Educational Research Review, 27*, 28-55. doi:10.1016/j.edurev.2018.10.002

Ferguson, R., & Shum, S. B. (2012). Social learning analytics: five approaches. In *Proceedings of the 2nd International Conference on Learning Analytics and Knowledge* (pp. 23-33). Academic Press.

Floridi, L., Cowls, J., Beltrametti, M., Chatila, R., Chazerand, P., Dignum, V., ... Schafer, B. (2018). AI4People—an ethical framework for a good AI society: Opportunities, risks, principles, and recommendations. *Minds and Machines*, *28*(4), 689–707. doi:10.1007/s11023-018-9482-5 PMID:30930541

Hamari, J., Koivisto, J., & Sarsa, H. (2014). Does gamification work? A literature review of empirical studies on gamification. In *2014 47th Hawaii international conference on system sciences* (pp. 3025-3034). IEEE.

Harnadi, B., & Widiantoro, A. D. (2024). Investigating the behavioral differences in the acceptance of MOOCs and E-learning technology. *Computers in Human Behavior Reports, 14*. doi:10.1016/j.chbr.2024.100403

Hill, H. (2019). *Humans in the Loop: The Future of AI in Education* [White Paper]. Chan Zuckerberg Initiative.

Johnson, W. L. (2016). Serious use of a serious game for language learning. *ReCALL*, *28*(2), 231–247.

Khowaja, K., & Salim, S. S. (2013). A systematic review of strategies and computer-based intervention (CBI) for reading comprehension of children with autism. *Research in Autism Spectrum Disorders, 7*(9), 1111-1121. doi:10.1016/j.rasd.2013.05.009

Kim, J.-H., Kim, M., Park, M., & Yoo, J. (2023). Immersive interactive technologies and virtual shopping experiences: Differences in consumer perceptions between augmented reality (AR) and virtual reality (VR). *Telematics and Informatics, 77*. doi:10.1016/j.tele.2022.101936

Kirsten, R. (2016). Computer-Based Instruction (CBI) Within Special Education. In Computer-Assisted and Web-Based Innovations in Psychology, Special Education, and Health. Academic Press. doi:10.1016/B978-0-12-802075-3.00009-7

Legaki, N.-Z., Xi, N., Hamari, J., Karpouzis, K., & Assimakopoulos, V. (2020). The effect of challenge-based gamification on learning: An experiment in the context of statistics education. *International Journal of Human-Computer Studies, 144*. doi:10.1016/j.ijhcs.2020.102496

Li, H., Zhang, T., & Jacqueline, D. (2023). Exploring factors influencing young children's learning from storybooks: Interactive and multimedia features. *Journal of Experimental Child Psychology, 233*. doi:10.1016/j.jecp.2023.105680

Lipton, Z. C. (2016). The Mythos of Model Interpretability. *ICML Workshop on Human Interpretability in Machine Learning*.

Lu, D., & Xie, Y.-N. (2024). The application of educational technology to develop problem-solving skills: A systematic review. *Thinking Skills and Creativity, 51*. doi:10.1016/j.tsc.2023.101454

Memarian, B., & Doleck, T. (2024). A scoping review of reinforcement learning in education. *Computers and Education Open, 6*. doi:10.1016/j.caeo.2024.100175

Molnar, C. (2019). The importance of data privacy in the age of artificial intelligence. *Berkeley Technology Law Journal, 34*(2), 1253–1286.

Mukul, E., & Büyüközkan, G. (2023). Digital transformation in education: A systematic review of education 4.0. *Technological Forecasting and Social Change, 194*. doi:10.1016/j.techfore.2023.122664

Ossa, L. A., Rost, M., Lorenzini, G., Shaw, D. M., & Elger, B. S. (2023). A smarter perspective: Learning with and from AI-cases. *Artificial Intelligence in Medicine, 135*. doi:10.1016/j.artmed.2022.102458

Perisic, A., Perisic, I., Lazic, M., & Perisic, B. (2023). The foundation for future education, teaching, training, learning, and performing infrastructure - The open interoperability conceptual framework approach. *Heliyon, 9*(6). doi:10.1016/j.heliyon.2023.e16836

Rajkomar, A., Hardt, M., Howell, M. D., Corrado, G., & Chin, M. H. (2018). Ensuring fairness in machine learning to advance health equity. *Annals of Internal Medicine, 169*(12), 866–872. doi:10.7326/M18-1990 PMID:30508424

Schwartz, K. (2019). AI & Education: 10 Projects that are shaping the future of education. *Forbes*.

Shi, Haller, Reeson, & Li. (2024). Decoding the dynamics of knowledge pricing: An empirical investigation of MOOC platform edX's pricing structure and signaling effects. *International Journal of Information Management Data Insights, 4*(1). doi:10.1016/j.jjimei.2024.100220

Sperling, K., Stenberg, C.-J., McGrath, C., Åkerfeldt, A., Heintz, F., & Stenliden, L. (2024). In search of artificial intelligence (AI) literacy in teacher education: A scoping review. *Computers and Education Open, 6*. doi:10.1016/j.caeo.2024.100169

Takaki, O., Hamamoto, N., Takefusa, A., Yokoyama, S., & Aida, K. (2022). Reasonable Setting Values for Anonymization Algorithms for Online Educational Data Analysis Support System. *Procedia Computer Science, 207*, 2556-2566. doi:10.1016/j.procs.2022.09.314

VanLehn, K., Graesser, A. C., Jackson, G. T., Jordan, P., Olney, A., & Rose, C. P. (2007). When are tutorial dialogues more effective than reading? *Cognitive Science, 31*(1), 3–62. doi:10.1080/03640210709336984 PMID:21635287

Vihos, J., Chute, A., Johnston, S., Pawliuk, B., Buro, K., Velupillai, N., & Sampaga, C. (2023). Undergraduate nursing student satisfaction with open educational resources in a professional communication course. *Teaching and Learning in Nursing, 18*(4), 468-473. doi:10.1016/j.teln.2023.04.008

Yalcinkaya, T., & Yucel, S. C. (2023a). Determination of nursing students' attitudes toward and readiness for mobile learning: A cross-sectional study. *Nurse Education Today, 120*. doi:10.1016/j.nedt.2022.105652

Yalcinkaya, T., & Yucel, S. C. (2023b). Mobile learning in nursing education: A bibliometric analysis and visualization. *Nurse Education in Practice, 71*. doi:10.1016/j.nepr.2023.103714

Zhang, Basham, & Yang. (2020). Understanding the implementation of personalized learning: A research synthesis. *Educational Research Review, 31*. doi:10.1016/j.edurev.2020.100339

Chapter 14
Integrate the Artificial Intelligence and Human to Develop the Food Processing Unit

G. Ajitha
Institute of Aeronautical Engineering, Hyderabad, India

R. J. Anandhi
Department of Information Science Engineering, New Horizon College of Engineering, Bangalore, India

Atul Singla
Lovely Professional University, Phagwara, India

Q. Mohammad
Hilla University College, Babylon, Iraq

S. Shalini
Anna University, Chennai, India

ABSTRACT

Among the numerous sorts of Industries 5.0, machine learning incorporates AI, which is both a necessary and promising component. Companies in the food, health, and pharmaceutical industries, among others, consistently provide excellent outcomes, which are good for customers. An AI system that provides data in a way that people can understand and use is proposed in this chapter. Therefore, the chapter's explanation of Food Industry 5.0 is based on the idea that AI and HR are converging. The result will be that businesses will have more information on the most recent innovations in the food industry, including how to save time and money while increasing output. As a result, the food industry can make a lot of money by preparing meals in the most promotional, sanitary, and healthful way possible.

DOI: 10.4018/979-8-3693-4268-8.ch014

1. INTRODUCTION

The cultivation and distribution of food, and provisions, have long been seen as both an essential human necessity and the pinnacle of agricultural production (Alshahrani, 2021). Every nation's prosperity depends on food industrial products (Fidan et al., 2023). Furthermore, it is a key component in the development of national and international economies (Kumar, Gudiseva, et al., 2022). Consequently, solutions for the food industry must be thoroughly researched and tested to ensure their effectiveness and safety when implemented correctly (Kumar et al., 2022). Along with other newly developed technologies, artificial intelligence (AI) has shown promise in recent decades for improving the ability to achieve ideas (Kumar et al., 2023). Consequently, research into the high-tech food industry and advanced agricultural techniques powered by AI is crucial (Mendhe et al. (2021)). The societal expectations are addressed and high-quality goods are produced on schedule using these tactics (Narsimhulu et al., 2022). By immediately using these cutting-edge advancements, the food industry may boost its income by making much more healthy foods. The highlighted area falls under each of the distinct categories (Veeraiah et al. (2022)). This study covers all the bases when it comes to current technology (Shukla & Tiwari, 2023), providing a synopsis of artificial intelligence (AI) and machine learning studies in the food businesses(Yedida et al., 2023). AI is used for more in these simple kinds of tasks. In addition, it might be useful for storing, preparing, and supplying food (Miorandi et al., 2012). Intelligent devices, like as robotics and smart drones, can help bring down the cost of packaging (Nath et al., 2023). In addition, it will promote the distribution of food supplies (Khan et al., 2023), the completion of work in dangerous environments, and the supply of items of very high quality (Motlagh et al., 2020). The two main areas where AI has made significant strides in the food business are food quality governance and food security management. Given the growing interest in using Industry 5.0 technology for a variety of possible categories (Pivarnik et al., 2016), they were surprised to see that relatively little prior work focused on food security as an application of these technologies (Fidan et al., 2023). This deduction highlights the need to conduct an assessment of Industry 5.0 tools and their potential applications across the entire food supply chain. The goal is to identify ways in which these tools can be used to improve the food system and ultimately benefit consumers. Automated collaborative work is the future of Industry 5.0. The present article set out to do just that—offer a high-level summary of the potential advantages of Industry 5.0 technology across the whole food supply chain, from production to distribution to consumption. It illustrated the advantages of utilizing these significant technologies—such as artificial intelligence, massive analysis of data, the Internet of Everything (IoE), and so on—in a manner that is centred on the human element to work together to incorporate it into the food system and achieve durability of the supply chain, quality, honesty, and privacy. As far as anybody can tell, no one has yet investigated this subject.

Nevertheless, a computerized and authentic approach, such as AI and repeatability, fixes this field's variegated and non-linear path of activity. Artificial intelligence (AI) raises awareness of food security by using computational approaches that represent cognitive abilities and creative solutions to many types of food business problems. Automation helps the food production lines, which in turn collect, store, analyse, and potentially improve the supply chain as well as conduct risk assessments on massive amounts of data. However, the industry becomes more susceptible to hacking as a result of putting such technologies into action. A synopsis of each component of this expert effort is provided in the following document. In Section 2, the system program, statistical research, intuitive conceptual structure, and graph-based technique—as well as the AI's distinctive qualities in the food industry—are covered. To ensure the drilling process's long-term sustainability, this section delves into AI and ML processes. In

Section 3, several unique visuals and figures are provided to suggest the use of AI for Industry 5.0. Section 4 continues to hold sway when it addresses the positive impacts of AI & the astute advances that contemporary businesses are embracing.

2. METHODOLOGY

A Multilayer Perceptron (MLP) is a kind of artificial neural network with feed-forward algorithms that takes a combination of inputs and uses them to construct a collection of outputs. An outlining characteristic of multi-level percolating (MLP) is the supervised diagram (DG) that combines all levels of recommendation and output. Typically, issues needing further preparation are the ones that MLP is usually used to resolve. Backpropagation (BP) is a network person who pretends to be an expert namely secondhand for this purpose. Numerous fields of power benefit from this method; any examples contain system interpretation, picture acknowledgement, and voice acknowledgement. One plausible reason for the MLP's stable make even the top of the food disposed of the area is allure dependability and ease of movement. To train a multi-coating perceptron (MLP) for product pose discovery (FP), support the combined data that holds sure appearance derived from product characteristics. Beyond that, knowledge methods like backpropagation and slope decline are wanted to change the network's characteristics. According to Equation (1), the advantage "P" shows the total of each worth at the consequence coating for a likely bud. A weight vector denoted by "x" and an input denoted by "W" is used here. The bias is represented by the letter "c" and the ignition function by the letter "g (.)".

$$P = g\left(\sum_{j=1}^{o} x_j w_j + c\right) \tag{1}$$

2.1 Food Processing Back Propagation Machine Learning

A BPNN's strength lies in its capacity to estimate the network's mean weights using a hybrid of the gradient descent and the chain rule methods. There should be minimal room for mistakes in the network's data classifications if it can correctly identify the input attributes. Analyzing how the gradient of the loss functions affects the connection to the ANN parameters is a crucial use of BPNN. From the output layer, the gradient is backpropagated to the next layers, where each node at each level has its slope predicted. There are many methods in which backpropagation may occur. Using the substance of every neuron 'O' and Eq. (2), calculate the result.

$$P_O = g(net_O) = g\left(c_O \sum_{j=1}^{o} x_{jO} p_j\right) \tag{2}$$

The "net O." here represents the total emission from the input stratum terminals. The entire number of input components is represented by "o," the weight coefficient between nodes "j" and "O" is denoted as "x_{jO}," and the function that triggered is g(.). Equation (3) is a popular tool for assessing the output layer inaccuracy.

$$F = U - P \tag{3}$$

Here, "U" stands for the desired output, "P" for the predicted production, and "F" for the error. After being informed of an error, one has to go backwards to previous layers, such as the input & hidden layer, to set the newly created input to the OO. The equation provides a formula for the updated weight (4).

$$x_O = x_p - ms \times \frac{\partial Ftotal}{\partial x} \tag{4}$$

The learning rate (ms), the gradient $\frac{\partial Ftotal}{\partial x}$, the previous weight ($x_p$), and the new weight ($x_O$) are all given in Eq. (4). To modify the BPNN network's weight, a delta rule is used.

2.2 Food processing RNN

Additionally, it has been demonstrated that recurrent neural networks (RNNs) are effective. RNNs are made up of artificial neural networks (ANNs) that interact with one another, producing directed graphs and sequences. In this way, the temporal progression of a time sequence can be represented. Unlike feed-forward neural networks, RNNs can use their internal state, or memory, to broaden the range of inputs they can process. The versatile use of RNN words allows for the passage into two large communities of entities sharing a common basic structure: the limiting desire and the unconstrained goal communities. RNNs are used as a parameter for every storage-based calculation and can store the results they produce. To get to the result, RNN does a series of computations at the input, hidden Eq. (5), and then the last layers.

$$i_j = f(i_{j-1}, y_j) \tag{5}$$

Here, "y_j" is the input state, "i_{j-1}" is the prior state, and "i_j" is the current state. The result is finally calculated using Equation (6).

$$P_j = X_{iP} i_k \tag{6}$$

The layer with the output weight is denoted by "X_{iP}" and the result after the activation function's use is "i_k"; furthermore, "P_j" is the result in Eq. (6). In Eq. (7), "X_{it}" represents the weighting factor for the input neuron and "X_{yi}" represents the value factor of the repeating neuron. The outcome determines whether the "tanh" function is enhanced or diminished by adjusting the network's internal structure.

$$i_k = tanh(X_{ii} i_{j-1} + X_{yi} y_j) \tag{7}$$

Research neural networks (RNNs) have been used in FP at the adoption level for many years. A well-known writer devised a system to evaluate the bread-kneading method. To demonstrate the technique's dynamic nature, the researchers have used RNN as an example model. They tested the suggested method's efficacy while keeping voltage and temperature in mind. They used the Bayesian regularization and Levenberg-Marquardt methods to understand their ANN architecture. When tested with kneading bread, RNN performed better, according to the final findings. Figure 1 displays the MLP method with the backpropagation network.

Figure 1. MLP back propagation network strategy

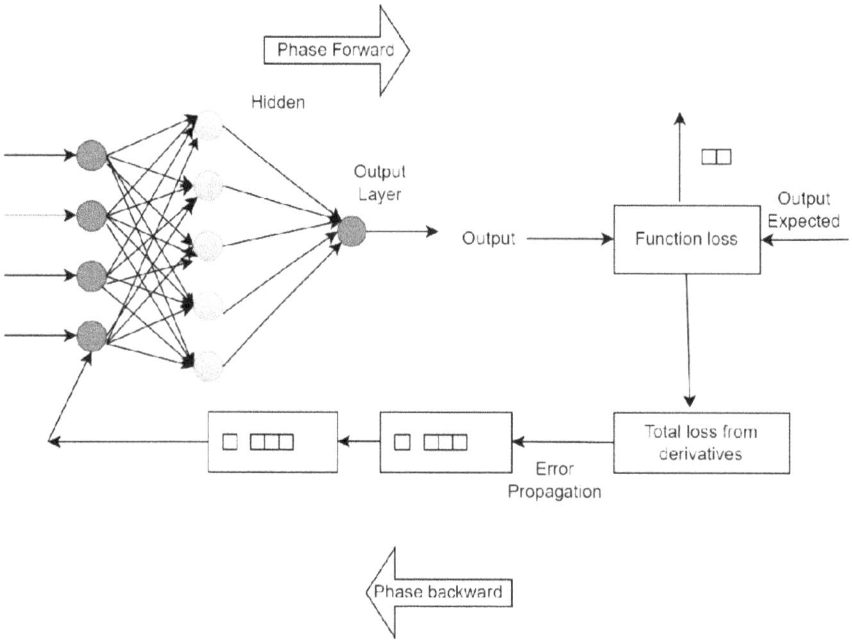

2.3 Food Processing DL

Deep learning (DL), the pinnacle of machine learning, allows for the systematic expression of data. One advantage is DL's powerful ability to easily recover pieces from raw data. Under some conditions, DL may improve classification accuracy while decreasing mistake rates. Countless parts are involved, including distortion, encoding, and decoding techniques, bunching, and more. Instantly after DL was introduced, its consumption levels skyrocketed, and it has been effectively used to tackle many academic challenges and expand into new application sectors like image processing and data analysis, among others. But there have also been major DL jobs in the FP industry. New developments in DL and substantial enhancements to FP have emerged. Give a quick example of a few of the main contributions. The use of convolutional neural networks (CNNs) to categorize food images into different classes is an innovative technique developed by a well-known researcher. Approaches proposed by the study's authors depend on a standard framework called "Deep Food." To determine the efficacy of their recommended technique, they reviewed the MLC-41 sample using a three-fold cross-validation methodology. Researchers compared the SMO classifier's performance with that of other popular prediction models after it had sorted the food photos. These models included Bayes Net and Random Forest.

Their reasoning was based on the fact that their suggested method works and that experiments in simulation prove the deep net architecture can handle multi-class segmentation. A state-of-the-art method for using CNN to predict meal calories and find out how common Multifood is was contributed by academics. The researchers looked through a dataset of thirty different kinds of meals; they used one for training and others to evaluate their method. The results of the presented research show that their proposed method is effective concerning memorization rate, reliability, and responsiveness.

3. RESULTS

Concerning data collection and analysis, the current study takes a methodical approach. Acquiring relevant data is the first phase. The next step is to conduct a pilot inquiry to better understand the current situation in the region. These research findings were retrieved from a wide variety of sources at precisely the right moment by using relevant search phrases, titles, and abstracts. The purpose of analyzing this data is to identify trends and opportunities for development in a more resilient industry. The current state of the food sector will also inform our recommendations, which will be based on the results of thorough investigations with plausible explanations. Based on the data gathered and the test classify the food business into four main categories (see Figure 2). Soil monitoring, rob cropping, and statistical evaluation are just a few examples of how artificial intelligence (AI) is being used in smart farming. Smart transport is the second category, and it's where artificial intelligence is having a game-changing impact on logistics. It is presently in use across a wide range of sectors, helping with things like traffic flow optimization and assisting vehicles including automobiles, trains, ships, and aeroplanes. All forms of transportation might be made safer, greener, smarter, and more efficient with the help of AI. For instance, self-driving cars using artificial intelligence might help reduce the number of accidents caused by human mistakes. The risks associated with these possibilities, however, are quite real, and include things like digital attacks, skewed transportation choices, and unanticipated outcomes and fraud. The openness of AI's decisions made while people aren't there raises ethical and employment concerns as well.

Intelligent processing is included in the third section. Companies in a wide variety of industries, including those dealing with food processing and handling, are interested in artificial intelligence. The FP and H industries are all affected by AI, both directly and indirectly. In a roundabout way, it helps farmers save money on item planning by better predicting the weather, which in turn helps farmers produce higher-quality material for food processing industries. Reduced transportation costs for food manufacturers are a direct result of AI's ability to help logistics businesses save costs. Regardless of the situation, it helps FP and H organizations reduce income. Intelligent distribution and consumption are FI's last areas of focus. It is clear from the label how the agricultural manufacturer will be used in FI. Machine learning (ML) may be useful for a variety of tasks, including logistics planning, demand forecasting, raw material collection, and delivery route mapping. Machine learning may eliminate roadblocks on distribution routes by improving the delivery agent's awareness of current and future traffic situations and providing them with real-time information about the optimal route. There is a plethora of applications designed specifically for the food service business that may aid with inventory management, serving quantity estimation, and recipe tracking in the present day.

This information may be used to do statistical analyses of overcrowding and the food products that are likely to be requested in the future. The selling of essential items over that period is combined with data from prior customer encounters, particularly information about meal alternatives, behaviours, and arguments, to provide these data points. The research leads us to assume that smart farming is becoming more and more in demand daily. Efforts to improve agricultural efficiency are receiving substantial funding from investors. Figure 3 shows the projected expansion of innovative agriculture over the next several decades. Figure 4 shows the future FI Investment forecasting to represent the bar chart. An insightful understanding of the intelligent business's investment forecast will be supported by this, and it will be easy to understand.

Figure 2. Technique mapping in AI and ML

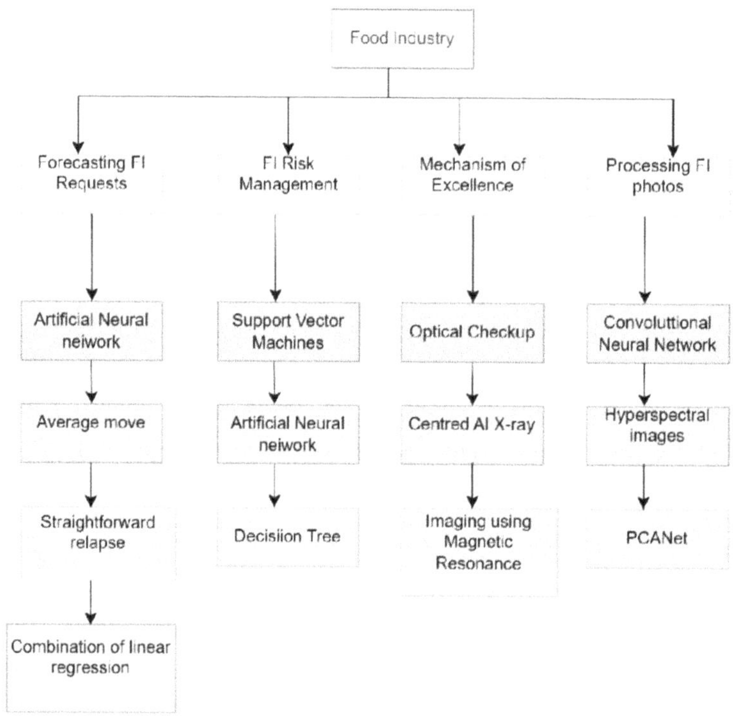

The food processing and manufacturing business needs a substantial amount of funding. When compared to human methods, AI systems can detect many manufacturing flaws in food far more rapidly. Furthermore, the area is known to rely heavily on research. Problems with cleanliness and security are at the top of the list of issues caused by the lack of computerization in the food processing chains, which are themselves hindered by global expansion. A user-friendly and inexpensive framework for a variety of artificial neural robotics projects is achieved when detectors are coupled with the microcontroller, which then creates output spikes. It has the potential to have significant positive effects on the food business. Artificial intelligence (AI) devices in the agro-based industry have combined machine learning with massive volumes of data to provide better information for decision-making and action-taking in the areas of agricultural outcomes, yield estimations, disease monitoring, and accessible features. Many industries stand to benefit from the automation and improvement of treatments, cost savings, and elimination of human error made possible by artificial intelligence and machine learning approaches. The kitchen staff at restaurants, cafés, and bars may use some help from AI and ML. These two divisions consistently provide several instances of AI in the food industry. Customers' and businesses' needs are always changing, therefore staying ahead of the competition is more important than ever.

Figure 3. Projected expansion of innovative agriculture

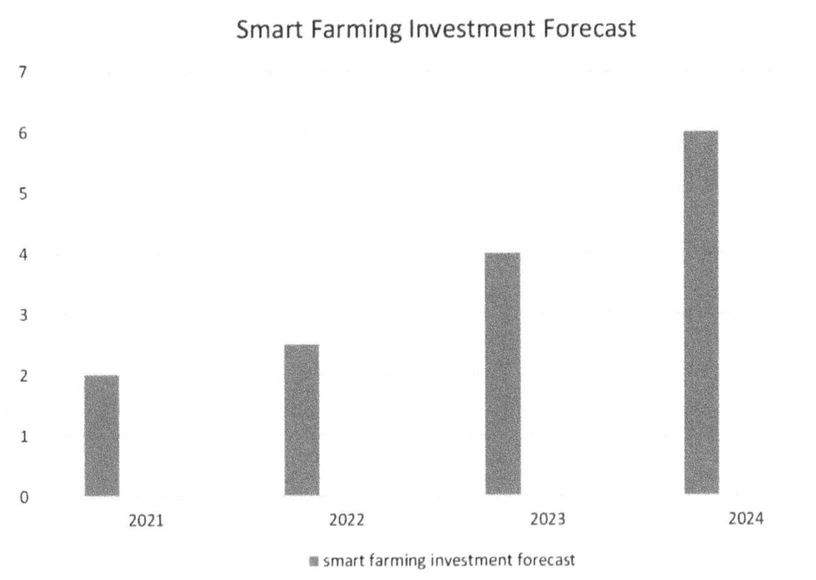

Figure 4. Future FI investment forecasting

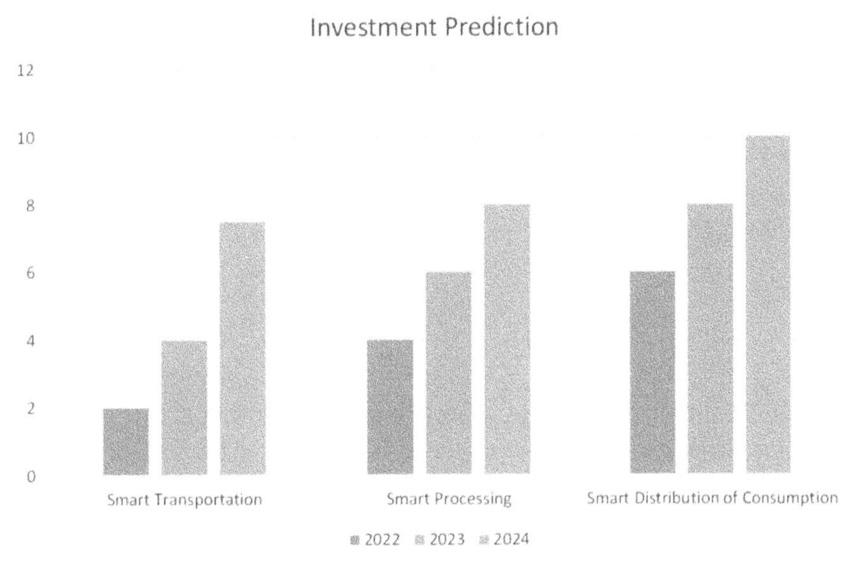

Automated technology is going to be a game-changer for the food business when it comes to protecting food standards and increasing industrial efficiency. The production of meals in the future will rely heavily on AI. Artificial intelligence also includes robotics. Businesses in the food and drink industry are making great strides thanks to innovative approaches to routine activities and streamlining internal processes to better meet the demands of their customers. Artificial intelligence (AI) is being used more and more to boost food production as the world moves beyond the COVID-19 pandemic. Since the human population is growing at a quicker rate than ever before, there is a greater need for AI that can improve speed, efficacy, and durability. In food presentation, the little details, such as size or colour, must be carefully considered. In the long run, these traits boost customer purchase rates because they let food providers make dependable decisions about how to cook different food products. Utilizing sensor capabilities like as cameras and near-infrared sensors, these state-of-the-art devices can see foodstuffs in a human-like manner. This is just one example of the complex features of AI; the food business uses a plethora of CCTV cameras. The use of specialized cameras equipped with face recognition and object recognition capabilities makes it possible to use this AI function to determine whether people are really serious about following food hygiene requirements.

4. CONCLUSION

The long-term effects of AI on the food industry are now the focus of academic research. There has been a lot of study on many different sorts of applications, but many of them are still in the early stages of development. Both DL and AI are useful tools in food processing, which involves tasks like grading, categorizing, forecasting, and quality evaluation. The use of these tactics has shown to be an effective approach for replicating difficult duties related to the cleanliness and safety of food services. Artificial intelligence (AI) and machine learning (ML) have provided humans with access to advanced technology in the real world, even though several ways have been devised to tackle the problems that have emerged in the food business. Artificial intelligence (AI) is capable of managing a wide variety of diverse systems that assess a multitude of factors that imply quality, appearance, texture, mainstream market popularity, and other characteristics. To produce a result that is accurate, trustworthy, and competent, as well as one that requires fewer human resources and helps the operator make long-range predictions about future occurrences, the one-of-a-kind method involves analyzing data patterns and refining the technique. The food industry has adopted the concept of artificial intelligence as a result of its ability to decrease and effectively complete each activity.

REFERENCES

Alshahrani, M. Y. (2021). Implementation of a blockchain system using improved Elliptic Curve Cryptography algorithm for the performance assessment of the students in the E-Learning platform. *Applied Sciences, 12*(1), 74. doi:10.3390/app12010074

Fidan, I., Huseynov, O., Ali, M. A., Alkunte, S., Rajeshirke, M., Gupta, A., Hasanov, S., Tantawi, K., Yasa, E., Yilmaz, O., Loy, J., Popov, V. V., & Popov, V. V. (2023). Recent inventions in additive manufacturing: Holistic review. *Inventions (Basel, Switzerland)*, *8*(4), 103. doi:10.3390/inventions8040103

Khan, M. A., Saleh, A. M., Waseem, M., & Sajjad, I. A. (2023). Artificial intelligence Enabled Demand Response: Prospects and challenges in smart grid environment. *IEEE Access : Practical Innovations, Open Solutions*, *11*, 1477–1505. doi:10.1109/ACCESS.2022.3231444

Kumar, S., Gudiseva, K., Iswarya, A., Rani, S., Prasad, K., & Sharma, Y. (2022). Automatic Music Generation System based on RNN Architecture. *2022 2nd International Conference on Technological Advancements in Computational Sciences (ICTACS)*. https://doi.org/10.1109/ICTACS56270.2022.9988652

Kumar, S., Raja, R., Mahmood, M. R., & Choudhary, S. (2023). A Hybrid Method for the Removal of RVIN Using Self Organizing Migration with Adaptive Dual Threshold Median Filter. *Sensing and Imaging*, *24*(1), 9. Advance online publication. doi:10.1007/s11220-023-00414-9

Kumar, S., Rani, S., Jain, A., Verma, C., Răboacă, M. S., Illés, Z., & Neagu, B. (2022). Face spoofing, age, gender and facial expression recognition using Advance Neural Network Architecture-Based Biometric System. *Sensors (Basel)*, *22*(14), 5160. doi:10.3390/s22145160 PMID:35890840

Mendhe, C. H., Henderson, N., Srivastava, G., & Mago, V. (2021). A scalable platform to collect, store, visualize, and analyze big data in real time. *IEEE Transactions on Computational Social Systems*, *8*(1), 260–269. doi:10.1109/TCSS.2020.2995497

Miorandi, D., Sicari, S., De Pellegrini, F., & Chlamtac, I. (2012). Internet of things: Vision, applications and research challenges. *Ad Hoc Networks*, *10*(7), 1497–1516. doi:10.1016/j.adhoc.2012.02.016

Motlagh, N. H., Mohammadrezaei, M., Hunt, J. D., & Zakeri, B. (2020). Internet of things (IoT) and the energy sector. *Energies*, *13*(2), 494. doi:10.3390/en13020494

Narsimhulu, K., Ramchander, N., & Swathi, A. (2022). *An AI Enabled Framework With Feature Selection for Efficient Heart Disease Prediction*. doi:10.1109/IC3I56241.2022.10073155

Nath, D., Kundu, I., Sharma, A., Shivhare, P., Afzal, A., Soudagar, M. E. M., & Park, S. G. (2023). Internet of Things integrated with solar energy applications: A state-of-the-art review. *Environment, Development and Sustainability*. Advance online publication. doi:10.1007/s10668-023-03691-2

Pivarnik, L. F., Richard, N., Gable, R. K., & Worobo, R. W. (2016). Knowledge and attitudes of produce and seafood processors and food safety educators regarding nonthermal processes. *Journal of Food Science Education*, *15*(4), 120–128. doi:10.1111/1541-4329.12093

Shukla, R. K., & Tiwari, A. (2023). Masked Face Recognition Using MobileNet V2 with Transfer Learning. *Computer Systems Science and Engineering*, *45*(1), 293–309. doi:10.32604/csse.2023.027986

Veeraiah, V., Pankajam, A., Vashishtha, E., Dhabliya, D., Karthikeyan, P., & Chandan, R. R. (2022, December). Efficient COVID-19 identification using deep learning for IoT. In *2022 5th International Conference on Contemporary Computing and Informatics (IC3I)* (pp. 128-133). IEEE. 10.1109/IC3I56241.2022.10073443

Yedida, V. S., Mehta, A., Vasudev, H., & Singh, S. (2023). *Role of numerical modeling in predicting the oxidation behavior of thermal barrier coatings*. IJIDEM. doi:10.1007/s12008-023-01306-8

Chapter 15
The Impact of Artificial Intelligence on Teacher-Learner Interaction in Virtual Education:
Addressing Challenges and Embracing Opportunities

Dalima Parwani
Sant Hirdaram Girls College, Bhopal, India

Manju Devnani
https://orcid.org/0009-0009-2368-1295
Sant Hirdaram Girls College, Bhopal, India

ABSTRACT

Artificial intelligence (AI) is transforming online education, offering personalized learning experiences and automating administrative tasks. This chapter explores AI's impact on teacher-learner interaction, highlighting opportunities and challenges. AI enables customized instruction, real-time communication, and immersive learning experiences. Yet, a cautious approach is needed to complement human expertise. AI addresses challenges like unequal access and engages diverse learners, revolutionizing content delivery and automating tasks. By combining AI with human insight, educators can create supportive virtual learning environments.

1. INTRODUCTION

Artificial Intelligence (AI) stands at the forefront of a technological revolution that is reshaping virtually every aspect of human society, and education is no exception. In recent years, AI has emerged as a powerful tool with the potential to revolutionize traditional educational paradigms, offering unprecedented opportunities to enhance teaching and learning processes.

DOI: 10.4018/979-8-3693-4268-8.ch015

The significance of AI in education lies in its capacity to personalize learning experiences, optimize instructional strategies, and provide valuable insights into student performance. Unlike traditional educational approaches, which often adopt a one-size-fits-all model, AI empowers educators to tailor instruction to the unique needs and preferences of individual learners. By analysing vast amounts of data, AI algorithms can identify patterns, predict learning trajectories, and offer personalized recommendations to optimize learning outcomes.

Moreover, AI has the potential to democratize access to education by breaking down geographical barriers and providing learners with anytime, anywhere access to educational resources. Virtual classrooms, online courses, and adaptive learning platforms powered by AI offer flexible learning options that cater to diverse learning styles and preferences. This democratization of education not only expands access to learning opportunities but also fosters inclusivity and diversity within educational settings.

Furthermore, AI holds the promise of transforming the role of educators from content providers to facilitators of learning. By automating routine tasks such as grading, lesson planning, and administrative duties, AI frees up valuable time for educators to focus on what matters most: fostering meaningful interactions with students, cultivating critical thinking skills, and nurturing creativity and innovation.

In essence, the significance of AI in revolutionizing education lies in its potential to unlock new possibilities for teaching and learning, empower educators and learners alike, and ultimately, shape the future of education in the digital age. As we embark on this transformative journey, it is essential to explore the opportunities and challenges that AI presents, and to harness its power responsibly to create a more equitable, accessible, and inclusive educational landscape.

1.1. Significance of Artificial Intelligence (AI) In Revolutionizing Education

Artificial intelligence is playing a vital role in upgrading the quality of higher education in numerous ways (Choi, 2020). AI-powered learning approaches have been employed to evaluate students' performance records, determine their strengths and weaknesses, and provide them with customized learning experiences that are tailored to their individual needs. This approach provides students with a tool kit model to gain knowledge more effectively with a productive outcome (Aldosari, 2020). AI-based technology such as Chatbots, Virtual Assistance tools, and Adaptive Learning Systems offer immersive and engaging learning experiences that allow students to discover complex theories and solutions in a more interactive and meaningful manner (Chaudhry et al., 2023; Pradana et al., 2023). In assessment and feedback, AI assists in grading and appraising student assignments, for example detecting similarities through Turnitin, monitoring students' participation and involvement in library resource utilization, providing faster and more precise feedback to students, and freeing up time for instructors to focus on other aspects of teaching (Essien et al., 2020).

Similarly, AI-powered chatbots offer learners immediate and personalized assistance for their academic and organizational needs, such as answering questions about course materials or providing information on course registration and addressing basic quarries. These systems successfully analyze student data to predict which students are at risk of dropping out or struggling academically. This filtration helps instructors and support staff identify and intervene with students at academic risk early, providing them with the help they need to succeed.

It has been identified that various AI applications, for example, Bit.ai, Mendeley, Turnitin, elinik.io, and Coursera tools and platforms support higher education research by analyzing large data sets, generating insights and predictions, and identifying patterns that may be difficult for human researchers to detect (Wenge, 2021).

As technology continues to evolve and improve, we can expect to see even more innovative and effective applications of AI in education, leading to more personalized, engaging, and effective learning experiences for students (Li et al., 2021).

This promising journey of AI significantly improves the performance and engagement of teachers in higher education. Since teaching staff Rahiman & Kodikal, Cogent Education (2024), 11: 2293431 https://doi.org/10.1080/2331186X.2023.2293431 Page 2 of 24 in higher education have a critical role both in administrative and academic and are completely engaged in regulatory, accreditation, and other important activities, the adoption of AI can help teachers automate administrative tasks, such as grading assignments, tracking attendance, and providing feedback to students, etc (Bisen et al., 2021). AI also helps teachers identify areas where they can improve their teaching skills and provide personalized professional development opportunities. For example, AI-powered coaching tools provide teachers with feedback on their teaching performance and suggest areas for improvement (Minkevics & Kampars, 2021).

Traditional teaching and assessment approaches prove insufficient in addressing these pressing issues. Furthermore, the absence of opportunities for international collaboration and cultural exchange in higher education compounds these challenges. To bridge these gaps, the integration of artificial intelligence (AI) emerges as a pivotal solution. AI algorithms have the capacity to analyze individual learning patterns, allowing for the tailoring of coursework to accommodate diverse preferences. The incorporation of predictive analytics effectively identifies students at risk, facilitating timely interventions to support their academic journey. AI-driven educational content delivery systems offer adaptability to students' pace, learning styles, and knowledge gaps, revolutionizing the approach to content dissemination.

Additionally, the automation of administrative tasks through AI provides the means to liberate faculty and staff from routine responsibilities, allowing them to focus on more impactful activities. Hence, the ongoing research actively contributes to the empowerment of the higher education system through the adoption of AI. The findings of this research endeavor will serve to assist institutional policymakers in recognizing how the adoption of new technology is perceived in higher education, enabling them to provide the necessary infrastructure and training to overcome specific challenges. Since the role of AI is inevitable in future education, current research aims to identify the level of awareness of faculty members on the applicability and adoption of artificial intelligence.

2. EVOLUTION OF VIRTUAL EDUCATION

In recent years, the landscape of knowledge acquisition and skill development has been reshaped by online education. With the rapid advancements in technology and the internet, traditional classrooms have relinquished their exclusivity as primary learning environments.

Online education has emerged as a versatile and easily accessible alternative, offering a myriad of learning opportunities to individuals from diverse age groups and backgrounds.

While the concept of online education has existed for decades, its popularity experienced a significant surge in the early 21st century. This surge was propelled by the advent of high-speed internet, powerful computing devices, and innovative learning platforms, which collectively acted as catalysts for its growth.

The effectiveness of education hinges on its ability to evolve and adapt to changing circumstances. While traditional educational settings have proven effective in the past, the digital age has brought about a new form of education: virtual education, which has significantly enhanced efficiency in contemporary learning environments.

Although many equate virtual education solely with online learning, its definition extends to any form of educational instruction that doesn't necessitate a physical classroom environment.

In today's educational landscape, virtual online education has made a profound impact and transformed educational practices. A timeline provided by Affordable-online-colleges.net outlines the evolution of virtual education and highlights its pioneering figures.

Institutions ranging from prestigious universities to local schools recognized the potential of online education in reaching a broader audience and providing greater flexibility in the learning process.

The Birth of E-Learning (1990s)

The digital learning revolution began with the advent of e-learning in the 1990s. The internet paved the way for online courses and educational resources, breaking down geographical barriers. Early e-learning materials were often basic, consisting of text-based content and simple graphics. However, this marked the first step towards a more accessible and flexible form of education.

Multimedia Integration (2000s)

As technology continued to advance, the 2000s saw the integration of multimedia elements into digital learning. Videos, animations, and interactive simulations enhanced the learning experience, catering to different learning styles. Learning Management Systems (LMS) also gained popularity, providing a centralized platform for course delivery, assessment, and student management.

Rise of Massive Open Online Courses (MOOCs)

The 2010s witnessed the rise of Massive Open Online Courses, or MOOCs, revolutionizing the accessibility of higher education. Platforms like Coursera, edX, and Khan Academy offered courses from top universities and educators globally. MOOCs not only democratized education but also allowed learners to progress at their own pace, promoting a self-directed learning approach.

Interactive Learning and Gamification

With the recognition of the importance of engagement in learning, the 2010s also saw the integration of gamification and interactive elements (See also: How Gamification Increases Engagement and Motivation in Digital Learning). Educational games and simulations made learning more enjoyable and effective, catering to younger audiences and promoting active participation.

Immersive Technologies (2020s and Beyond)

As we step into the 2020s, digital learning has reached new heights with the advent of immersive technologies. Virtual Reality (VR) and Augmented Reality (AR) have transformed traditional classrooms into virtual landscapes, providing learners with immersive and interactive experiences. Virtual classrooms allow students to collaborate, engage in real-time discussions, and even conduct virtual experiments.

2.1 Artificial Intelligence and Its Applications in Various Sectors

Artificial intelligence (AI) is experiencing rapid expansion across various industries, permeating countless applications. Companies and individuals leverage AI to streamline repetitive tasks, analyse vast volumes of data, and enhance the efficiency of existing programs. From Google's algorithms to self-driving vehicles to Amazon's Alexa, AI has become an integral part of our daily lives, shaping our interactions with technology.

Here are several examples of artificial intelligence applications driving technological progress:

2.1.1 ChatGPT

- The debut of ChatGPT showcased the potential of future chatbots, engaging users in conversations to address inquiries and even debate concepts.
- ChatGPT represents an evolved iteration of AI chatbots, which have been widely embraced by numerous companies for round-the-clock customer assistance and swift issue resolution.
- With ongoing advancements in AI technology, it's anticipated that the language processing capabilities of chatbots will become increasingly refined, further enhancing their effectiveness in communication.

2.1.2 Agriculture

- AI's significance in agriculture has been remarkable. Utilizing computer vision and machine learning, applications have emerged capable of identifying soil deficiencies and offering planting advice.
- Precision agriculture, driven by AI, empowers farmers to leverage weather pattern analysis for accurate forecasting and optimal planting schedules. AI aids in selecting suitable crops, combating pest infestations, and assessing soil conductivity and pH levels.
- The integration of AI with robotics further revolutionizes agriculture, enabling faster and more efficient crop harvesting compared to traditional human labour methods.

2.1.3 Ecommerce

- The ecommerce sector has embraced AI extensively, leveraging its capabilities to predict trends, evaluate performance, and streamline inventory management processes.
- AI's adeptness at tracking user behavior and validating data has proven instrumental in combating credit card fraud and counterfeit online reviews, bolstering trust and security within the ecommerce landscape.
- AI-driven "recommendation engines" personalize the shopping experience by suggesting products tailored to individual browsing histories and preferences, enhancing customer engagement and satisfaction.

- Virtual assistants and chatbots contribute to the ecommerce ecosystem, providing interactive and responsive customer support to address inquiries and streamline purchasing experiences.

2.1.4 Education

- While education is still dominated by human personnel, artificial intelligence helps boost educators' potential. AI facilitates automation in various repetitive and data-intensive tasks within education, including grading homework, scheduling meetings, managing multiple online courses concurrently, and sending personalized communications to students.
- Additionally, AI contributes to the creation or digitization of lectures and study guides, streamlining content delivery and accessibility.
- Chatbot-style AIs are increasingly prevalent in education, offering quick responses to routine inquiries and freeing up educators' time for more complex tasks and personalized student interactions.

2.1.5 Finance

- The finance industry extensively integrates AI across various functions and levels. Customers benefit from AI-driven services providing information about their banking and investment accounts, enhancing accessibility and transparency.
- Banks and credit card companies employ AI to identify alterations in transaction patterns, effectively detecting and preventing fraudulent activities.
- Lenders utilize artificial intelligence to forecast and evaluate borrowers' risk profiles, facilitating informed lending decisions.
- Venture capital firms leverage AI to derive personalized insights and enhance decision-making regarding financial risk management.
- Robo-advisors and financial management services capitalize on AI to automate trading processes, offering efficient and algorithm-driven investment solutions to clients.

2.1.6 HealthCare

- Artificial intelligence has made significant inroads into the medical field, enhancing various aspects of healthcare delivery. AI aids administrative tasks such as data processing, meeting scheduling, file organization, and transcription of medical notes, streamlining operations for healthcare administrators.
- One of the most notable applications of AI in healthcare is robotic-assisted surgeries, which offer enhanced precision, reduced invasiveness, minimal error margins, and 24/7 availability compared to traditional surgeries.
- AI contributes to medical diagnoses by utilizing wearable devices to track health parameters and detect issues before patients are symptomatic. Moreover, AI assists in interpreting medical scans, such as MRIs, enabling faster and more accurate identification of harmful abnormalities.
- Pharmaceutical companies leverage AI to analyze historical and contemporary data, facilitating the discovery of new potential drugs and accelerating the drug development process.

2.1.7 Marketing

- Artificial intelligence plays a crucial role in marketing strategies across various industries, offering capabilities for swift data analysis and insight generation. Marketing teams utilize AI to generate comprehensive campaign reports, enhancing decision-making processes and assessing campaign performance effectively. AI enhances customer engagement by personalizing messages and delivering targeted content based on individual preferences and behaviors.
- Online retargeting campaigns are optimized through AI, allowing for dynamic adjustments based on user interactions and browsing history.
- AI-driven systems enable marketing teams to pivot advertising methodologies mid-campaign, adapting to new insights and market trends in real-time.
- Chatbots contribute to marketing efforts by facilitating interactive customer interactions, with language processing aiding in analyzing and producing marketing content.

2.1.8 Social Media

Social media platforms represent another significant application of artificial intelligence, with companies like Meta and Twitter harnessing AI to analyze vast amounts of data and derive actionable insights. AI enables various functions on social media platforms, including:

- Tracking user behavior to inform marketing and advertisement strategies, allowing companies to target audiences more effectively.
- Monitoring comments and interactions to suggest new posts and accounts to follow, enhancing user engagement and discovery.
- Determining trending topics and discussions in real-time, enabling timely and relevant content creation.
- Generating targeted content based on demographic and behavioral data, ensuring personalized user experiences.
- Combatting cyberbullying and identifying harmful or illegal content through AI-powered content moderation tools, promoting a safer online environment.

2.1.9 Household

- Automated driving programs used by companies like Tesla, Audi, and Volvo, which rely on AI for autonomous navigation and collision avoidance.
- Email filtering systems that utilize AI to identify and block spam and illicit content, enhancing user experience and security.
- Smart devices equipped with facial recognition technology for user authentication and transaction security.
- Domestic robots such as automated vacuums and lawn mowers, which leverage AI to navigate spaces, avoid obstacles, and optimize performance.
- Virtual assistants like Siri, Amazon Alexa, and Google Assistant, as well as advanced home security systems, which rely on artificial intelligence for natural language processing, task automation, and personalized assistance.

2.2 Applications of AI in Education

2.2.1. Plagiarism Detection: AI-powered plagiarism detection tools, such as Turnitin and Grammarly, analyse student submissions to identify instances of plagiarism by comparing them against a vast database of academic sources and previously submitted work.

2.2.2. Exam Integrity: AI algorithms can monitor students during online exams to detect suspicious behaviour, such as cheating or unauthorized collaboration. These systems use techniques like facial recognition, eye tracking, and keystroke analysis to ensure exam integrity.

2.2.3. Chabot's for Enrolment and Retention: Universities deploy AI-powered chatbots on their websites and messaging platforms to assist prospective students with enrollment inquiries, provide information about courses and programs, and support current students with academic advising and retention efforts.

2.2.4. Learning Management Systems (LMS): AI-enhanced LMS platforms personalize learning experiences by recommending relevant resources, adapting content to individual learning styles, tracking student progress, and providing real-time feedback to both students and instructors.

2.3.5. Transcription of Faculty Lectures: AI transcription tools, such as Otter.ai and Rev.com, automatically transcribe faculty lectures and discussions in real-time or post-event. These transcriptions can be used for accessibility purposes, note-taking, and content review.

2.3.6. Enhanced Online Discussion Boards: AI-powered discussion platforms, like Packback and Piazza, facilitate engaging online discussions by automatically generating questions, moderating threads, and providing personalized feedback to students based on their contributions.

2.3.7. Analyzing Student Success Metrics: AI algorithms analyze vast amounts of student data, including grades, attendance, engagement, and demographic information, to identify patterns and predict student success or at-risk behaviors. This enables proactive interventions and targeted support for students.

2.3.8. Academic Research: AI technologies, such as machine learning and natural language processing, assist researchers in analyzing large datasets, discovering patterns in academic literature, generating hypotheses, and even automating aspects of the research process, such as data collection and analysis.

2.3.9. Connected Campuses: AI-powered campus management systems integrate various administrative functions, such as student records, scheduling, facilities management, and transportation, to create connected and efficient campus ecosystems that enhance the overall student experience.

These examples demonstrate how AI is transforming various aspects of higher education, from administrative tasks to teaching and learning processes, ultimately improving efficiency, effectiveness, and student outcomes.

2.4. Benefits of AI in Education

The integration of artificial intelligence (AI) in education brings forth numerous benefits that positively impact students' learning experiences. This section highlights some of the key advantages of AI in education:

2.4.1. Personalized Learning: AI-powered educational platforms have the capability to analyse vast amounts of data to understand students' learning styles, preferences, and knowledge gaps. With this information, AI can provide personalized learning experiences by delivering tailored content, resources, and assessments to each student. Personalized learning allows students to progress at their own pace, focus on areas where they need improvement, and explore advanced concepts when ready. This individualized approach enhances student engagement, motivation, and overall learning outcomes.

2.4.2. Immediate and Constructive Feedback: AI enables the provision of timely and constructive feedback to students. Automated grading systems powered by AI algorithms can assess assignments, quizzes, and exams quickly, providing students with immediate feedback on their performance. This prompt feedback allows students to understand their strengths and weaknesses, identify areas for improvement, and make necessary adjustments in real-time. By addressing gaps in understanding promptly, students can enhance their learning and make progress more effectively.

2.4.3. Enhanced Collaboration and Interaction: AI technologies facilitate collaborative learning environments. Intelligent tutoring systems and virtual learning assistants can support group discussions, provide guidance, and encourage collaboration among students. These AI-powered tools can simulate real-world scenarios, promote active participation, critical thinking, and problem-solving skills. By fostering collaboration and interaction, AI empowers students to learn from each other, exchange ideas, and develop essential teamwork skills.

2.4.4. Wealth of Educational Resources: AI can efficiently curate and organize vast amounts of educational content, making it easily accessible to students. AI-powered educational platforms can recommend relevant resources, such as textbooks, articles, videos, and interactive learning materials, based on students' individual needs and preferences. This access to a wide range of educational resources empowers students to explore diverse topics, deepen their understanding, and engage with various learning materials beyond traditional classroom resources.

2.4.5. Intelligent Learning Analytics: AI enables advanced data analytics that can provide valuable insights into students' learning progress, patterns, and areas of improvement. By analysing data on student performance, AI algorithms can identify trends and patterns, allowing educators to make data-informed decisions. Intelligent learning analytics can help educators identify struggling students, personalize interventions, and develop targeted instructional strategies. This data-driven approach supports evidence-based teaching practices and enhances the overall effectiveness of educational interventions.

2.4.6. Continuous Learning Support: AI-powered virtual learning assistants can provide round-the clock support to students. These assistants can answer questions, provide explanations, and offer guidance, ensuring that students have access to learning support regardless of time or location. Continuous learning support helps students overcome barriers and challenges in their learning process, reinforcing their confidence and motivation.

The integration of AI in education offers a range of benefits that enhance students' learning experiences. Personalized learning, immediate feedback, enhanced collaboration, access to educational resources, intelligent learning analytics, and continuous learning support are some of the advantages that AI brings to education. By leveraging AI technologies, educators can create dynamic and engaging learning environments that cater to the unique needs and preferences of students, leading to improved learning outcomes and student success.

3. CHALLENGES IN TEACHER-LEARNER INTERACTION IN VIRTUAL EDUCATION

The COVID-19 pandemic has ushered in a "new normal" way of living, necessitating adaptations in our lifestyles, work routines, and interactions. As part of this adjustment, there has been a noticeable increase in parental expenditure on electronic devices for home-based learning, reflecting a shift towards online education as emphasized by governmental directives. With the closure of traditional educational institutions, online learning has emerged as a vital alternative to ensure the continuity of education during these unprecedented times.

Universities in Malaysia have moved their classes online to ensure continuity to the teaching and learning process and minimize the spread of Covid-19 infection (Salina, Mazlina, & Wafa, 2020). In this regard, the main concern is to ensure all students receive education online of the same quality as traditional learning sessions when learning is done remotely.

Presently, there are a lot of technologies available for online teaching and learning processes but sometimes they create certain issues and challenges (or constraints). Some examples of technical issues are downloading errors, issues with installation, login problems, and problems with audio and video (Dhawan, 2020).

3.1. Obstacles Faced By Teachers and Learners in Virtual Classrooms

Several researchers had conducted studies related to teachers or lecturers' and students' perceptions of online teaching and learning amid the Covid-19 pandemic. Some of the issues and challenges that have been faced by teachers or lecturers and students while using online teaching and learning approach among others are (Dhawan, 2020; Misha, Gupta, and Shree, 2020; Rapanta et al. 2020; Selvanathan, Atikah, & Alyani, 2020):

3.1.1. Accessibility

It is said that students without reliable internet access and technology struggle to participate in digital learning. Limited internet access is challenging to the students in rural areas for their studies, which also resulted in delay for the task submission (Selvanathan, Atikah, & Alyani, 2020). However, for those who do have access to technology, learning online can be more effective in many ways.

3.1.2. Affordability

Online education is often viewed as a more economical option due to reduced expenses associated with transportation, lodging, and overall institution-based learning costs.

3.1.3. Flexibility

It is another interesting aspect of online learning; a learner can schedule or plan their time for completion of courses available online. However, sometimes student finds online teaching has so much of time and flexibility that students never find time to do it (Dhawan, 2020).

3.1.4. Learning Pedagogy

Integrating traditional face-to-face lectures with technology gives rise to blended learning and flipped classrooms, potentially enhancing students' learning outcomes. However, despite these benefits, some students perceive online teaching as monotonous and lacking engagement. Personalized attention and interactive dialogue are challenging to achieve in online settings. Moreover, lecturers have reported difficulties in conducting practical classes online during lockdowns, as it necessitates systematic demonstration of procedures in the students' presence.

3.1.5. Life-Long Learning

Students have the opportunity to engage in continuous learning and skill development, as they can access educational resources anytime and anywhere. However, the full potential of online learning is often hindered by the lack of practical application of learned concepts.

However, challenges such as limited internet accessibility, including network availability and financial constraints on purchasing data packages, pose significant barriers to some students' engagement with online learning.

3.2 Limitations of Current Virtual Education Platforms in Facilitating Meaningful Interaction

Online programs possess notable strengths and provide unparalleled access to high-quality education; however, they also harbor inherent weaknesses that may jeopardize the success of such programs. These challenges can be categorized into six main areas:

3.2.1. Technology

3.2.1.1. Equity and Access to Technology

For any online program to thrive, it necessitates accessible technology for its students. The absence of access, whether due to economic constraints or logistical challenges, may exclude otherwise eligible students from participating in the course. This poses a significant concern, particularly in rural and economically disadvantaged areas. Moreover, from an administrative standpoint, if students cannot afford the technology required by the institution, they may opt out of the program. Additionally, internet accessibility is not ubiquitous, and in certain regions of the United States and other countries, accessing the internet can be costly. Some users pay a fixed monthly fee for their internet connection, while others are billed based on their online usage. If participants' online time is constrained by their internet access affordability, equitable instruction and participation in the online program may not be feasible for all students.

3.2.1.2. Computer Literacy

Both students and instructors must possess a basic level of computer literacy to effectively engage in an online learning environment. This includes proficiency in using various search engines, navigating the World Wide Web, and familiarity with tools such as Newsgroups, FTP procedures, and email. Without these foundational technology skills, individuals may struggle to succeed in an online program. A student or faculty member who lacks proficiency in using the system may impede the overall success of the program.

Limitations of Technology

The success of an online program hinges on the reliability and user-friendliness of the technology utilized. However, even the most advanced technology is not infallible. It is not a matter of if, but when, equipment failures will occur within an online program. While technology is intended to seamlessly integrate into the learning process, breakdowns can happen at any point along the system. For instance, the server hosting the program could crash, disrupting access for all participants. Networked computers used by participants may encounter technical issues, hindering access to the class. Individual PCs can experience various problems that impede students' access. Furthermore, internet connections may fail, or the hosting institution's network may become overwhelmed, leading to slowdowns or complete failures. In such scenarios, technology ceases to be seamless and reliable, potentially detracting from the learning experience.

3.2.2. The Students

While online education can serve as an effective alternative for mature, self-disciplined learners, it may not be suitable for those who require more guidance and support. Online asynchronous learning empowers students to take charge of their educational journey and offers flexibility in study schedules, particularly beneficial for non-traditional learners. However, this places a greater onus on students to manage their learning independently. To thrive in an online program, students must demonstrate strong organizational skills, self-motivation, and effective time management abilities to keep pace with the course requirements. Consequently, online education may not be suitable for younger students, such as those in elementary or secondary school, and other individuals who rely heavily on structured guidance and struggle to assume the responsibilities inherent in the online learning paradigm.

3.2.3. The Facilitator

3.2.3.1. The Lack of Essential Online Skills

Effective in-person teaching skills may not necessarily translate into effective online instruction. If instructors lack adequate training in online delivery methods and techniques, the success of the online program may be compromised. An instructor must possess strong written communication skills and proficiency in the language of instruction to ensure the efficacy of the online course. Without adequately prepared facilitators, the online program's quality may suffer.

An online instructor must compensate for the absence of physical presence by fostering a supportive atmosphere in the Virtual Classroom where all students feel encouraged to participate, knowing that their instructor is accessible. Failure to establish such an environment can result in alienation among students and between students and the instructor.

3.2.4. The Online Environment

3.2.4.1. Level of Interaction

The potential of online learning is most evident in the high level of synergy fostered by active dialogue among participants, a key source of learning in a Virtual Classroom. However, in larger classes (20 or more students), the level of synergy tends to diminish along the learning continuum, eventually transitioning into independent study to accommodate the larger class size. At this stage, dialogue and interaction among participants and the facilitator become limited, indicating that the medium is not fully utilized to its potential.

3.2.4.2. Subjects Inappropriate for Online Instruction

Despite the recent excitement surrounding online programs, it is crucial to acknowledge that certain subjects are not suitable for online instruction due to limitations inherent in the electronic medium. Examples include hands-on subjects such as public speaking, surgery, dental hygiene, and sports, where physical movement and practice are integral to achieving the learning objectives. These subjects are ideally taught in a traditional face-to-face learning environment. Hybrid courses may offer a temporary solution by making certain aspects of the course more accessible to a wider audience who may face challenges attending campus.

3.2.5. The Curriculum

The design and development of the curriculum for any online program are crucial for its success. Often, in the rush to establish distance education initiatives, institutions overlook the significance of the curriculum and the necessity for qualified professionals to craft it. What works in traditional classroom settings may not necessarily translate effectively to an online environment, where learning dynamics and instructional methods differ significantly. Online curricula need to prioritize student dialogue through written communication and foster group interaction and engagement. Traditional lecture-based approaches are incompatible with the success of online programs. However, by adapting or creating curricula tailored to the online medium, high-quality education can be delivered effectively.

This is an exciting era for the intersection of technology and education. Online programs present technologically-driven instructional platforms that broaden learning opportunities and offer quality education through diverse formats and modes. Particularly for adult learners seeking to continue their education amidst work, family, and other commitments, online programs provide a convenient solution. Higher education institutions recognize the indispensable role of online programs in extending educational access to diverse populations. To ensure the success of an online program, careful consideration and balance are required in areas such as curriculum design, facilitation, technology integration, and student engagement, leveraging the strengths of this format while mitigating potential weaknesses.

3.3. Addressing Issues Such as Lack of Personalization, Communication Barriers, and Technical Difficulties

To address the issue of lack of personalization, educational institutions can implement adaptive learning technologies that tailor the learning experience to individual students' needs and preferences. This might involve using AI algorithms to analyze students' learning styles, strengths, and weaknesses, and then providing customized learning materials and activities accordingly. Additionally, instructors can incorporate more interactive and collaborative elements into their teaching methods, allowing students to engage with the material in ways that resonate with their unique learning preferences.

Communication barriers can be overcome by fostering a more inclusive and interactive online learning environment. This could involve providing clear guidelines for communication channels and expectations, encouraging active participation from all students, and utilizing various communication tools such as discussion forums, video conferencing, and instant messaging. Moreover, instructors can make themselves more accessible to students by offering regular office hours, providing prompt feedback on assignments, and being responsive to student inquiries and concerns.

4. CASE STUDIES

4.1. Embracing AI for Enhanced Teaching and Wellbeing: A Case Study at Basingstoke College of Technology

The Basingstoke College of Technology (BCoT) has embarked on a forward-thinking journey to integrate Artificial Intelligence (AI) into its educational practices, demonstrating a pioneering approach to leveraging technology to enhance teaching efficiency and foster human skills development among students.

4.1.1. AI Integration and Teacher Workload Reduction

At the forefront of this initiative is the application of AI tools, notably Google Bard and Teachermatic, aimed at reducing teachers' administrative burdens. Since June 2023, BCoT teachers have reported an average time saving of 5.1 hours per week, a substantial reduction that has been redirected towards more effective teaching and nurturing essential human skills in students. This shift has been instrumental in addressing the growing concern of teacher burnout and workload, critical factors in teacher retention and educational quality.

4.1.2. Ethical Framework and Controlled Prototypes

Recognizing the ethical implications of AI, BCoT established an AI Ethics Group comprising Teaching and Learning, IT Systems, and GDPR teams. This group convenes monthly to ensure that AI applications align with the college's strategy and ethical standards. From February to December, the college executed a phased implementation, including controlled planning prototypes with teachers, student learning enhancements, and the development of an AI Misuse Policy. These steps ensured a responsible and measured integration of AI within the educational framework.

4.1.3. Innovative Approaches in Planning and Assessment

The application of AI has been particularly transformative in planning and resource creation. Teachers received training and support in using Sequence of Learning Prompts and other AI-generated aids, which facilitated efficient planning and administration tasks. Additionally, BCoT undertook a significant shift in assessment methodologies. The traditional reliance on essays gave way to more diverse formats like podcasts, blogs, and real-world projects, prompted by the capabilities of AI tools like Snapchat's My AI in answering standard essay questions. This evolution in assessment reflects a commitment to authenticity and relevance in student evaluation.

4.1.4. Professional Development and Support

Professional development has been a cornerstone of BCoT's AI strategy. Staff Continuous Professional Development (CPD) sessions on AI were conducted regularly, supplemented by Learning Coach and Technologist support, both online and in-person. This approach ensured that teachers were not only familiar with AI tools but could also apply them effectively in their teaching practices.

4.1.5. Impact on Teaching and Learning

The use of AI at BCoT has had a tangible impact on teaching and learning dynamics. Case studies like Chef Lecturer Chris Swain illustrate the profound effect of AI in transforming teaching approaches. Utilizing ChatGPT, Chris transformed his culinary notes and ideas into a comprehensive curriculum swiftly, freeing him to focus more on engaging and interactive teaching. Such applications underline AI's role as a facilitator of enriched teaching experiences and the development of non-technical skills like communication and emotional intelligence.

4.1.6. Future Directions and Ethical Considerations

BCoT continues to navigate the evolving landscape of AI in education. The college is committed to enhancing digital literacy and ethical AI usage among students, preparing them for the future workplace. The journey includes ongoing exploration of AI in assessment feedback and personalized learning, always within the college's ethical and strategic framework.

In conclusion, BCoT's application of AI in education serves as a model for how technology can empower educators, enrich the learning experience, and ensure a balanced focus on both technological proficiency and essential human skills development.

4.2. Berlitz Empowered 500,000 Language Learners Using Azure AI Speech

Berlitz, a language education company, recognized the increasing demand for flexible learning options and aimed to maintain its emphasis on spoken language practice in an online setting. Collaborating with Microsoft, Berlitz leveraged Azure AI Speech technology to achieve this goal, as outlined in a case study.

Azure AI Speech, particularly its pronunciation assessment capabilities, addressed the shortcomings of traditional speech-to-text solutions. This transition led to a significantly enhanced student experience and enabled Berlitz to reach a broader audience of learners.

Berlitz also utilized Azure AI Speech Studio and text-to-speech features to augment its capabilities, offering a cost-effective voice generation tool. This innovation allowed learners to interact with various accents and speaker profiles, overcoming previous constraints related to budget, scheduling, and geographical barriers for adult learners.

By leveraging Azure AI speech tools, Berlitz effectively reduced its product development costs and accelerated its time to market, enabling investments in other areas of product innovation and customer support.

Nicolas Potel, Director of Learning Experience at Berlitz, highlighted the importance of selecting a speech-to-text solution with minimal false negatives, ensuring the acceptance of most correct responses.

This criterion was essential for Berlitz, emphasizing the significance of technology in meeting their objectives.

Results:

- Enhanced student experience through pronunciation assessment for 500,000 learners.
- Improved accessibility for a diverse range of learner profiles.
- Successful launch of new products, reaching thousands of new customers.

4.3 Brainly: Enabling Global Education With 24/7 Access to Expert Study Help for Students Worldwide

Brainly, an online learning platform, recognized the challenges students faced when seeking homework help, particularly on mobile devices, and aimed to streamline the learning process. Collaborating with Google Cloud, Brainly utilized its Vision AI technology, as documented in a case study.

Through this partnership, students were empowered to photograph their questions and receive instant, relevant answers. Leveraging Vision AI's multilingual capabilities significantly improved engagement and garnered high satisfaction rates. The technology's ability to recognize text in multiple languages enabled Brainly to serve a global audience, ensuring students worldwide could benefit from the platform.

Scalability was a critical aspect of Google Cloud's contribution to the implementation. The platform effectively managed the surge in demand driven by remote learning, enabling Brainly to support students globally.

Brainly's collaboration with Google Cloud resulted in a solution that fosters more accessible and equitable learning experiences.

Bill Salak, CTO of Brainly, highlighted the importance of democratizing access to education through technology: "We're using Google Cloud technology to build a solution that democratizes access to education and helps students who often get left behind."

Results:

- Achieved a 70% student satisfaction rate
- Experienced a 6x boost in engagement with photo queries
- Increased revenue from subscriptions

5. BEST PRACTICES

5.1 Personalized Learning and Adaptive Platforms

AI is increasingly employed in education to individualize learning experiences for students, tailoring educational content based on their unique skills, interests, and learning preferences. By analyzing student performance data, AI identifies patterns of learning difficulties or gaps in understanding.

Adaptive platforms leverage AI and machine learning (ML) algorithms to assess extensive amounts of student performance data, allowing for the evaluation of their strengths and weaknesses. This information is then combined with individual needs, preferences, and learning styles to craft customized learning paths.

For example, if a student demonstrates proficiency in a particular subject, the platform may bypass basic lessons and progress to more advanced content. Conversely, if a student encounters challenges with a concept, the platform can offer additional resources and adjust the pace to accommodate their learning requirements.

Moreover, adaptive platforms take into account students' diverse learning styles, such as visual or auditory preferences, delivering content in the most effective manner for each learner. This personalized approach to learning not only enhances comprehension but also fosters student motivation and engagement.

The Benefits for Students

Traditional, one-size-fits-all learning approaches can be frustrating for students who have varied learning styles. This often leads to disengagement and a lack of motivation, as students may struggle to find relevance or interest in the material. Many students require additional support on certain topics to keep pace with their peers.

Table 1. Benefits and challenges of personalized learning and adaptive platforms

Benefits	Challenges
Customized Learning Experience: Personalized learning allows students to progress through the curriculum at their own pace, ensuring that they fully understand a topic before moving on to the next one. This customized approach can lead to better learning outcomes.	**Resource-Intensive**: Implementing Personalized learning often requires significant investments in technology, infrastructure, and continuing professional development. Not all institutions may have the resources to adopt personalized learning fully.
Improved Student Engagement: When students can learn in a way that aligns with their interests, they are more likely to stay engaged and motivated, leading to a deeper grasp of the subject matter.	**Faculty development and Support**: Teachers play a central role in personalized learning environments. They need training and ongoing support to effectively implement this approach, create personalized learning plans, and manage diverse student needs.
Addressing Diverse Learning Needs: Classrooms often consist of students with varying levels of knowledge and abilities. Personalized learning helps address the diverse learning needs of students, providing additional support to those who need it and allowing advanced learners to explore more challenging material.	**Curriculum and Content Adaptation**: Personalized learning requires a curriculum that can be easily adapted to individual learners. Developing or curating such flexible content can, however, be challenging.
Self-directed Learning: Personalized learning encourages students to take ownership of their learning and become more self-directed learners. They learn how to set goals, monitor their progress, and make decisions about their learning path(s).	**Data Privacy and Security**: Personalized learning relies on collecting and analyzing student data. Ensuring the privacy and security of these data is crucial to protect students' information from potential breaches or misuse.
Data-Driven Instruction: Personalized learning relies on data and analytics to understand students' strengths and weaknesses. Academics can use these data to make informed decisions about instructional strategies and interventions.	**Technical Issues**: The use of technology in personalized learning can be susceptible to technical glitches and interruptions. Reliability and seamless integration of technology are essential for a smooth personalized learning experience.
Flexibility and Accessibility: Personalized learning can be implemented in various settings and modalities, including classrooms, online platforms, and blended learning environments. It also allows for greater accessibility for students with special needs, refugee contexts, or those in remote areas.	**Balancing Structure and Freedom**: Some students may struggle with the freedom to choose their learning path and may need academic advising.
Lifelong Learning Skills: By engaging in personalized learning experiences, students can develop essential skills and graduate outcomes such as critical thinking, problem solving, and independent learning, which are valuable beyond their academic journey.	**Assessment and Accountability**: Traditional forms of standardized assessment may not align well with personalized learning approaches. Finding effective ways to assess (summative and formative) and measure student progress in personalized settings can be rather complex.

5.2 Intelligent Tutoring Systems

An intelligent instructional system has the capability to observe a learner's problem-solving actions and behaviors across multiple sessions, allowing it to infer the learner's knowledge, beliefs, and attitudes based on a cognitive theory.

Intelligent tutoring involves modelling expert cognitive processes, detecting student errors, diagnosing knowledge gaps, providing instruction tailored to the student's knowledge level, offering hints and feedback, and delivering didactic instruction in a timely manner during problem-solving activities.

Intelligent tutoring systems (ITSs) aim to replicate the methods and dialogue of human tutors, providing real-time instructional interactions personalized to individual students. These systems possess domain knowledge as well as knowledge about the student and effective teaching strategies, aiming to emulate the qualities of a skilled human teacher.

The implementation of ITSs involves incorporating computational mechanisms and knowledge representations from artificial intelligence, computational linguistics, and cognitive science fields.

In practice, an ITS is educational software with an artificial intelligence component that monitors students' progress, providing tailored feedback and hints. By analyzing a student's performance data, the system can identify areas of strength and weakness, offering additional exercises or instruction as needed.

ITSs are also referred to as Intelligent Computer-Aided Instruction (ICAI) and Knowledge-Based Tutoring Systems (KBTS).

Table 2. Benefits and challenges of intelligent tutoring systems

Benefits	Challenges
Enhanced Learning Outcomes: ITS can provide personalized and adaptive instruction, tailored to individual student needs, which can lead to improved learning outcomes and academic performance.	**Development and Implementation**: Designing and developing effective ITS requires significant time, training, resources, and expertise in both pedagogy and technology
Individualized Learning: ITS can offer personalized feedback and guidance to students, allowing them to progress at their own pace and focus on areas where they need additional support	**Data Privacy and Security**: ITS collect and analyze large amounts of student data, raising concerns about data privacy, security, and the ethical use of personal information.
Continuous Assessment: ITS can provide real-time assessment and feedback, enabling students to monitor their progress and identify areas for improvement.	**Bias and Discrimination**: If not properly designed and trained, ITS can perpetuate biases and discrimination, as the underlying algorithms may replicate biases present in the training data.
Immediate Feedback: ITS can offer immediate feedback on students' responses, allowing them to correct their mistakes and reinforce their understanding in real time	**Technical Limitations**: ITS may face limitations in accurately understanding and interpreting students' responses, especially in complex or ambiguous situations, leading to potential gaps in instructional support.
Access to Quality Education: ITS can provide access to quality education in remote or underserved areas, reaching students who may not have access to traditional educational resources.	**Teacher–Student Relationship**: The use of ITS may impact the traditional teacher–student relationship, as students may rely more on the system for instruction and guidance, potentially reducing interpersonal interactions.
Cost and Time Efficiency: ITS can reduce the cost and time associated with one-on-one tutoring by automating certain aspects of instruction and support.	**User Acceptance and Engagement**: ITS may face resistance or low user acceptance from students and academics, who may prefer traditional instructional methods or perceive the system as impersonal or less effective
Long-term Knowledge Retention: ITS can employ spaced repetition and other cognitive techniques (Cognitive Load Theory) to promote long-term retention of knowledge and skills	**Integration with Existing Systems**: Integrating ITS with existing educational technologies, infrastructure, and curricula can present technical and logistical challenges, requiring careful planning and coordination.

decisions. This transparency can enhance trust, accountability, and understanding, empowering stakeholders to engage meaningfully with AI technologies in education.

6.4 Responsibility and Accountability

The complex nature of AI systems can often blur the lines of accountability, leading to gaps or ambiguities in determining who is responsible for their design, development, deployment, use, or impact. In cases where AI systems cause harm or errors, it may be challenging to attribute accountability to any specific human agent, as these systems operate based on algorithms and data-driven decision-making.

To address this issue, it's crucial to establish clear accountability frameworks and delineate roles and responsibilities among different stakeholders involved in the AI ecosystem. This includes developers, educators, policymakers, administrators, and others. By defining clear lines of responsibility, specifying standards for ethical conduct, and implementing mechanisms for oversight and accountability, stakeholders can ensure that AI systems are deployed responsibly and that any potential harms or errors are addressed promptly and appropriately.

7. ETHICAL CONSIDERATIONS AND FUTURE DIRECTIONS

7.1 Ethical Implications of Using AI in Education

The integration of AI in education poses several challenges and ethical considerations that demand careful attention:

1. Data Privacy Concerns: The utilization of AI in education necessitates the collection and analysis of vast amounts of student data, raising concerns about privacy and data protection. Educators must ensure that data collection practices are transparent, consent-based, and compliant with relevant regulations, such as GDPR or COPPA. Additionally, robust security measures should be implemented to safeguard sensitive information from unauthorized access or misuse.
2. Biases in AI Algorithms: AI algorithms may inadvertently perpetuate biases present in the data they are trained on, leading to unfair or discriminatory outcomes. To address this challenge, educators must regularly audit AI systems for bias, diversify training data to mitigate biases, and implement algorithmic transparency measures to enhance accountability and fairness. Moreover, ongoing education and awareness efforts are essential to help stakeholders recognize and mitigate bias in AI applications.
3. Accessibility Issues: AI-powered tools and platforms may inadvertently exclude students with disabilities or diverse learning needs if they are not designed with accessibility in mind. Educators should prioritize accessibility considerations throughout the development and implementation of AI solutions, ensuring that they adhere to accessibility standards and guidelines. This may involve incorporating features such as screen readers, keyboard navigation, and adjustable font sizes to accommodate diverse learners effectively.

By addressing these challenges and ethical considerations, educators can harness the transformative potential of AI in education while ensuring that it remains inclusive, equitable, and ethically responsible.

7.2 The Future of AI in Education and Potential Innovations

The future of AI in education holds immense potential for revolutionizing teacher-learner interaction and enhancing the overall learning experience. Here are some speculative insights into future innovations:

Personalized Learning Experiences: AI will continue to evolve to provide more personalized learning experiences tailored to individual student needs, preferences, and learning styles. Advanced algorithms will analyze vast amounts of student data to deliver customized content, adaptive learning paths, and targeted interventions, ensuring that each student receives instruction at their own pace and level of understanding.

Intelligent Tutoring Systems: The development of intelligent tutoring systems (ITS) powered by AI will enable more interactive and responsive teaching experiences. These systems will not only provide personalized instruction but also offer real-time feedback, adaptive scaffolding, and customized learning pathways to support student mastery of complex concepts and skills.

Collaborative Learning Environments: AI-driven collaborative learning environments will foster greater collaboration, creativity, and critical thinking among students. Virtual classrooms equipped with AI-powered tools and features, such as intelligent chatbots, virtual reality simulations, and collaborative problem-solving platforms, will enable students to engage in collaborative projects, peer-to-peer feedback, and group discussions in immersive and interactive settings.

Augmented Reality and Virtual Reality: Augmented reality (AR) and virtual reality (VR) technologies will play an increasingly prominent role in education, offering immersive and experiential learning experiences. AI algorithms will enhance AR/VR simulations by providing intelligent guidance, contextually relevant information, and adaptive learning scenarios, allowing students to explore complex concepts in engaging and interactive ways.

Ethical AI and Responsible Use: As AI becomes more integrated into education, there will be a growing emphasis on ethical AI principles and responsible use practices. Educators, policymakers, and technology developers will collaborate to establish ethical guidelines, privacy safeguards, and transparency measures to ensure that AI technologies are used ethically, equitably, and responsibly in educational settings.

The potential innovations of AI in education are vast and promising, with the potential to revolutionize teaching and learning. Here are some speculative insights into potential future innovations:

Adaptive Learning Systems: AI-powered adaptive learning systems will continue to evolve, providing personalized learning experiences tailored to each student's individual needs, preferences, and learning styles. These systems will leverage advanced algorithms to analyze vast amounts of student data, including academic performance, behavior, and preferences, to deliver customized content, adaptive learning paths, and targeted interventions in real time.

Intelligent Virtual Assistants: Intelligent virtual assistants powered by AI will become increasingly prevalent in educational settings, providing students with on-demand access to personalized support, guidance, and resources. These virtual assistants will use natural language processing (NLP) and machine learning algorithms to interact with students, answer questions, provide feedback, and assist with various learning tasks, enhancing student engagement and learning outcomes.

Automated Grading and Feedback: AI-driven automated grading and feedback systems will streamline the assessment process, enabling educators to assess student work more efficiently and provide timely, personalized feedback. These systems will use machine learning algorithms to analyze student responses,

Compilation of References

Ababneh, M., Aljarrah, A., Karagozlu, D., & Ozdamli, F. (2021). Guiding the students in high school by using machine learning. *TEM Journal*, *10*(1), 384–391. doi:10.18421/TEM101-48

Abbas, N. B., & Ryan, M.-L. (2004). Narrative as virtual reality: Immersion and interactivity in literature and electronic media. *The Yearbook of English Studies*, *34*, 277. doi:10.2307/3509518

Abdullah, Al-Ansi, Jaboob, Garad, & Al-Ansi. (2023). Analyzing augmented reality (AR) and virtual reality (VR) recent development in education. *Social Sciences & Humanities Open, 8*(1). doi:10.1016/j.ssaho.2023.100532

Adane, M. D., Deku, J. K., & Asare, E. K. (2023). Performance Analysis of Machine Learning Algorithms in Prediction of Student Academic Performance. *Journal of Advances in Mathematics and Computer Science*, *38*(5), 74–86. doi:10.9734/jamcs/2023/v38i51762

Ahmad, A., Waseem, M., Liang, P., Fahmideh, M., Aktar, M. S., & Mikkonen, T. (2023). *Towards Human-Bot Collaborative Software Architecting with ChatGPT*. 10.48550/arXiv.2302.14600.

Ahmed, K., & Mesonovich, M. (2019). Learning management systems and student performance. *International Journal of Sustainable Energy Development*, *7*(1), 582–591.

Akyıldız, S. T. (2019). Do 21st Century Teachers Know about Heutagogy or Do They Still Adhere to Traditional Pedagogy and Andragogy? *International Journal of Progressive Education*, *15*(6).

Alabbasi, D. (2022). Factors influencing students engagement in virtual classrooms and their impact on satisfaction. *Information Sciences Letters*, *11*(4), 1203–1215. doi:10.18576/isl/110420

Al-Ayyoub, M., Jararweh, Y., Daraghmeh, M., & Althebyan, Q. (2015). Multi-agent based dynamic resource provisioning and monitoring for cloud computing systems infrastructure. *Cluster Computing*, *18*(2), 919–932. doi:10.1007/s10586-015-0449-5

Alberola, J. M., del Val, E., Sanchez-Angui, V., Palomares, A., & Dolores, T. M. (2016). An artificial intelligence tool for heterogeneous team formation in the classroom. *Knowledge-Based Systems*, *101*, 1–14. doi:10.1016/j.knosys.2016.02.010

Ali, M. F., Jayakody, D. N. K., & Li, Y. (2022). Recent trends in underwater Visible Light Communication (UVLC) systems. *IEEE Access : Practical Innovations, Open Solutions*, *10*, 22169–22225. doi:10.1109/ACCESS.2022.3150093

Aljanabi, M. (2023). ChatGPT: Future directions and open possibilities. *Mesopotamian Journal of Cybersecurity*, 16-17.

Alkhatlan, A., & Kalita, J. (2018). Intelligent tutoring systems: A comprehensive historical survey with recent developments. *arXiv preprint arXiv:1812.09628*. https://doi.org/ doi:10.5120/ijca2019918451

Allam, Z., Dey, G., & Jones, D. S. (2020). Artificial intelligence (AI) provided early detection of the coronavirus (COVID-19) in China and will influence future urban health policy internationally. *AI*, *1*(2), 156–165. doi:10.3390/ai1020009

Al-Obaydi, L. H., Pikhart, M., & Klimova, B. (2023). ChatGPT and the General Concepts of Education: Can Artificial Intelligence-Driven Chatbots Support the Process of Language Learning? *International Journal of Emerging Technologies in Learning, 18*(21), 39–50. doi:10.3991/ijet.v18i21.42593

Al-Rasheedi, M., Gueymard, C. A., Al-Khayat, M., Ismail, A., Lee, J. A., & Al-Duaj, H. (2020). Performance evaluation of a utility-scale dual-technology photovoltaic power plant at the Shagaya Renewable Energy Park in Kuwait. *Renewable & Sustainable Energy Reviews, 133*, 110139. doi:10.1016/j.rser.2020.110139

Alruwais, N., & Zakariah, M. (2023). Student-Engagement Detection in Classroom Using Machine Learning Algorithm. *Electronics (Basel), 12*(731), 731. doi:10.3390/electronics12030731

Alsawaier, R. S. (2018). The effect of gamification on motivation and engagement. *The International Journal of Information and Learning Technology, 35*(1), 56–79. doi:10.1108/IJILT-02-2017-0009

Alshahrani, M. Y. (2021). Implementation of a blockchain system using improved Elliptic Curve Cryptography algorithm for the performance assessment of the students in the E-Learning platform. *Applied Sciences, 12*(1), 74. doi:10.3390/app12010074

AlShaikh, R., Al-Malki, N., & Almasre, M. (2024). The implementation of the cognitive theory of multimedia learning in the design and evaluation of an AI educational video assistant utilizing large language models. *Heliyon, 10*(3). doi:10.1016/j.heliyon.2024.e25361

AlshaterM. M. (2022). Exploring the role of artificial intelligence in enhancing academic performance: A case study of ChatGPT. SSRN 2022. doi:10.2139/ssrn.4312358

Altrabsheh, N., Gaber, M. M., & Cocea, M. (2016). *SA-E: Sentiment Analysis for Education. Portsmouth University Research Portal*. Pure.

Ampatzidis, Y., Partel, V., & Costa, L. (2020). Agroview: Cloud-based application to process, analyze and visualize UAV-collected data for precision agriculture applications utilizing artificial intelligence. *Computers and Electronics in Agriculture, 174*, 105457. doi:10.1016/j.compag.2020.105457

Ananth, P. V. K., Muralikrishnan, K., & Chatterjee, A. (2021). Asset performance monitoring and maintenance management in cement manufacturing. In CRC Press eBooks (pp. 225–261). doi:10.1201/9781003106791-7

Anuyahong, B., Rattanapong, C., & Patcha, I. (2023). Analyzing the Impact of Artificial Intelligence in Personalized Learning and Adaptive Assessment in Higher Education. *International Journal of Innovation and Scientific Research, 10*(4), 88–93. Advance online publication. doi:10.51244/IJRSI.2023.10412

Arafat, M. Y., & Moh, S. (2019). Routing Protocols for Unmanned aerial vehicle networks: A survey. *IEEE Access : Practical Innovations, Open Solutions, 7*, 99694–99720. doi:10.1109/ACCESS.2019.2930813

Aragon, S. (2016). *Teacher Shortages: What We Know*. Teacher Shortage Series.

Aria, M., & Cuccurullo, C. (2017). Bibliometrix : An R-tool for comprehensive science mapping analysis. *Journal of Informetrics, 11*(4), 959–975. doi:10.1016/j.joi.2017.08.007

Arslan, K. (2020). Eğitimde yapay zekâ ve uygulamaları [Artificial intelligence and applications in education]. *Batı Anadolu Eğitim Bilimleri Dergisi, 11*(1), 71–88.

Artificial Intelligence in education. (2021). Using heart rate variability (HRV) as a biomarker to assess emotions objectively. *Computers and Education: Artificial Intelligence, 2*, 100011.

Atila, O., & Şengür, A. (2021). Attention guided 3D CNN-LSTM model for accurate speech based emotion recognition. *Applied Acoustics*, *182*, 108260. doi:10.1016/j.apacoust.2021.108260

Audureau, E., Carrat, F., Layese, R., Cagnot, C., Asselah, T., Guyader, D., Larrey, D., De Lédinghen, V., Ouzan, D., Zoulim, F., Roulot, D., Tran, A., Bronowicki, J.-P., Zarski, J.-P., Riachi, G., Calès, P., Péron, J.-M., Alric, L., Bourlière, M., . . . Nahon, P. (2020). Personalized surveillance for hepatocellular carcinoma in cirrhosis – using machine learning adapted to HCV status. *Journal of Hepatology, 73*(6), 1434-1445. doi:10.1016/j.jhep.2020.05.052

Aversa, R., Panza, N., & Tasquier, L. (2015). An Agent-Based Platform for Cloud Applications Performance Monitoring. *An Agent-based Platform for Cloud Applications Performance Monitoring*. doi:10.1109/CISIS.2015.79

Aversa, R., Tasquier, L., & Venticinque, S. (2013). *Agents Based Monitoring of Heterogeneous Cloud Infrastructures*. doi:10.1109/UIC-ATC.2013.52

Awuor, O. G. (2023). Assessment of existing cyber-attack detection models for web-based systems. *Global Journal of Engineering and Technology Advances, 15*(1), 70–89. doi:10.30574/gjeta.2023.15.1.0075

Azazi, N. A. N., Hussin, N. A. M., & Selvanathan, M. (2020). Students learning experiences during COVID-19: Work from home period in Malaysian higher learning institutions. *Teaching Public Administration*, 1-10. DOI:. doi:101177/0144739420977900

Babtain, A. (2021). The effect of Mcgraw-hill education connect on students' academic performance. *International Journal of Emerging Technologies in Learning*, *16*(3), 86–113. doi:10.3991/ijet.v16i03.17995

Bachiri, Y. A., Mouncif, H., & Bouikhalene, B. (2023). Artificial Intelligence Empowers Gamification: Optimizing Student Engagement and Learning Outcomes in E-learning and MOOCs. *International Journal of Engineering Pedagogy, 13*(8), 4–19. doi:10.3991/ijep.v13i8.40853

Badini, S., Regondi, S., Frontoni, E., & Pugliese, R. (2023). *Assessing the capabilities of ChatGPT to improve additive manufacturing troubleshooting*. Advanced Industrial and Engineering Polymer Research. doi:10.1016/j.aiepr.2023.03.003

Baidoo-AnuD.AnsahO. (2023). *Education in the Era of Generative Artificial Intelligence (AI): Understanding the Potential Benefits of ChatGPT in Promoting Teaching and Learning*. doi:10.2139/ssrn.4337484

Bai, S., Hew, K. F., & Huang, B. (2020). Does gamification improve student learning outcome? Evidence from a meta-analysis and synthesis of qualitative data in educational contexts. *Educational Research Review*, *30*, 100322. doi:10.1016/j.edurev.2020.100322

Baker, T., Smith, L., & Anissa, N. (2019). *Educ-AI-tion rebooted? Exploring the future of artificial intelligence in schools and colleges*. https://media.nesta.org.uk/documents/Future_of_AI_and_education_v5_WEB.pdf

Baker, R. S., & Inventado, P. S. (2014). Educational data mining and learning analytics. In J. Larusson & B. White (Eds.), *Learning analytics: From research to practice* (pp. 61–75). Springer. doi:10.1007/978-1-4614-3305-7_4

Balula, A., & Moreira, A. (2014). *Evaluation of online higher education: Learning, interaction and technology*. Springer., doi:10.1007/978-3-319-05425-4

Banerjee, I., Perera, I., & Choudhury, J. (2013). Introducing immersive technologies for learning: A study evaluating the readiness for using virtual worlds for learning and teaching in an Indian University. *2013 Sixth International Conference on Contemporary Computing (IC3)*. 10.1109/IC3.2013.6612202

Bansal, H. and Khan, R. (2018). A review paper on human-computer interaction. *Int. J. Adv. Res. Comput. Sci. Softw. 8*(53). . doi:10.23956/ijarcsse.v8i4.630

Bansal, R. (2017). Challenges and future trends in commerce education in India. *International Journal of Techno-Management Research*, *5*(3), 25–35.

Bansal, R., Dadhich, V., & Ahmad, N. (2014). Indian commodity market–A performance review. *International Journal of Management and Commerce*, *1*(5), 19–34.

Bantugan, B. S., Li, X., Liu, L., Liu, Y., Wang, X., Yang, M., & Zhang, X. (2024). The Adoption of Artificial Intelligence of Selected International Chinese Educators Enrolled as Graduate Students in the College of Education of St. Paul University Manila. *International Journal of Innovation and Scientific Research*, *11*(2), 133–146. doi:10.51244/IJRSI.2024.1102011

Barata, G., Gama, S., Jorge, J., & Gonçalves, D. (2016). Early prediction of student profiles based on performance and gaming preferences. *IEEE Transactions on Learning Technologies*, *9*(3), 272–284. doi:10.1109/TLT.2016.2541664

Becker, S. A., Brown, M., Dahlstrom, E., Davis, A., DePaul, K., Diaz, V., & Pomerantz, J. (2018). *NMC horizon report: 2018 higher education edition*. Educause.

Benotti, L., Martínez, M. C., & Schapachnik, F. (2014). Engaging high school students using chatbots. In *Proceedings of the 2014 Innovation and Technology in Computer Science Education Conference*. ACM. 10.1145/2591708.2591728

Bergdahl, N. (2022). Engagement and disengagement in online learning. *Computers & Education*, *188*, 104561. Advance online publication. doi:10.1016/j.compedu.2022.104561

Berman, N. B., & Artino, A. R. Jr. (2018). Development and initial validation of an online engagement metric using virtual patients. *BMC Medical Education*, *18*(1), 213. doi:10.1186/s12909-018-1322-z PMID:30223825

Berry, S. (2019). The role of video and text chat in a virtual classroom: How technology impacts community. In *Educational Technology and Resources for Synchronous Learning in Higher Education* (pp. 173–187). IGI Global. doi:10.4018/978-1-5225-7567-2.ch009

Bhardwaj, P. K., Gupta, P., Panwar, H., Siddiqui, M. K., Morales-Menendez, R., & Bhaik, A. (2021). Application of Deep Learning on Student Engagement in E-learning Environments. *Computers & Electrical Engineering*, *93*, 93. doi:10.1016/j.compeleceng.2021.107277 PMID:36567679

Bhujade, S., Kamaleshwar, T., Jaiswal, S., & Babu, D. V. (2022). Deep learning application of image recognition based on self-driving vehicle. In Communications in computer and information science (pp. 336–344). doi:10.1007/978-3-031-07012-9_29

Biradar, N., & Hosalli, G. (2024). Segmentation and Detection of Crop Pests using Novel U-Net with Hybrid Deep Learning Mechanism. *Pest Management Science*, ps.8083. Advance online publication. doi:10.1002/ps.8083 PMID:38506377

Bird, S., Klein, E., & Loper, E. (2009). *Natural language processing with Python: Analyzing text with the natural language toolkit*. O'Reilly Media, Inc.

Bishop, L. (2023). A computer wrote this paper: What chatgpt means for education, research, and writing. *Research and Writing*.

Blaine, A. M. (2019). Interaction and presence in the virtual classroom: An analysis of the perceptions of students and teachers in online and blended Advanced Placement courses. *Computers & Education*, *132*, 31–43. doi:10.1016/j.compedu.2019.01.004

Blaschke, L. M. (2012). *Heutagogy and Lifelong Learning: A Review of Heutagogical Practice and Self-Determined Learning*. . doi:10.19173/irrodl.v13i1.1076

Boateng, S. L., Obed, K. A. P., Boateng, R., Budu, J., Marfo, J. S., & Asamoah, P. (2024). Educational technologies and elementary level education – A bibliometric review of scopus indexed journal articles. *Heliyon, 10*(7). doi:10.1016/j.heliyon.2024.e28101

Bommineni, V. L., Bhagwagar, S., Balcarcel, D., Davatzikos, C., & Boyer, D. (2023). Performance of ChatGPT on the MCAT: the road to personalized and equitable premedical learning. MedRxiv, 2023-03. doi:10.1101/2023.03.05.23286533

Bond, M., Buntins, K., Bedenlier, S., Zawacki-Richter, O., & Kerres, M. (2020). Mapping Research in Student Engagement and Educational Technology in Higher Education: A systematic evidence map. *International Journal of Educational Technology in Higher Education*, *17*(1), 2. doi:10.1186/s41239-019-0176-8

BonsuE.Baffour-KoduahD. (2023). *From the consumers' side: Determining students' perception and intention to use ChatGPT in Ghanaian higher education.* doi:10.2139/ssrn.4387107

Boulton, C. A., Hughes, E., Kent, C., Smith, J. R., & Williams, H. T. P. (2019). Student engagement and well-being over time at a higher education institution. *PLoS One*, *14*(11), e0225770. Advance online publication. doi:10.1371/journal.pone.0225770 PMID:31774878

Bozkurt, Xiao, Lambert, Pazurek, Crompton, Koseoglu, & Jandrić. (2023). Speculative futures on ChatGPT and generative artificial intelligence (AI): A collective reflection from the educational landscape. *Asian J. Distance Educ.*

Bozkurt, A., Karadeniz, A., Baneres, D., Guerrero-Roldán, A. E., & Rodríguez, M. E. (2021). Artificial intelligence and reflections from educational landscape: A review of AI Studies in half a century. *Sustainability (Basel)*, *13*(2), 800. doi:10.3390/su13020800

Brigham, T. J. (2015). An introduction to gamification: Adding game elements for engagement. *Medical Reference Services Quarterly*, *34*(4), 471–480. doi:10.1080/02763869.2015.1082385 PMID:26496401

Brull, S., & Finlayson, S. (2016). Importance of gamification in increasing learning. *Journal of Continuing Education in Nursing*, *47*(8), 372–375. doi:10.3928/00220124-20160715-09 PMID:27467313

Buckley, K., Fairman, K., Pogge, E., & Raney, E. (2022). Use of Learning Management System Data to Predict Student Success in a Pharmacy Capstone Course. *American Journal of Pharmaceutical Education, 86*(4). doi:10.5688/ajpe8594

Bulgakova, D. (2023). The prohibited artificial intelligence practice. *Teorìâ Ta Praktika Sudovoï Ekspertizi Ì Kriminalìstiki, 32*(3), 89–112. https://doi.org/ doi:10.32353/khrife.3.2023.06

Bulger, M., Mayer-Schönberger, V., & Padilla, N. (2016). Principled artificial intelligence: Mapping consensus in ethical and rights-based approaches to principles for AI. SSRN *Electronic Journal*. doi:10.2139/ssrn.2903242

Bulut, O., & Wongvorachan, T. (2022). Feedback Generation through Artificial Intelligence. In The Open/Technology in Education, Society, and Scholarship Association Conference (Vol. 2, No. 1, pp. 1-9). doi:10.18357/otessac.2022.2.1.125

Burgos, D., Tattersall, C., & Koper, R. (2007). Representing adaptive and adaptable units of learning: How to model personalized eLearning in IMS Learning Design. *Computers and Education: E-learning. Theory into Practice*, 41–56.

Burke, K., Fanshawe, M., & Tualaulelei, E. (2022). We can't always measure what matters: Revealing opportunities to enhance online student engagement through pedagogical care. *Journal of Further and Higher Education*, *46*(3), 287–300. doi:10.1080/0309877X.2021.1909712

Burton, J. K., Moore, D. M. M., & Magliaro, S. G. (2004). Behaviorism and instructional cancers. *The Lancet. Oncology*, *21*(1).

Calonge, D. S., Firuz, K., & Gurrib, I. (2023). New Era of Artificial Intelligence in Education: Towards a Sustainable Multifaceted Revolution. *Sustainability (Basel), 15*(16), 12451. doi:10.3390/su151612451

Cao, J., Crews, J. M., Lin, M., Burgoon, J. K., & Nunamaker, J. F. Jr. (2008). An empirical investigation of virtual Interaction in supporting learning. *The Data Base for Advances in Information Systems, 39*(3), 51–68. doi:10.1145/1390673.1390680

Carey, P. (2018). The impact of institutional culture, policy and process on student engagement in university decision-making. *Perspectives, 22*(1), 11–18. doi:10.1080/13603108.2016.1168754

Carver, D. L. (2014). *Analysis of student perceptions of the psychosocial learning environment in online and face-to-face career and technical education courses*. Old Dominion University Libraries.

Casanova, Vicente Vicente, Prieto, Pescador, Hernández Sánchez, Almaraz Menéndez, & Morales. (2016). Toxicology learning through the use of open educational resources: The European "TOX-OER" Project. *Toxicology Letters, 258*, S302-S303. . doi:10.1016/j.toxlet.2016.06.2111

Casas-Roma, J., & Conesa, J. (2021). A literature review on artificial intelligence and ethics in online learning. *Intelligent Systems and Learning Data Analytics in Online Education*, 111-131.

Celik, I. (2023). Towards Intelligent-TPACK: An empirical study on teachers' professional knowledge to ethically integrate artificial intelligence (AI)-based tools into education. *Computers in Human Behavior, 138*. doi:10.1016/j.chb.2022.107468

Cents-Boonstra, M., Lichtwarck-Aschoff, A., Lara, M. M., & Denessen, E. (2021). Patterns of motivating teaching behaviour and student engagement: A microanalytic approach. *European Journal of Psychology of Education, 5*(1), 1–5. doi:10.1007/s10212-021-00543-3

Cesari, V., Galgani, B., Gemignani, A., & Menicucci, D. (2021). Enhancing qualities of consciousness during online learning via multisensory interactions. *Behavioral Sciences (Basel, Switzerland), 11*(5), 57. doi:10.3390/bs11050057 PMID:33919379

Çetin, M., & Aktaş, A. (2021). Yapay zeka ve eğitimde gelecek senaryoları [Artificial intelligence and future scenarios in education]. *OPUS International Journal of Society Researches, 18*, 4225-4268. doi:10.26466/opus.911444

Chae, H., Kim, M., Kim, C., Jeong, W., Kim, H., Lee, J., & Yeo, J. (2023). TUTORING: instruction-grounded conversational agent for language learners. In *Proceedings of the AAAI Conference on Artificial Intelligence* (Vol. 37, No. 13, pp. 16413–16415). 10.1609/aaai.v37i13.27063

Chakraborty, M., & Nafukho, F. M. (2015). *Strategies for virtual learning environments: Focusing on teaching presence and teaching immediacy.* Internet Learning. doi:10.18278/il.4.1.1

Chang, C.-W. (2009). Efficacy of interaction among college students in a web-based environment. *Journal of Educational Technology Development and Exchange, 2*(1). Advance online publication. doi:10.18785/jetde.0201.02

Chassignol, M., Khoroshavin, A., Klimova, A., & Bilyatdinova, A. (2018). Artificial Intelligence trends in education: A narrative overview. *Procedia Computer Science, 136*, 16–24. doi:10.1016/j.procs.2018.08.233

Chen, L., Zeng, S., & Wang, W. (2021). The influence of emotion and learner control on multimedia learning. *Learning and Motivation, 76*. doi:10.1016/j.lmot.2021.101762

Cheney, A. W., McClannon, T., Bolt, L., & Sanders, R. L. (2019). Perceptions of presence and community in immersive online learning environments. In *Emerging Technologies in Virtual Learning Environments* (pp. 116–131). IGI Global. doi:10.4018/978-1-5225-7987-8.ch006

Chen, K., & Li, S. (2021). Sequential, typological, and academic dynamics of self-regulated learners: Learning analytics of an undergraduate chemistry online course. *Computers and Education: Artificial Intelligence*, *2*, 100024. doi:10.1016/j.caeai.2021.100024

Chen, L., Chen, P., & Lin, Z. (2020). Artificial intelligence in education: A review. *IEEE Access : Practical Innovations, Open Solutions*, *8*, 75264–75278. doi:10.1109/ACCESS.2020.2988510

Chen, W. (2020). Knowledge-aware learning analytics for smart learning. *Procedia Computer Science*, *159*, 1957–1965. doi:10.1016/j.procs.2019.09.368

Chen, X., Siau, K., & Nah, F. F. H. (2012). Empirical comparison of 3-D virtual world and face-to-face classroom for higher education. *Journal of Database Management*, *23*(3), 30–49. doi:10.4018/jdm.2012070102

Chen, X., Xie, H., & Hwang, G. J. (2020). A multi-perspective study on artificial intelligence in education: Grants, conferences, journals, software tools, institutions, and researchers. *Computers and Education: Artificial Intelligence*, *1*, 100005. doi:10.1016/j.caeai.2020.100005

Chen, X., Xie, H., Zou, D., & Hwang, G. (2020). Application and theory gaps during the rise of Artificial Intelligence in Education. Computers and Education. *Artificial Intelligence*, *1*, 100002.

Cho, M.-H., & Tobias, S. (2016). Should instructors require discussion in online courses? Effects of online discussion on community of inquiry, learner time, satisfaction, and achievement. *International Review of Research in Open and Distance Learning*, *17*(2). Advance online publication. doi:10.19173/irrodl.v17i2.2342

Christopoulos, A., Conrad, M., & Shukla, M. (2016). How do students 'really' interact with virtual worlds? - the influence of proper induction for virtual interactions. *Proceedings of the 8th International Conference on Computer Supported Education*. 10.5220/0005755700430054

Christopoulos, A., Conrad, M., & Shukla, M. (2018). Increasing student engagement through virtual interactions: How? *Virtual Reality (Waltham Cross)*, *22*(4), 353–369. doi:10.1007/s10055-017-0330-3

Čižmešija, A., Horvat, D., & Vukovac, P. (2021). Improving student engagement and course completion using chatbot application. *INTED2021 Proceedings*, 8346-8354.

Coates, H. (2016). *Student Engagement in Campus-Based and Online Education*. Routledge.

Coglianese, C., & Lai, A. (2022). Assessing Automated Administration. *U of Penn Law School, Public Law Research Paper*, (22-28). doi:10.1093/oxfordhb/9780197579329.013.30

Conati, C., Gašević, D., Chen, G., Khosravi, H., Kay, J., Martinez-Maldonado, R., Sadiq, S., Knight, S., Shum, S. B., & Tsai, Y.-S. (2022). Explainable Artificial Intelligence in education. *Computers and Education: Artificial Intelligence*, *3*. doi:10.1016/j.caeai.2022.100074

Connell, J. P. (1990). *Context, self, and action: A motivational analysis of self-system processes across the life span*. University of Chicago Press.

Crawford, K., Dobbe, R., Dryer, T., Fried, G., Green, B., Kaziunas, E., ... Salehi, N. (2019). *AI now report 2019*. Academic Press.

Cucinotta, D., & Vanelli, M. (2020). WHO declares COVID-19 a pandemic. *Acta Biomedica*, *91*(1), 157. doi:10.23750/abm.v91i1.9397 PMID:32191675

Cui, Y., Song, X., Hu, Q., Li, Y., Sharma, P., & Khapre, S. (2022). Human-robot interaction in higher education for predicting student engagement. *Computers & Electrical Engineering*, *99*, 99. doi:10.1016/j.compeleceng.2022.107827

Cunningham-Nelson, S., Boles, W., Trouton, L., & Margerison, E. (2019). A review of chatbots in education: Practical steps forward. *30th annual conference for the Australasian association for engineering education (AAEE 2019): Educators becoming agents of change: Innovate, integrate.* Motivate: Engineers Australia.

Cunningham-Nelson, S., Boles, W., Trouton, L., & Margerison, E. (2019). A review of chatbots in education: practical steps forward. In *30th Annual Conference for the Australasian Association for Engineering Education (AAEE 2019): Educators Becoming Agents of Change: Innovate, Integrate, Motivate* (pp. 299-306). Engineers Australia.

D'Alba, A., Najmi, A., Gratch, J., & Bigenho, C. (2011). Virtual learning environments. The oLTECx: A study of participant attitudes and experiences. *International Journal of Gaming and Computer-Mediated Simulations*, *3*(1), 33–50. doi:10.4018/jgcms.2011010103

Dai, H., Liu, Z., Liao, W., Huang, X., Wu, Z., Zhao, L., . . . Li, X. (2023). Chataug: Leveraging chatgpt for text data augmentation. arXiv preprint arXiv:2302.13007.

Damasceno, A. L. de B., Ribeiro, D. dos S., & Barbosa, S. D. J. (2019). What the literature and instructors say about the analysis of student interaction logs on virtual learning environments. *2019 IEEE Frontiers in Education Conference (FIE).*

Das, S., Roy, S., Bose, R., Acharjya, P. P., & Mondal, H. (2022). Analysis of Student Sentiment Dynamics to Evaluate Teachers Performance in Online Course using Machine Learning. In *2022 International Conference on Applied Artificial Intelligence and Computing (ICAAIC)* (pp. 668-673). IEEE. 10.1109/ICAAIC53929.2022.9792958

Davis, L., & Hase, S. (2001). *The River of Learning in the Workplace. Proceedings of Research to reality: Putting VET research to Work: Australian Vocational Education and Training Research Association (AVETRA).*

De Freitas, S., Rebolledo-Mendez, G., Liarokapis, F., Magoulas, G., & Poulovassilis, A. (2010). Learning as immersive experiences: Using the four-dimensional framework for designing and evaluating immersive learning experiences in a virtual world. *British Journal of Educational Technology*, *41*(1), 69–85. doi:10.1111/j.1467-8535.2009.01024.x

De Meester, A., van Duyse, F., Aelterman, N., de Muynck, G. J., & Haerens, L. (2020). An experimental, video-based investigation into the motivating impact of choice and positive feedback among students with different motor competence levels. *Physical Education and Sport Pedagogy*, *25*(4), 361–378. doi:10.1080/17408989.2020.1725456

de Oliveira Durso, S., & Arruda, E. P. (2022). Artificial intelligence in distance education: A systematic literature review of Brazilian studies. *Problems of Education in the 21st Century, 80*(5), 679-692.

de Souza Zanirato Maia, J., Bueno, A. P. A., & Sato, J. R. (2023). Applications of Artificial Intelligence Models in Educational Analytics and Decision Making: A Systematic Review. *WORLD (Oakland, Calif.)*, *4*(2), 288–313. doi:10.3390/world4020019

Dede, C. (2010). Comparing frameworks for 21st century skills. 21st Century Skills. *Rethinking How Students Learn*, *51*, 51–76.

Dee, D., Uppala, S., Simmons, A. J., Berrisford, P., Poli, P., Kobayashi, S., Andræ, U., Balmaseda, M., Balsamo, G., Bauer, P., Bechtold, P., Beljaars, A., Van De Berg, L., Bidlot, J., Bormann, N., Delsol, C., Dragani, R., Fuentes, M., Geer, A., ... Vitart, F. (2011). The ERA-Interim reanalysis: Configuration and performance of the data assimilation system. *Quarterly Journal of the Royal Meteorological Society*, *137*(656), 553–597. doi:10.1002/qj.828

Delfino, M., & Persico, D. (2007). Online or face-to-face? Experimenting with different techniques in teacher training. *Journal of Computer Assisted Learning*, *23*(5), 351–365. doi:10.1111/j.1365-2729.2007.00220.x

Della-Ventura, V. M. (2017). Creating inspiring learning environments employing digital technologies: A case study of the effectiveness of WhatsApp in music education. Springer.

Dewan, M. A. A., Lin, F., Wen, D., Murshed, M., and Uddin, Z. (2018). *IEEE smart world, ubiquitous intelligence & computing, advanced & trusted computing, scalable computing & communications, cloud & big data computing, internet of people and smart city innovation SmartWorld/SCALCOM/UIC/ATC/CBDCom/IOP/SCI)*. IEEE.

Dewan, M. A. A., Murshed, M., & Lin, F. (2019). Engagement detection in online learning: A review. *Smart Learning Environments*, *6*(1), 2–8. doi:10.1186/s40561-018-0080-z

Dhawan, S. (2020). Online learning: A panacea in the time of COVID-19 crisis. *Journal of Educational Technology Systems*, *49*(1), 5–22. doi:10.1177/0047239520934018

Dicheva, C., & Dicheva, D. (2017). Gamifying education: what is known, what is believed and what remains uncertain: a critical review. *International Journal of Educational Technology in Higher Education*, *14*(1), 1–36. doi:10.1186/s41239-017-0042-5

Dicheva, D., Dichev, C., Agre, G., & Angelova, G. (2015). Gamification in Education: A Systematic Mapping Study. *Journal of Educational Technology & Society*, *18*(3), 75–88. doi:10.1109/EDUCON.2014.6826129

Dikshit, S., Atiq, A., Shahid, M., Dwivedi, V., & Thusu, A. (2023). The use of artificial intelligence to optimize the routing of vehicles and reduce traffic congestion in urban areas. *ICST Transactions on Energy Web*, *10*. Advance online publication. doi:10.4108/ew.4613

Dillahunt, T., Wang, B., Teasley, S., West, R., & Zhang, P. (2019). *Confronting Bias in AI: Practical considerations for educators*. Retrieved from https://edtechbooks.org/ai/bias

Dixson, M. (2015). Measuring student engagement in the online course: The online student engagement scale (OSE). *Online Learning : the Official Journal of the Online Learning Consortium*, *19*(4). Advance online publication. doi:10.24059/olj.v19i4.561

Dogan, M. E., Goru Dogan, T., & Bozkurt, A. (2023). The use of artificial intelligence (AI) in online learning and distance education processes: A systematic review of empirical studies. *Applied Sciences (Basel, Switzerland)*, *13*(5), 3056. doi:10.3390/app13053056

Domínguez, A., Saenz-De-Navarrete, J., De-Marcos, L., Fernández-Sanz, L., Pagés, C., & Martínez-Herráiz, J. J. (2013). Gamifying Learning Experiences: Practical Implications and Outcomes. *Computers & Education*, *63*(1), 380–392. doi:10.1016/j.compedu.2012.12.020

Douglas, J., Douglas, A., & Barnes, B. (2006). Measuring Student Satisfaction at a UK University. *Quality Assurance in Education*, *14*(3), 251–267. doi:10.1108/09684880610678568

Downing, J., & Dyment, J. (2018). Online initial teacher education students' perceptions of using web conferences to support professional conversations. *The Australian Journal of Teacher Education*, *43*(4), 68–91. doi:10.14221/ajte.2018v43n4.5

Driskell, J. E., & Dwyer, D. J. (1984). Microcomputer Videogame Based Training. *Technology*, *24*(2), 11–16.

Duin, A. H., & Tham, J. (2020). The Current State of Analytics: Implications for Learning Management System (LMS) Use in Writing Pedagogy. *Computers and Composition*, *55*. doi:10.1016/j.compcom.2020.102544

Dutta, S., Mia, I., & Azad, M. A. K. (2017). Artificial Intelligence in Education: Challenges and Opportunities for Sustainable Development. In *2017 4th International Conference on Electrical Engineering and Information & Communication Technology (ICEEICT)* (pp. 1-6). IEEE.

Dwivedi, Y. K., Kshetri, N., Hughes, L., Slade, E. L., Jeyaraj, A., Kar, A. K., & Wright, R. (2023). So what if ChatGPT wrote it? Multidisciplinary perspectives on opportunities, challenges and implications of generative conversational AI for research, practice and policy. *International Journal of Information Management, 71*, 102642. doi:10.1016/j.ijinfomgt.2023.102642

Eisenhardt, K. M., & Martin, J. A. (2000). Dynamic capabilities: What are they? *Strategic Management Journal, 21*(10–11), 1105–1121. doi:10.1002/1097-0266(200010/11)21:10/11<1105::AID-SMJ133>3.0.CO;2-E

Elkhodr, M., Gide, E., Wu, R., & Darwish, O. (2023). ICT students' perceptions towards ChatGPT: An experimental reflective lab analysis. *STEM Education, 3*(2), 70–88. doi:10.3934/steme.2023006

El-Sabagh, H. A. (2021). Adaptive e-learning environment based on learning styles and its impact on development students' engagement. *International Journal of Educational Technology in Higher Education, 18*(1), 53. doi:10.1186/s41239-021-00289-4

Ertel, W. (2017). *Introduction to artificial intelligence. Undergraduate topics in Computer Science* (2nd ed.). Springer. doi:10.1007/978-3-319-58487-4

Esten. (2019). *"Uzaktan Öğretimde Yapay Zekâ" Başlıklı Eğitimde Yapay Zekâ Çalıştayı Sonuç Raporu* [Final Report of Artificial Intelligence in Education Workshop titled "Artificial Intelligence in Distance Education"]. https://tasam.org/tr-TR/Icerik/51444/uzaktan_ogretimde_yapay_zekâ_ egitimde_yapay_zekâ_calistayi_-_5_sonuc_raporu

Falloon, G. (2010). Using avatars and virtual environments in learning: What do they have to offer? *British Journal of Educational Technology, 41*(1), 108–122. doi:10.1111/j.1467-8535.2009.00991.x

Fang, Y., Roscoe, R. D., & McNamara, D. S. (2023). Artificial intelligence-based assessment in education. In *Handbook of artificial intelligence in education* (pp. 485–504). Edward Elgar Publishing. doi:10.4337/9781800375413.00033

Fazil, A. W., Hakimi, M., Shahidzay, A. K., & Hasas, A. (2024). Exploring the Broad Impact of AI Technologies on Student Engagement and Academic Performance in University Settings in Afghanistan. *RIGGS: Journal of Artificial Intelligence and Digital Business, 2*(2), 56–63. doi:10.31004/riggs.v2i2.268

Fellnhofer, K. (2019). Toward a taxonomy of entrepreneurship education research literature: A bibliometric mapping and visualization. *Educational Research Review, 27*, 28-55. doi:10.1016/j.edurev.2018.10.002

Felszeghy, S., Pasonen-Seppänen, S., Koskela, A., Nieminen, P., Härkönen, K., Paldanius, K. M., Gabbouj, S., Ketola, K., Hiltunen, M., Lundin, M., Haapaniemi, T., Sointu, E., Bauman, E. B., Gilbert, G. E., Morton, D., & Mahonen, A. (2019). Using online game-based platforms to improve student performance and engagement in histology teaching. *BMC Medical Education, 19*(1), 1–11. doi:10.1186/s12909-019-1701-0 PMID:31331319

Ferguson, R., & Shum, S. B. (2012). Social learning analytics: five approaches. In *Proceedings of the 2nd International Conference on Learning Analytics and Knowledge* (pp. 23-33). Academic Press.

Fernandes, C. W., Rafatirad, S., & Sayadi, H. (2023). Advancing personalized and adaptive learning experience in education with artificial intelligence. In *2023 32nd Annual Conference of the European Association for Education in Electrical and Information Engineering (EAEEIE)* (pp. 1-6). IEEE. 10.23919/EAEEIE55804.2023.10181336

Fernandez, P. (2023). Through the looking glass: Envisioning new library technologies AI-text generators as explained by ChatGPT. *Library Hi Tech News, 40*(3), 11–14. doi:10.1108/LHTN-02-2023-0017

Fidan, I., Huseynov, O., Ali, M. A., Alkunte, S., Rajeshirke, M., Gupta, A., Hasanov, S., Tantawi, K., Yasa, E., Yilmaz, O., Loy, J., Popov, V. V., & Popov, V. V. (2023). Recent inventions in additive manufacturing: Holistic review. *Inventions (Basel, Switzerland), 8*(4), 103. doi:10.3390/inventions8040103

Figueroa-Flores, J. F. (2016). Gamification and game-based learning: Two strategies for the 21st-century learner. *World Journal of Educational Research (Los Angeles, Calif.)*, *3*(2), 507–522. doi:10.22158/wjer.v3n2p507

Firat, M. (2023). *How ChatGPT can transform autodidactic experiences and open education*. OSFPREPRINTS.

Floridi, L., Cowls, J., Beltrametti, M., Chatila, R., Chazerand, P., Dignum, V., ... Schafer, B. (2018). AI4People—an ethical framework for a good AI society: Opportunities, risks, principles, and recommendations. *Minds and Machines*, *28*(4), 689–707. doi:10.1007/s11023-018-9482-5 PMID:30930541

Fredricks, J. A., Blumenfeld, P. C., & Paris, A. H. (2015). School engagement: Potential of the concept, state of the evidence. *Review of Educational Research*, *74*(1), 59–109. doi:10.3102/00346543074001059

Frieder, S., Pinchetti, L., Griffiths, R. R., Salvatori, T., Lukasiewicz, T., Petersen, P. C., Chevalier, A., & Berner, J. (2023). Mathematical capabilities of chatgpt. *arXiv* arXiv:2301.13867.

Friend, B., Patrick, S., Schneider, C., & Vander Ark, T. (2017). *What's possible with personalized learning? An overview of personalized learning for schools, families & communities*. iNACOL.

Fryer, L. K., Nakao, K., & Thompson, A. (2019). Chatbot learning partners: Connecting learning experiences, interest and competence. *Computers in Human Behavior*, *93*, 279–289. doi:10.1016/j.chb.2018.12.023

Furrer, C., & Skinner, E. (2003). Sense of relatedness as a factor in children's academic engagement and performance. *Journal of Educational Psychology*, *95*(1), 148–162. doi:10.1037/0022-0663.95.1.148

Fütterer, T., Fischer, C., Alekseeva, A., Chen, X., Tate, T., Warschauer, M., & Gerjets, P. (2023). ChatGPT in education: Global reactions to AI innovations. *Scientific Reports*, *13*(1), 15310. doi:10.1038/s41598-023-42227-6 PMID:37714915

Gallini, J. K., & Barron, D. (2001). Participants' perceptions of web-infused environments: A survey of teaching beliefs, learning approaches, and communication. *Journal of Research on Technology in Education*, *34*(2), 139–156. doi:10.1080/15391523.2001.10782341

Garett, R., & Young, S. D. (2019). Health care gamification: A study of game mechanics and elements. *Technology. Knowledge and Learning*, *24*(3), 341–353. doi:10.1007/s10758-018-9353-4

Garrison, D. R., Anderson, T., & Archer, W. (2003). A theory of critical inquiry in online distance education. Handbook of Distance Education, 1(4), 113-127.

Ghosh, R., Rude-Parkins, C., & Kerrick, S. A. (2012). Collaborative problem-solving in virtual environments: Effect of social interaction, social presence, and sociability on critical thinking. In *The Next Generation of Distance Education* (pp. 191–205). Springer US. doi:10.1007/978-1-4614-1785-9_13

Ghulam, S. T., & Abushammala, H. (2023). Challenges and opportunities in the management of electronic waste and its impact on human health and environment. *Sustainability (Basel)*, *15*(3), 1837. doi:10.3390/su15031837

Gibbs, W. J. (1998). Implementing on-line learning environments. *Journal of Computing in Higher Education*, *10*(1), 16–37. doi:10.1007/BF02946984

Gill, S. S., Xu, M., Patros, P., Wu, H., Kaur, R., Kaur, K., Fuller, S., Singh, M., Arora, P., Parlikad, A. K., Stankovski, V., Abraham, A., Ghosh, S. K., Lutfiyya, H., Kanhere, S. S., Bahsoon, R., Rana, O., Dustdar, S., Sakellariou, R., ... Buyya, R. (2024). Transformative effects of ChatGPT on modern education: Emerging Era of AI Chatbots. *Internet of Things and Cyber-Physical Systems*, *4*, 19–23. doi:10.1016/j.iotcps.2023.06.002

GilsonA.SafranekC.HuangT.SocratesV.ChiL.TaylorR. A.ChartashD. (2022). How Well Does ChatGPT Do When Taking the Medical Licensing Exams? The Implications of Large Language Models for Medical Education and Knowledge Assessment. medRxiv.

Gligorea, I., Cioca, M., Oancea, R., Gorski, A. T., Gorski, H., & Tudorache, P. (2023). Adaptive learning using artificial ıntelligence in e-learning: A literature review. *Education Sciences*, *13*(12), 1216. doi:10.3390/educsci13121216

Goel, A. K., & Polepeddi, L. (2017). *Jill watson: A virtual teaching assistant for online education.* Presented to the Learning Engineering for Online Learning Workshop, Harvard University. https://smartech.gatech.edu/bitstream/handle/1853/59104/goelpolepeddiharvardvolume-v7.1.pdf?sequence=1&isAllowed=y

Gomede, E., Gaffo, F. H., Briganó, G., de Barros, R., & Mendes, L. (2018). Application of computational intelligence to improve education in smart cities. *Sensors (Basel)*, *18*(1), 267. Advance online publication. doi:10.3390/s18010267 PMID:29346288

González, C. S., N. Gómez, V. Navarro, M. Cairos, C. Quirce, P. Toledo, and N. Marrero-Gordillo. (2016). Learning Healthy Lifestyles through Active Videogames, Motor Games and the Gamification of Educational Activities. *Computers in Human Behavior, 55*(Part A), 529–551. doi:10.1016/j.chb.2015.08.052

González-Calatayud, V., Prendes-Espinosa, P., & Roig-Vila, R. (2021). Artificial intelligence for student assessment: A systematic review. *Applied Sciences (Basel, Switzerland)*, *11*(12), 5467. doi:10.3390/app11125467

Gopalakrishna & Venugopal. (2023). Assessment on the Intricacies of English Speaking Abilities by Rural Students in India. In *English Language Competence in Rural Youth: Improving Job Readiness.* Current Publications.

Grzonka, D., Kołodziej, J., & Jakóbik, A. (2019). Agent–based monitoring of the task scheduling in computational clouds. *Journal of Intelligent & Fuzzy Systems*, *37*(6), 7481–7492. doi:10.3233/JIFS-179355

Habeeb, Rahman, & Rashmi. (2023). Revolutionizing education: Artificial intelligence empowered learning in higher education. *Cogent Education.* doi:10.1080/2331186X.2023.2293431

Hafez, M. G., & El-Gamel, M. (2016). Agent-Based Cloud Computing: A Survey. *Agent-based Cloud Computing. Survey (London, England)*, 285–292. Advance online publication. doi:10.1109/FiCloud.2016.48

Halaweh. (2023). ChatGPT in education: Strategies for responsible implementation. *Contemp. Educ. Technol., 15*(2).

Haleem, A., Javaid, M., & Singh, R. P. (2022). An era of ChatGPT as a significant futuristic support tool: A study on features, abilities, and challenges. *BenchCouncil Transactions on Benchmarks, Standards and Evaluations, 2*(4), 100089.

Halili, S. H., Rahman, N. H. A., & Razak, R. A. (2018). Traditional versus virtual learning: How engaged are the students in learning English literature? *Indonesian Journal of Applied Linguistics*, *8*(1). Advance online publication. doi:10.17509/ijal.v8i1.11467

Hamari, J., Koivisto, J., & Sarsa, H. (2014). Does gamification work? A literature review of empirical studies on gamification. In *2014 47th Hawaii international conference on system sciences* (pp. 3025-3034). IEEE.

Hamari, J., Koivisto, J., & Sarsa, H. (2014). Does Gamification Work? A Literature Review of Empirical Studies on Gamification. *Proceedings of the Annual Hawaii International Conference on System Sciences.* 10.1109/HICSS.2014.377

Handelsman, M. M., Briggs, W. L., Sullivan, N., & Towler, A. (2005). A Measure of College Student Course Engagement. *The Journal of Educational Research*, *98*(3), 184–192. doi:10.3200/JOER.98.3.184-192

Hao, Y., Helo, P., & Gunasekaran, A. (2019). Cloud platforms for remote monitoring system: A comparative case study. *Production Planning and Control*, *31*(2–3), 186–202. doi:10.1080/09537287.2019.1631459

Harati, H., Sujo-Montes, L., Tu, C. H., Armfield, S. J., & Yen, C. J. (2021). Assessment and learning in knowledge spaces (ALEKS) adaptive system impact on students' perception and self-regulated learning skills. *Education Sciences*, *11*(10), 603. doi:10.3390/educsci11100603

Harnadi, B., & Widiantoro, A. D. (2024). Investigating the behavioral differences in the acceptance of MOOCs and E-learning technology. *Computers in Human Behavior Reports, 14*. doi:10.1016/j.chbr.2024.100403

Haseski, H. I. (2019). What do Turkish pre-service teachers think about artificial intelligence? *International Journal of Computer Science Education in Schools*, *3*(2), 3–23. doi:10.21585/ijcses.v3i2.55

Headden, S. (2013). The promise of personalized learning: Blending the human touch with technological firepower. *Education Next*, *13*(4), 14–21.

Heagney, M., & Benson, R. (2017). How mature-age students succeed in higher education: Implications for institutional support. *Journal of Higher Education Policy and Management*, *39*(3), 216–234. doi:10.1080/1360080X.2017.1300986

Hearst, M. A., Dumais, S. T., Osuna, E., Platt, J., & Schölkopf, B. (1998). Support vector machines. *IEEE Intelligent Systems & their Applications*, *13*(4), 18–28. doi:10.1109/5254.708428

Hernández-Lara, A. B., & Serradell-López, E. (2018). Student interactions in online discussion forums: Their perception on learning with business simulation games. *Behaviour & Information Technology*, *37*(4), 419–429. doi:10.1080/0144929X.2018.1441326

Hew, K. F, Chen, Q, & Tang.Y. (2018). Understanding Student Engagement in Large-Scale Open Online Courses: A Machine Learning Facilitated Analysis of Student's Reflections in 18 Highly Rated MOOCs. *International Review of Research in Open and Distributed Learning, 193.*

He, W. (2013). Examining students' online interaction in a live video streaming environment using data mining and text mining. *Computers in Human Behavior*, *29*(1), 90–102. doi:10.1016/j.chb.2012.07.020

Hew, K. F. (2016). Promoting engagement in online courses: What strategies can we learn from three highly rated MOOCS? *British Journal of Educational Technology*, *47*(2), 320–341. doi:10.1111/bjet.12235

He, X., & Yin, J. (2022). Research on application of artificial intelligence technology in administrative innovation smart management system. In *2022 International Conference on Education, Network and Information Technology (ICENIT)* (pp. 379-382). IEEE. 10.1109/ICENIT57306.2022.00093

Hien, H. T., Cuong, P.-N., Nam, L. N. H., Nhung, H. L. T. K., & Thang, L. D. (2018). Intelligent assistants in higher-education environments: the FIT-EBot, A chatbot for administrative and learning Support. In *Proceedings of the 9th International Symposium on Information and Communication Technology*. ACM. 10.1145/3287921.3287937

Hill, H. (2019). *Humans in the Loop: The Future of AI in Education* [White Paper]. Chan Zuckerberg Initiative.

Hill, M. (2024). *Find the path to what's possible*. McGraw Hill. https://www.mheducation.com/

Hinojo-Lucena, F. J., Aznar-Díaz, I., Cáceres-Reche, M. P., & Romero-Rodríguez, J. M. (2019). Artificial intelligence in higher education: A bibliometric study on its impact in the scientific literature. *Education Sciences*, *9*(1), 51. doi:10.3390/educsci9010051

Hoc, J. M. (2000). From human-machine interaction to human-machine cooperation. *Ergonomics*, *43*(7), 833–843. doi:10.1080/001401300409044 PMID:10929820

Holmes, W., Bialik, M., & Fadel, C. (2023). *Artificial intelligence in education*. Globethics Publications., doi:10.58863/20.500.12424/4276068

Holmes, W., Porayska-Pomsta, K., Holstein, K., Sutherland, E., Baker, T., Shum, S. B., Santos, O. C., Rodrigo, M. T., Cukurova, M., Bittencourt, I. I., & Koedinger, K. R. (2021). Ethics of AI in education: Towards a community-wide framework. *International Journal of Artificial Intelligence in Education*, 1–23. doi:10.1007/s40593-021-00239-1

Holzinger, A., Saranti, A., Angerschmid, A., Retzlaff, C. O., Gronauer, A., Pejaković, V., Medel-Jiménez, F., Krexner, T., Gollob, C., & Stampfer, K. (2022). Digital transformation in smart farm and forest operations needs Human-Centered AI: Challenges and future directions. *Sensors (Basel)*, *22*(8), 3043. doi:10.3390/s22083043 PMID:35459028

Hong, W. C. H. (2023). The impact of ChatGPT on foreign language teaching and learning: Opportunities in education and research. *Journal of Educational Technology and Innovation*, *5*(1).

Hooda, M., Rana, C., Dahiya, O., Rizwan, A., & Hossain, M. S. (2022). Artificial intelligence for assessment and feedback to enhance student success in higher education. *Mathematical Problems in Engineering*, 1–19. doi:10.1155/2022/5215722

Hrastinski, S., Olofsson, A. D., Arkenback, C., Ekström, S., Ericsson, E., Fransson, G., Jaldemark, J., Ryberg, T., Öberg, L., Fuentes, A., Gustafsson, U., Humble, N., Mozelius, P., Sundgren, M., & Utterberg, M. (2019). Critical Imaginaries and Reflections on Artificial Intelligence and Robots in Postdigital K-12 Education. *Postdigital Science and Education*, *2019*(1), 427–445. doi:10.1007/s42438-019-00046-x

Huang, A.Y. Q., Lub, O. H. T., Yan, S. J. H. (2022). Effects of Artificial Intelligence–Enabled personalized recommendations on learners' learning engagement, motivation, and outcomes in a flipped classroom. *Computers & Education, 194.*

Huang, A. Y., Lu, O. H., & Yang, S. J. (2023). Effects of artificial Intelligence–Enabled personalized recommendations on learners' learning engagement, motivation, and outcomes in a flipped classroom. *Computers & Education*, *194*, 104684. doi:10.1016/j.compedu.2022.104684

HuaT. K. (2022). A short review on machine learning. Authorea Preprints.

Hughes, M., & Daykin, N. (2002). Towards constructivism: Investigating students' perceptions and learning as a result of using an online environment. *Innovations in Education and Teaching International*, *39*(3), 217–224. doi:10.1080/13558000210150036

Hung, A. C. Y. (2017). A critique and defense of gamification. *Journal of Interactive Online Learning*, *15*(1).

Hutchison, L. F. (2012). Addressing the STEM teacher shortage in American schools: Ways to recruit and retain effective STEM teachers. *Action in Teacher Education*, *34*(5–6), 541–550. doi:10.1080/01626620.2012.729483

Hwang, G. J., & Chien, S. Y. (2022). Definition, roles, and potential research issues of the metaverse in education: An artificial intelligence perspective. *Computers and Education: Artificial Intelligence*, *3*, 100082. doi:10.1016/j.caeai.2022.100082

Hwang, G.-J., Tu, Y.-F., & Tang, K.-Y. (2022). AI in Online-Learning Research: Visualizing and Interpreting the Journal Publications from 1997 to 2019. *International Review of Research in Open and Distance Learning*, *23*(1), 104–130. doi:10.19173/irrodl.v23i1.6319

Hwang, G., Xie, H., Wah, B. W., & Gašević, D. (2020). Vision, challenges, roles and research issues of Artificial Intelligence in Education. *Computers and Education. Artificial Intelligence*, *1*, 100001.

Hwang, G., Yang, L., & Wang, S. (2013). A concept map-embedded educational computer game for improving students' learning performance in natural science courses. *Computers & Education*, *69*, 121–130. doi:10.1016/j.compedu.2013.07.008

İşler, B., & Kiliç, M. (2021). The use and development of artificial intelligence in education. *e-Journal of New Media*, *5*(1), 1-11.

Jackson, P. C. (1985). *Introduction to artificial intelligence* (2nd ed.). Dover Publications, Inc.

Jainani, K., & Khan, R. (2021). *The Impact of Customer Relationship Management on Customer Satisfaction and Retention.* https://www.academia.edu/59302555/The_Impact_Of_Customer_Relationship_Management_On_Customer_Satisfaction_And_Retention_The_Mediation_Of_Service_Quality

Jain, J., Jain, A., Srivastava, S. K., Verma, C., Răboacă, M. S., & Illés, Z. (2022). Improved Security of E-Healthcare Images Using Hybridized Robust Zero-Watermarking and Hyper-Chaotic System along with RSA. *Mathematics*, *10*(7), 1071. doi:10.3390/math10071071

Jalil, S., Rafi, S., LaToza, T. D., Moran, K., & Lam, W. (2023). ChatGPT and Software Testing Education: Promises & Perils. *arXiv* 2023, arXiv:2302.03287. doi:10.1109/ICSTW58534.2023.00078

Jarvela, S., Kirschner, P. A., Hadwin, A., Jarvenoja, H., Malmberg, J., Miller, M., & Laru, J. (2016). Socially shared regulation of learning in CSCL: Understanding and prompting individual and group-level shared regulatory activities. *International Journal of Computer-Supported Collaborative Learning*, *11*(3), 263–280. doi:10.1007/s11412-016-9238-2

Javaid, M., Haleem, A., Singh, R. P., & Suman, R. (2021). Artificial Intelligence Applications for Industry 4.0: A Literature-Based Study. *Journal of Industrial Integration and Management*, *07*(01), 83–111. doi:10.1142/S2424862221300040

Johnson, R., & Miller, C. (2021). Immersive Learning Environments: Exploring the Role of AI in Virtual Reality Education. *Educational Technology Research and Development*, *18*(3), 201–215.

Johnson, W. L. (2016). Serious use of a serious game for language learning. *ReCALL*, *28*(2), 231–247.

Jones, B., & Wang, L. (2019). Enhancing Teacher-Student Communication Through AI-Powered Virtual Assistants. *International Journal of Virtual Learning Environments*, *7*(1), 112–127.

Jordan, M. I., & Mitchell, T. M. (2015). Machine learning: Trends, perspectives, and prospects. *Science*, *349*(6245), 255–260. doi:10.1126/science.aaa8415 PMID:26185243

Jung, G., & Sim, K. M. (2011). *Agent-Based Adaptive Resource Allocation on the Cloud Computing Environment*. Agent-based Adaptive Resource Allocation on the Cloud Computing Environment. doi:10.1109/ICPPW.2011.18

Kahu, E. R., & Nelson, K. (2018). Student engagement in the educational interface: Understanding the mechanisms of student success. *Higher Education Research & Development*, *37*(1), 58–71. doi:10.1080/07294360.2017.1344197

Kahu, E. R., Picton, C., & Nelson, K. (2019). Pathways to engagement: A longitudinal study of the first-year student experience in the educational interface. *Higher Education*, *79*(4), 657–673. doi:10.1007/s10734-019-00429-w

Kaledio, P., Robert, A., & Frank, L. (2024). The Impact of Artificial Intelligence on Students' Learning Experience. *SSRN*. Advance online publication. doi:10.2139/ssrn.4716747

Kapralos, B., Hogan, M., Pribetic, A. I., & Dubrowski, A. (2011). Virtual simulations and serious games in a laptop-based university: Gauging faculty and student perceptions. *Interactive Technology and Smart Education*, *8*(2), 106–120. doi:10.1108/17415651111141821

Karabchuk, T., & Roshchina, Y. (2023). Predictors of student engagement: The role of universities' or importance of students' background? *European Journal of Higher Education*, *13*(3), 327–346. doi:10.1080/21568235.2022.2035240

Karlgren, K. (2005). *Intelligent tutoring systems (its)*. Academic Press.

Karsenti, T. (2019). Artificial intelligence in education: The urgent need to prepare teachers for tomorrow's schools. *Formation et Profession*, *27*(1), 112–116. doi:10.18162/fp.2019.a167

Kazi, K. S. (2023). Detection of Malicious Nodes in IoT Networks based on Throughput and ML. *Journal of Electrical and Power System Engineering*, *9*(1), 22–29.

Kazi, V., & ... . (2023). Deep Learning, YOLO and RFID based smart Billing Handcart. *Journal of Communication Engineering & Systems*, *13*(1), 1–8.

Kebritchi, M., Lipschuetz, A., & Santiague, L. (2017). Issues and challenges for teaching successful online courses in higher education. *Journal of Educational Technology Systems*, *46*(1), 4–29. doi:10.1177/0047239516661713

Khanal, P. (2013). Making virtual learning interactive and meaningful: Implications of constructivism for adult students. *International Journal of Research Studies in Education*, *2*(4). Advance online publication. doi:10.5861/ijrse.2013.302

Khan, H. M., Ahmad, S., Javed, R., & Nasir, N. (2023). The significance of Artificial Intelligence in business and accounting: A Bibliometric analysis. *Pakistan Journal of Humanities and Social Sciences*, *11*(2). Advance online publication. doi:10.52131/pjhss.2023.1102.0417

Khan, H., Kushwah, K. K., Khare, K., Mahobia, S. K., & Thakur, J. S. (2023). Methods of Evaluation and Assessment in Digital Learning. In *Mobile and Sensor-Based Technologies in Higher Education* (pp. 83–110). IGI Global. doi:10.4018/978-1-6684-5400-8.ch004

Khan, I., Ahmad, A. R., Jabeur, N., & Mahdi, M. N. (2021). An artificial intelligence approach to monitor student performance and devise preventive measures. *Smart Learning Environments*, *8*(1), 1–18. doi:10.1186/s40561-021-00161-y

Khan, M. A., Saleh, A. M., Waseem, M., & Sajjad, I. A. (2023). Artificial intelligence Enabled Demand Response: Prospects and challenges in smart grid environment. *IEEE Access : Practical Innovations, Open Solutions*, *11*, 1477–1505. doi:10.1109/ACCESS.2022.3231444

Khan, M., Mehran, M. T., Haq, Z. U., Ullah, Z., Naqvi, S. R., Ihsan, M., & Abbass, H. (2021). Applications of artificial intelligence in COVID-19 pandemic: A comprehensive review. *Expert Systems with Applications*, *185*, 115695. doi:10.1016/j.eswa.2021.115695 PMID:34400854

Khowaja, K., & Salim, S. S. (2013). A systematic review of strategies and computer-based intervention (CBI) for reading comprehension of children with autism. *Research in Autism Spectrum Disorders*, *7*(9), 1111-1121. doi:10.1016/j.rasd.2013.05.009

Kigo, N. (2016). *An agent based system for monitoring and measuring performance of public cloud applications for users*. http://erepository.uonbi.ac.ke/handle/11295/97834

Kim, J.-H., Kim, M., Park, M., & Yoo, J. (2023). Immersive interactive technologies and virtual shopping experiences: Differences in consumer perceptions between augmented reality (AR) and virtual reality (VR). *Telematics and Informatics*, *77*. doi:10.1016/j.tele.2022.101936

Kim, H. S., Kim, N. Y., & Cha, Y. (2021). Is it beneficial to use AI chatbots to improve learners' speaking performance? *Journal of ASIA TEFL*, *18*(1), 161–178. doi:10.18823/asiatefl.2021.18.1.10.161

Kim, S., Jang, Y., Choi, S., Kim, W., Jung, H., Kim, S., & Kim, H. (2021). Analyzing teacher competency with TPACK for K-12 AI education. *Kunstliche Intelligenz*, *35*(2), 139–151. doi:10.1007/s13218-021-00731-9

Kindermann, T. A. (1993). Natural peer groups as contexts for individual development: The case of children's motivation in school. *Developmental Psychology*, *29*(6), 970–977. doi:10.1037/0012-1649.29.6.970

Kirsten, R. (2016). Computer-Based Instruction (CBI) Within Special Education. In Computer-Assisted and Web-Based Innovations in Psychology, Special Education, and Health. Academic Press. doi:10.1016/B978-0-12-802075-3.00009-7

Kitamura, F. C. (2023). ChatGPT is shaping the future of medical writing but still requires human judgment. *Radiology*, *307*(2), e230171. doi:10.1148/radiol.230171 PMID:36728749

Kiy, H. (2023). A study on writing experience with ChatGPT of college students. *The Korean Society of Culture and Convergence*, *45*(9), 853–868. doi:10.33645/cnc.2023.09.45.09.853

Kolli, S., Ranjani, M., Kavitha, P., Daniel, D., & Chandramauli, A. (2023). *Prediction of Water Quality Parameters by IoT and Machine Learning*. doi:10.1109/ICCCI56745.2023.10128475

Komalavalli, K., Hemalatha, R., & Dhanalakshmi, S. (2020). A survey of artificial intelligence in smart phones and its applications among the students of higher education in and around Chennai City. *Shanlax International Journal of Education*, *8*(3), 89–95. doi:10.34293/education.v8i3.2379

Koppala Venugopal, Vital, Das, Jena, & Mohapatro. (2023). Usage Determinants of Mobile Applications Impelling Students Group: Assessment through Machine Learning Models and Regression. *Vytapeni, Vetrani, Instalace Journal*, *11*(11), 151-178. https://vvijournal.com/volume-11-issue-112023/

Kop, R. (2011). The challenges to connective learning on open online networks: Learning experiences during a massive open online course. *International Review of Research in Open and Distance Learning*, *12*(3), 19–38. doi:10.19173/irrodl.v12i3.882

Kosba, E., Dimitrova, V., & Boyle, R. (2007). Adaptive feedback generation to support teachers in web-based distance education. *User Modeling and User-Adapted Interaction*, *17*(4), 379–413. doi:10.1007/s11257-007-9031-z

Krasnova, T., & Ananjev, A. (2015). Students' perception of learning in the online discussion environment. *Mediterranean Journal of Social Sciences*. Advance online publication. doi:10.5901/mjss.2015.v6n6s1p202

Krishnamurthy, K., Selvaraj, N., Gupta, P., Cyriac, B., Dhurairaj, P., Abdullah, A., Krishnapillai, A., Lugova, H., Haque, M., Xie, S., & Ang, E. T. (2022). Benefits of gamification in medical education. *Clinical Anatomy (New York, N.Y.)*, *35*(6), 795–807. doi:10.1002/ca.23916 PMID:35637557

Krithika, L. B., & Lakshmi, P. G. G. (2016). Student Emotion Recognition System (SERS) for e-learning improvement based on learner concentration metric. *Procedia Computer Science*, *85*, 767–776. doi:10.1016/j.procs.2016.05.264

Kumar, S., Gudiseva, K., Iswarya, A., Rani, S., Prasad, K., & Sharma, Y. (2022). Automatic Music Generation System based on RNN Architecture. *2022 2nd International Conference on Technological Advancements in Computational Sciences (ICTACS)*. 10.1109/ICTACS56270.2022.9988652

Kumar, A. (2022). Study and analysis of different segmentation methods for brain tumor MRI application. *Multimedia Tools and Applications*, *82*(5), 7117–7139. doi:10.1007/s11042-022-13636-y PMID:35991584

Kumar, K., & Saini, R. (2022). Data-driven internet of things and cloud computing enabled hydropower plant monitoring system. *Sustainable Computing : Informatics and Systems*, *36*, 100823. doi:10.1016/j.suscom.2022.100823

Kumar, S., Raja, R., Mahmood, M. R., & Choudhary, S. (2023). A Hybrid Method for the Removal of RVIN Using Self Organizing Migration with Adaptive Dual Threshold Median Filter. *Sensing and Imaging*, *24*(1), 9. Advance online publication. doi:10.1007/s11220-023-00414-9

Kumar, S., Rani, S., Jain, A., Verma, C., Răboacă, M. S., Illés, Z., & Neagu, B. (2022). Face spoofing, age, gender and facial expression recognition using Advance Neural Network Architecture-Based Biometric System. *Sensors (Basel)*, *22*(14), 5160. doi:10.3390/s22145160 PMID:35890840

Kumar, S., Singh, S., & Kumar, J. (2019). *Gender Classification Using Machine Learning with Multi-Feature Method*. doi:10.1109/CCWC.2019.8666601

Kung, T. H., Cheatham, M., Medenilla, A., Sillos, C., De Leon, L., Elepaño, C., Madriaga, M., Aggabao, R., Diaz-Candido, G., Maningo, J., & Tseng, V. (2023). Performance of ChatGPT on USMLE: Potential for AI-assisted medical education using large language models. *PLOS Digital Health*, *2*(2), e0000198. doi:10.1371/journal.pdig.0000198 PMID:36812645

Kurzweil, R., Richter, R., Kurzweil, R., & Schneider, M. L. (1990). *The age of intelligent machines* (Vol. 580). MIT Press.

Kurzweil, R., Richter, R., Kurzweil, R., & Schneider, M. L. (1990). *The age of intelligent machines, 580*. MIT Press.

Kutubuddin, K. (2022). Big data and HR Analytics in Talent Management: A Study. *Recent Trends in Parallel Computing*, *9*(3), 16–26.

Kuzilek, J., Hlosta, M., Herrmannova, D., Zdrahal, Z., & Wolff, A., A. (2015). OU analysis: analysing at-risk students at the Open University. *Proceedings of First International Workshop on Visual Aspects of Learning Analytics and Knowledge Conference (LAK 2015)*, 1–16.

Labadze, L., Grigolia, M., & Machaidze, L. (2023). Role of AI chatbots in education: Systematic literature review. *International Journal of Educational Technology in Higher Education*, *20*(1), 56. doi:10.1186/s41239-023-00426-1

Lainjo, B., & Tsmouche, H. (2023). The impact of artificial intelligence on higher learning institutions. *International Journal of Education, Teaching, and Social Sciences*, *3*(2), 96–113. doi:10.47747/ijets.v3i2.1028

Lamb, R. L., Etopio, E., Hand, B., & Yoon, S. Y. (2019). Virtual reality simulation: Effects on academic performance within two domains of writing in science. *Journal of Science Education and Technology*, *28*(4), 371–381. doi:10.1007/s10956-019-09774-y

Landers, R. N., Bauer, K. N., Callan, R. C., & Armstrong, M. B. (2015). Psychological theory and the gamification of learning. *Gamification in education and business*, 165-186.

Lapadat, J. C. (2006). Written interaction: A key component in online learning. *Journal of Computer-Mediated Communication, 7*(4). doi:10.1111/j.1083-6101.2002.tb00158.x

Lathuililere, S., Masse, B., Mesejo, P., & Horaud, R. (2019). Neural network-based reinforcement learning for audio-visual gaze control in human-robot interaction. *Pattern Recognition Letters*, *118*, 61–71. doi:10.1016/j.patrec.2018.05.023

Law, N. W. Y. (2019). Human development and augmented intelligence. In *The 20th International conference on artificial intelligence in education (AIED 2019)*. Springer.

Leach, L. (2016). Enhancing student engagement in one institution. *Journal of Further and Higher Education*, *40*(1), 23–47. doi:10.1080/0309877X.2013.869565

Lee, S. W.-Y. (2013). Investigating students' learning approaches, perceptions of online discussions, and students' online and academic performance. *Computers & Education*, *68*, 345–352. doi:10.1016/j.compedu.2013.05.019

Legaki, N.-Z., Xi, N., Hamari, J., Karpouzis, K., & Assimakopoulos, V. (2020). The effect of challenge-based gamification on learning: An experiment in the context of statistics education. *International Journal of Human-Computer Studies*, *144*. doi:10.1016/j.ijhcs.2020.102496

Li, H., Zhang, T., & Jacqueline, D. (2023). Exploring factors influencing young children's learning from storybooks: Interactive and multimedia features. *Journal of Experimental Child Psychology*, *233*. doi:10.1016/j.jecp.2023.105680

Li, J., Li, P., & Niu, W. (2020). Artificial intelligence applications in upper gastrointestinal cancers. *The Lancet. Oncology*, *21*(1), e4. doi:10.1016/S1470-2045(19)30721-1 PMID:31908305

Li, M. (2018). Online peer review using Turnitin PeerMark. *Journal of Response to Writing*, *4*(2), 99–117.

Li, M., & Li, J. (2017). Online peer review using Turnitin in first-year writing classes. *Computers and Composition*, *46*, 21–38. doi:10.1016/j.compcom.2017.09.001

Lin, M. P.-C., & Chang, D. (2020). Enhancing post-secondary writers' writing skills with a chatbot. *Journal of Educational Technology & Society*, *23*(1), 78–92. https://www.jstor.org/stable/26915408

Lin, P. H., Wooders, A., Wang, J. T. Y., & Yuan, W. M. (2018). Artificial intelligence, the missing piece of online education? *IEEE Engineering Management Review*, *46*(3), 25–28. doi:10.1109/EMR.2018.2868068

Lin, S. Y., & Overbaugh, R. C. (2007). The effect of student choice of online discussion format on tiered achievement and student satisfaction. *Journal of Research on Technology in Education*, *39*(4), 399–415. doi:10.1080/15391523.2007.10782489

Lipton, Z. C. (2016). The Mythos of Model Interpretability. *ICML Workshop on Human Interpretability in Machine Learning*.

Littlejohn, A., Milligan, C., & Margaryan, A. (2011). Collective learning in the workplace: Important knowledge-sharing behaviours. *International Journal of Advanced Corporate Learning*, *4*(4), 26–31. doi:10.3991/ijac.v4i4.1801

Liu, C. H., & Matthews, R. (2005). Vygotsky's philosophy: Constructivism and its criticisms examined. *International Education Journal*, *6*(3), 386–399.

Liu, Y., Yu, W., Dillon, T. S., Rahayu, W., & Li, M. (2022). Empowering IoT predictive maintenance solutions with AI: A distributed system for manufacturing Plant-Wide monitoring. *IEEE Transactions on Industrial Informatics*, *18*(2), 1345–1354. doi:10.1109/TII.2021.3091774

Livera, A., Paphitis, G., Pikolos, L., Papadopoulos, I., Montes-Romero, J., Lopez-Lorente, J., Makrides, G., Sutterlueti, J., & Georghiou, G. E. (2022). Intelligent Cloud-Based Monitoring and Control Digital Twin for photovoltaic power plants. *2022 IEEE 49th Photovoltaics Specialists Conference (PVSC)*. 10.1109/PVSC48317.2022.9938505

LiY.DuanY. (2023). The ethical performance of artificial general intelligence models based on DIKWP. doi:10.13140/RG.2.2.36224.10242

Liyakat, K. K. S. (2023). Detecting Malicious Nodes in IoT Networks Using Machine Learning and Artificial Neural Networks. *2023 International Conference on Emerging Smart Computing and Informatics (ESCI)*, 1-5, 10.1109/ESCI56872.2023.10099544

Liyakat, K. K. S. (2023). Machine Learning Approach Using Artificial Neural Networks to Detect Malicious Nodes in IoT Networks. In P. K. Shukla, H. Mittal, & A. Engelbrecht (Eds.), *Computer Vision and Robotics. CVR 2023. Algorithms for Intelligent Systems*. Springer. doi:10.1007/978-981-99-4577-1_3

Liyakat, K. K. S. (2024). Machine Learning Approach Using Artificial Neural Networks to Detect Malicious Nodes in IoT Networks. In S. K. Udgata, S. Sethi, & X. Z. Gao (Eds.), *Intelligent Systems. ICMIB 2023. Lecture Notes in Networks and Systems* (Vol. 728). Springer. doi:10.1007/978-981-99-3932-9_12

Looi, C.-K. (2005). Exploring the affordances of online chat for learning. *International Journal of Learning Technology*, *1*(3), 322. doi:10.1504/IJLT.2005.006520

Lowell, V. L., & Alshammari, A. (2019). Experiential learning experiences in an online 3D virtual environment for mental health interviewing and diagnosis role-playing: A comparison of perceived learning across learning activities. *Educational Technology Research and Development. Educational Technology Research and Development*, *67*(4), 825–854. doi:10.1007/s11423-018-9632-8

Lu, D., & Xie, Y.-N. (2024). The application of educational technology to develop problem-solving skills: A systematic review. *Thinking Skills and Creativity, 51*. doi:10.1016/j.tsc.2023.101454

Luan, H., Geczy, P., Lai, H., Gobert, J., Yang, S. J., Ogata, H., Baltes, J., Guerra, R., Li, P., & Tsai, C. C. (2020). Challenges and future directions of big data and artificial intelligence in education. *Frontiers in Psychology, 11*, 580820. doi:10.3389/fpsyg.2020.580820 PMID:33192896

Luckin, R. (2017). Towards artificial intelligence-based assessment systems. *Nature Human Behaviour, 1*(3), 28. doi:10.1038/s41562-016-0028

Lu, J. (2004). *A personalized e-learning material recommender system* [Paper presentation]. *2nd International Conference on Information Technology and Applications (ICITA).*

Lyu, H. (2020). How are students immersed by providing virtual reality technology? The role of psychological distance in online flipped class. *International Journal of Information and Education Technology (IJIET), 10*(1), 79–83. doi:10.18178/ijiet.2020.10.1.1343

Machha Babitha, Ms., C Sushma, et al. (2022). Trends of Artificial Intelligence for online exams in education. *International Journal of Early Childhood Special Education, 14*(01), 2457–2463.

Malinka, K., Perešíni, M., Firc, A., Hujňák, O., & Januš, F. (2023). On the educational impact of ChatGPT: Is Artificial Intelligence ready to obtain a university degree? *arXiv* 2023, arXiv:2303.11146. doi:10.1145/3587102.3588827

Manjakkal, L., Jain, A., Nandy, S., Goswami, S. K., Carvalho, J. T., Pereira, L., See, C. H., Pillai, S. C., & Hogg, R. A. (2023). Sustainable electrochemical energy storage devices using natural bast fibres. *Chemical Engineering Journal, 465*, 142845. doi:10.1016/j.cej.2023.142845

Manou, E., Lazari, E.-C., Thomopoulou, G.-E., Agrogiannis, G., Kavantzas, N., & Lazaris, A. C. (2021). Participation and interactivity in synchronous E-learning pathology course during the COVID-19 pandemic. *Advances in Medical Education and Practice, 12*, 1081–1091. doi:10.2147/AMEP.S317854 PMID:34584484

Maphosa, V., & Maphosa, M. (2023). Artificial intelligence in higher education: A bibliometric analysis and topic modeling approach. *Applied Artificial Intelligence, 37*(1), 2261730. doi:10.1080/08839514.2023.2261730

Maqableh, W., Alzyoud, F. Y., & Zraqou, J. (2023). The use of facial expressions in measuring students' interaction with distance learning environments during the COVID-19 crisis. *Visual Informatics, 7*(1), 1–17. doi:10.1016/j.visinf.2022.10.001 PMID:36312746

Marchand, G. C., & Gutierrez, A. P. (2012). The role of emotion in the learning process: Comparisons between online and face-to-face learning settings. *The Internet and Higher Education, 15*(3), 150–160. doi:10.1016/j.iheduc.2011.10.001

Mason, M. (2008). What is complexity theory and what are its implications for educational change? *Educational Philosophy and Theory, 40*(1), 35–49. doi:10.1111/j.1469-5812.2007.00413.x

Matheri, A. N., Belaid, M., Ntuli, F., Nabadda, E., & Ngila, J. C. (2022). Sustainable circularity and intelligent data-driven operations and control of the wastewater treatment plant. *Physics and Chemistry of the Earth/Physics and Chemistry of the Earth. Parts a/B/C, 126*, 103152. doi:10.1016/j.pce.2022.103152

Matthew, N. O. S., Tolulope, J. A., Abayomi, A. A., & Sarhan, M. M. (2021). Artificial intelligence in education. *International Journal of Scientific Advances, 2*(1), 5–11. doi:10.51542/ijscia.v2i1.2

Mbakwe, A. B., Lourentzou, I., Celi, L. A., Mechanic, O. J., & Dagan, A. (2023). ChatGPT passing USMLE shines a spotlight on the flaws of medical education. *PLOS Digital Health, 2*(2), e0000205. doi:10.1371/journal.pdig.0000205 PMID:36812618

McGorry, S. Y. (2003). Measuring quality in online programs. *The Internet and Higher Education*, *6*(2), 159–177. doi:10.1016/S1096-7516(03)00022-8

Meera, A., & Swamynathan, S. (2013). Agent based Resource Monitoring System in IaaS Cloud Environment. *Procedia Technology*, *10*, 200–207. doi:10.1016/j.protcy.2013.12.353

Memarian, B., & Doleck, T. (2024). A scoping review of reinforcement learning in education. *Computers and Education Open, 6*. doi:10.1016/j.caeo.2024.100175

Mendhe, C. H., Henderson, N., Srivastava, G., & Mago, V. (2021). A scalable platform to collect, store, visualize, and analyze big data in real time. *IEEE Transactions on Computational Social Systems*, *8*(1), 260–269. doi:10.1109/TCSS.2020.2995497

Menon, V. A., Prasad, A., & Boobalakrishnan, N. (2022). "Kathakali" & Virtual Reality: An Experiment. *International Journal of Art & Design*, *6*(2), 118–130. doi:10.5281/ZENODO.7437385

Miorandi, D., Sicari, S., De Pellegrini, F., & Chlamtac, I. (2012). Internet of things: Vision, applications and research challenges. *Ad Hoc Networks*, *10*(7), 1497–1516. doi:10.1016/j.adhoc.2012.02.016

Mishra, L., Gupta, T., & Shree, A. (2020). *Online teaching-learning in higher education during lockdown period of Covid-a9 pandemic*. International Journal of Educational Research Design. doi:10.1016/j.ijedro.2020.100012

Molesworth, M. (2004). Collaboration, reflection and selective neglect: campus-based marketing students' experiences of using a virtual learning environment. *Innovations in Education and Teaching International, 41*(1), 79–92. doi:10.1080/1470329032000172739

MollickE. R.MollickL. (2023). Using AI to implement effective teaching strategies in classrooms: Five strategies, including prompts. Including Prompts (March 17, 2023). https://doi.org/doi:10.2139/ssrn.4391243

Molnar, C. (2019). The importance of data privacy in the age of artificial intelligence. *Berkeley Technology Law Journal*, *34*(2), 1253–1286.

Montenegro-Rueda, M., Fernández-Cerero, J., Fernández-Batanero, J. M., & López-Meneses, E. (2023). Impact of the Implementation of ChatGPT in Education: A Systematic Review. *Computers*, *12*(8), 153. doi:10.3390/computers12080153

Motlagh, N. H., Mohammadrezaei, M., Hunt, J. D., & Zakeri, B. (2020). Internet of things (IoT) and the energy sector. *Energies*, *13*(2), 494. doi:10.3390/en13020494

Motta, I., & Quaresma, M. (2023). Increasing Transparency to Design Inclusive Conversational Agents (CAs): Perspectives and Open Issues. In *Proceedings of the 5th International Conference on Conversational User Interfaces* (pp. 1-4). 10.1145/3571884.3604304

Mukul, E., & Büyüközkan, G. (2023). Digital transformation in education: A systematic review of education 4.0. *Technological Forecasting and Social Change, 194*. doi:10.1016/j.techfore.2023.122664

Müller, A. C., & Guido, S. (2017). *Introduction to Machine Learning with Python, A Guide for Data Scientists*. O'Reilly.

Murshed, M., Dewan, M. A. A., Lin, F., & Wen, D. (2019). *Engagement detection in e-learning environments using convolutional neural networks. In 2019 IEEE Intl Confon Dependable, autonomic and Secure Computing, Intl Conf on pervasive intelligence and computing, Intl Conf on cloud and big data computing, intl Confon Cyber Science and Technology Congress*. IEEE. doi:10.1109/DASC/PiCom/CBDCom/CyberSciTech.2019.00028

Mussman, K. (2016). *Prior Lake-Savage Area Schools: U.S. Department of Education Green Ribbon Schools.Prior Lake-Savage Area*. U.S. Department of Education.

Nabiyev, V., & Erümit, A. K. (2020). Yapay zekanın temelleri [Fundamentals of artificial intelligence]. In V. Nabiyev & A. K. Erümit (Eds.), *Eğitimde yapay zeka kuramdan uygulamaya* [Artificial intelligence in education from theory to practice] (pp. 2–37). Pegem Academy. doi:10.14527/9786257052986.01

Narsimhulu, K., Ramchander, N., & Swathi, A. (2022). *An AI-enabled Framework With Feature Selection for Efficient Heart Disease Prediction*. https://doi.org/ doi:10.1109/IC3I56241.2022.10073155

Nath, D., Kundu, I., Sharma, A., Shivhare, P., Afzal, A., Soudagar, M. E. M., & Park, S. G. (2023b). Internet of Things integrated with solar energy applications: A state-of-the-art review. *Environment, Development and Sustainability*. Advance online publication. doi:10.1007/s10668-023-03691-2

Nelson, C., Boles, W., Trouton, L., & Margerison, E. (2019). A review of chatbots in education: Practical steps forward. In *30th Annual Conference for the Australasian Association for Engineering Education (AAEE 2019): Educators Becoming Agents of Change: Innovate, Integrate, Motivate*. Engineers Australia.

Ng, D. T. K., Ching, A. C. H., & Law, S. W. (2023). Online learning in management education amid the pandemic: A bibliometric and content analysis. *International Journal of Management Education, 21*(2), 100796. doi:10.1016/j.ijme.2023.100796

Nicholas, J. A., Chan, H. W., & Baker, M. A. B. (2019, February). Machine learning: Applications of artificial intelligence to imaging and diagnosis. *Biophysical Reviews, 11*(1), 111–118. doi:10.1007/s12551-018-0449-9 PMID:30182201

Okuno, H. G., Nakadai, K., & Kitano, H. (2002). Social interaction of humanoid robot based on audio-visual tracking. *The International conference on industrial, engineering and other applications of applied intelligent systems*, 725-735.

Osetskyi, V., Vitrenko, A., Tatomyr, I., Bilan, S., & Hirnyk, Y. (2020). Artificial intelligence application in education: Financial implications and prospects. *Financial and Credit Activity Problems of Theory and Practice, 2*(33), 574-584.

Osetskyi, V., Vitrenko, A., Tatomyr, I., Bilan, S., & Hirnyk, Y. (2020). Artificial intelligence application in education: Financial implications and prospects. *Financial and Credit Activity Problems of Theory and Practice, 2*(33), 574-584. doi:10.18371/fcaptp.v2i33.207246

Ossa, L. A., Rost, M., Lorenzini, G., Shaw, D. M., & Elger, B. S. (2023). A smarter perspective: Learning with and from AI-cases. *Artificial Intelligence in Medicine, 135*. doi:10.1016/j.artmed.2022.102458

Ouyang, F., & Jiao, P. (2021) Artificial intelligence in education: The three paradigms. *Computers and Education: Artificial Intelligence, 2*.

Owan, V. J., Abang, K. B., Idika, D. O., Etta, E. O., & Bassey, B. A. (2023). Exploring the potential of artificial intelligence tools in educational measurement and assessment. *Eurasia Journal of Mathematics, Science and Technology Education, 19*(8), em2307. Advance online publication. doi:10.29333/ejmste/13428

Panadero, E., & Jarvela, S. (2015). Socially shared regulation of learning: A review. *European Psychologist, 20*(3), 190–203. doi:10.1027/1016-9040/a000226

Pandey, A. K., & Gelin, R. (2017). Humanoid robots in education: a short review. In A. Goswami & P. Vadakkepat (Eds.), *Humanoid robotics: a reference* (pp. 1–16). Springer. doi:10.1007/978-94-007-7194-9_113-1

Park, C., & Kim, D.-G. (2020). Perception of instructor presence and its effects on learning experience in online classes. *Journal of Information Technology Education, 19*, 475–488. doi:10.28945/4611

Patuzzi, F., Prando, D., Vakalis, S., Rizzo, A. M., Chiaramonti, D., Tirler, W., Mimmo, T., Gasparella, A., & Baratieri, M. (2016). Small-scale biomass gasification CHP systems: Comparative performance assessment and monitoring experiences in South Tyrol (Italy). *Energy, 112*, 285–293. doi:10.1016/j.energy.2016.06.077

Pedro, F., Subosa, M., Rivas, A., & Valverde, P. (2019). *Artificial intelligence in education: Challenges and opportunities for sustainable development*. UNESCO. https://repositorio.minedu.gob.pe/bitstream/handle/20.500.12799/6533/Artificial%20intelligence%20in%20education%20challenges%20and%20opportunities%20for%20sustainable%20development.pdf?sequence=1&isAllowed=y

Peel, M. (2000). "Nobody Cares": The challenge of isolation in school to university transition. *Journal of Institutional Research*, *9*(1), 22–34.

Pelletier, K., Brown, M., Brooks, D. C., McCormack, M., Reeves, J., Arbino, N., Bozkurt, A., Crawford, S., Czerniewicz, L., Gibson, R., Linder, K., Mason, J., & Mondelli, V. (2021). *2021 EDUCAUSE horizon report teaching and learning edition*. EDUCAUSE.

Peng, W. (2017). Research on model of student engagement in online learning. *Eurasia Journal of Mathematics, Science and Technology Education*, *13*(7), 2869–2882. doi:10.12973/eurasia.2017.00723a

Perisic, A., Perisic, I., Lazic, M., & Perisic, B. (2023). The foundation for future education, teaching, training, learning, and performing infrastructure - The open interoperability conceptual framework approach. *Heliyon, 9*(6). doi:10.1016/j.heliyon.2023.e16836

Perkins. (2023). Academic integrity considerations of AI Large Language Models in the post-pandemic era: ChatGPT and beyond. *J. Univ. Teach. Learn. Pract., 20*(2).

Pervez, A., & Bansal, R. (2019). Capital adequacy, risk and bank performance: Evidence from India. *Journal of Xi'an University of Architecture & Technology*, *XI*(XII), 199–212.

Pillai, S., & Sharma, A. (2023). Hybrid unsupervised web-attack detection and classification – A deep learning approach. *Computer Standards & Interfaces*, *86*, 103738. doi:10.1016/j.csi.2023.103738

Pivarnik, L. F., Richard, N., Gable, R. K., & Worobo, R. W. (2016). Knowledge and attitudes of produce and seafood processors and food safety educators regarding nonthermal processes. *Journal of Food Science Education*, *15*(4), 120–128. doi:10.1111/1541-4329.12093

Pliakos, K., Joo, S. H., Park, J. Y., Cornillie, F., Vens, C., & Van den Noortgate, W. (2019). Integrating machine learning into item response theory for addressing the cold start problem in adaptive learning systems. *Computers & Education*, *137*, 91–103. doi:10.1016/j.compedu.2019.04.009

Polat, A. Horzum, M. B. ve Akgün, Ö. E. (2013). Uzaktan eğitim öğrencilerinin sorgulama topluluğu algılarının akademik motivasyon açısından incelenmesi [Examining distance education students' perceptions of community of inquiry in terms of academic motivation]. *Kapadokya Education Journal*, *1*(1), 53–65.

Popenici, S. A., & Kerr, S. (2017). Exploring the impact of artificial intelligence on teaching and learning in higher education. *Research and Practice in Technology Enhanced Learning*, *12*(1), 22. doi:10.1186/s41039-017-0062-8 PMID:30595727

Pranaya & Venugopal. (2023). Impact of Mother Tongue on Students' speaking Abilities in English Language at Rural Places. In *English Language Competence in Rural Youth: Improving Job Readiness*. Current Publications.

Rahman, M. M., & Watanobe, Y. (2023). ChatGPT for Education and Research: Opportunities, Threats, and Strategies. *Applied Sciences (Basel, Switzerland)*, *13*(9), 5783. doi:10.3390/app13095783

Rajkomar, A., Hardt, M., Howell, M. D., Corrado, G., & Chin, M. H. (2018). Ensuring fairness in machine learning to advance health equity. *Annals of Internal Medicine*, *169*(12), 866–872. doi:10.7326/M18-1990 PMID:30508424

Ramakrishnan, A., Ottmar, E., LoCasale-Crouch, J., & Whitehill, J. (2019). Toward automated classroom observation: Predicting positive and negative climate. *14th IEEE International Conference on Automatic Face & Gesture Recognition (FG 2019),* 1-8. 10.1109/FG.2019.8756529

Ramasamy, V., Singsen, D., & Walia, G. S. (2024). Fostering Student Engagement and Success in STEM Education: An AI-Driven Exploration of High Impact Practices from Cross-Disciplinary General Education Courses. *Journal of Engineering Education Transformations, 37*(2).

Ramesh, P., Dutta, S. J., Neog, S. S., Baishya, P., & Bezbaruah, I. (2019). Implementation of Predictive Maintenance Systems in Remotely Located Process Plants under Industry 4.0 Scenario. In Springer series in reliability engineering (pp. 293–326). doi:10.1007/978-3-030-36518-9_12

Rathore, B. (2023). Future of AI & generation alpha: ChatGPT beyond boundaries. *Eduzone: Int. Peer Rev. Refer. Multidiscip. J., 12*(1), 63–68.

Reed, P., Watmough, S., & Duvall, P. (2015). Assessment analytics using Turnitin & Grademark in an undergraduate medical curriculum. *Journal of Perspectives in Applied Academic Practice*, *3*(2), 92–108. doi:10.14297/jpaap.v3i2.159

Rickabaugh, J. (2016). *Tapping the power of personalized learning: A roadmap for school leaders*. ASCD.

Riedl, M. O. (2019). Human-centered artificial intelligence and machine learning. *Human Behavior and Emerging Technologies*, *1*(1), 33–36. doi:10.1002/hbe2.117

Ritzhaupt, A. D., Poling, N., Frey, C., Kang, Y., & Johnson, M. (2016). A phenomenological study of games, simulations, and virtual environments courses: What are we teaching and How? *International Journal of Gaming and Computer-Mediated Simulations*, *8*(3), 59–73. doi:10.4018/IJGCMS.2016070104

Rivera, E. S., & Garden, C. L. P. (2021). Gamification for student engagement: A framework. *Journal of Further and Higher Education*, *45*(7), 999–1012. doi:10.1080/0309877X.2021.1875201

Rivers, C., & Holland, A. (2022). Management education and artificial intelligence: Toward personalized learning. In *The future of management education* (pp. 184–204). Routledge. doi:10.4324/9781003095903-14

Robertson, J., & Despa, J. O. (2006). Ghostwriter: Educational drama and presence in a virtual environment. *Journal of Computer-Mediated Communication, 8*(1). doi:10.1111/j.1083-6101.2002.tb00159.x

Rogers, S. L., Hollett, R., Li, Y. R., & Speelman, C. P. (2022). An evaluation of virtual reality role-play experiences for helping-profession courses. *Teaching of Psychology*, *49*(1), 78–84. doi:10.1177/0098628320983231

Rolfe, V. (2011). Can Turnitin be used to provide instant formative feedback? *British Journal of Educational Technology*, *42*(4), 701–710. doi:10.1111/j.1467-8535.2010.01091.x

Roll, I., Russell, D. M., & Gašević, D. (2018). Learning at scale. *International Journal of Artificial Intelligence in Education*, *28*(4), 471–477. doi:10.1007/s40593-018-0170-7

Russell, S. J., & Norvig, P. (2016). *Artificial intelligence: a modern approach*. Pearson.

Rutledge, C., Walsh, C. M., Swinger, N., Auerbach, M., Castro, D., Dewan, M., Khattab, M., Rake, A., Harwayne-Gidansky, I., Raymond, T. T., Maa, T., & Chang, T. P. (2018). Gamification in action: Theoretical and practical considerations for medical educators. *Academic Medicine*, *93*(7), 1014–1020. doi:10.1097/ACM.0000000000002183 PMID:29465450

Salam, A., Ullah, F., Amin, F., & Abrar, M. (2023). Deep Learning Techniques for Web-Based Attack Detection in Industry 5.0: A Novel approach. *Technologies*, *11*(4), 107. doi:10.3390/technologies11040107

Santiteerakul, S., Sopadang, A., Tippayawong, K. Y., & Tamvimol, K. (2020). The role of smart technology in sustainable agriculture: A case study of Wangree Plant Factory. *Sustainability (Basel), 12*(11), 4640. doi:10.3390/su12114640

Sari, J. M., & Purwanta, E. (2021). The implementation of artificial intelligence in STEM-based creative learning in the society 5.0 Era. *Tadris J. Kegur. dan Ilmu Tarb, 6*(2), 433-440.

Šćepanović, S., Žarić, N. A. Đ. A., & Matijević, T. (2015, September). Gamification in higher education learning–state of the art, challenges and opportunities. In *Proc. 6th Int. Conf. e-Learn* (pp. 128-134). Academic Press.

Schfer, L. (2003). Storytelling in virtual environments. *Virtual Reality (Waltham Cross), 7*(1), 1–1. doi:10.1007/s10055-003-0115-8

Schuster, K., Hoffmann, M., Bach, U., Richert, A., & Jeschke, S. (2014). Diving in? How users experience virtual environments using the virtual theatre. In Design, User Experience, and Usability. User Experience Design for Diverse Interaction Platforms and Environments (pp. 636–646). Springer International Publishing. doi:10.1007/978-3-319-07626-3_60

Schwartz, K. (2019). AI & Education: 10 Projects that are shaping the future of education. *Forbes.*

Şenocak, D. (2020). Açık ve uzaktan öğrenme ortamlarında yapay zekâ: Sunduğu fırsatlar ve yarattığı endişeler [Artificial intelligence in open and distance learning environments: Opportunities and concerns]. *Journal of Open Education Applications and Research, 6*(3), 56–78.

Seo, K., Tang, J., Roll, I., Fels, S., & Yoon, D. (2021). The impact of artificial intelligence on learner–instructor interaction in online learning. *International Journal of Educational Technology in Higher Education, 18*(1), 1–23. doi:10.1186/s41239-021-00292-9 PMID:34778540

Sepang, K. M., Santosa, M. H., & Suprianti, G. A. P. (2021). Exploring influence of Virtual Reality-based English learning activities towards secondary students' English writing achievement. *The Art of Teaching English as a Foreign Language, 1*(1), 63–74. doi:10.36663/tatefl.v1i1.88

Sera, L., & Wheeler, E. (2017). Game on: The gamification of the pharmacy classroom. *Currents in Pharmacy Teaching & Learning, 9*(1), 155–159. doi:10.1016/j.cptl.2016.08.046 PMID:29180148

Shafique, R., Aljedaani, W., Rustam, F., Lee, E., Mehmood, A., & Choi, G. S. (2023). Role of artificial ıntelligence in online education: A systematic mapping study. *IEEE Access : Practical Innovations, Open Solutions*, 1. Advance online publication. doi:10.1109/ACCESS.2023.3278590

Shahid, W. B., Aslam, B., Abbas, H., Khalid, S. B., & Afzal, H. (2022). An enhanced deep learning based framework for web attacks detection, mitigation and attacker profiling. *Journal of Network and Computer Applications, 198*, 103270. doi:10.1016/j.jnca.2021.103270

Shaik, T., Tao, X., Li, Y., Dann, C., Mcdonald, J., Redmond, P., & Galligan, L. (2022). A Review of the Trends and Challenges in Adopting Natural Language Processing Methods for Education Feedback Analysis. *IEEE Access : Practical Innovations, Open Solutions, 10*, 56720–56739. doi:10.1109/ACCESS.2022.3177752

Sharma, K., Giannakos, M., & Dillenbourg, P. (2020). Eye-tracking and artificial intelligence to enhance motivation and learning. *Smart Learning Environments, 7*(1), 13. Advance online publication. doi:10.1186/s40561-020-00122-x

SharmaP.JoshiS.GautamS.FilipeV.ReisM. J. (2019). Student engagement detection using emotion analysis, eye tracking and head movement with machine learning. *ARXIV preprint* arxiv:1909.12913.

Sharma, S., Zavarsky, P., & Butakov, S. (2020b). *Machine Learning based Intrusion Detection System for Web-Based Attacks.* doi:10.1109/BigDataSecurity-HPSC-IDS49724.2020.00048

Shawar, B. A., & Atwell, E. S. (2007). Chatbots: Are they really useful*? J. Lang. Technol Comput. Linguist.*, *22*(1), 29–29. doi:10.21248/jlcl.22.2007.88

Shellenbarger, S. (2019). Flashcards get smarter so you can, too. *Wall Street Journal.* https://www.wsj.com/articles/flashcards-get-smarter-so-you-can-too-1430253560

Shi, Haller, Reeson, & Li. (2024). Decoding the dynamics of knowledge pricing: An empirical investigation of MOOC platform edX's pricing structure and signaling effects. *International Journal of Information Management Data Insights, 4*(1). doi:10.1016/j.jjimei.2024.100220

Shoufan, A. (2023). Exploring students' perceptions of ChatGPT: Thematic analysis and follow-up survey. *IEEE Access : Practical Innovations, Open Solutions*, *11*, 38805–38818. doi:10.1109/ACCESS.2023.3268224

Shukla, R. K., & Tiwari, A. (2023). Masked Face Recognition Using MobileNet V2 with Transfer Learning. *Computer Systems Science and Engineering*, *45*(1), 293–309. doi:10.32604/csse.2023.027986

Sim, K. M. (2012). Agent-Based cloud computing. *IEEE Transactions on Services Computing*, *5*(4), 564–577. doi:10.1109/TSC.2011.52

Sim, M. S., & Rahmat, N. H. (2022). Online group interactions in online classrooms: Does experience matter? *International Journal of Academic Research in Business & Social Sciences*, *12*(8). Advance online publication. doi:10.6007/IJARBSS/v12-i8/13185

Simpson, O. (2010). Can we do better? CWP Retention Literature Review, Report to the Centre for Widening Participation, Open University.

Sinatra, G. M., Heddy, B. C., & Lombardi, D. (2015). The Challenges of Defining and Measuring Student Engagement. *Educational Psychologist*, *50*(1), 1–13. doi:10.1080/00461520.2014.1002924

Singh, C., Rao, M. S., Mahaboobjohn, Y. M., Kotaiah, B., & Kumar, T. R. (2022). Applied machine tool data condition to predictive smart maintenance by using artificial intelligence. In Communications in computer and information science (pp. 584–596). doi:10.1007/978-3-031-07012-9_49

Singh, T., & Mishra, J. (2021). Learning with artificial intelligence systems: application, challenges, and opportunities. *Impact of AI technologies on teaching, learning, and research in higher education*, 236–253. doi:10.4018/978-1-7998-4763-2.ch015

Singh, D. (2023). ChatGPT: A new approach to revolutionise organisations. *Int. J. New Media Stud.*, *10*(1), 57–63.

Singh, S. V. (2023). *The Prospects for Advancing Adaptive Learning Technology through AI Methods. In 2023 Future of Educational Innovation-Workshop Series Data in Action.* IEEE. doi:10.1109/IEEECONF56852.2023.10105111

Sinha, S., Rogat, T. K., Adams-Wiggins, K. R., & Hmelo-silver, C. E. (2004). Collaborative group engagement in a computer-supported inquiry learning environment. *International Journal of Computer-Supported Collaborative Learning*, *10*(3), 273–307. doi:10.1007/s11412-015-9218-y

Sivakumar, S., Neeraja, B., Jamuna Rani, M., Anandaram, H., Ramya, S., Padhan, G., & Gurusamy, S. (2022). Machine learning approach on time series for PV-solar energy. *Advances in Materials Science and Engineering*, 2022.

Skinnner, B. F. (1984). The Shame of American Education. *The American Psychologist*, *39*(9), 947–954. doi:10.1037/0003-066X.39.9.947

Small, F., Dowell, D., & Simmons, P. (2012). Teacher communication preferred over peer interaction: Student satisfaction with different tools in a virtual learning environment. *Journal of International Education in Business*, *5*(2), 114–128. doi:10.1108/18363261211281735

Smith, A. (2020). Leveraging Personalized Learning Algorithms in Online Education: A Case Study. *Journal of Educational Technology*, *15*(2), 45–62.

Sobania, D., Briesch, M., Hanna, C., & Petke, J. (2023). An analysis of the automatic bug fixing performance of chatgpt. arXiv preprint arXiv:2301.08653. doi:10.1109/APR59189.2023.00012

Song, P., & Wang, X. (2020). A bibliometric analysis of worldwide educational artificial intelligence research development in recent twenty years. *Asia Pacific Education Review*, *21*(3), 473–486. doi:10.1007/s12564-020-09640-2

Sperling, K., Stenberg, C.-J., McGrath, C., Åkerfeldt, A., Heintz, F., & Stenliden, L. (2024). In search of artificial intelligence (AI) literacy in teacher education: A scoping review. *Computers and Education Open, 6*. doi:10.1016/j.caeo.2024.100169

Stott, A., & Neustaedter, C. (2013). Analysis of Gamification in Education. *Technical Report 2013-0422-01*.

Sukhadia, A., Upadhyay, K., Gundeti, M., Shah, S., & Shah, M. (2020). Optimization of smart traffic governance system using artificial intelligence. *Augmented Human Research*, *5*(1), 13. Advance online publication. doi:10.1007/s41133-020-00035-x

Sun, Q., Abdourazakou, Y., & Norman, T. J. (2017). LearnSmart, adaptive teaching, and student learning effectiveness: An empirical investigation. *Journal of Education for Business*, *92*(1), 36–43. doi:10.1080/08832323.2016.1274711

Surameery, N. M. S., & Shakor, M. Y. (2023). Use ChatGPT to solve programming bugs. *Int. J. Inf. Technol. Comput. Eng.*, *3*(01), 17–22.

Swan, K. (2001). Virtual interaction: Design factors affecting student satisfaction and perceived learning in asynchronous online courses. *Distance Education*, *22*(2), 306–331. doi:10.1080/0158791010220208

Swartzwelder, K., Murphy, J., & Murphy, G. (2019). The impact of text-based and video discussions on student engagement and interactivity in an online course. *The Journal of Educators Online*, *16*(1). Advance online publication. doi:10.9743/jeo.2019.16.1.13

Takaki, O., Hamamoto, N., Takefusa, A., Yokoyama, S., & Aida, K. (2022). Reasonable Setting Values for Anonymization Algorithms for Online Educational Data Analysis Support System. *Procedia Computer Science, 207*, 2556-2566. doi:10.1016/j.procs.2022.09.314

Tan, Y., Min, D., Li, Y., Li, W., Hu, N., Chen, Y., & Qi, G. (2023). Evaluation of ChatGPT as a question answering system for answering complex questions. arXiv preprint arXiv:2303.07992.

Tandel, G. S., Balestrieri, A., Jujaray, T., Khanna, N. N., Saba, L., & Suri, J. S. (2020). Multiclass magnetic resonance imaging brain tumor classification using artificial intelligence paradigm. *Computers in Biology and Medicine*, *122*, 103804. doi:10.1016/j.compbiomed.2020.103804 PMID:32658726

Tang, K. Y., Chang, C. Y., & Hwang, G. J. (2023). Trends in artificial intelligence-supported e-learning: A systematic review and co-citation network analysis (1998–2019). *Interactive Learning Environments*, *31*(4), 2134–2152. doi:10.1080/10494820.2021.1875001

Tangney, S. (2014). Student-centred Learning: A Humanist Perspective. *Teaching in Higher Education*, *19*(3), 266–275. doi:10.1080/13562517.2013.860099

Tanrıkulu, F. (2022). Students' perceptions about the effects of collaborative digital storytelling on writing skills. *Computer Assisted Language Learning*, *35*(5–6), 1090–1105. doi:10.1080/09588221.2020.1774611

Tariq, A., Awan, M. J., Alshudukhi, J., Alam, T. M., Alhamazani, K. T., & Meraf, Z. (2022). Software measurement by using artificial intelligence. *Journal of Nanomaterials*, *2022*, 1–10. doi:10.1155/2022/7283171

Taşçı, G., & Çelebi, M. (2020). Eğitimde yeni bir paradigma: Yükseköğretimde yapay zekâ [A new paradigm in education: Artificial intelligence in higher education]. *OPUS International Journal of Society Researches*, *16*(29), 2346–2370. doi:10.26466/opus.747634

TateT. P.DoroudiS.RitchieD.XuY.UciM. W. (2023). Educational research and AI-generated writing: Confronting the coming tsunami. EdArXiv. doi:10.35542/osf.io/4mec3

Tawafak, R. M., Alfarsi, G., & Khudayer, B. H. (2022). Artificial intelligence effectiveness and impact within COVID-19. In *ITM web of conferences* (Vol. 42, p. 01008). EDP Sciences. doi:10.1051/itmconf/20224201008

Tcha-Tokey, K., Christmann, O., Loup-Escande, E., Loup, G., & Richir, S. (2018). Towards a model of User eXperience in immersive virtual environments. *Advances in Human-Computer Interaction*, *2018*, 1–10. doi:10.1155/2018/7827286

Tcha-Tokey, K., Christmann, O., Loup-Escande, E., & Richir, S. (2016). Proposition and validation of a questionnaire to measure the user experience in immersive virtual environments. *The International Journal of Virtual Reality : a Multimedia Publication for Professionals*, *16*(1), 33–48. doi:10.20870/IJVR.2016.16.1.2880

Tekerek, A., & Bay, Ö. F. (2019). Design and implementation of an artificial intelligence-based web application firewall model. *Neural Network World*, *29*(4), 189–206. doi:10.14311/NNW.2019.29.013

Tham, J., Duin, A. H., Gee, L., Ernst, N., Abdelqader, B., & McGrath, M. (2018). Understanding virtual reality: Presence, embodiment, and professional practice. *IEEE Transactions on Professional Communication*, *61*(2), 178–195. doi:10.1109/TPC.2018.2804238

Thoms, B. (2011). A dynamic social feedback system to support learning and social interaction in higher education. *IEEE Transactions on Learning Technologies*, *4*(4), 340–352. doi:10.1109/TLT.2011.9

Thurzo, M., Strunga, M., Urban, R., Surovková, J., & Afrashtehfar, K. I. (2023). Impact of artificial intelligence on dental education: A review and guide for curriculum update. *Education Sciences*, *13*(2), 150. doi:10.3390/educsci13020150

Timms, M. J. (2016). Letting artificial intelligence in education out of the box: Educational cobots and smart classrooms. *International Journal of Artificial Intelligence in Education*, *26*(2), 701–712. doi:10.1007/s40593-016-0095-y

Torrato, J. B., Aguja, S. E., & Prudente, M. S. (2021). Using web video conferencing to conduct a program as a proposed model for teacher leadership and academic vitality in the Philippines. *Education Sciences*, *11*(658), 1–30. doi:10.3390/educsci11110658

Trowler, V. (2010). *Student Engagement Literature Review*. The Higher Education Academy. doi:10.1037/0022-0663.85.4.571

Truta, C., Parv, L., & Topala, I. (2018). Academic Engagement and Intention to Drop Out: Levers for Sustainability in Higher Education. *Sustainability (Basel)*, *10*(12), 4637. Advance online publication. doi:10.3390/su10124637

Tu, C. H., Yen, C. J., Sujo-Montes, L., & Roberts, G. A. (2015). Gaming Personality and Game Dynamics in Online Discussion Instructions. *Educational Media International*, *52*(3), 155–172. doi:10.1080/09523987.2015.1075099

Utama, I. B. K. Y., Pamungkas, R. F., Faridh, M. M., & Jang, Y. M. (2023). Intelligent IoT platform for multiple PV plant monitoring. *Sensors (Basel)*, *23*(15), 6674. doi:10.3390/s23156674 PMID:37571458

Uzun, N. B., Aktaş, M., & Akay, C. (2023). Measurement and Evaluation Challenges in Distance Education: Systematic Review and Qualitative Meta-Synthesis. *Journal of Educational Technology*, *19*(4). Advance online publication. doi:10.26634/jet.19.4.19368

van Dis, E. A., Bollen, J., Zuidema, W., van Rooij, R., & Bockting, C. L. (2023). ChatGPT: Five priorities for research. *Nature*, *614*(7947), 224–226. doi:10.1038/d41586-023-00288-7 PMID:36737653

van Gaalen, A. E., Brouwer, J., Schönrock-Adema, J., Bouwkamp-Timmer, T., Jaarsma, A. D. C., & Georgiadis, J. R. (2021). Gamification of health professions education: A systematic review. *Advances in Health Sciences Education : Theory and Practice*, *26*(2), 683–711. doi:10.1007/s10459-020-10000-3 PMID:33128662

Vanichvasin, P. (2022). Impact of Chatbots on Student Learning and Satisfaction in the Entrepreneurship Education Programme in Higher Education Context. *International Education Studies*, *15*(6), 15. doi:10.5539/ies.v15n6p15

VanLehn, K., Graesser, A. C., Jackson, G. T., Jordan, P., Olney, A., & Rose, C. P. (2007). When are tutorial dialogues more effective than reading? *Cognitive Science*, *31*(1), 3–62. doi:10.1080/03640210709336984 PMID:21635287

Vargas-Murillo, A. R., Pari-Bedoya, I. N. M. A., & Guevara-Soto, F. J. (2023). Challenges and Opportunities of AI-Assisted Learning: A Systematic Literature Review on the Impact of ChatGPT Usage in Higher Education. *International Journal of Learning. Teaching and Educational Research*, *22*(7), 122–135. doi:10.26803/ijlter.22.7.7

Veeraiah, V., Pankajam, A., Vashishtha, E., Dhabliya, D., Karthikeyan, P., & Chandan, R. R. (2022, December). Efficient COVID-19 identification using deep learning for IoT. In *2022 5th International Conference on Contemporary Computing and Informatics (IC3I)* (pp. 128-133). IEEE. 10.1109/IC3I56241.2022.10073443

Venugopal, K., & Das, S. (2023). Prediction Analysis of Gen Zers' Attitudes on Ecological Consciousness. In *Sustainable Science and Intelligent Technologies for Societal Development*. IGI Global.

Verma, N., Getenet, S., Dann, C., & Shaik, T. (2023). Designing an artificial intelligence tool to understand student engagement based on teacher's behaviours and movements in video conferencing. *Computers and Education: Artificial Intelligence*, *5*, 100187. doi:10.1016/j.caeai.2023.100187

Vihos, J., Chute, A., Johnston, S., Pawliuk, B., Buro, K., Velupillai, N., & Sampaga, C. (2023). Undergraduate nursing student satisfaction with open educational resources in a professional communication course. *Teaching and Learning in Nursing, 18*(4), 468-473. doi:10.1016/j.teln.2023.04.008

Virgiawan, M., Suryani, N., & Sutimin, L. A. (2020). The effectiveness of guided writing combined with virtual reality video as teaching media on students' writing achievement. *International Journal of Linguistics. Literature and Translation*, *3*(10), 41–47. doi:10.32996/ijllt.2020.3.10.5

Walter, A., Finger, R., Huber, R., & Buchmann, N. (2017). Smart farming is key to developing sustainable agriculture. *Proceedings of the National Academy of Sciences of the United States of America*, *114*(24), 6148–6150. doi:10.1073/pnas.1707462114 PMID:28611194

Wang, K., Zuo, M., Yu, S., Luo, H., Yan, Y., & Ouyang, H. (2021). Use Machine Learning to Predict Primary School Students' Level of Learning Engagement. *ICETM'21: 2021 4th International Conference on Education Technology Management*. 10.1145/3510309.3510313

Wang, L.-C. C. (2014). Student Perceptions of Using Instant Messaging Software to Facilitate Synchronous Online Class Interaction in a Graduate Teacher Education Course. *Journal of Computing in Teacher Education*, 15–21.

Wang, R., Sun, Z., & Zhou, Y. (2023, June). Research on the new model of" Internet+ education" based on artificial intelligence. In *International Conference on Mathematics, Modeling, and Computer Science (MMCS2022)* (Vol. 12625, pp. 187-192). SPIE. 10.1117/12.2670426

Wan, J., Reddy, M., & Longman, D. (2011). Understanding student engagement in 3D virtual learning environments. *International Journal of Technology Enhanced Learning*, *3*(5), 468. doi:10.1504/IJTEL.2011.042099

Wei, H.-C., Peng, H., & Chou, C. (2015). Can more interactivity improve learning achievement in an online course? Effects of college students' perception and actual use of a course-management system on their learning achievement. *Computers & Education*, *83*, 10–21. doi:10.1016/j.compedu.2014.12.013

White, G. (2020). Adaptive learning technology relationship with student learning outcomes. *Journal of Information Technology Education*, *19*, 113–130. doi:10.28945/4526

Whitehill, J., Serpell, Z., Lin, Y., Foster, A., & Movellan, J. R. (2014). The faces of engagement: Automatic recognition of student engagement from facial expressions. *IEEE Transactions on Affective Computing*, *5*(1), 86–98. doi:10.1109/TAFFC.2014.2316163

Whitton, N., & Moseley, A. (2014). Deconstructing Engagement: Rethinking Involvement in Learning. *Simulation & Gaming*, *45*(4–5), 266–275. doi:10.1177/1046878114554755

Williams, L., & Lahman, M. (2011). Online discussion, student engagement, and critical thinking. *Journal of Political Science Education*, *7*(2), 143–162. doi:10.1080/15512169.2011.564919

Xia, Q., Chiu, T. K. F., Lee, M., Temitayo, I., Dai, Y., & Chai, C. S. (2022). A self-determination theory design approach for inclusive and diverse artificial intelligence (AI) K-12 education. *Computers & Education*, *189*, 104582. Advance online publication. doi:10.1016/j.compedu.2022.104582

Xu, A., Liu, Z., Guo, Y., Sinha, V., & Akkiraju, R. (2017). A new chatbot for customer service on social media. In *Proceedings of the 2017 CHI Conference on Human Factors in Computing Systems*. ACM. 10.1145/3025453.3025496

Xu, B. (2021). Artificial intelligence teaching system and data processing method based on big data. *Complexity*, *2021*, 1–11. doi:10.1155/2021/1961061

Xu, W., Meng, J., Raja, S. K. S., Priya, M. P., & Kiruthiga Devi, M. (2023). Artificial intelligence in constructing personalized and accurate feedback systems for students. *International Journal of Modeling, Simulation, and Scientific Computing*, *14*(01), 2341001. doi:10.1142/S1793962323410015

Xu, X., Dugdale, D. M., Wei, X., & Mi, W. (2023). Leveraging Artificial Intelligence to Predict Young Learner Online Learning Engagement. *American Journal of Distance Education*, *37*(3), 185–198. doi:10.1080/08923647.2022.2044663

Yakin, A. A., Apriani, E., Obaid, A. J., & Elngar, A. A. (2023). Transforming online learning management: Generative models on ChatGPT to enhance Online Student Engagement Scale. [Jurnal Pendidikan dan Kependidikan]. *IDARAH*, *7*(2), 135–148. doi:10.47766/idarah.v7i2.1514

Yalcinkaya, T., & Yucel, S. C. (2023a). Determination of nursing students' attitudes toward and readiness for mobile learning: A cross-sectional study. *Nurse Education Today, 120*. doi:10.1016/j.nedt.2022.105652

Yalcinkaya, T., & Yucel, S. C. (2023b). Mobile learning in nursing education: A bibliometric analysis and visualization. *Nurse Education in Practice, 71*. doi:10.1016/j.nepr.2023.103714

Yang, S. J., Ogata, H., Matsui, T., & Chen, N. S. (2021). Human-centered artificial intelligence in education: Seeing the invisible through the visible. *Computers & Education: Artificial Intelligence*, *2*, 100008.

Yang, X., Xu, Y., Kuang, L., Wang, Z., Gao, H., & Wang, X. (2022). An information fusion approach to intelligent traffic signal control using the joint methods of multiagent reinforcement learning and artificial intelligence of things. *IEEE Transactions on Intelligent Transportation Systems*, *23*(7), 9335–9345. doi:10.1109/TITS.2021.3105426

Yan, H. (2022). Design of online music education system based on artificial intelligence and multiuser detection algorithm. *Computational Intelligence and Neuroscience*, *2022*, 1–11. doi:10.1155/2022/9083436 PMID:35371210

Yedida, V. S., Mehta, A., Vasudev, H., & Singh, S. (2023). *Role of numerical modeling in predicting the oxidation behavior of thermal barrier coatings*. IJIDEM. doi:10.1007/s12008-023-01306-8

Yue, T. (2023). Democratizing Financial Knowledge with ChatGPT by OpenAI: Unleashing the Power of Technology. SSRN *Electronic Journal*. doi:10.2139/ssrn.4346152

Yu, H., Miao, C., Leung, C., & White, T. J. (2017). Towards AI-powered personalization in MOOC learning. *NPJ Science of Learning*, *2*(15), 1–5. doi:10.1038/s41539-017-0016-3 PMID:30631461

Zacharis, N. Z. (2016). Predicting student academic performance in blended learning using artificial neural networks. *International Journal of Artificial Intelligence & Applications*, *7*(5), 17–29. doi:10.5121/ijaia.2016.7502

Zadeh, L. A. (1973). Outline of a new approach to the analysis of complex systems and decision processes. *IEEE Transactions on Systems, Man, and Cybernetics*, *SMC-3*(1), 28–44. doi:10.1109/TSMC.1973.5408575

Zainuddin, Z., Chu, S. K. W., Shujahat, M., & Perera, C. J. (2020). The impact of gamification on learning and instruction: A systematic review of empirical evidence. *Educational Research Review*, *30*, 100326. doi:10.1016/j.edurev.2020.100326

Zawacki-Richter, O., Marín, V. I., Bond, M., & Gouverneur, F. (2019). Systematic review of research on artificial intelligence applications in higher education – Where are the educators? *International Journal of Educational Technology in Higher Education*, *16*(39), 1–27. doi:10.1186/s41239-019-0171-0

Zemčík, M. T. (2019). A brief history of chatbots. *DEStech Transactions on Computer Science and Engineering*. . doi:10.12783/dtcse/aicae2019/31439

Zhang, Basham, & Yang. (2020). Understanding the implementation of personalized learning: A research synthesis. *Educational Research Review*, *31*. doi:10.1016/j.edurev.2020.100339

Zheng, B., & Warschauer, M. (2015). Participation, interaction, and academic achievement in an online discussion environment. *Computers & Education*, *84*, 78–89. doi:10.1016/j.compedu.2015.01.008

Zheng, J., Xing, W., & Zhu, G. (2019). Examining sequential patterns of self- and socially shared regulation of STEM learning in a CSCL environment. *Computers & Education*, *136*, 34–48. doi:10.1016/j.compedu.2019.03.005

Zhou, C., Li, Q., Li, C., Yu, J., Liu, Y., & Wang, G. (2023). *A comprehensive survey on pre-trained foundation models: A history from bard to ChatGPT.* arXiv preprint arXiv:2302.09419.

Zhu, H. (2020). Big data and artificial intelligence modelling for drug discovery. *Annual Review of Pharmacology and Toxicology*, *60*(1), 573–589. doi:10.1146/annurev-pharmtox-010919-023324 PMID:31518513

Zoroayka, V. S. (2018). Design and implementation of a chatbot in online higher education settings. *Issues in Information Systems*, *19*(4).

Related References

To continue our tradition of advancing academic research, we have compiled a list of recommended IGI Global readings. These references will provide additional information and guidance to further enrich your knowledge and assist you with your own research and future publications.

Aburezeq, I. M., & Dweikat, F. F. (2017). Cloud Applications in Language Teaching: Examining Pre-Service Teachers' Expertise, Perceptions and Integration. *International Journal of Distance Education Technologies*, *15*(4), 39–60. doi:10.4018/IJDET.2017100103

Acharjya, B., & Das, S. (2022). Adoption of E-Learning During the COVID-19 Pandemic: The Moderating Role of Age and Gender. *International Journal of Web-Based Learning and Teaching Technologies*, *17*(2), 1–14. https://doi.org/10.4018/IJWLTT.20220301.oa4

Adams, J. L., & Thomas, S. K. (2022). Non-Linear Curriculum Experiences for Student Learning and Work Design: What Is the Maximum Potential of a Chat Bot? In S. Ramlall, T. Cross, & M. Love (Eds.), *Handbook of Research on Future of Work and Education: Implications for Curriculum Delivery and Work Design* (pp. 299–306). IGI Global. https://doi.org/10.4018/978-1-7998-8275-6.ch018

Adera, B. (2017). Supporting Language and Literacy Development for English Language Learners. In J. Keengwe (Ed.), *Handbook of Research on Promoting Cross-Cultural Competence and Social Justice in Teacher Education* (pp. 339–354). Hershey, PA: IGI Global. doi:10.4018/978-1-5225-0897-7.ch018

Ahamer, G. (2017). Quality Assurance for a Developmental "Global Studies" (GS) Curriculum. In I. Management Association (Ed.), Educational Leadership and Administration: Concepts, Methodologies, Tools, and Applications (pp. 438-477). Hershey, PA: IGI Global. https://doi.org/ doi:10.4018/978-1-5225-1624-8.ch023

Ahamer, G. (2017). Quality Assurance for a Developmental "Global Studies" (GS) Curriculum. In I. Management Association (Ed.), Educational Leadership and Administration: Concepts, Methodologies, Tools, and Applications (pp. 438-477). Hershey, PA: IGI Global. https://doi.org/ doi:10.4018/978-1-5225-1624-8.ch023

Akayoğlu, S., & Seferoğlu, G. (2019). An Analysis of Negotiation of Meaning Functions of Advanced EFL Learners in Second Life: Negotiation of Meaning in Second Life. In M. Kruk (Ed.), *Assessing the Effectiveness of Virtual Technologies in Foreign and Second Language Instruction* (pp. 61–85). IGI Global. https://doi.org/10.4018/978-1-5225-7286-2.ch003

Akella, N. R. (2022). Unravelling the Web of Qualitative Dissertation Writing!: A Student Reflects. In A. Zimmerman (Ed.), *Methodological Innovations in Research and Academic Writing* (pp. 260–282). IGI Global. https://doi.org/10.4018/978-1-7998-8283-1.ch014

Alegre de la Rosa, O. M., & Angulo, L. M. (2017). Social Inclusion and Intercultural Values in a School of Education. In S. Mukerji & P. Tripathi (Eds.), *Handbook of Research on Administration, Policy, and Leadership in Higher Education* (pp. 518–531). Hershey, PA: IGI Global. doi:10.4018/978-1-5225-0672-0.ch020

Alexander, C. (2019). Using Gamification Strategies to Cultivate and Measure Professional Educator Dispositions. *International Journal of Game-Based Learning*, *9*(1), 15–29. https://doi.org/10.4018/IJGBL.2019010102

Anderson, K. M. (2017). Preparing Teachers in the Age of Equity and Inclusion. In I. Management Association (Ed.), Medical Education and Ethics: Concepts, Methodologies, Tools, and Applications (pp. 1532-1554). Hershey, PA: IGI Global. doi:10.4018/978-1-5225-0978-3.ch069

Awdziej, M. (2017). Case Study as a Teaching Method in Marketing. In D. Latusek (Ed.), *Case Studies as a Teaching Tool in Management Education* (pp. 244–263). Hershey, PA: IGI Global. doi:10.4018/978-1-5225-0770-3.ch013

Bakos, J. (2019). Sociolinguistic Factors Influencing English Language Learning. In N. Erdogan & M. Wei (Eds.), *Applied Linguistics for Teachers of Culturally and Linguistically Diverse Learners* (pp. 403–424). IGI Global. https://doi.org/10.4018/978-1-5225-8467-4.ch017

Banas, J. R., & York, C. S. (2017). Pre-Service Teachers' Motivation to Use Technology and the Impact of Authentic Learning Exercises. In L. Tomei (Ed.), *Exploring the New Era of Technology-Infused Education* (pp. 121–140). Hershey, PA: IGI Global. doi:10.4018/978-1-5225-1709-2.ch008

Barton, T. P. (2021). Empowering Educator Allyship by Exploring Racial Trauma and the Disengagement of Black Students. In C. Reneau & M. Villarreal (Eds.), *Handbook of Research on Leading Higher Education Transformation With Social Justice, Equity, and Inclusion* (pp. 186–197). IGI Global. https://doi.org/10.4018/978-1-7998-7152-1.ch013

Benhima, M. (2021). Moroccan English Department Student Attitudes Towards the Use of Distance Education During COVID-19: Moulay Ismail University as a Case Study. *International Journal of Information and Communication Technology Education*, *17*(3), 105–122. https://doi.org/10.4018/IJICTE.20210701.oa7

Beycioglu, K., & Wildy, H. (2017). Principal Preparation: The Case of Novice Principals in Turkey. In I. Management Association (Ed.), Educational Leadership and Administration: Concepts, Methodologies, Tools, and Applications (pp. 1152-1169). Hershey, PA: IGI Global. https://doi.org/ doi:10.4018/978-1-5225-1624-8.ch054

Bharwani, S., & Musunuri, D. (2018). Reflection as a Process From Theory to Practice. In M. Khosrow-Pour, D.B.A. (Ed.), Encyclopedia of Information Science and Technology, Fourth Edition (pp. 1529-1539). Hershey, PA: IGI Global. doi:10.4018/978-1-5225-2255-3.ch132

Bhushan, A., Garza, K. B., Perumal, O., Das, S. K., Feola, D. J., Farrell, D., & Birnbaum, A. (2022). Lessons Learned From the COVID-19 Pandemic and the Implications for Pharmaceutical Graduate Education and Research. In C. Ford & K. Garza (Eds.), *Handbook of Research on Updating and Innovating Health Professions Education: Post-Pandemic Perspectives* (pp. 324–345). IGI Global. https://doi.org/10.4018/978-1-7998-7623-6.ch014

Bintz, W., Ciecierski, L. M., & Royan, E. (2021). Using Picture Books With Instructional Strategies to Address New Challenges and Teach Literacy Skills in a Digital World. In L. Haas & J. Tussey (Eds.), *Connecting Disciplinary Literacy and Digital Storytelling in K-12 Education* (pp. 38–58). IGI Global. https://doi.org/10.4018/978-1-7998-5770-9.ch003

Bohjanen, S. L., Cameron-Standerford, A., & Meidl, T. D. (2018). Capacity Building Pedagogy for Diverse Learners. In J. Keengwe (Ed.), *Handbook of Research on Pedagogical Models for Next-Generation Teaching and Learning* (pp. 195–212). Hershey, PA: IGI Global. doi:10.4018/978-1-5225-3873-8.ch011

Brewer, J. C. (2018). Measuring Text Readability Using Reading Level. In M. Khosrow-Pour, D.B.A. (Ed.), Encyclopedia of Information Science and Technology, Fourth Edition (pp. 1499-1507). Hershey, PA: IGI Global. doi:10.4018/978-1-5225-2255-3.ch129

Brookbanks, B. C. (2022). Student Perspectives on Business Education in the USA: Current Attitudes and Necessary Changes in an Age of Disruption. In A. Zhuplev & R. Koepp (Eds.), *Global Trends, Dynamics, and Imperatives for Strategic Development in Business Education in an Age of Disruption* (pp. 214–231). IGI Global. doi:10.4018/978-1-7998-7548-2.ch011

Brown, L. V., Dari, T., & Spencer, N. (2019). Addressing the Impact of Trauma in High Poverty Elementary Schools: An Ecological Model for School Counseling. In K. Daniels & K. Billingsley (Eds.), *Creating Caring and Supportive Educational Environments for Meaningful Learning* (pp. 135–153). IGI Global. https://doi.org/10.4018/978-1-5225-5748-7.ch008

Brown, S. L. (2017). A Case Study of Strategic Leadership and Research in Practice: Principal Preparation Programs that Work – An Educational Administration Perspective of Best Practices for Master's Degree Programs for Principal Preparation. In V. Wang (Ed.), *Encyclopedia of Strategic Leadership and Management* (pp. 1226–1244). Hershey, PA: IGI Global. doi:10.4018/978-1-5225-1049-9.ch086

Brzozowski, M., & Ferster, I. (2017). Educational Management Leadership: High School Principal's Management Style and Parental Involvement in School Management in Israel. In V. Potocan, M. Üngan, & Z. Nedelko (Eds.), *Handbook of Research on Managerial Solutions in Non-Profit Organizations* (pp. 55–74). Hershey, PA: IGI Global. doi:10.4018/978-1-5225-0731-4.ch003

Cahapay, M. B. (2020). Delphi Technique in the Development of Emerging Contents in High School Science Curriculum. *International Journal of Curriculum Development and Learning Measurement, 1*(2), 1–9. https://doi.org/10.4018/IJCDLM.2020070101

Camacho, L. F., & Leon Guerrero, A. E. (2022). Indigenous Student Experience in Higher Education: Implementation of Culturally Sensitive Support. In P. Pangelinan & T. McVey (Eds.), *Learning and Reconciliation Through Indigenous Education in Oceania* (pp. 254–266). IGI Global. https://doi.org/10.4018/978-1-7998-7736-3.ch016

Cannaday, J. (2017). The Masking Effect: Hidden Gifts and Disabilities of 2e Students. In P. Dickenson, P. Keough, & J. Courduff (Eds.), *Preparing Pre-Service Teachers for the Inclusive Classroom* (pp. 220–231). Hershey, PA: IGI Global. doi:10.4018/978-1-5225-1753-5.ch011

Cederquist, S., Fishman, B., & Teasley, S. D. (2022). What's Missing From the College Transcript?: How Employers Make Sense of Student Skills. In Y. Huang (Ed.), *Handbook of Research on Credential Innovations for Inclusive Pathways to Professions* (pp. 234–253). IGI Global. https://doi.org/10.4018/978-1-7998-3820-3.ch012

Cockrell, P., & Gibson, T. (2019). The Untold Stories of Black and Brown Student Experiences in Historically White Fraternities and Sororities. In P. Hoffman-Miller, M. James, & D. Hermond (Eds.), *African American Suburbanization and the Consequential Loss of Identity* (pp. 153–171). IGI Global. https://doi.org/10.4018/978-1-5225-7835-2.ch009

Cohen, M. (2022). Leveraging Content Creation to Boost Student Engagement. In T. Driscoll III, (Ed.), *Designing Effective Distance and Blended Learning Environments in K-12* (pp. 223–239). IGI Global. https://doi.org/10.4018/978-1-7998-6829-3.ch013

Contreras, E. C., & Contreras, I. I. (2018). Development of Communication Skills through Auditory Training Software in Special Education. In M. Khosrow-Pour, D.B.A. (Ed.), Encyclopedia of Information Science and Technology, Fourth Edition (pp. 2431-2441). Hershey, PA: IGI Global. doi:10.4018/978-1-5225-2255-3.ch212

Cooke, L., Schugar, J., Schugar, H., Penny, C., & Bruning, H. (2020). Can Everyone Code?: Preparing Teachers to Teach Computer Languages as a Literacy. In J. Mitchell & E. Vaughn (Eds.), *Participatory Literacy Practices for P-12 Classrooms in the Digital Age* (pp. 163–183). IGI Global. https://doi.org/10.4018/978-1-7998-0000-2.ch009

Cooley, D., & Whitten, E. (2017). Special Education Leadership and the Implementation of Response to Intervention. In F. Topor (Ed.), *Handbook of Research on Individualism and Identity in the Globalized Digital Age* (pp. 265–286). Hershey, PA: IGI Global. doi:10.4018/978-1-5225-0522-8.ch012

Cosner, S., Tozer, S., & Zavitkovsky, P. (2017). Enacting a Cycle of Inquiry Capstone Research Project in Doctoral-Level Leadership Preparation. In I. Management Association (Ed.), Educational Leadership and Administration: Concepts, Methodologies, Tools, and Applications (pp. 1460-1481). Hershey, PA: IGI Global. doi:10.4018/978-1-5225-1624-8.ch067

Crawford, C. M. (2018). Instructional Real World Community Engagement. In M. Khosrow-Pour, D.B.A. (Ed.), Encyclopedia of Information Science and Technology, Fourth Edition (pp. 1474-1486). Hershey, PA: IGI Global. doi:10.4018/978-1-5225-2255-3.ch127

Crosby-Cooper, T., & Pacis, D. (2017). Implementing Effective Student Support Teams. In P. Dickenson, P. Keough, & J. Courduff (Eds.), *Preparing Pre-Service Teachers for the Inclusive Classroom* (pp. 248–262). Hershey, PA: IGI Global. doi:10.4018/978-1-5225-1753-5.ch013

Curran, C. M., & Hawbaker, B. W. (2017). Cultivating Communities of Inclusive Practice: Professional Development for Educators – Research and Practice. In C. Curran & A. Petersen (Eds.), *Handbook of Research on Classroom Diversity and Inclusive Education Practice* (pp. 120–153). Hershey, PA: IGI Global. doi:10.4018/978-1-5225-2520-2.ch006

Dass, S., & Dabbagh, N. (2018). Faculty Adoption of 3D Avatar-Based Virtual World Learning Environments: An Exploratory Case Study. In I. Management Association (Ed.), Technology Adoption and Social Issues: Concepts, Methodologies, Tools, and Applications (pp. 1000-1033). Hershey, PA: IGI Global. https://doi.org/ doi:10.4018/978-1-5225-5201-7.ch045

Davison, A. M., & Scholl, K. G. (2017). Inclusive Recreation as Part of the IEP Process. In C. Curran & A. Petersen (Eds.), *Handbook of Research on Classroom Diversity and Inclusive Education Practice* (pp. 311–330). Hershey, PA: IGI Global. doi:10.4018/978-1-5225-2520-2.ch013

DeCoito, I. (2018). Addressing Digital Competencies, Curriculum Development, and Instructional Design in Science Teacher Education. In M. Khosrow-Pour, D.B.A. (Ed.), Encyclopedia of Information Science and Technology, Fourth Edition (pp. 1420-1431). Hershey, PA: IGI Global. https://doi.org/ doi:10.4018/978-1-5225-2255-3.ch122

DeCoito, I., & Richardson, T. (2017). Beyond Angry Birds™: Using Web-Based Tools to Engage Learners and Promote Inquiry in STEM Learning. In I. Levin & D. Tsybulsky (Eds.), *Digital Tools and Solutions for Inquiry-Based STEM Learning* (pp. 166–196). Hershey, PA: IGI Global. doi:10.4018/978-1-5225-2525-7.ch007

Delmas, P. M. (2017). Research-Based Leadership for Next-Generation Leaders. In R. Styron Jr & J. Styron (Eds.), *Comprehensive Problem-Solving and Skill Development for Next-Generation Leaders* (pp. 1–39). Hershey, PA: IGI Global. doi:10.4018/978-1-5225-1968-3.ch001

Demiray, U., & Ekren, G. (2018). Administrative-Related Evaluation for Distance Education Institutions in Turkey. In K. Buyuk, S. Kocdar, & A. Bozkurt (Eds.), *Administrative Leadership in Open and Distance Learning Programs* (pp. 263–288). Hershey, PA: IGI Global. doi:10.4018/978-1-5225-2645-2.ch011

Dickenson, P. (2017). What do we Know and Where Can We Grow?: Teachers Preparation for the Inclusive Classroom. In P. Dickenson, P. Keough, & J. Courduff (Eds.), *Preparing Pre-Service Teachers for the Inclusive Classroom* (pp. 1–22). Hershey, PA: IGI Global. doi:10.4018/978-1-5225-1753-5.ch001

Ding, Q., & Zhu, H. (2021). Flipping the Classroom in STEM Education. In J. Keengwe (Ed.), *Handbook of Research on Innovations in Non-Traditional Educational Practices* (pp. 155–173). IGI Global. https://doi.org/10.4018/978-1-7998-4360-3.ch008

Dixon, T., & Christison, M. (2021). Teaching English Grammar in a Hybrid Academic ESL Course: A Mixed Methods Study. In K. Kelch, P. Byun, S. Safavi, & S. Cervantes (Eds.), *CALL Theory Applications for Online TESOL Education* (pp. 229–251). IGI Global. https://doi.org/10.4018/978-1-7998-6609-1.ch010

Donne, V., & Hansen, M. (2017). Teachers' Use of Assistive Technologies in Education. In L. Tomei (Ed.), *Exploring the New Era of Technology-Infused Education* (pp. 86–101). Hershey, PA: IGI Global. doi:10.4018/978-1-5225-1709-2.ch006

Donne, V., & Hansen, M. A. (2018). Business and Technology Educators: Practices for Inclusion. In I. Management Association (Ed.), Business Education and Ethics: Concepts, Methodologies, Tools, and Applications (pp. 471-484). Hershey, PA: IGI Global. https://doi.org/ doi:10.4018/978-1-5225-3153-1.ch026

Dos Santos, L. M. (2022). Completing Student-Teaching Internships Online: Instructional Changes During the COVID-19 Pandemic. In M. Alaali (Ed.), *Assessing University Governance and Policies in Relation to the COVID-19 Pandemic* (pp. 106–127). IGI Global. https://doi.org/10.4018/978-1-7998-8279-4.ch007

Dreon, O., Shettel, J., & Bower, K. M. (2017). Preparing Next Generation Elementary Teachers for the Tools of Tomorrow. In M. Grassetti & S. Brookby (Eds.), *Advancing Next-Generation Teacher Education through Digital Tools and Applications* (pp. 143–159). Hershey, PA: IGI Global. doi:10.4018/978-1-5225-0965-3.ch008

Durak, H. Y., & Güyer, T. (2018). Design and Development of an Instructional Program for Teaching Programming Processes to Gifted Students Using Scratch. In J. Cannaday (Ed.), *Curriculum Development for Gifted Education Programs* (pp. 61–99). Hershey, PA: IGI Global. doi:10.4018/978-1-5225-3041-1.ch004

Egorkina, E., Ivanov, M., & Valyavskiy, A. Y. (2018). Students' Research Competence Formation of the Quality of Open and Distance Learning. In V. Mkrttchian & L. Belyanina (Eds.), *Handbook of Research on Students' Research Competence in Modern Educational Contexts* (pp. 364–384). Hershey, PA: IGI Global. doi:10.4018/978-1-5225-3485-3.ch019

Ekren, G., Karataş, S., & Demiray, U. (2017). Understanding of Leadership in Distance Education Management. In I. Management Association (Ed.), Educational Leadership and Administration: Concepts, Methodologies, Tools, and Applications (pp. 34-50). Hershey, PA: IGI Global. https://doi.org/ doi:10.4018/978-1-5225-1624-8.ch003

Elmore, W. M., Young, J. K., Harris, S., & Mason, D. (2017). The Relationship between Individual Student Attributes and Online Course Completion. In K. Shelton & K. Pedersen (Eds.), *Handbook of Research on Building, Growing, and Sustaining Quality E-Learning Programs* (pp. 151–173). Hershey, PA: IGI Global. doi:10.4018/978-1-5225-0877-9.ch008

Ercegovac, I. R., Alfirević, N., & Koludrović, M. (2017). School Principals' Communication and Co-Operation Assessment: The Croatian Experience. In I. Management Association (Ed.), Educational Leadership and Administration: Concepts, Methodologies, Tools, and Applications (pp. 1568-1589). Hershey, PA: IGI Global. https://doi.org/ doi:10.4018/978-1-5225-1624-8.ch072

Everhart, D., & Seymour, D. M. (2017). Challenges and Opportunities in the Currency of Higher Education. In K. Rasmussen, P. Northrup, & R. Colson (Eds.), *Handbook of Research on Competency-Based Education in University Settings* (pp. 41–65). Hershey, PA: IGI Global. doi:10.4018/978-1-5225-0932-5.ch003

Farmer, L. S. (2017). Managing Portable Technologies for Special Education. In V. Wang (Ed.), *Encyclopedia of Strategic Leadership and Management* (pp. 977–987). Hershey, PA: IGI Global. doi:10.4018/978-1-5225-1049-9.ch068

Farmer, L. S. (2018). Optimizing OERs for Optimal ICT Literacy in Higher Education. In J. Keengwe (Ed.), *Handbook of Research on Mobile Technology, Constructivism, and Meaningful Learning* (pp. 366–390). Hershey, PA: IGI Global. doi:10.4018/978-1-5225-3949-0.ch020

Ferguson, B. T. (2019). Supporting Affective Development of Children With Disabilities Through Moral Dilemmas. In S. Ikuta (Ed.), *Handmade Teaching Materials for Students With Disabilities* (pp. 253–275). IGI Global. doi:10.4018/978-1-5225-6240-5.ch011

Fındık, L. Y. (2017). Self-Assessment of Principals Based on Leadership in Complexity. In I. Management Association (Ed.), Educational Leadership and Administration: Concepts, Methodologies, Tools, and Applications (pp. 978-991). Hershey, PA: IGI Global. https://doi.org/ doi:10.4018/978-1-5225-1624-8.ch047

Flor, A. G., & Gonzalez-Flor, B. (2018). Dysfunctional Digital Demeanors: Tales From (and Policy Implications of) eLearning's Dark Side. In I. Management Association (Ed.), The Dark Web: Breakthroughs in Research and Practice (pp. 37-50). Hershey, PA: IGI Global. https://doi.org/ doi:10.4018/978-1-5225-3163-0.ch003

Floyd, K. K., & Shambaugh, N. (2017). Instructional Design for Simulations in Special Education Virtual Learning Spaces. In T. Kidd & L. Morris Jr., (Eds.), *Handbook of Research on Instructional Systems and Educational Technology* (pp. 202–215). Hershey, PA: IGI Global. doi:10.4018/978-1-5225-2399-4.ch018

Freeland, S. F. (2020). Community Schools: Improving Academic Achievement Through Meaningful Engagement. In R. Kronick (Ed.), *Emerging Perspectives on Community Schools and the Engaged University* (pp. 132–144). IGI Global. https://doi.org/10.4018/978-1-7998-0280-8.ch008

Ghanbarzadeh, R., & Ghapanchi, A. H. (2019). Applied Areas of Three Dimensional Virtual Worlds in Learning and Teaching: A Review of Higher Education. In I. Management Association (Ed.), *Virtual Reality in Education: Breakthroughs in Research and Practice* (pp. 172-192). IGI Global. https://doi.org/10.4018/978-1-5225-8179-6.ch008

Giovannini, J. M. (2017). Technology Integration in Preservice Teacher Education Programs: Research-based Recommendations. In M. Grassetti & S. Brookby (Eds.), *Advancing Next-Generation Teacher Education through Digital Tools and Applications* (pp. 82–102). Hershey, PA: IGI Global. doi:10.4018/978-1-5225-0965-3.ch005

Good, S., & Clarke, V. B. (2017). An Integral Analysis of One Urban School System's Efforts to Support Student-Centered Teaching. In J. Keengwe & G. Onchwari (Eds.), *Handbook of Research on Learner-Centered Pedagogy in Teacher Education and Professional Development* (pp. 45–68). Hershey, PA: IGI Global. doi:10.4018/978-1-5225-0892-2.ch003

Guetzoian, E. (2022). Gamification Strategies for Higher Education Student Worker Training. In C. Lane (Ed.), *Handbook of Research on Acquiring 21st Century Literacy Skills Through Game-Based Learning* (pp. 164–179). IGI Global. https://doi.org/10.4018/978-1-7998-7271-9.ch009

Hamidi, F., Owuor, P. M., Hynie, M., Baljko, M., & McGrath, S. (2017). Potentials of Digital Assistive Technology and Special Education in Kenya. In C. Ayo & V. Mbarika (Eds.), *Sustainable ICT Adoption and Integration for Socio-Economic Development* (pp. 125–151). Hershey, PA: IGI Global. doi:10.4018/978-1-5225-2565-3.ch006

Hamim, T., Benabbou, F., & Sael, N. (2022). Student Profile Modeling Using Boosting Algorithms. *International Journal of Web-Based Learning and Teaching Technologies, 17*(5), 1–13. https://doi.org/10.4018/IJWLTT.20220901.oa4

Henderson, L. K. (2017). Meltdown at Fukushima: Global Catastrophic Events, Visual Literacy, and Art Education. In R. Shin (Ed.), *Convergence of Contemporary Art, Visual Culture, and Global Civic Engagement* (pp. 80–99). Hershey, PA: IGI Global. doi:10.4018/978-1-5225-1665-1.ch005

Hudgins, T., & Holland, J. L. (2018). Digital Badges: Tracking Knowledge Acquisition Within an Innovation Framework. In I. Management Association (Ed.), Wearable Technologies: Concepts, Methodologies, Tools, and Applications (pp. 1118-1132). Hershey, PA: IGI Global. https://doi.org/ doi:10.4018/978-1-5225-5484-4.ch051

Hwang, R., Lin, H., Sun, J. C., & Wu, J. (2019). Improving Learning Achievement in Science Education for Elementary School Students via Blended Learning. *International Journal of Online Pedagogy and Course Design, 9*(2), 44–62. https://doi.org/10.4018/IJOPCD.2019040104

Jančec, L., & Vodopivec, J. L. (2019). The Implicit Pedagogy and the Hidden Curriculum in Postmodern Education. In J. Vodopivec, L. Jančec, & T. Štemberger (Eds.), *Implicit Pedagogy for Optimized Learning in Contemporary Education* (pp. 41–59). IGI Global. https://doi.org/10.4018/978-1-5225-5799-9.ch003

Janus, M., & Siddiqua, A. (2018). Challenges for Children With Special Health Needs at the Time of Transition to School. In I. Management Association (Ed.), Autism Spectrum Disorders: Breakthroughs in Research and Practice (pp. 339-371). Hershey, PA: IGI Global. doi:10.4018/978-1-5225-3827-1.ch018

Jesus, R. A. (2018). Screencasts and Learning Styles. In M. Khosrow-Pour, D.B.A. (Ed.), Encyclopedia of Information Science and Technology, Fourth Edition (pp. 1548-1558). Hershey, PA: IGI Global. doi:10.4018/978-1-5225-2255-3.ch134

John, G., Francis, N., & Santhakumar, A. B. (2022). Student Engagement: Past, Present, and Future. In S. Ramlall, T. Cross, & M. Love (Eds.), *Handbook of Research on Future of Work and Education: Implications for Curriculum Delivery and Work Design* (pp. 329–341). IGI Global. https://doi.org/10.4018/978-1-7998-8275-6.ch020

Karpinski, A. C., D'Agostino, J. V., Williams, A. K., Highland, S. A., & Mellott, J. A. (2018). The Relationship Between Online Formative Assessment and State Test Scores Using Multilevel Modeling. In M. Khosrow-Pour, D.B.A. (Ed.), Encyclopedia of Information Science and Technology, Fourth Edition (pp. 5183-5192). Hershey, PA: IGI Global. doi:10.4018/978-1-5225-2255-3.ch450

Kats, Y. (2017). Educational Leadership and Integrated Support for Students with Autism Spectrum Disorders. In I. Management Association (Ed.), Educational Leadership and Administration: Concepts, Methodologies, Tools, and Applications (pp. 101-114). Hershey, PA: IGI Global. https://doi.org/ doi:10.4018/978-1-5225-1624-8.ch007

Kaya, G., & Altun, A. (2018). Educational Ontology Development. In M. Khosrow-Pour, D.B.A. (Ed.), Encyclopedia of Information Science and Technology, Fourth Edition (pp. 1441-1450). Hershey, PA: IGI Global. doi:10.4018/978-1-5225-2255-3.ch124

Keough, P. D., & Pacis, D. (2017). Best Practices Implementing Special Education Curriculum and Common Core State Standards using UDL. In P. Dickenson, P. Keough, & J. Courduff (Eds.), *Preparing Pre-Service Teachers for the Inclusive Classroom* (pp. 107–123). Hershey, PA: IGI Global. doi:10.4018/978-1-5225-1753-5.ch006

Kilburn, M., Henckell, M., & Starrett, D. (2018). Factors Contributing to the Effectiveness of Online Students and Instructors. In M. Khosrow-Pour, D.B.A. (Ed.), Encyclopedia of Information Science and Technology, Fourth Edition (pp. 1451-1462). Hershey, PA: IGI Global. doi:10.4018/978-1-5225-2255-3.ch125

Koban Koç, D. (2021). Gender and Language: A Sociolinguistic Analysis of Second Language Writing. In E. Hancı-Azizoglu & N. Kavaklı (Eds.), *Futuristic and Linguistic Perspectives on Teaching Writing to Second Language Students* (pp. 161–177). IGI Global. https://doi.org/10.4018/978-1-7998-6508-7.ch010

Konecny, L. T. (2017). Hybrid, Online, and Flipped Classrooms in Health Science: Enhanced Learning Environments. In I. Management Association (Ed.), Flipped Instruction: Breakthroughs in Research and Practice (pp. 355-370). Hershey, PA: IGI Global. https://doi.org/ doi:10.4018/978-1-5225-1803-7.ch020

Kupietz, K. D. (2021). Gaming and Simulation in Public Education: Teaching Others to Help Themselves and Their Neighbors. In N. Drumhiller, T. Wilkin, & K. Srba (Eds.), *Simulation and Game-Based Learning in Emergency and Disaster Management* (pp. 41–62). IGI Global. https://doi.org/10.4018/978-1-7998-4087-9.ch003

Kwee, C. T. (2022). Assessing the International Student Enrolment Strategies in Australian Universities: A Case Study During the COVID-19 Pandemic. In M. Alaali (Ed.), *Assessing University Governance and Policies in Relation to the COVID-19 Pandemic* (pp. 162–188). IGI Global. https://doi.org/10.4018/978-1-7998-8279-4.ch010

Lauricella, S., & McArthur, F. A. (2022). Taking a Student-Centred Approach to Alternative Digital Credentials: Multiple Pathways Toward the Acquisition of Microcredentials. In D. Piedra (Ed.), *Innovations in the Design and Application of Alternative Digital Credentials* (pp. 57–69). IGI Global. https://doi.org/10.4018/978-1-7998-7697-7.ch003

Llamas, M. F. (2019). Intercultural Awareness in Teaching English for Early Childhood: A Film-Based Approach. In E. Domínguez Romero, J. Bobkina, & S. Stefanova (Eds.), *Teaching Literature and Language Through Multimodal Texts* (pp. 54–68). IGI Global. https://doi.org/10.4018/978-1-5225-5796-8.ch004

Lokhtina, I., & Kkese, E. T. (2022). Reflecting and Adapting to an Academic Workplace Before and After the Lockdown in Greek-Speaking Cyprus: Opportunities and Challenges. In A. Zhuplev & R. Koepp (Eds.), *Global Trends, Dynamics, and Imperatives for Strategic Development in Business Education in an Age of Disruption* (pp. 126–148). IGI Global. https://doi.org/10.4018/978-1-7998-7548-2.ch007

Lovell, K. L. (2017). Development and Evaluation of Neuroscience Computer-Based Modules for Medical Students: Instructional Design Principles and Effectiveness. In J. Stefaniak (Ed.), *Advancing Medical Education Through Strategic Instructional Design* (pp. 262–276). Hershey, PA: IGI Global. doi:10.4018/978-1-5225-2098-6.ch013

Maher, D. (2019). The Use of Course Management Systems in Pre-Service Teacher Education. In J. Keengwe (Ed.), *Handbook of Research on Blended Learning Pedagogies and Professional Development in Higher Education* (pp. 196–213). IGI Global. https://doi.org/10.4018/978-1-5225-5557-5.ch011

Makewa, L. N. (2019). Teacher Technology Competence Base. In L. Makewa, B. Ngussa, & J. Kuboja (Eds.), *Technology-Supported Teaching and Research Methods for Educators* (pp. 247–267). IGI Global. https://doi.org/10.4018/978-1-5225-5915-3.ch014

Mallett, C. A. (2022). School Resource (Police) Officers in Schools: Impact on Campus Safety, Student Discipline, and Learning. In G. Crews (Ed.), *Impact of School Shootings on Classroom Culture, Curriculum, and Learning* (pp. 53–70). IGI Global. https://doi.org/10.4018/978-1-7998-5200-1.ch004

Marinho, J. E., Freitas, I. R., Leão, I. B., Pacheco, L. O., Gonçalves, M. P., Castro, M. J., Silva, P. D., & Moreira, R. J. (2022). Project-Based Learning Application in Higher Education: Student Experiences and Perspectives. In A. Alves & N. van Hattum-Janssen (Eds.), *Training Engineering Students for Modern Technological Advancement* (pp. 146–164). IGI Global. https://doi.org/10.4018/978-1-7998-8816-1.ch007

McCleskey, J. A., & Melton, R. M. (2022). Rolling With the Flow: Online Faculty and Student Presence in a Post-COVID-19 World. In S. Ramlall, T. Cross, & M. Love (Eds.), *Handbook of Research on Future of Work and Education: Implications for Curriculum Delivery and Work Design* (pp. 307–328). IGI Global. https://doi.org/10.4018/978-1-7998-8275-6.ch019

McCormack, V. F., Stauffer, M., Fishley, K., Hohenbrink, J., Mascazine, J. R., & Zigler, T. (2018). Designing a Dual Licensure Path for Middle Childhood and Special Education Teacher Candidates. In D. Polly, M. Putman, T. Petty, & A. Good (Eds.), *Innovative Practices in Teacher Preparation and Graduate-Level Teacher Education Programs* (pp. 21–36). Hershey, PA: IGI Global. doi:10.4018/978-1-5225-3068-8.ch002

McDaniel, R. (2017). Strategic Leadership in Instructional Design: Applying the Principles of Instructional Design through the Lens of Strategic Leadership to Distance Education. In V. Wang (Ed.), *Encyclopedia of Strategic Leadership and Management* (pp. 1570–1584). Hershey, PA: IGI Global. doi:10.4018/978-1-5225-1049-9.ch109

McKinney, R. E., Halli-Tierney, A. D., Gold, A. E., Allen, R. S., & Carroll, D. G. (2022). Interprofessional Education: Using Standardized Cases in Face-to-Face and Remote Learning Settings. In C. Ford & K. Garza (Eds.), *Handbook of Research on Updating and Innovating Health Professions Education: Post-Pandemic Perspectives* (pp. 24–42). IGI Global. https://doi.org/10.4018/978-1-7998-7623-6.ch002

Meintjes, H. H. (2021). Learner Views of a Facebook Page as a Supportive Digital Pedagogical Tool at a Public South African School in a Grade 12 Business Studies Class. *International Journal of Smart Education and Urban Society, 12*(2), 32–45. https://doi.org/10.4018/IJSEUS.2021040104

Melero-García, F. (2022). Training Bilingual Interpreters in Healthcare Settings: Student Perceptions of Online Learning. In J. LeLoup & P. Swanson (Eds.), *Handbook of Research on Effective Online Language Teaching in a Disruptive Environment* (pp. 288–310). IGI Global. https://doi.org/10.4018/978-1-7998-7720-2.ch015

Meletiadou, E. (2022). The Use of Peer Assessment as an Inclusive Learning Strategy in Higher Education Institutions: Enhancing Student Writing Skills and Motivation. In E. Meletiadou (Ed.), *Handbook of Research on Policies and Practices for Assessing Inclusive Teaching and Learning* (pp. 1–26). IGI Global. https://doi.org/10.4018/978-1-7998-8579-5.ch001

Memon, R. N., Ahmad, R., & Salim, S. S. (2018). Critical Issues in Requirements Engineering Education. In I. Management Association (Ed.), Computer Systems and Software Engineering: Concepts, Methodologies, Tools, and Applications (pp. 1953-1976). Hershey, PA: IGI Global. doi:10.4018/978-1-5225-3923-0.ch081

Mendenhall, R. (2017). Western Governors University: CBE Innovator and National Model. In K. Rasmussen, P. Northrup, & R. Colson (Eds.), *Handbook of Research on Competency-Based Education in University Settings* (pp. 379–400). Hershey, PA: IGI Global. doi:10.4018/978-1-5225-0932-5.ch019

Mense, E. G., Griggs, D. M., & Shanks, J. N. (2018). School Leaders in a Time of Accountability and Data Use: Preparing Our Future School Leaders in Leadership Preparation Programs. In E. Mense & M. Crain-Dorough (Eds.), *Data Leadership for K-12 Schools in a Time of Accountability* (pp. 235–259). Hershey, PA: IGI Global. doi:10.4018/978-1-5225-3188-3.ch012

Mense, E. G., Griggs, D. M., & Shanks, J. N. (2018). School Leaders in a Time of Accountability and Data Use: Preparing Our Future School Leaders in Leadership Preparation Programs. In E. Mense & M. Crain-Dorough (Eds.), *Data Leadership for K-12 Schools in a Time of Accountability* (pp. 235–259). Hershey, PA: IGI Global. doi:10.4018/978-1-5225-3188-3.ch012

Mestry, R., & Naicker, S. R. (2017). Exploring Distributive Leadership in South African Public Primary Schools in the Soweto Region. In I. Management Association (Ed.), Educational Leadership and Administration: Concepts, Methodologies, Tools, and Applications (pp. 1041-1064). Hershey, PA: IGI Global. doi:10.4018/978-1-5225-1624-8.ch050

Monaghan, C. H., & Boboc, M. (2017). (Re) Defining Leadership in Higher Education in the U.S. In V. Wang (Ed.), *Encyclopedia of Strategic Leadership and Management* (pp. 567–579). Hershey, PA: IGI Global. doi:10.4018/978-1-5225-1049-9.ch040

Morall, M. B. (2021). Reimagining Mobile Phones: Multiple Literacies and Digital Media Compositions. In C. Moran (Eds.), *Affordances and Constraints of Mobile Phone Use in English Language Arts Classrooms* (pp. 41-53). IGI Global. https://doi.org/10.4018/978-1-7998-5805-8.ch003

Mthethwa, V. (2022). Student Governance and the Academic Minefield During COVID-19 Lockdown in South Africa. In M. Alaali (Ed.), *Assessing University Governance and Policies in Relation to the COVID-19 Pandemic* (pp. 255–276). IGI Global. https://doi.org/10.4018/978-1-7998-8279-4.ch015

Muthee, J. M., & Murungi, C. G. (2018). Relationship Among Intelligence, Achievement Motivation, Type of School, and Academic Performance of Kenyan Urban Primary School Pupils. In M. Khosrow-Pour, D.B.A. (Ed.), Encyclopedia of Information Science and Technology, Fourth Edition (pp. 1540-1547). Hershey, PA: IGI Global. https://doi.org/ doi:10.4018/978-1-5225-2255-3.ch133

Naranjo, J. (2018). Meeting the Need for Inclusive Educators Online: Teacher Education in Inclusive Special Education and Dual-Certification. In D. Polly, M. Putman, T. Petty, & A. Good (Eds.), *Innovative Practices in Teacher Preparation and Graduate-Level Teacher Education Programs* (pp. 106–122). Hershey, PA: IGI Global. doi:10.4018/978-1-5225-3068-8.ch007

Nkabinde, Z. P. (2017). Multiculturalism in Special Education: Perspectives of Minority Children in Urban Schools. In J. Keengwe (Ed.), *Handbook of Research on Promoting Cross-Cultural Competence and Social Justice in Teacher Education* (pp. 382–397). Hershey, PA: IGI Global. doi:10.4018/978-1-5225-0897-7.ch020 trainer. She has published papers in International and national Journals and participated in more than 20 national and international conferences, Seminars, FDPs, Workshops. She served as a question paper setter in various autonomous colleges. She has also delivered various guest talks and soft skill training in various schools and colleges.

Ayşin Gaye Üstün is an Asst. Prof. at Vocational School at Sinop University, Turkey. She earned her doctoral degree from the Department of Computer Education and Instructional Technology at Atatürk University, Turkey. Her academic interest areas are open and distance education environments, artificial intelligence, coding education and instructional design.

Arun V. P. is a driven and accomplished professional with a diverse educational background and extensive hands-on experience across various industries. Graduating with honors, Arun earned his Master of Business Administration (M.B.A) with a specialization in Human Resources and Marketing from the renowned Sona School of Management in Salem in 2018, where he excelled academically with an impressive 8.3 Cumulative Grade Point Average (CGPA). Before pursuing his MBA, Arun laid a solid foundation by obtaining a Bachelor of Engineering degree from Kongu Engineering College in 2014. Throughout his academic journey, Arun displayed an unwavering commitment to learning and personal growth, actively seeking opportunities to expand his knowledge and skills beyond the confines of traditional education. He sought practical experiences to complement his theoretical understanding, such as a 45-day summer internship focused on conducting a feasibility study for R-Doc Sustainability in the market. Additionally, Arun broadened his horizons through a 7-day industrial visit to Malaysia and Singapore, immersing himself in diverse cultural and professional environments. Arun's academic pursuits were further enriched by his involvement in hands-on projects, including a comprehensive study on Employee Job Satisfaction at Roots Cast Private Limited. These practical experiences not only honed his analytical and problem-solving skills but also showcased his proactive approach to learning and professional development.

Koppala Venugopal, a professor in Management Studies at Aditya Institute of Technology and Management at Srikakulam, has had an adroit experience of academic, Research and community service. He has contributed 5 Projects, 2 patents, 10 books, 70 publications, 48 paper presentations, 56 resource talks and 12 memberships. He is guiding 4 scholars from various universities. His exceptional interest industry interface has made his efforts dexterous.

Renu Vij is an expert of Behavioral analytics, behavioral Pyschology.She has been in mentoring since last 16 years, having strong Scopus indexed research papers. She is well known influential women who contributed in society.

Mehmet Yavuz completed his undergraduate education at Fırat University, Department of Computer Education. He completed his master's and doctoral studies at Atatürk University, Department of Computer and Instructional Technologies. He is still working as an Assistant Professor at Bingöl University, Faculty of Economics and Administrative Sciences, Department of Management Information Systems. His research interests include digital transformation, distance education and artificial intelligence.

Index